Optimizing Socio-Economic Systems in the Union State of Russia and Belarus: R & D, Higher Education, and Labor Markets in the Digital Economy

Collective Scientific Monograph

Edited by

Galina V. Astratova
Department of Regional Economics
Innovative Entrepreneurship and Economics (REIE&E)
Institute of Economics and Management
School of Public Administration and Entrepreneurship (SPAE)
Ural Federal University (UrFU), Yekaterinburg 620002
Sverdlovsk Region, Russian Federation

Maxim V. Vlasov
Department of Regional Economics
Innovative Entrepreneurship and Economics (REIE&E)
Institute of Economics and Management
School of Public Administration and Entrepreneurship (SPAE)
Ural Federal University (UrFU), Yekaterinburg 620002
Sverdlovsk Region, Russian Federation

Chigozirim Ndubuisi Onwusiribe
School of Public Administration and Entrepreneurship (SPAE)
Ural Federal University (UrFU), Yekaterinburg 620002
Sverdlovsk Region, Russian Federation

&

Longinus D.N. Nnadozie
Department of Agribusiness Management
Michael Okpara University of Agriculture, Umudike
Umuahia 7267, Abia State
Federal Republic of Nigeria

Optimizing Socio-Economic Systems in the Union State of Russia and Belarus: R & D, Higher Education, and Labor Markets in the Digital Economy
Collective Scientific Monograph

Editors: Galina V. Astratova, Maxim V. Vlasov, Chigozirim Ndubuisi Onwusiribe & Longinus D.N. Nnadozie

ISBN (Online): 979-8-89881-561-5

ISBN (Print): 979-8-89881-562-2

ISBN (Paperback): 979-8-89881-563-9

Published by Bentham Science Publishers Pte. Ltd. Singapore, in collaboration with
Eureka Conferences, USA.

First published in 2026.

Bentham Science Publishers Pte. Ltd.
No. 9 Raffles Place
Office No. 26-01
Singapore 048619
Singapore
Email: subscriptions@benthamscience.net

BENTHAM
SCIENCE

CONTENTS

FOREWORD

In an era defined by rapid technological advancement, geopolitical realignment, and unprecedented economic integration challenges, the quest to understand and optimize complex socio-economic systems has never been more critical. The Union State of Russia and Belarus represents a fascinating case study in economic integration, one that exists at the intersection of historical ties, contemporary geopolitical realities, and forward-looking digital transformation.

This volume, meticulously compiled under the leadership of Professors Galina V. Astratova, Maxim Vlasov, and Chigozirim Onwusiribe, emerges as a vital contribution to our understanding of how integrated economies can navigate the complexities of the digital age. It brings together a remarkable assembly of scholars across multiple disciplines, merging theoretical frameworks with practical applications to address pressing questions about optimal development pathways in interconnected economic systems.

What distinguishes this work is its comprehensive approach to examining the intricate relationships between seemingly disparate yet fundamentally connected sectors: the research and development services market, higher education systems, and evolving labor markets. The authors have admirably tackled the challenge of identifying optimal parameters for these systems' functioning through sophisticated methodological approaches, data mining, multifactor analysis, and economic-mathematical modeling, resulting in a work of substantial theoretical and practical significance.

Moreover, this book emphasizes the importance of fostering innovation ecosystems that leverage the unique strengths of both nations. By highlighting successful case studies and best practices, the authors provide a roadmap for enhancing collaboration between government, academia, and industry, which is essential for driving sustainable economic growth.

The timing of this research is particularly noteworthy. As economies worldwide reassess traditional models of growth and development in light of digital transformation, the insights presented here extend well beyond the specific case of the Russia-Belarus Union State. The mechanisms designed and analyzed throughout these pages offer valuable frameworks for policymakers, academic institutions, and economic strategists globally who are grappling with similar challenges of integration and optimization.

The authors' interdisciplinary expertise shines through in their treatment of creative human capital development—perhaps the most critical element in any knowledge economy. Their exploration of how educational institutions must evolve to meet emerging labor market demands while simultaneously driving innovation presents a balanced view that acknowledges both the transformative potential and inherent challenges of digitalization.

For researchers, this book provides a rigorous analytical foundation; for practitioners, it offers actionable insights into designing systems that can thrive amid constant change. The extensive international collaboration evident in this work also serves as a powerful reminder that academic inquiry transcends political boundaries, bringing together diverse perspectives in the service of shared knowledge advancement.

As we navigate the complex terrain of economic development in the twenty-first century, works like this—grounded in data, enriched by interdisciplinary thinking, and focused on practical applications—will prove indispensable guides. The authors have made a significant contribution to our collective understanding of how socio-economic systems can be optimally designed not just to weather change, but to harness it for sustainable development, ensuring that both Russia and Belarus can emerge as leaders in the global digital economy.

Inna V. Krakovetskaya
Department of National Research
Tomsk State University
Tomsk 634050, Tomsk Oblast
Russian Federation

PREFACE

The book addresses the optimal development of complex socio-economic systems within the Union State of Russia and Belarus, focusing on the research sector, higher education, and the labour market in the digital economy. The main scientific problem it tackles is identifying the optimal parameters for these systems' functioning, using methods such as data mining, multifactor analysis, and economic and mathematical modelling. The project aims to develop technologies for designing these systems based on the author's achievements in economic modelling and various analytical methods.

The most important aspects of modernity are considered, including 1) the mechanisms of development of complex socio-economic systems in new economic conditions (using the example of the Union State of the Russian Federation and the Republic of Belarus); 2) the problems and prospects of digitalization of the economy in new economic conditions; 3) topical issues of human capital development in the digital economy. The results of the authors' long-term theoretical and applied research are presented. The book is intended for specialists in the fields of education and science, research and teaching staff, graduate students, and undergraduates studying the problems of digitalization, modern higher education, and the labour market, as well as students of economic, sociological, and managerial specialties in Russia and Belarus.

Galina V. Astratova
Department of Regional Economics
Innovative Entrepreneurship and Economics (REIE&E)
Institute of Economics and Management
School of Public Administration and Entrepreneurship (SPAE)
Ural Federal University (UrFU), Yekaterinburg 620002
Sverdlovsk Region, Russian Federation

Maxim V. Vlasov
Department of Regional Economics
Innovative Entrepreneurship and Economics (REIE&E)
Institute of Economics and Management
School of Public Administration and Entrepreneurship (SPAE)
Ural Federal University (UrFU), Yekaterinburg 620002
Sverdlovsk Region, Russian Federation

Chigozirim Ndubuisi Onwusiribe
School of Public Administration and Entrepreneurship (SPAE)
Ural Federal University (UrFU), Yekaterinburg 620002
Sverdlovsk Region, Russian Federation

&

Longinus D.N. Nnadozie
Department of Agribusiness Management
Michael Okpara University of Agriculture, Umudike
Umuahia 7267, Abia State
Federal Republic of Nigeria

ACKNOWLEDGEMENT

The ideological inspirer and organizer of the team of authors for writing this book, as well as the developer of the general research methodology and the author of a number of research methods (for example, consumer behavior) was Professor Galina V. Astratova, whose range of research interests is extremely wide: from the problems of public administration to market management mechanisms of the R&D sector, higher education, digital economy and labour market.

An irreplaceable contribution to mathematical data processing and the development of new research methods was made by Dr. Chigozirim N. Onwusiribe and Professor Maxim V. Vlasov. A significant contribution to the literary and scientific translation of Russian-language texts, as well as the technical editing of electronic files, was made by Dr. Chigozirim N. Onwusiribe and Longinus D.N. Nnadozie. Each of the authors of the chapters and sections has made a full-fledged contribution to the writing of this monograph, as they are recognized experts in the stated problems. For example, Professor Natalia A. Simchenko and Associate Professor Airat M. Izmailov specialize in the sectoral problems of the labor market in the context of digitalization, as well as topical issues of the innovation infrastructure of the Union State of Russia and Belarus.

Professor Evgeny V. Sinitsyn and Associate Professor Viola A. Larionova are well-known experts in the field of mathematical modeling of socio-economic systems and innovation infrastructure.

Representatives of Belarus, Associate Professors – Irina A. Shamardina, Lyubov I. Tararyshkina, Boris A. Zhalezko – are also known for their work on a wide range of economic problems of Belarus and Russian-Belarusian economic relations.

INTRODUCTION

Galina V. Astratova, Chigozirim Ndubuisi Onwusiribe, Maxim V. Vlasov

In 2024, exactly 25 years have passed since the creation of the Union State of the Russian Federation and the Republic of Belarus, one of the most successful integration entities in the post-Soviet space in the 21st century1. In the context of the global formation of the knowledge economy and the digital transformation of society, as well as the creation of a unified scientific and technological space in the Union State of Russia and Belarus, a particular relevance are the issues of finding a source of financing for these transformations and, accordingly, state regulation, coordination and interaction of the higher professional education system, R & D and the labour market, which reflect the results of our earlier research[2].

The current situation is due to a number of factors described in detail in our previous studies[3], namely:

1. The global change in the role of the public sector and the importance of government regulation in sectors of national economies.
2. The introduction of digital (information) technologies into the business models of organizations in the commercial and non-profit sectors, which has become global and universal, defining the format of "digital life";
3. Changes in the formats of educational institutions, changes in the nature of the work of researchers and teaching staff of universities, as well as changes in the nature and conditions of students' education.
4. Changing consumer behaviour in the digital environment in general and in the educational services market, in particular.
5. A change in the role of human capital in society due to changes in the requirements for the qualifications and competencies of employees related to the knowledge, skills, and abilities of an individual in the digital environment, which led to a significant change in the nature of the work of employees in both commercial and non-commercial sectors.
6. The transformation of the innovation infrastructure of the Union State of the Russian Federation and the Republic of Belarus into a key factor in import substitution, sustainable development, and growth in new economic conditions.

1: The Union State: 25 years of integration – results and new tasks. June 06, 2024. – [Electronic resource]. [Available From: https://forumspb.com/programme/businessprogramme/131433/#broadcast] (accessed: 06.06.2024). (In Russ.).

2: Astratova, 2023b; Astratova, et al., 2022; Bengraf, et al., 2024; etc.

3: Astratova, et al., 2024; Astratova & Bekshaev, 2024; Astratova & Izmailov, 2024; Astratova & Sinitsyn, et al. 2024; Astratova, 2023 and 2023b; Astratova, et al., 2023; Astratova et al., 2022; Astratova et al., 2021; Bengraf, et al., 2024; Larionova et al., 2019; Simchenko et al., 2023; Shamardina, 2022; Sinitsyn et al., 2022; Tararyshkina, 2019; Tolmachev et al., 2019; Yanovskaya & Simchenko, 2024; Zhalezko et al., 2020; etc.

At the same time, both in the Russian Federation and in the Republic of Belarus, there are many controversial issues related to digitalization that need to be resolved in the very near future:

1. The nature of work, employment structure, and unemployment in the context of the use of digital/ information technologies;
2. Factors of discrimination and benefits for employees due to the use of digital / information technologies;
3. Problems of the use of digital/information technologies by civil servants, *etc*., where theory and practice are in the process of active formation.

Obviously, these issues should become an urgent research problem and be considered by scientists in the very near future.

Consequently, the need for a comprehensive, interdisciplinary study of complex socio-economic systems – higher professional education, R & D, and the labour market of the Union State of the Russian Federation and the Republic of Belarus—and the problems of sectoral state regulation of these systems in the context of the digitalization of the economy are becoming increasingly urgent. That is why the team of authors of this monograph attempted to consider some aspects of the stated problems.

The collective monograph presented to the readers is structured into four interconnected parts, addressing the core challenges of integration and digital transformation:

Part 1: General issues of integration and socio-economic systems examines the theoretical aspects of complex socio-economic system development, including mathematical models and mechanisms; traces the historical creation and evolution of the Union State; analyzes modern directions of Russian-Belarusian economic cooperation; and assesses key indicators within the R & D sector, Higher Education System (HES), and labour market of the Russian and Belarusian digital economy. These issues are described in detail in chapters:

CHAPTER 1 THEORETICAL ASPECTS OF THE DEVELOPMENT OF COMPLEX SOCIOECONOMIC SYSTEMS(MATHEMATICAL MODELS AND MECHANISMS).

CHAPTER 2 THE HISTORY OF THE UNION STATE OF THE RUSSIAN FEDERATION AND THE REPUBLIC OF BELARUS: CREATION AND EVOLUTION

CHAPTER 3 MODERN DIRECTIONS OF ECONOMIC COOPERATION BETWEEN THE RUSSIAN FEDERATION AND THE REPUBLIC OF BELARUS

CHAPTER 4 SOME ASPECTS OF THE MAIN INDICATORS ASSESSMENT IN THE CONTEXT OF THE COMPLEX SOCIO-ECONOMIC SYSTEMS DEVELOPMENT (R&D SECTOR, HES, AND THE LABOR MARKET) IN THE RUSSIAN AND BELARUSIAN DIGITAL ECONOMY

CHAPTER 5 ASSESSMENT OF THE DEVELOPMENT PROCESSES OF COMPLEX SOCIOECONOMIC SYSTEMS IN THE DIGITAL ECONOMY OF THE UNION STATE

Part 2: Development of the Science, Technology, and Innovation (STI) sector focuses on the innovative infrastructure of the Union State as a key factor for import substitution and development; explores public management of this infrastructure in the digital economy; identifies bottlenecks limiting public administration effectiveness in HES and R & D; analyzes economic mechanisms for stimulating scientific and innovative activity; discusses indicative planning in innovation activity management; and addresses the challenges of creative human capital. These issues are described in detail in chapters:

CHAPTER 6 INNOVATIVE INFRASTRUCTURE OF THE UNION STATE OF THE RUSSIAN FEDERATION AND THE REPUBLIC OF BELARUS AS A KEY FACTOR OF IMPORT SUBSTITUTION AND DEVELOPMENT IN NEW ECONOMIC CONDITIONS

CHAPTER 7 PUBLIC MANAGEMENT OF THE USRB INNOVATION INFRASTRUCTURE IN THE DIGITAL ECONOMY

CHAPTER 8 IDENTIFICATION OF BOTTLENECKS LIMITING THE EFFECTIVENESS OF PUBLIC ADMINISTRATION IN HES AND R&D SECTORS IN RUSSIA AND BELARUS

CHAPTER 9 ECONOMIC MECHANISMS FOR STIMULATING THE SCIENTIFIC AND INNOVATIVE ACTIVITY OF THE USRB

CHAPTER 10 INDICATIVE PLANNING IN THE PROCESS OF SMA'S MANAGEMENT OF INNOVATION ACTIVITY AT THE USRB

CHAPTER 11 THE CHALLENGES OF CREATIVE HUMAN CAPITAL IN THE DIGITAL ECONOMY

Part 3: Development of the higher education system and interaction investigates sectoral state regulation of higher education amid digitalization; consumer behavior characteristics, motives, and impact factors in the digital educational environment; the application of Artificial Intelligence and Data Analytics in educational process organization and quality assessment; comprehensive semantic and sentiment analysis for evaluating digital educational technologies in Russian universities; and human capital development within the integrated R & D and higher education context of the Union State digital economy. These issues are described in detail in chapters:

CHAPTER 12 SECTORAL STATE REGULATION OF THE HIGHER EDUCATION SYSTEM IN RUSSIA AND BELARUS IN THE CONTEXT OF DIGITALIZATION

CHAPTER 13 CONSUMER BEHAVIOR IN THE DIGITAL EDUCATIONAL ENVIRONMENT: MAIN CHARACTERISTICS, MOTIVES, AND IMPACT FACTORS

CHAPTER 14 ARTIFICIAL INTELLIGENCE AND DATA ANALYTICS IN THE ORGANIZATION OF THE EDUCATIONAL PROCESS AND QUALITY ASSESSMENT OF HIGHER EDUCATION

CHAPTER 15 EVALUATING DIGITAL EDUCATIONAL TECHNOLOGIES: A COMPREHENSIVE SEMANTIC AND SENTIMENT ANALYSIS IN RUSIAN

UNIVERSITIES

CHAPTER 16 HUMAN CAPITAL DEVELOPMENT IN THE CONTEXT OF INTEGRATING R & D AND HIGHER EDUCATION IN THE USRB DIGITAL ECONOMY

Part 4: Other cooperation issues between Russia and Belarus explores the labour market as a complex socio-economic system through mathematical modelling; the socio-technological nature of labour organization in the Union State's digital environment; the use of digital technologies in state and municipal administration; and synthesizes policies for advancing socio-economic integration and innovation. These issues are described in detail in chapters:

CHAPTER 17 THE LABOUR MARKET AS A COMPLEX SOCIO-ECONOMIC SYSTEM: SOME ASPECTS OF MATHEMATICAL MODELLING IN THE LABOUR MARKET OF THE UNION STATE

CHAPTER 18 THE SOCIO-TECHNOLOGICAL NATURE OF THE ORGANIZATION OF LABOR IN THE DIGITAL ENVIRONMENT OF THE UNION STATE

CHAPTER 19 THE USE OF DIGITAL TECHNOLOGIES IN THE STATE AND MUNICIPAL ADMINISTRATION OF THE RUSSIAN FEDERATION AND THE REPUBLIC OF BELARUS

CHAPTER 20. POLICY SYNTHESIS: ADVANCING SOCIO-ECONOMIC INTEGRATION AND INNOVATION IN THE UNION STATE OF RUSSIA AND BELARUS

List of Contributors

Airat M. Izmailov	Department of Digital Economics, Volga State University of Telecommunications and Informatics, Samara 443090, Middle Volga region, Russian Federation
Boris A. Zhalezko	Department of Marketing, Belarusian National Technical University, Minsk 220013, Republic of Belarus
Chigozirim N. Onwusiribe	School of Public Administration and Entrepreneurship (SPAE), Ural Federal University (UrFU), Yekaterinburg 620002, Sverdlovsk Region, Russian Federation
Evgeny V. Sinitsyn	Department of Management, Institute of Economics and Management, Ural Federal University (UrFU), Yekaterinburg 620002, Sverdlovsk Region, Russian Federation
Galina V. Astratova	Department of Regional Economics, Innovative Entrepreneurship and Economics (REIE&E), Institute of Economics and Management, School of Public Administration and Entrepreneurship (SPAE), Ural Federal University (UrFU), Yekaterinburg 620002, Sverdlovsk Region, Russian Federation
Irina A. Shamardina	Marketing Department, Belarusian National Technical University, Minsk 220013, Republic of Belarus
Longinus D.N. Nnadozie	Department of Agribusiness Management, Michael Okpara University of Agriculture, Umudike, Umuahia 7267, Abia State, Federal Republic of Nigeria
Lyubov I. Tararyshkina	Department of Eurasian Studies, Belarusian State University, Minsk 220030, Republic of Belarus
Maxim V. Vlasov	Department of Regional Economics, Innovative Entrepreneurship and Economics (REIE&E), Institute of Economics and Management, School of Public Administration and Entrepreneurship (SPAE), Ural Federal University (UrFU), Yekaterinburg 620002, Sverdlovsk Region, Russian Federation
Natalia A. Simchenko	Department of Economic Theory and Economic Policy, St. Petersburg State University, St. Petersburg 199034, Russian Federation
Viola A. Larionova	Department of Economics and Management of Construction and Real Estate Market, Ural Federal University (UrFU), Yekaterinburg 620002, Sverdlovsk Region, Russian Federation

CHAPTER 1

Theoretical Aspects of the Development of Complex Socio-Economic Systems (Mathematical Models and Mechanisms)

Evgeny V. Sinitsyn[1,*] and **Viola A. Larionova**[2]

[1] *Department of Management, Ural Federal University (UrFU), Yekaterinburg 620002, Sverdlovsk Region, Russian Federation*

[2] *Department of Economics and Management of Construction and Real Estate Market, Ural Federal University (UrFU), Yekaterinburg 620002, Sverdlovsk Region, Russian Federation*

Abstract: This chapter explores the theoretical foundations and methodological approaches to modeling and managing complex Socio-Economic Systems (SES). It examines simulation modeling as a powerful analytical tool for understanding system dynamics under conditions of uncertainty and environmental variability. The chapter discusses the challenges in developing accurate simulation models for SES, including parameter selection, adequacy assessment, and verification methods. Special attention is given to different classes of complex systems and their corresponding mathematical models, from deterministic to stochastic networks. The chapter also presents optimization methods for finding equilibrium states in multi-stakeholder systems, including Pareto optimization and the Groves group selection mechanism for resolving conflicts of interest. The proposed methodological framework enables policymakers to design effective economic mechanisms and control parameters that maximize system-wide efficiency while balancing the interests of all participants. This approach supports strategic decision-making in the rapidly changing environment of modern socio-economic systems.

Keywords: Decision-making, Economic mechanisms, Pareto optimization, Simulation modeling, Socio-economic systems, Stochastic networks, System optimization.

INTRODUCTION

Management of socio-economic systems is associated with significant difficulties associated with both the complexity of the system itself, characterized by many elements and the presence of cause-and-effect relationships of the system with the

* **Corresponding Author Evgeny V. Sinitsyn:** Department of Management, Ural Federal University (UrFU), Yekaterinburg 620002, Sverdlovsk Region, Russian Federation; E-mail: sinitsyn_ev@mail.ru

Galina V. Astratova, Maxim V. Vlasov, Chigozirim Ndubuisi Onwusiribe & Longinus D.N. Nnadozie (Eds.)

external environment, and the non-linearity of the processes occurring within it (Astratova & Klimuk, 2022; Bertalanffy, 1962).

At present, one of the key strategic state goals is to increase the effectiveness of managerial decisions in influencing socio-economic processes in a rapidly changing external environment[1] (Pasmurtseva, 2020). As it is well known, decision-making on the choice of a development strategy for a Socio-Economic System (SES) is based on a systematic approach to forecasting the future behaviour of the system, considering retrospective information, existing regularities of its dynamics, internal and external relations, opportunities and risks (Ansoff, 1989; Ermicheva, 2008; Lazimov & Nazarov, 2023; Pasmurtseva, 2020; *etc.*). Among the methods of research of complex SES, there are expert analysis methods, such as SWOT-analysis, Delphi method, structural and hierarchical expertise; methods of statistical analysis, including descriptive and inductive statistics, including factor analysis, correlation, and regression analysis; as well as a wide range of mathematical modelling methods (Golovko, 2020).

Among the methods of mathematical modelling, simulation modelling occupies a special place as a reliable tool for the analysis of complex SES, allowing for the study of their dynamics under conditions of uncertainty. In case of poorly structured interrelationships and variable external influences, Simulation Modelling (SM) allows a significant increase in the understanding of the development of the complex processes, and the results of the research can become the basis for management decision-making.

SM is a special case of mathematical modelling and represents the most effective tool for analysing the dynamics of the considered SES. These systems are characterized by high structural and functional complexity, the presence of formalized and non-formalized links with the external environment, uncertainty in predictive assumptions, and reactions to external influences.

Since the 1960s of the XX century, the rapid development of information technologies and experimental approaches to the management of socio-economic and production systems has contributed to the widespread use of SM, due to its practical significance as a tool for making managerial decisions. The theoretical foundations of SM include a set of methodological approaches and provisions, intuitive and formal methods, mathematical tools, and software for modelling and studying complex systems (Emelianov *et al.*, 2002; Bertalanffy, 1962).

---

1 Decree of the President of the Russian Federation of 21.07.2020 № 474 "On the National Development Goals of the Russian Federation for the period until 2030". Publication number: 0001202007210012. Date of publication: 21.07.2020. - [Electronic resource]. URL: http://static.government.ru/media/acts/files/1202007210012.pdf (date of reference: 22.04.2024). (In Russ.).

Terminologically, "simulation" is interpreted as the reproduction of real characteristics of objects, phenomena, or processes using a speculative abstract or physical model. Simulation allows us to understand the nature of a phenomenon, describe the processes occurring in the original object, and predict the future state of the object without resorting to experiments on the real object (Bertalanffy, 1962; Emelianov *et al.*, 2002; Naylor, 1975; *etc.*).

SM uses abstract models described by logical and mathematical relationships that represent causal relationships between the properties of the object and external factors, and in the case of complex systems, the relationships between the elements of the system. Mathematically, the simulation model is a logical and mathematical description of the system $U = \{u_1, u_2. .u_k\}$ and dependencies of its functional properties (G) on endogenous and exogenous parameters, $V = \{v_1, v_2. .v_k\}$.

In a broad context, the goal of SM is to find such a function G that not only describes with a given accuracy the state of the system U at a known set of parameters V, but also steadily predicts the future state of the system when varying the parameters. The functional dependence G can be expressed in various ways using a number of analytical expressions, differential equations, sign graphs, state maps, networks, *etc.* Based on a properly constructed model, an inverse problem can be solved to determine the values of the system parameters that ensure the transition of the system to a given state with optimal characteristics. Optimization methods are used to solve this type of problem (Emelianov *et al.*, 2002).

Let us pay attention to some key problems in the development of SM to describe complex SES under conditions of risk and uncertainty of the external environment. At the current stage of economic development, SES are characterized by complexity, interconnectedness with other systems, instability, and susceptibility to the influence of many factors at both local and global levels. In this regard, the task of complex reproduction of such system characteristics in SM is practically impossible and significantly complicates calculations. It follows that when developing a model, it is necessary to include only those properties of the original object that largely determine the behaviour of the object within the set of research objectives. From this point of view, the sufficiency criterion for selecting the configuration of reproducible system properties is the optimal ratio between the relative calculation error and its labour intensity. As a rule, to simulate the properties of the original object, several simulation models are created, which are compared with each other according to this criterion, and then the best model is selected.

The same problem arises when selecting the internal and external parameters of the system. It is important to understand which parameters should be considered when building the model. Here, the criterion of sufficiency is the degree of influence of these parameters on reproducible properties. The quality of the model is determined based on completeness and sufficiency of considering the various parameters of the system to describe the change in properties when varying the parameters with a given accuracy. In addition to the set of parameters, the range of their variation should be defined, which in turn indicates the domain of definition of the simulation model. The larger the model definition domain and the greater the number of system characteristics, the more complex the model will be, but the greater the number of characteristics and parameters, the more expensive it may be to implement the model.

The adequacy of the model is assessed based on the accuracy of the prediction of the system characteristics at various parameter values, but, as a rule, the adequacy of the model decreases when the model definition domain is expanded. The complexity of the model depends not only on the complexity of the system to be reproduced, but also on the total number of properties and parameters included in the model, as well as on the degree of accuracy required in determining the values of reproducible properties of the system. If the model has a large dimensionality, it is transformed into a hierarchical modular structure, each module of which is described separately, and the relationship between input parameters and output characteristics of the module is specified.

The control of complex systems is modelled with the help of system modules generating control actions. The creation of a conceptual model implies the algorithmization of control actions on the system as a whole and its constituent modules, as well as on the processes occurring in it. Control actions can initiate several processes within the system.

The external environment is also defined in the form of system modules that generate external influences that cause perturbations in the system and move it to another state based on certain rules. External influences lead to successive changes in the state of a complex system, including simultaneous changes to several system modules with parallel processes.

Based on the collection of initial data on the real system, the initial values of the system parameters are determined, which can be either deterministic or stochastic. For deterministic parameters, specific values of the real system act as initial values, while for stochastic parameters, the initial value is usually defined as their average value, or the frequency distribution of a random variable is specified. Distribution laws are determined empirically by analysing frequency histograms, comparing them with theoretical distributions, and selecting the best fit to the experimental data. Subsequent verification is carried out using Pearson's criterion of agreement (Emelianov *et al.*, 2002).

The next stage of modelling is the determination of input parameters and output parameters of all modules of the system, as well as their functional dependencies. Correlation and regression or dispersion analyses are used to identify the types of dependencies. The statistical significance of multiple regression coefficients is checked based on t-statistics, in the absence of statistical data on the functioning of the system in previous periods (for example, if it is a new system), functional dependencies are established by the researcher based on expert opinion on the predicted values of parameters and output characteristics of the system modules. For discrete parameters, their values are specified, and for stochastic parameters, the range of change is specified.

Thus, as a result of the conceptual description of the model, the functional algorithm of the system module is formally described, and certainty regarding input parameters and output characteristics is achieved. When the system is affected by control factors, the algorithms can be executed in parallel or sequentially, and the output characteristics of one module can act as input characteristics for another module. The whole set of developed algorithms with given initial values and ranges of input parameter changes represents a formalized description of the dynamics of evolution of a complex system under the influence of various changes in the external environment and system control.

Due to the peculiarities of the processes occurring in complex control systems, several classes of such systems can be distinguished, for which specialized mathematical models and modelling tools have been developed. For example, in complex software control systems, all processes are executed in parallel and use common system resources. The functional scheme of such a system includes a set of algorithms of all modules with specified initial values and limitations of active resources.

For systems with a structural type of control, the state of the system U at a time t is characterized by the output characteristics of all modules of the system (t). The functional algorithm of the system describes the sequential change in the system's state within the N-dimensional state space. The dynamics of the system's development are characterized by the trajectories connecting the points of the corresponding system states.

In the case of stochastic systems (networks) with discrete sets of states, the change in the system state occurs continuously over time. At any point, the state of the system can be determined by an identification function that distinguishes one state of the system from another. Functional algorithms for such systems have been developed to describe mass service systems in which the identifying feature is the number of requests for service. In the absence of random external influences, the algorithm can be presented in the form of differential equations that determine the change in the system state using transient and output functions (Naylor, 1975).

If in a stochastic network the state of the system is determined at discrete moments of time, such a system is called an automaton. An automaton changes its state as a result of the influence of an input signal at certain time intervals (cycles). In this case, the new state of the automaton is determined both by the impact of the input signal on the system and its previous state.

If the transitions of the system from one state to another are given by a continuous function of time, then a stochastic system is a stochastic network with a continuous set of states. The change of the system state occurs according to the probability distribution of states, and the output signal is determined by the probability distribution of outputs. To study the operation of stochastic automata, a special mathematical tool was created, which is known as a Markov chain (Morimoto, 1963).

The above classification of complex systems is not exhaustive. It is necessary to clarify the objectives of IM, the types of models being developed, and the choice of methods used to simulate various classes of complex systems. The IM method is selected based on the parameters, the type of control action, and the method of setting the time in the model. When changing time with a constant step Δt, the new state of the system module and itsoutput characteristicsare determined at the moments oftime $t_0 + \Delta tk$, where $k = 1,2,3....$

The second way to specify time is to limit the system to the moment of occurrence of a special state of the system. For example, the occurrence of external influences, the moment of reaction, and changes in the state of the system. In this case, the possible future events and special states of the system that may occur during the entire forecasting period are analysed, and the moments of time t_k, through which time flows in the model, are fixed.

To implement simulation models, various software tools based on modelling languages are used to solve various classes of IM problems. Simulation languages, by their structure, are problem-oriented (procedural) algorithmic languages designed to describe the behaviour of complex systems in time, based on event-driven algorithms. Unlike general-purpose programming languages, they use abstract conceptualization terms and can automate such operations as time modelling, execution of quasi-parallel algorithms, random event generation process, and collection and processing of statistical data. Currently, several modelling languages are used for software implementation of discrete (GPSS, SIMULA, SIMSCRIPT), continuous (MIMIC, ARTON), and composite (Rustle, NEDIS, UMS) models. In addition, there are ready-made software packages (GPSSWorld, Extend, Arena, Simulink) that allow the user to set model parameters, conduct experiments, and generate reports in various formats using built-in standard tools and graphical interfaces.

The reliability of the model is verified by comparison of the results obtained during the experiments with the properties of the real system. In the case of deterministic systems, the measure of adequacy is the deviation of certain properties of the model from the properties of the original system. If the deviation does not exceed the maximum permissible value, the model is considered adequate for the system. In the case of a stochastic system, the minimum acceptable probability is established at which the deviation of the properties of the model from the properties of the original is within the acceptable error.

However, direct comparison of the properties of the model and the original object can be difficult due to the lack of data on the future characteristics of the system under study or the inability to establish precise criteria for the validity of the model. In such cases, expert analysis of IM results is relied upon. During such an analysis, inconsistencies between the model and the system under study are identified, sources of discrepancies are studied, input parameters and modules with errors in the formulation of the algorithm are identified, and the correctness of the measurement of output characteristics and their sensitivity to changes in input parameters is checked.

If significant errors are identified in the process of creating a conceptual model and formalizing the functional processes of the system, then the model is adjusted both at the global level and at the local level, if it is necessary to introduce changes to individual modules of the system. An important aspect for the further application of the created model is to determine the area of its suitability, that is, the conditions under which this model can be used to predict the development of SES. Restrictions are imposed both on the range of changes in the input parameters of the model, including the parameters of external control actions, and on the output characteristics.

The developed simulation model of the SES allows computer experiments to determine the output characteristics of the system at different values of internal and external parameters within a given definition area. The purpose of the experiments is to determine such combinations of system parameters that achieve the maximum criteria for the effectiveness or optimality of the system functioning. These criteria are set based on the technical characteristics of the system and the required values of the output characteristics of the system. Experiments are conducted according to a plan based on scientific hypotheses and systematically study the effect of various system parameters on output characteristics under various external conditions. The result of the experiments is the modelling of the most favourable state of the SES and the conditions of transition to this state under the influence of control parameters, considering the uncertainty of the external environment.

The search for the optimal structure and parameters of the SES is based on the Pareto optimization method (Bula, *et al.*, 2017) and can be formulated by us as determining the economic mechanism of influence on the system (*a*) and the corresponding set of external control parameters (*x*) in such a way that the multidimensional objective function *W* (*a*) in equation 1 the impact on the system has reached its maximum value:

$$max\ \{W(a): a \in \prod\},\ a \in A, \qquad \textbf{(1)}$$

where $\prod$ is the set of Pareto-optimal solutions.

The target multivariate function of the control action efficiency *W(a)* in equation 1 has the following form:

$$W(x) = \sum_{i=1}^{n} l_i\, w_i\, (x),\ i=(1,n), \qquad \textbf{(2)}$$

where l_i – importance coefficients of strategic objectives $w_1, w_2, w_3 \ldots w_n$.

The set of strategic goals of the state policy in the sphere of management of various SES is determined based on the priorities of the concept of long-term socio-economic development of the state as presented in equation 2. Thus, the permissible parameters of the external control impact on the system should satisfy the following conditions as specified in equation 3:

$$M^* = maxW(a) = maxW(x),\ a \in A,\ x \in X. \qquad \textbf{(3)}$$

In addition, the economic mechanisms of public administration should be interconnected to ensure the maximum system-wide efficiency criteria. Accounting of the results of control measures on the system should be based on the harmonization of the interests of all parties involved. In this case, legal, economic, and administrative norms form a combination of external control parameters within a particular economic mechanism.

By outlining the vectors of economic behaviour of the various actors in equation 4:

d_i – vector of economic behaviour of the main actors of the processes

occurring within the socio-economic system ($d_i \in D$);

c_i – vector of economic behaviour of the subject of the Federation, ($c_i \in C$);

b_i – vector of economic behaviour of local governments ($b_i \in B$);

g_i – vector of economic behaviour of consumers ($g_i \in G$),

At a given combination of external parameters, *k*, it is possible to determine the full set of probable consequences of control actions on the system:

$$x = f\,(k,\ d_i, \ldots\ d_n,\ c_i, \ldots\ c_n,\ b_i, \ldots\ b_n,\ g_i, \ldots\ g_n). \qquad \textbf{(4)}$$

Let *S, U, V, and Z* be the preference functions of various participants in the economic processes taking place in the system. In this case, each participant strives to maximize the result preference function.

The mechanism for optimizing the system and coordinating the preferences of participants involves determining the balance of interests and responsibilities of all parties in equation 5. In this case, the optimal option should correspond to the highest value of the sum of the utility functions of all parties:

$$max\ Q(a) = max\ Q(x) = max\ F\ (S(x),\ U(x),\ V(x),\ Z(x)) \qquad \textbf{(5)}$$

In the case of a conflict of interest, the problem of finding economic equilibrium is solved using the Groves group selection mechanism (Groves, 1973). It assumes the possibility of compensating one or the other party for damage from a certain unfavourable outcome. Then the optimal transformation corresponds to the parameters of the instrument, characterized by maximizing all preference functions:

$max\ \{[S(x),\ U(x),\ V(x),\ Z(x)]: x \in X\}$,

$max\ \{[S(a),\ U(a),\ V(a),\ Z(a)]: a \in A\}$.

The method proposed by the authors makes it possible to find effective means of managing the socio-economic condition and making optimal decisions based on the coordination of the interests and responsibilities of all stakeholders. Similar positions on this issue are also set out in the study of models of the state strategic management system and the problems of their implementation (Pasmurtseva, 2020), as well as the digital transformation of public administration as a strategic public good (Nazarenko and Novikova, 2023).

CONCLUSION

The theoretical exploration of complex socio-economic systems presented in this chapter underscores the critical importance of simulation modeling as a methodological approach for understanding and managing these systems under conditions of uncertainty. The development of adequate simulation models requires careful consideration of system properties, parameters, and their functional dependencies, with a focus on achieving an optimal balance between model complexity and predictive accuracy. The chapter has demonstrated that effective management of socio-economic systems necessitates a comprehensive approach to modeling that accounts for both deterministic and stochastic elements, as well as the complex interrelationships between system modules. The classification of systems based on their control mechanisms—structural, stochastic networks, and automata—provides a framework for selecting appropriate mathematical tools and modeling languages for different types of socio-economic phenomena.

Of particular significance is the proposed optimization methodology based on Pareto principles and the Groves group selection mechanism, which enables the coordination of interests among various stakeholders within the system. This approach acknowledges that optimal control of socio-economic systems requires not only technical efficiency but also the balancing of potentially conflicting preferences among participants. The practical implications of this theoretical framework extend to policy formulation and strategic decision-making at various levels of governance. By employing simulation models that capture the essential dynamics of socio-economic systems, policymakers can test various combinations of control parameters to identify those that maximize system-wide effectiveness while respecting the constraints imposed by stakeholder interests and external environmental factors. As socio-economic systems continue to grow in complexity and interconnectedness, the methodological approaches outlined in this chapter will become increasingly valuable. Future research directions may include the refinement of these methods to incorporate emerging technologies such as artificial intelligence and big data analytics, which could further enhance the predictive power of simulation models and their usefulness in guiding strategic interventions in complex socio-economic systems.

In conclusion, the theoretical aspects discussed in this chapter provide a solid foundation for understanding and managing the development of complex socio-economic systems through mathematical modeling and optimization mechanisms, offering valuable insights for researchers, policymakers, and practitioners in the field of socio-economic system management.

CHAPTER 2

The History of the Union State of the Russian Federation and the Republic of Belarus: Creation and Evolution

Lyubov I. Tararyshkina[1,*]

[1] *Department of Eurasian Studies, Belarusian State University, Minsk 220030, Republic of Belarus*

Abstract: This chapter examines the historical development and evolving structure of the Union State of the Russian Federation and the Republic of Belarus (USRB), one of the most significant integration projects in Eurasia. The analysis traces the USRB's origins from the 1990 Agreement between the Russian and Belarusian Soviet Socialist Republics through subsequent treaties that established increasingly closer cooperation based on principles of sovereignty, territorial integrity, and peaceful relations. The chapter details how the 1999 Treaty on the Establishment of the Union State, which came into force in 2000, created the foundation for comprehensive integration across economic, political, and social spheres. The research demonstrates how the USRB experience served as a blueprint for broader regional integration, particularly in the formation of the Eurasian Economic Union (EAEU). It analyzes the implementation of numerous Union State programs in sectors including defense, customs infrastructure, agriculture, space technology, medicine, and environmental protection, highlighting the 35:65 funding ratio between Belarus and Russia. Special attention is given to the 28 union integration programs agreed upon in 2021, which represent a new phase in bilateral integration focusing on legislative harmonization, market unification, and coordinated policies across multiple sectors. The chapter concludes that the USRB functions as a crucial mechanism for ensuring economic security within the EAEU customs territory, while the ongoing implementation of integration programs continues to strengthen scientific, technological, and innovative development between Belarus and Russia, serving as a model for deeper Eurasian integration.

Keywords: Belarus-Russia integration, Bilateral treaties, Customs harmonization, EAEU, Supranational cooperation, Union State, Union programs.

INTRODUCTION

A particularly prominent example of a complicated socio-economic system is the supranational formation of the Union State of the Russian Federation and the

* **Corresponding author Lyubov I. Tararyshkina:** Department of Eurasian Studies, Minsk 220030, Republic of Belarusian State University, Belarus; E-mail: tararyshkina@rambler.ru

Galina V. Astratova, Maxim V. Vlasov, Chigozirim Ndubuisi Onwusiribe & Longinus D.N. Nnadozie (Eds.)

Republic of Belarus (USRB), which is currently the most prominent integration project in Eurasia. The favourable situation that supports the effective functioning of the Union State of the Russian Federation and the Republic of Belarus was preceded by considerable preliminary work on good-neighbourly cooperation and interstate cooperation. The Union State of the Russian Federation and the Republic of Belarus has its initial basis in the Agreement between the Russian Soviet Federative Socialist Republic and the Belarusian Soviet Socialist Republic of December 18, 1990[1], which stipulates, "The Parties recognize each other as sovereign states and undertake not to take any action that would be to the detriment of the state sovereignty of the other Party".

Then, treaties were adopted in the framework of the Treaty of Friendship, Good-Nepourish and Cooperation between the Russian Federation and the Republic of Belarus of February 21, 1995[2], the Treaty on the Formation of Community of Belarus and Russia of April 2, 1996[3], the Treaty on the Union of the Republic of Belarus and the Russian Federation of April 2, 1997[4], on development of friendly relations and cooperation based on the principle of respect for State sovereignty and territorial integrity, inviolability of borders, peaceful resolution of disputes and non-use or threat of use of force, equality, non-interference in internal affairs, respect for human rights and fundamental freedoms, and conscientious fulfilment of obligations.

In December 1998, the Presidents of the Republic of Belarus and the Russian Federation signed a Declaration on Further Unity of Russia and Belarus[5] in addition to a Treaty between the Russian Federation and the Republic of Belarus on Equal Rights of Citizens and an Agreement on Creating Equal Conditions for Business Entities of the Allied States. These reports described concrete steps for the realization of actual bilateral interstate integration.

The Treaty on the Establishment of the Union State was signed on December 8, 1999 came into force on January 26 2000[6], and the Action Program of the Repub-

---

1 The Agreement between the Russian Soviet Federative Socialist Republic and the Belarusian Soviet Socialist Republic dated December 18, 1990 [Electronic resource]. // Consultant Plus. Belarus / YurSpektr LLC, National Center for Legal Information. Republic Belarus. – Minsk, 2024. (accessed: 04/22/2024). (In Russian).

2 The Treaty of Friendship, Good-neighborliness and cooperation between the Russian Federation and the Republic of Belarus dated February 21, 1995 [Electronic resource] // Consultant Plus. Belarus / YurSpektr LLC, National Center for Legal Information. Republic Belarus.– Minsk, 2024. (accessed: 04/22/2024). (In Russian).

3 Education Agreement] Communities of Belarus and Russia dated April 2, 1996 [Electronic resource] // Consultant Plus. Belarus / YurSpektr LLC, National Center for Legal Information. Rep. Belarus.–Minsk, 2024. (accessed: 04/22/2024). (In Russian).

4 The Agreement on the Union of Belarus and Russia dated April 2, 1997 [Electronic resource] // Consultant Plus. Belarus / YurSpektr LLC, National Center for Legal Information. Republic Belarus.– Minsk, 2024. (accessed: 04/22/2024). (In Russian).

5 The Agreement on the Union of Belarus and Russia dated April 2, 1997 [Electronic resource] // Consultant Plus. Belarus / YurSpektr LLC, National Center for Legal Information. Republic Belarus.– Minsk, 2024. (accessed: 04/22/2024). (In Russian).

6 The Treaty on the establishment of the Union State of December 8, 1999 [signed in Moskve08.12.1999] // National Register of Legal Acts of the Republic of Belarus, 14.01.2000, No. 4, 2/118, "Vedomosti of the National Assembly of the Republic of Belarus", 2000, No. 1-2, art. 1. (In Russian).

lic of Belarus and the Russian Federation for implementation of the Treaty on the Establishment of the Union State established the aims, objectives and main ideological directions for constructing the Union State[7] of Belarus and Russia which were included in the legal framework of the Treaty on the Eurasian Economic Union the Treaty of the EAEU on May 29, 2024[8] (hereinafter known as the EAEU Agreement) with the mechanisms for its implementation under the conditions of the customs territory of the Eurasian Economic Union (EAEU).

The findings of a comparative analysis of the basic provisions of the Treaty on the Establishment of the Union State and the EAEU Agreement are set forth in our previous study (Astratova *et al.*, 2024). It is found that the strategic approaches outlined in the Treaty on the Establishment of the Union State to facilitate closer integration of the economies of Belarus and Russia by employing common competition rules and standards for consumer protection, a uniform monetary, currency, tax and pricing policies; a single trade and customs tariff policy in regard to third countries, international organizations and associations, and other ideological directions were encapsulated in the provisions of the EAEU Agreement.

The integration strategic objective is to ensure the free movement of goods, services, capital, and labour. Moreover, in the EAEU, there is considerable emphasis on the coordinated, aligned, or unified policy in the sectoral economy. The basis for establishing the Customs Union of the Republic of Belarus, the Republic of Kazakhstan, and the Russian Federation was the Agreement between the Governments of Belarus and Russia on the completion of unification and creating a unified system of tariff and non-tariff regulation in the Union State, dated January 29, 2001[9].

The Agreement establishes the intention to apply a single customs tariff (import and export) when trading with third countries. The customs regulation experience in the Union State became the basis for supranational customs legislation in the Eurasian Economic Union (EAEU). The EAEU customs territories rely on customs regulation principles, customs regulation, and customs administration

7 The Action Program of the Republic of Belarus and the Russian Federation for the implementation of the provisions of the Treaty on the Establishment of the Union State [adopted in Moscow on 08.12.1999)] // Zvyazda, No. 236, 1999, "Soviet Belarus", No. 296, 1999. (In Russian).

8 The Treaty on the Eurasian Economic Union 01.10.2019) (with amendments and additions, intro. effective from 04/05/2022). – [Electronic resource] : [signed in Astana on 05/29/2014] // Consultant Plus. Belarus / YurSpektr LLC, National Center for Legal Information. Rep. Belarus.– Minsk, 2024. (accessed: 04/22/2024). (In Russian).

9 Agreement between the Government of the Republic of Belarus and the Government of the Russian Federation on the completion of unification and creation of a unified system of tariff and non-tariff regulation in the Union State dated January 29, 2001// National Register of Legal Acts of the Republic of Belarus, 2002, No. 41, 3/335. (In Russian).

rules and practices developed in the USRB. Therefore, the integration effort of Russia and Belarus in the Union state laid the foundation for forming and reaching the strategic aim of Eurasian integration by going to a "five" format (Tararyshkina, 2019).

According to Article 32 of the Treaty on the Establishment of the Union State of December 8, 1999, the USRB's budget is intended to fund Union State programs and projects, its operations, including the maintenance of its organs. The Union State has adopted and is proceeding to implement several dozen sectoral programs in health care, industry, transport, educational services, *etc.*, and it is continuing to develop and implement new projects to strengthen union integration. The revenue part of the USRB's budget is made up of fixed contributions from its participating states from the national budgetary resources of Belarus and Russia, and from non-tax revenue. The contributions to the USRB budget are treated as macroeconomic indicators and are expressed as the equity contributions of the Republic of Belarus and the Russian Federation - 35:65.

The Union State programs are implemented in accordance with the Procedure for development and implementation of Union State programs, approved by Resolution No. 7 (as amended on September 14, 2022 No. 19)[10] of the Council of Ministers of the Union State, rather, 57 Union State Programs, over the 2000s, have included development of new technologies and innovative products in the following fields: radio electronics, microelectronics, microwave electronics, optoelectronics, microsystem engineering, thermal imaging technologies; defence and security and compliance; customs infrastructure and customs processing technology; agriculture and food processing; space technologies, devices and instruments; high performance computing and software; collaborative action to respond to the Chernobyl emergency; the manufacture of chemical fibres, yarn and composite materials; hydrometeorology and environmental protection; diesel powered automotive and agricultural vehicles; medicine and pharmacology; protection of common information resources; social relations and labour relations. A funded Stem Cells project, methods of treatment using cells and tissue engineering have been developed, and studies have been undertaken in medical universities in Belarus and Russia to prepare specialists in regenerative medicine[11].

---

10 On the Procedure for the development and implementation of programs of the Union State and the List of joint programs, subprograms, projects and activities [Electronic resource]: Resolution of the Council of Ministers of the Union State dated October 11, 2000 No. 7 (ed. dated 09/14/2022 No. 19). URL: http://bii.by/tx.dll?d=71011 . (accessed: 04/20/2024). (In Russian).

11 Union programs and projects // Union State [Electronic resource]// Access mode: http:// https://www.postkomsg.com/programs . (accessed: 04/20/2024). (InRussian).

In 2024, total financing as part of the activities of the Standing Committee, including Union State programs, will be over 6 billion Russian rubles. The implementation of six of the seven programs has continued which were started after 2023 in the area of national security: "Improvement of the border security of the Union State", "Improvement of military infrastructure facilities planned for joint use in the interests of ensuring the regional grouping of troops (forces) of the Republic of Belarus and the Russian Federation" and "Modernization of logistics facilities planned for joint use in the interests of ensuring the regional grouping of troops (forces) of the Republic of Belarus and the Russian Federation". This year, it is also planned to implement high-tech programs: from space activity - Complex - SG, in the field of microelectronics - Intel auto, and in the area of photonics - Component-F[12]. The 28 union integration programs of Belarus and Russia agreed upon in the Decree of the Supreme state Council con 6 dated 4 November 2021, "On the Main directions for the implementation of the provisions of the Treaty on the Establishment of the Union State for 2021-2023"[13], have a new direction of developing the bilateral integration of Belarus and Russia.

Customs cooperation occupies an important position in the framework of the implementation of the 28 Union Programs. In accordance with the Agreement on Harmonization of Customs Legislation of the Russian Federation and the Republic of Belarus and Cooperation in the Customs Sphere of March 4, 2022[14], the customs authorities cooperate in such areas as information interaction and mutual exchange of information; operation of an Interstate Center for Coordinating Risk Management, analytics, and monitoring of customs activities; joint customs inspection; categorizing entities performing customs operations; cooperating with mobile groups of customs authorities of the Parties; regulation of the institution of authorized economic operator. Implementation of the described customs transformation directions in the context of "joint integration" in the customs territory of the EAEU will make it possible to achieve a cohesive framework for customs regulation.

---

12 In 2024, nine programs of the Union State will be implemented [Electronic resource]//Access mode: https://www.sb.by/articles/vot-taki--komponenty.html . (accessed: 04/22/2024). (In Russian).

13 On the main directions of implementation of the provisions of the Treaty on the Establishment of the Union State for 2021-2023 [Electronic resource]: Decree of the Supreme State Council of the Union State, November 4, 2021 No. 6, Minsk – Moscow// Consultant Plus. Belarus / YurSpektr LLC, National Center for Legal Information. Rep. Belarus. – Minsk, 2024. (InRussian).

14 Agreement on harmonization of customs legislation of the Russian Federation and the Republic of Belarus and cooperation in the customs sphere from March 4, 2022 [Electronic resource] // Consultant Plus. Belarus / YurSpektr LLC, National Center for Legal Information. Republic Belarus.–Minsk, 2024. (accessed: 04/22/2024). (In Russian).

In addition, it should be stressed that in the contexts of the implementation of the 28 Union Programs, considerable significance is also attached to a set of measures in a vast range of industry and sphere issues, including 1) unification of legislation of both countries in various industries of an economy; 2) bringing alignment to business conditions; 3) creating common financial and energy markets; 4) creating a transport space; 5) harmonising the labour market, *etc.*

Additionally, it is important in the context of the outlined developments that the Union programs envisage the creation of a common scientific and technological space, as well as a unified industrial, innovative, educational, migration, and agricultural policy in this sense. Both countries adopted a number of legislative acts that have to do with the innovative and scientific and technological development of the national economies and individual sectors and areas right up until 2020, which were extended to 2025, and then again extended to 2030. The implementation of such inheritance of directions would not only contribute to strengthening the bilateral union integration of Belarus and Russia but also deepen Eurasian integration through the economic interaction and cooperation between the USRB and the EAEU.

Therefore, the analysis of the historical stages along with an economic and legal rationale for the creation and development of the Union State of the Russian Federation and the Republic of Belarus shows that the USRB serves as a rampart to ensure economic security in the customs territory of the EAEU. The execution of 28 Union programs will further enhance the scientific, technological, and innovative development of the national economies and particular components of the Union State of Belarus and Russia.

CONCLUSION

The evolution of the Union State of the Russian Federation and the Republic of Belarus represents one of the most successful examples of post-Soviet integration, demonstrating how historical, cultural, and economic ties can be leveraged to create robust supranational structures. From its conceptual origins in the 1990 Agreement through its formal establishment in 1999-2000 and subsequent development, the USRB has consistently provided a framework for deepening bilateral cooperation while respecting the sovereignty of both member states.

The analysis presented in this chapter reveals several significant findings. First, the USRB has served as a crucial testing ground for integration mechanisms that were later adopted by the broader Eurasian Economic Union, particularly in areas of customs regulation, tariff policy, and cross-border cooperation. The experience gained through the Union State directly informed the construction of the EAEU's legal and institutional architecture, highlighting the USRB's role as an integration laboratory within the post-Soviet space.

Second, the implementation of numerous sectoral programs across industries ranging from microelectronics to agriculture, from space technologies to healthcare, illustrates the comprehensive nature of the integration process. The coordinated budget system, with its established 35:65 contribution ratio between Belarus and Russia, has provided stable financing for these initiatives, demonstrating a consistent political commitment to the integration project despite changing geopolitical circumstances.

Third, the adoption of the 28 union integration programs in 2021 marks a significant new phase in the development of the Union State. These programs address fundamental aspects of economic integration, including legislative harmonization, market alignment, unified industrial and innovation policies, and coordinated approaches to energy, transport, and labor markets. This renewed commitment to integration comes at a critical juncture in international relations and reflects both countries' strategic decision to deepen their alliance in response to external challenges.

Looking forward, the Union State faces both opportunities and challenges. On one hand, the continued implementation of the integration programs promises to create a more cohesive economic space with reduced barriers to trade, investment, and labor mobility. The shared scientific and technological space envisioned in these programs could enhance the competitive position of both countries in critical industries, including microelectronics, photonics, and advanced manufacturing. On the other hand, the integration process must navigate complex questions of national sovereignty, economic asymmetry, and alignment with other regional integration initiatives, particularly the EAEU. The success of the Union State will depend on maintaining the careful balance between deepening cooperation and respecting the distinct national interests of both member states.

In conclusion, the Union State of the Russian Federation and the Republic of Belarus stands as a significant achievement in post-Soviet integration. Its historical development, institutional structures, and ambitious integration agenda provide valuable insights into the dynamics of regional cooperation. As both countries continue to implement their shared vision of integration through the 28 union programs and other initiatives, the USRB is likely to remain a central pillar of Eurasian integration and a key mechanism for ensuring economic security and prosperity in an increasingly complex global environment.

CHAPTER 3

Modern Directions of Economic Cooperation Between the Russian Federation and the Republic of Belarus

Irina A. Shamardina[1,*]

[1] *Marketing Department, Belarusian National Technical University, Minsk 220013, Republic of Belarus*

Abstract: This chapter examines the modern economic cooperation between the Russian Federation and the Republic of Belarus, analyzing their integration within the framework of the Union State. It explores the historical foundations and current dynamics of their bilateral relations, with particular focus on trade flows, investment patterns, and sectoral collaboration in areas such as manufacturing, energy, transportation, and education. The analysis reveals significant growth in bilateral trade turnover, which increased 2.6 times from 2005 to 2021, despite asymmetries in economic size and structure. The chapter details how Russia remains Belarus's key trading partner, accounting for nearly half of Belarus's foreign trade, while Belarus represents about 5% of Russia's trade turnover. Special attention is given to the implementation of 28 union programs across 11 sectors that form the backbone of their integration agenda for 2024-2026. The research also highlights challenges to full economic integration, including differences in institutional structures, sectoral legislation, and the predominance of the public sector in Belarus. Nevertheless, it concludes that global and regional developments, including sanctions against Russia and mutual policies of import substitution, are likely to accelerate cooperation between the two states, with digital transformation and the formation of a unified information space serving as key drivers of future integration.

Keywords: Belarus-Russia trade, Bilateral investment, Economic integration, Educational harmonization, Import substitution, Sectoral cooperation, Union State.

INTRODUCTION

Cooperation between the two states the Russian Federation and the Republic of Belarus has various prerequisites, including a common language, as well as geographical, cultural, political, and social factors, as well as deep historical roots.

* **Corresponding author Irina A. Shamardina:** Marketing Department, Belarusian National Technical University, Minsk 220013, Republic of Belarus; E-mail: gorira@yandex.by

Galina V. Astratova, Maxim V. Vlasov, Chigozirim Ndubuisi Onwusiribe & Longinus D.N. Nnadozie (Eds.)

In the modern world economy, the internationalization of states is expressed in integration processes and formalized in relevant agreements. Internationalization is also facilitated by various international ratings comparing the economies of different countries Table **1**.

Table 1. The economic situation of the Russian Federation and the Republic of Belarus in 2023 in the global context, compiled by the authors based on the source.

Name of indicators	Russian Federation	Republic of Belarus
GDPonPPP $ bn.	4,649.7	202.0
GDP per capita, PPP$	31,967	21,709

(Dutta *et al.*, 2024, pp. 87 and 179)

Table **1** shows that both fraternal countries have good potential for mutually beneficial cooperation. After the collapse of the USSR, the countries continued to strengthen their relations within the framework of the activities of the CIS, then the Union State. As noted above, the signing of the agreement on the creation of the USRB in the 90s took place as part of the deepening of integration processes between these states, which are already members of the CIS.

The rapprochement of the Slavic countries was based on a willingness to cooperate more closely in various fields and increase the potential for cooperation and mutual benefit. Parameters indicating the effectiveness of such decisions are contained, first, in the statistics of trade relations[1].

Thus, over the period from 2005 to 2021, the total trade turnover between the two countries increased from $15,995.6 million up to $4, 3003,565.39 million, that is, 2.6 times since and maintains an upward trend. It should also be noted that under the conditions of Western economic sanctions against Russia, not only the division of foreign trade into “friendly” countries (including Belarus) and “unfriendly countries” took place, but also a noticeable increase in the total turnover of the Russian Federation. Thus, in the fundamental work of Alexander Knobel (Knobel&Firanchuk, 2023), it is noted that in 2022, Russia's total trade turnover amounted to $850.5 billion, and the positive balance increased to $332.4 billion. At the same time, exports reached a record level of $591.5 billion

1 Despite the fact that the Union of the Russian Federation and the Republic of Belarus has been functioning since the late 90s, statistics reflecting trade flows between the countries have been presented on the official websites of central banks since 2000. At the same time, in the period from 2005 to 2011, the balance of payments were compiled according to the MFB Methodology in the 5th edition, and with the transition in 2009 to the sixth edition of the Methodology, the recalculation of indicators was carried out until 2005. In addition, separate publications of central banks and the Standing Committee of the SG on the balance of Payments of the two countries for the period after 2021. There were none at the time of writing this monograph.

(+19.9%), and imports amounted to $259.1 billion, stabilizing at the end of 2022 at new levels: supplies from the UK and USA fell 6–7 times, from other large "unfriendly" countries by one and a half to two times; but most significantly Geographically close neutral countries Turkey and Kazakhstan have increased supplies to the Russian market.

Returning to trade with Belarus, it should be noted that due to the different sizes of the economies, the volume of trade is uneven. Russia remains a key partner of Belarus: the total foreign trade turnover of goods in 2021 amounted to $78.9 billion, of which almost half (49.9%) is accounted for by trade with the Russian Federation. The share of the Republic of Belarus in the trade turnover of the Russian Federation amounted to 4.9%.

In the period from 2005 to 2021, there was a negative balance of trade in goods and services in the balance of payments of the Republic of Belarus on an ongoing basis. The deficit of trade in goods between the Republic of Belarus and the Russian Federation has increased from $3.5 billion (5.7% of GDP) for 2020 to $7.4 billion. (10.8% of GDP) for 2021, mainly due to the outstripping growth of imports (by 44.6%) compared with the growth of exports (by 26.0%)[2].

There was an increase in exports by individual commodity groups (except fuel and energy products), which affected the supply of metals and products made from them (by $1.2 billion), chemical industry products (by $0.9 billion), machinery, equipment, and vehicles (by $0.6 billion). The most important for the Belarusian economy are supplies from Russia of mineral products (97.7%), ferrous and non-ferrous metals (73.9 and 54.6%), wood (54.1%), building materials (49.3%), machinery and equipment (40.1%).

In turn, the share of the Republic of Belarus as a consumer country of Russian goods is 4.7% of the total exports of the Russian Federation. The Belarusian market is the most significant for Russian exporters of textiles, leather raw materials, machinery, equipment, and vehicles; construction materials: the share of supplies to Belarus in the total volume of Russian exports for these commodity groups is 26.3%; 25.9%; 11.4% and 10.6%, respectively (Zhalezko *et al.*, 2020).

Exports of Belarusian goods to Russia increased by more than a quarter (by $3.3 billion), up to $16.0 billion, accounting for 23.4% of GDP and 41.0% of total exports of goods of the Republic of Belarus.

---

2 Source: Balance of payments of the Republic of Belarus with the Russian Federation. The official website of the National Bank of the Republic of Belarus. –[Electronic resource]. URL: https://www.nbrb.by/bel/statistics/balpaybelrus (accessed: 02/28/2024). (In Russian).

The growth dynamics of 40.6% is provided by an increase in the supply of machinery and equipment. The main part of Belarusian exports to Russia is represented by machinery, equipment, and vehicles ($4.8 billion), with a share of 30.7% in total imports and supplies of Belarusian food products to the Russian market ($4.6 billion or 29.3% of Russia's total imports from Belarus). The demand of Russian consumers for intermediate goods from the Republic of Belarus is stable: imports of chemical industry products – $2.0 billion, metals and products – $ 1.3 billion[3].

The share of the Republic of Belarus in the total imports of the Russian Federation amounted to 5.3%. The most significant segments of the Russian market for Belarusian suppliers are: food (12.1% of total Russian imports), wood (9.3%), building materials (8.4%), and textiles (6.5%).

Over the period 2005-2021, the volume of trade in services between the two countries increased by more than 2 times. The balance of mutual trade in services for 2021 was positive for the Republic of Belarus in the amount of $326.9 million, or 0.5% of GDP. Its formation was mainly influenced by telecommunications, computers, information services ($216.7 million), and services for processing material resources belonging to other parties ($124.3 million) and transportation services ($39.6 million). The largest negative balance with Russia was in construction services ($140.7 million). Exports of services to the Russian Federation in 2021 amounted to $1.9 billion, or 2.7% of GDP (18.2% of total exports of services of the Republic of Belarus), and increased by 21.7%, primarily due to an increase in exports of telecommunications, computer and information services (1.4 times), transport services (by 27.5%) and construction services (by 16.4%). The structure of exports of services from the Republic of Belarus to the Russian Federation in 2020 and 2021 is shown in Fig. (**1**).

The main types of services purchased from residents of the Russian Federation remained transportation services (31.4%), construction services (26.6%), and travel services (9.3%). The structure of imports of services to the Republic of Belarus from the Russian Federation in 2020 and 2021 is shown in Fig. (**2**).

It should be noted that the problem of modernization and development of railway infrastructure is important in ensuring the development of foreign trade. In 2023, rail transportation of Belarusian foreign trade goods to Russian ports increased 2.3 times compared to the level of 2022. The governments of both sides have set a

3 The balance of payments and the international investment position of the Union State for 2021/ - [Electronic resource] / The Central Bank of the Russian Federation and the National Bank of the Republic of Belarus. – 2022. -49 with . URL: https://www.cbr.ru/content/document/ file/71387/union_state_pb.pdf (accessed: 02/28/2024). (In Russian).

priority for the development of infrastructure sections of Russian Railways and the Belarusian Railway to ensure the transportation of promising volumes of goods from Belarus to the ports of the northwestern region of Russia.

Building regional economic relations is a priority for both countries. Cooperation is being established with all regions. For this purpose, joint working groups have been created, which include representatives of almost 60 regions. Currently, regional cooperation is regulated by more than 70 agreements, and more than 300 agreements have been concluded between the regions, districts, and cities of both countries. There are 11 branches of the Embassy of the Republic of Belarus in Russia: in Yekaterinburg, Kazan, Kaliningrad, Krasnoyarsk, Nizhny Novgorod, Novosibirsk, Rostov-on-Don, St. Petersburg, Smolensk, Ufa, and Khabarovsk.

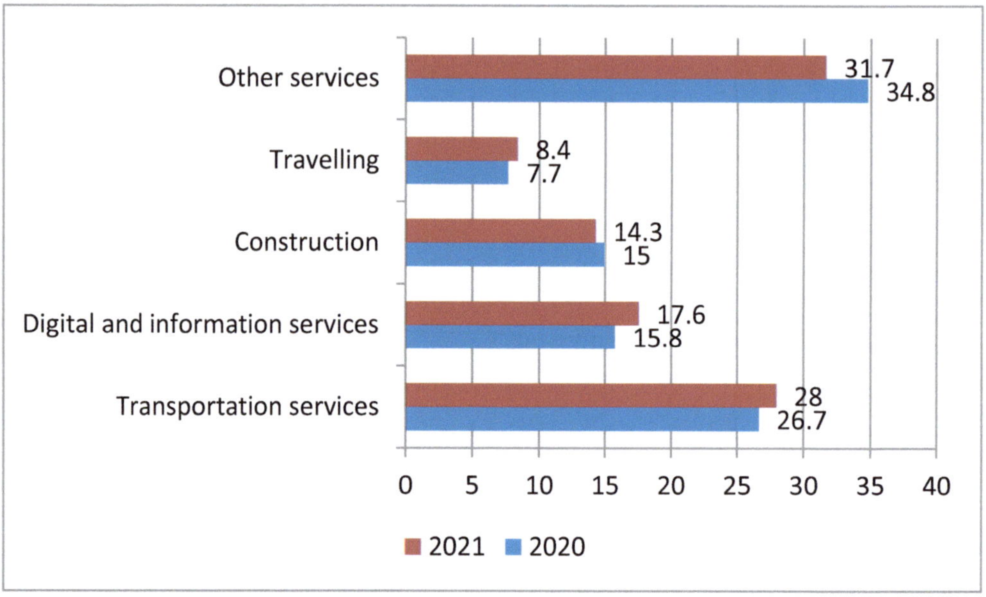

Fig. (1). Structure of services exports from the Republic of Belarus to the Russian Federation in 2020 and 2021[4], %.

---

4 The balance of payments and the international investment position of the Union State for 2021/ - [Electronic resource] / The Central Bank of the Russian Federation and the National Bank of the Republic of Belarus. – 2022. -49 with . URL: https://www.cbr.ru/content/document/file/71387/union_state_pb.pdf (accessed: 02/28/2024).(InRussian).

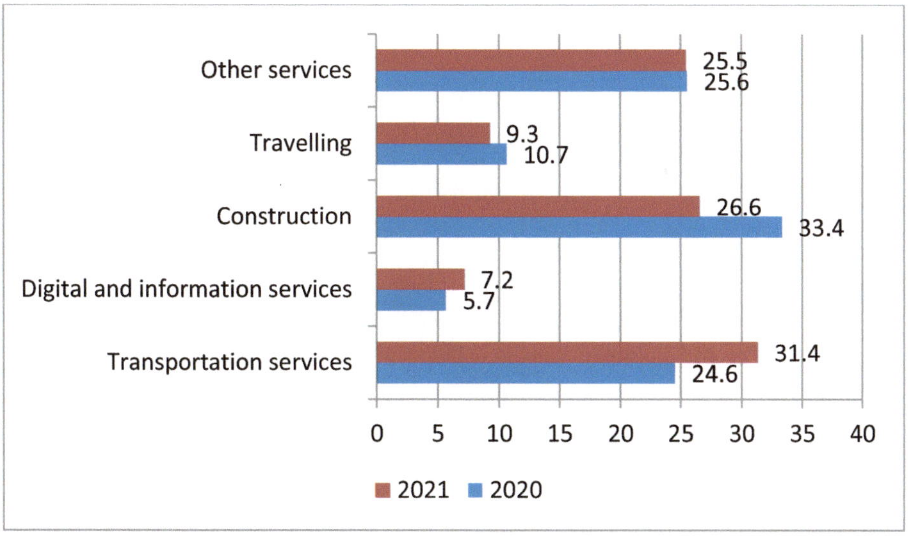

Fig. (2). Structure of imports of services to the Republic of Belarus from the Russian Federation in 2020 and 2021[5], %.

Cooperation between the two countries is developing not only in trade, but also in mechanical engineering, petrochemistry, energy, transport, construction, and the agro-industrial complex. More than 8000 Belarusian and Russian enterprises cooperate closely in the areas of raw materials supply and joint production. For example, about half of the truck parts of the Minsk Automobile Plant are manufactured in Russia[6].

Forty-five joint ventures and 154 retail chains with Belarusian capital are registered on the territory of 40 subjects of Russia. There are more than 2,000 organizations with Russian capital and about 1,300 joint ventures in the Republic of Belarus (Siparo, 2023).

Russia is also one of the main investors in the Belarusian economy; the volume Of Foreign Direct Investment (FDI) is about 45% of the total share of FDI in the

5 The balance of payments and the international investment position of the Union State for 2021/ - [Electronic resource] / The Central Bank of the Russian Federation and the National Bank of the Republic of Belarus. – 2022. -49 with . URL: https://www.cbr.ru/content/document/file/71387/union_state_pb.pdf (accessed: 02/28/2024).(In Russian).

6 Source: the official website of the Minsk Automobile Plant. – [Electronic resource] . URL: https://maz.by /-(accessed: 04/22/2024).(InRussian).

republic. More than 60 different investment projects are being implemented in Belarus. Cooperation continues on the implementation of the SRB programs: "Autoelectronics", "Safety-SG", "Electronmash-65", Microtech-SG, "Optics SG". The Russian Federation and the Republic of Belarus are actively involved in joint projects in the fields of crop production, animal husbandry, and land reclamation.

A number of key institutions and developments within the framework of the USRB have no analogues yet, including in the EAEU format. In particular, within the framework of the Union State of the Russian Federation and the Republic of Belarus, institutions of the Union budget and union ownership (for infrastructure facilities, intellectual products) have developed and are developing, which are not yet typical of other integration structures. The budget of the Union State funds union programs in various fields (space, information technology, microelectronics, agriculture, border security, overcoming the consequences of the Chernobyl disaster, *etc.*).

Equal rights of citizens of the two countries are ensured, and a unified system of social guarantees has been created. Today, Russian and Belarusian citizens have almost the same opportunities for employment, choice of place of residence, education, medical care, and social security. When crossing the Belarusian-Russian border, Belarusians and Russians do not need to pass border control, customs inspection, or receive and fill out a migration card[7].

At the supranational level, the interaction of states is determined by the Action Program of the Russian Federation and the Republic of Belarus on the implementation of the provisions of the Agreement on the Establishment of the USRB[8] and the Main Directions for the implementation of the provisions of the Agreement on the Establishment of the USRB (hereinafter – the Main Directions).

During the period 2021-2023, five integrated information platforms were created, including on traceability and labelling of goods, transport control, veterinary and phytosanitary control; currency and customs regulation were harmonized; measures to ensure information security in the financial sector were developed; uniform rules for access to public procurement, competition rules and trade activities were developed; approaches to the formation of a unified industrial

7 The Union State [Electronic resource] / The official website of the President of the Republic of Belarus. URL: https://president.gov.by/ru/belarus/economics/integracija/sojuznoe-gosudarstvo. (accessed: 02/28/2024).(InRussian).

8 The Program of Actions of the Russian Federation and the Republic of Belarus on the implementation of the provisions of the Treaty on the Establishment of the Union State [Electronic resource] / Website of the Union State. URL: https://soyuz.by/programma-deystviy-rossiysky-federacii-i-respubliki-belarus-po-realizacii-polozheniy-dogovora-o-sozdanii-soyuznogo-gosudarstva. (accessed: 02/28/2024).(InRussian).

policy, joint investment projects are being implemented; the conditions of work in the transport and communication markets have been formed; the conditions for mutual access of tour operators to the market of tourist services have been determined.

A number of measures have been implemented in other areas; several dozen different agreements, laws, decrees, and resolutions have been signed and adopted. Among other things, equal rights have been provided to citizens of Belarus and Russia in the social and labor sphere, and the permissive employment procedure has been abolished[9].

Currently, the Main Directions for 2024-2026 have been approved[10]. According to the program document, the cooperation will be aimed at further forming a regulatory framework for the development of joint economic potential and sectoral cooperation in various fields, the development of specific projects in the fields of industry, agriculture, healthcare, transport, education, statistics, sports and tourism, scientific and technical cooperation, and in the information space.

All these areas for the new three-year period are structured, as already noted above, into 11 sections and 28 union programs[11], including macroeconomic, tax and customs policy, financial market, cooperation in trade and consumer protection, the functioning of unified energy markets, and the safe operation of nuclear energy facilities. The document also contains a block on humanitarian cooperation, including the creation of a common information space.

The integration of countries in the field of education is being actively implemented. Belarusians can enrol in Russian universities on equal terms with Russian citizens, both by general competition and within the government quota.

According to Belstat[12], the peak figures of Belarusian students in Russian universities were recorded in 2011 – 21.2 thousand (only 3.6 thousand of them studied full–time), and by 2022 their number approached 6.3 thousand (3.9

---

9 The Supreme Council approved the Main directions for the implementation of the provisions of the Treaty on the Establishment of the Union State for 2024-2026 [Electronic resource] / BELTA News Agency. URL: https://www.belta.by/society/view/vgs-utverdil-osnovnye-napravlenija-realizatsii-polozhenij-dogovora-o-sozdanii-sojuznogo-gosudarstva-na-612363-2024/. (accessed: 02/28/2024). (In Russian).

10 Decree No. 2 dated January 29, 2024 "On the main directions of implementation of the provisions of the Treaty on the Establishment of the Union State for 2024-2026" [Electronic resource] / Website of the Union State. URL: https://soyuz.by/projects/dekrety-vysshego-gosudarstvennogo-sov-ta-soyuznogo-gosudarstva/dekret-ot-29-yanvarya-2024-g-2-ob-osnovnyh-napravleniyah-realizacii-polozheniy-dogovora-o-s-zdanii-soyuznogo-gosudarstva-na-2024-2026-gody. (accessed: 02/28/2024). (In Russian).

11 The Supreme Council approved the Main directions for the implementation of the provisions of the Treaty on the Establishment of the Union State for 2024-2026 [Electronic resource] / BELTA News Agency. URL: https://www.belta.by/society/view/vgs-utverdil-osnovnye-napravlen-ja-realizatsii-polozhenij-dogovora-o-sozdanii-sojuznogo-gosudarstva-na-612363-2024/. (accessed: 02/28/2024). (In Russian).

12 It will become easier for Belarusians to enroll in Russian universities[Electronic resource] / Sputnik Belarus News Agency. URL:https://sputnik.by/20230217/postupit-v-vuzy-rossii-belorusam-stanet-prosche-1072428208.html (accessed: 02/28/2024). (In Russian).

thousand – full-time students). In the early 2010s, the highest number of Russian students in Belarusian universities was also recorded. In 2011, there were 1.8 thousand (1.4 thousand full–time students), and in 2022, 1.1 thousand (843 full–time students). However, in the Department of International Cooperation of the Ministry of Science and Higher Education of Russia in February 2023, it was reported that twice as many Belarusian students study in Russia – about 12.5 thousand. The ministry also assured that this indicator has not changed significantly in the last 5 years[13].

In April 2021, the Ministry of Education and Science of the Russian Federation simplified admission to universities for applicants from Belarus, with the opportunity to count the results of the Belarusian Centralized testing as the result of an entrance test conducted by universities independently. This allowed Belarusian students to enrol in Russian universities on budget places within the allocated quotas or on a paid basis without passing the Unified State Exam. In general, the possibility of studying on a budget basis for Belarusian students in Russia has increased. If in 2015 only 91 quotas were allocated for Belarusian students, then in 2023. The number of quotas has increased to 1300[14].

Many issues in the field of education remain unresolved, starting from the education system as a whole (Russia has been with the Bologna process since 2003, Belarus has been an observer since 2015, which was reflected, for example, in obtaining the first stage of higher education in Russia, where a bachelor's degree is awarded, and in Belarus – a specialist), the principles of student recruitment (in Russia – based on the Unified State Exam, in Belarus – centralized testing, centralized examination), before the distribution of university graduates (in Belarus, trained specialists must work for two years at a fixed place, in Russia there is no such requirement).

Nevertheless, considerable attention is paid to the issue of training highly qualified specialists in the scientific, technological and economic spheres, since it is assumed that the unification of education standards will create a solid foundation for further integration of the economies and social systems of Russia and Belarus, will form a common understanding of technological, economic and political processes (Shamardina, 2022; Zhalezko, *et al.*, 2020).

---

13 It will become easier for Belarusians to enroll in Russian universities[Electronic resource] / Sputnik Belarus News Agency. URL:https://sputnik.by/20230217/postupit-v-vuzy-rossii-belorusam-stanet-prosche-1072428208.html (accessed: 02/28/2024). (In Russian).

14 The Russian government has increased the tuition quota for Belarusian students by 43%[Electronic resource] /Ministry of Science and Higher Education of the Russian Federation. URL: https://static.minobrnauki.gov.ru/press-center/news/mezhdunarodnoe-sotrudnichestvo/50741 (accessed: 02/28/2024). (In Russian).

Despite the obvious progress of cooperation between the Russian Federation and the Republic of Belarus, there are certain problems in the formation of a single economic space. Among these is the asymmetry of integration processes, which can be explained by the different size of the two economies (significant differences in GDP, territory, population, resource potential, economic policy, *etc.*), greater involvement of some areas in integration compared to others, *etc.* The natural process of cooperation is hindered by the predominance of the public sector over the private sector in Belarus, differences in the sectoral legislation of both countries, and the institutional structure.

In the light of modern global and regional events, the reorientation of economies to the eastern vector of development, the strengthening of the interdependence of economies as a result of sanctions restrictions, and the expressed policy of import substitution within the USRB, closer cooperation between states in all directions is seen in the near future. The vector activating these processes will be the formation of a unified information space, the implementation of the results of digital transformation, including in the educational sphere.

CONCLUSION

The economic cooperation between the Russian Federation and the Republic of Belarus represents a significant case of regional integration with far-reaching implications. Despite the challenges posed by asymmetric economies, differing institutional frameworks, and regulatory disparities, both nations have demonstrated remarkable progress in building mutual economic ties and advancing their integration agenda within the Union State framework.

The substantial growth in bilateral trade turnover increasing 2.6 times from 2005 to 2021 reflects the deepening economic interdependence between the two countries. Russia's position as Belarus's primary trading partner and a major source of foreign direct investment underscores the strategic importance of this relationship to the Belarusian economy. Simultaneously, Belarus has carved out important niches in the Russian market, particularly in machinery, food products, and services sectors. The implementation of coordinated policies across multiple domains from industrial cooperation and energy markets to financial systems and social guarantees signals the comprehensive nature of integration efforts. The approval of Main Directions for 2024-2026, encompassing 28 union programs across 11 key sectors, provides a clear roadmap for future collaboration and reflects political commitment to the integration process.

Current geopolitical realities, particularly Western sanctions against Russia and the consequent reorientation toward eastern markets, have created additional impetus for strengthening bilateral economic ties. The shared emphasis on import substitution and technological sovereignty is likely to accelerate integration in high-priority sectors such as manufacturing, agriculture, and digital technologies.

Looking forward, the formation of a unified information space and digital transformation appear to be the most promising vectors for deepening integration. These developments, coupled with ongoing harmonization in education and professional qualification systems, will be crucial for cultivating the human capital necessary to support joint economic initiatives. While challenges remain in reconciling differences in economic structures and governance models, the trajectory of Belarus-Russia economic cooperation suggests a continuing evolution toward a more integrated economic space that serves the strategic interests of both nations in an increasingly complex global environment.

CHAPTER 4

Some Aspects of the Main Indicators Assessment in the Context of the Complex Socio-economic Systems Development (R & D sector, HES, and the labor market) in the Russian and Belarusian Digital Economy

Galina V. Astratova[1,*], **Boris A. Zhalezko**[2] and **Airat M. Izmailov**[3]

[1] *Department of Regional Economics, Innovative Entrepreneurship and Economics (REIE&E), Institute of Economics and Management, School of Public Administration and Entrepreneurship (SPAE), Ural Federal University (UrFU), Yekaterinburg 620002, Sverdlovsk Region, Russian Federation*

[2] *Department of Marketing, Belarusian National Technical University, Minsk 220013, Republic of Belarus*

[3] *Department of Digital Economics, Volga State University of Telecommunications and Informatics, Samara 443090, Middle Volga region, Russian Federation*

Abstract: This chapter examines the assessment methodologies and indicators used to evaluate Complex Socio-Economic Systems (CSES) development in the context of Russian and Belarusian digital economies, with particular focus on R & D, Higher Education Systems (HES), and labor markets. The chapter begins by establishing the theoretical foundation of indicators and indices, explaining their importance for measuring progress toward Sustainable Development Goals. It then analyzes specific indicator systems applied to evaluate scientific and technological development, including technological equipment measures, the ICT Development Index, and various university ranking methodologies. The authors present comparative data showing the relative positions of Russia and Belarus in global technological advancement rankings, revealing significant gaps between these countries and world leaders. Special attention is given to university rankings, where Russian institutions (with Moscow State University leading) are making progress but still lag behind Western counterparts, while Belarusian universities remain in lower tiers. The chapter further explores the digitalization of educational environments through electronic information and educational resources, examining how these technologies affect institutional effectiveness and rankings. Finally, the authors review labor market indicators in the

* **Corresponding author Galina V. Astratova:** Department of Regional Economics, Innovative Entrepreneurship and Economics (REIE&E), Institute of Economics and Management, School of Public Administration and Entrepreneurship (SPAE), Ural Federal University (UrFU), Yekaterinburg 620002, Sverdlovsk Region, Russian Federation; E-mail: galina_28@mail.ru

Galina V. Astratova, Maxim V. Vlasov, Chigozirim Ndubuisi Onwusiribe & Longinus D.N. Nnadozie (Eds.)

digital economy context, discussing various measurement approaches, including composite indices that reflect intellectual development and creative work characteristics. The research concludes that while numerous methodologies exist, each has limitations that may distort empirical findings, particularly in transformational economies like Russia and Belarus.

Keywords: Complex socio-economic systems, Digital economy, Higher education rankings, Indicators assessment, Labor market metrics, R & D development, and Technological advancement indices.

INTRODUCTION

In its most general form, the indicator is derived from primary data that do not allow correct interpretation of changes in the external and/or internal environment of an economic entity, and secondly, correctly interprets the state and/or dynamics of changes in a number of variables. Economic, social, and environmental Indicators are used when it is necessary to describe "... phenomena or conditions of the natural environment" (Laverov, 2004, p. 43); and they "... always point to something that is beyond direct consideration" (Tarasova & Kruchina, 2006, p. 127). Together with indicators in socio-economic research, it is customary to use aggregated (weighted) indicators called indices, the use of which is justified in cases where the causal relationships between variables are well understood (Laverov, 2004, p. 43-76). The use of indices and indicators is due to many reasons, such as:

- The high cost (unavailability) of direct observation of the phenomenon under study;
- The importance of decisions for forecasting or developing strategic plans.
- Facilitating access to information for different categories and groups of users.
- Standardization and unification of the exchange of scientific and technical information.
- Simplification of data analysis and interpretation of observed phenomena, *etc.* (Borodin, 2023; Dudina & Tarasova, 2022; Laverov, 2004; Zhalezko *et al.*, 2022; *etc.*).

Accordingly, indicators of the development of Complex Socio-Economic Systems (hereinafter referred to as CSES) are necessary to be able to measure, track (monitor), access, and analyze the pace, dynamics, and effectiveness of the movement of countries, regions, industries, and business entities towards achieving the Sustainable Development Goals (hereinafter referred to as SDGs). Moreover, development indicators allow adjusting the strategy and tactics of achieving the SDGs. It is also important that many development indicators appear due to the fact that often the measurement of quality of life, happiness, personal hopes and personal progress, ethnicity and cultural affiliation, appearance or intelligence are absent from the generally accepted SDG indicator system, which does not allow "... to make the concepts of a safe and equitable space for humanity and the SDGs more inclusive and comprehensive" (Custodio, *et al.*, 2023, p. 1).

Currently, the most developed indicators in the scientific literature characterize the achievement of SDGs. In this regard, two methods of their construction are known:

- *Creation of a development indicators system*, where each individual indicator illustrates individual aspects of SDGs achievement. As a rule, economic, social, environmental, and institutional subsystems of indicators are distinguished.
- *Development of an integral (aggregated) indicator* or index that allows assessing the degree of sustainability of socio-economic development. Usually, the aggregation of indicators is implemented based on three groups of CSES indicators: environmental, ecological-economic, and ecological-socio-economic (Laverov, 2004, p. 43-76).

With regard to such CSES as R & D, higher education, and the labor market in the context of digitalization, it should be noted that, on the one hand, these systems are reflected in separate SDGs indicators, for example:

A. Social indicators. Promoting education, training, and public awareness;
B. Human Development Index (HDI) that evaluates the level of average achievements of a country by three indicators: 1) a long and healthy life; 2) knowledge; 3) a decent standard of living (Tarasova & Kruchina, 2006, p. 138).

On the other hand, these CSES (R & D, higher education, and the labor market in the context of digitalization), due to their complexity, have their own indicators for assessing their development. Moreover, in the context of the development of the knowledge economy and the information society, the indicators of R & D and higher education are often considered together (Chugunov, 2011).

For example, to determine the place of a country in the world ranking of scientific and technological development, you can use two "sets" of indicators:

- Knowledge intensity (input parameters, which usually include the share of R & D expenditures in the country's GDP; the absolute number of researchers; the specific number of researchers in the country);

- Scientific output (output parameters, or effectiveness/efficiency and competitiveness) (Chugunov, 2011, p. 13).

With the implementation of digitalization in the world, an impressive number of methods and methodologies have been proposed for calculating various indicators and indices used for comparative analysis of the information development of countries, the use of ICT in various sectors of national economies, and the introduction of e-government technologies. However, researchers usually rely on three basic indicator systems:

- The indicator of technological equipment – integrates data on five types of technical means using special statistical methods: personal computers, mobile phones, the Internet, fax machines, and televisions;
- Transparency of communications – assesses the degree of use of ICT in the processes of interaction between government, business, and the public, both among themselves and within each of the individual communication groups;
- The Information Society Index (ISI) – allows measuring national information capabilities and information capital, defining indicators such as: computer, information, social, and Internet infrastructure (Chugunov, 2011; Sergeev & Artyushkin, 2016; Shtrik, 2002, *etc*.)

In addition, individual consulting companies and rating agencies are developing their own methods and methodologies for measuring the level of scientific and technological development of countries. For example, Global Finance conducts an annual ranking of countries according to the level of scientific and technological activity, as well as the ability to create and use advanced technologies. To calculate the annual ranking of countries, this company uses the following groups of indicators:

- Internet users as a percentage of the country's population and LTE (4G) users as a percentage of the population;
- An indicator of digital competitiveness that measures a country's current technological environment and its prospects for future success;
- The share of GDP spent on R & D, reflecting the government's investment in future technological progress and the desire to compete for this future evolution (Getzoff, 2023).

The combination of these three sets of indicators makes it possible to rank countries by the level of technological capabilities and the level of ownership of these technologies by the population. The resulting annual ranking of countries gives an idea of the technological state of the countries (Table **1**).

Table 1. The most technologically advanced countries and territories of the world, according to global finance in 2023, compiled by the authors based on M. Getzoff (2023).

Rating	Country	Total Score
1	South Korea	6.63
2	USA	4.94
3	Taiwan	4.90
4	Denmark	4.79
5	Switzerland	4.68
...	...	...
38	China	– 0.23
...	...	...
44	Russian Federation	– 0.98
...	...	...
53	South Africa	– 3.54
...	...	...
57	Ukraine	– 4.49

As can be seen from (Table **1**), according to the level of technological development, the Russian Federation is not even among the "ten" technologically developed countries, taking 44th place, and the Republic of Belarus is not even in the top hundred.

According to Global Finance experts, compared with 2022, in 2023 the differences became more pronounced in terms of digital competitiveness and investment in R & D (Getzoff, 2023). Obviously, Russia and Belarus have something to work on to expand their Internet base and LTE penetration.

Also in recent decades, the ICT Development Index (IDI) has been separately identified and calculated – this is an index published by the International Telecommunication Union of the United Nations, using many indicators (the number of people using the Internet; % of the population covered by the 3G mobile network; coverage of 3G and 4G/LTE networks; Internet traffic per subscription; *etc.*) and allowing measure the digital divide and compare the effectiveness of ICTs both within and between countries (Table **2**).

Table **2** shows that the Russian Federation and the Republic of Belarus are not on the list of the best countries in the ICT Development Index (IDI).

Table 2. The ranking of countries according to the ICT Development Index (IDI), compiled by the authors based on the source[1].

Rating	Country	Total Score
1	Singapore	97.4
2	Estonia	96.9
3	Finland	96.7
4	USA	96.6
5	Malaysia	94.5
...	...	...
	Russian Federation	88.9
...	...	...
	Republic of Belarus	86.9

In the context of global competition and the struggle for a place in world rankings, there are also higher educational institutions, where, as we noted earlier, governments are no longer key players, and competition has taken on an institutional character, which "... led to a multi-level form of competition and the transformation of universities into full-fledged business competitors"(Astratova, *et al.*, 2021, p. 27). This thesis is confirmed by the research results of other authors (Brennan, 2004; Global HES Rep, 2022; Musselin, 2018, *etc.*).

In order to stand out in the competition, in the 60s of the XX century, the editors of US News decided to invest in educational ratings as a tool for competitive distinction and identification (Espeland, 2015). The decision turned out to be successful and led to the tradition of annual university rankings. By now, the ratings of THE, QS, ARWU, and a number of others are known. Over the past twenty years, universities from the USA and Great Britain have been consistently in the "top ten" universities in the world (Table **3**).

1 Source: ICT Development Index 2023. International Telecommunication Union. Retrieved 2024-01-01. – [Electronic resource]. URL: https://www.itu.int/itu-d/reports/statistics/IDI2023/ (accessed: 25.05.2024).

Table 3. The "top ten" universities in the world and the place of leading Russian and Belarusian universities in the world university ranking in 2023, according to the (TimesHigherEducation)[2].

Rating	Name, Country, Region	Number of Students, TOTAL	Number of Students per 1 Teaching Staff Member	Number of International Students	The Ratio of Women to Men
1.	University of Oxford, UK	20 965	10.6	42%	48: 52
2.	Harvard University, USA	21 887	9.6	25%	50: 50
3.	University of Cambridge, UK	20 185	11.3	39%	47: 53
4.	Stanford University, USA	16 164	7.1	24%	46: 54
5.	Massachusetts Institute of Technology, USA	11 415	8.2	33%	40: 60
	California Institute of Technology, USA	2 237	6.2	34%	37: 63
6.	Princeton University, USA	8 279	8.0	23%	46: 54
7.	University of California, Berkeley, USA	40 921	18.4	24%	52: 48
8.	Yale University United States, USA	13 482	5.9	21%	52: 48
9.	Imperial College London, UK	8 545	11.2	61%	40: 60
...	-	-	-	-	-
163.	Moscow State University (MSU), Russia	32 625	10.0	36%	50: 50
201-250	Moscow University of Physics and Technology (MIPT), Russia	6 083	11.5	20%	н / д
301-350	Peter the Great St. Petersburg Polytechnic University, Russia	16 375	9.7	32%	41: 59
401-500	Higher School of Economics, Russia	32 102	17.5	11%	н / д
...	-	-	-	-	-
1201-1500	Ural Federal University (UrFU), Russia	26 370	13.1	17%	50: 50
...	-	-	-	-	-
1501+	Belarusian State University (BSU), Belarus	14 082	7.9	18%	60:40

As follows from Table 3, the permanent leader in the rating of THE is Lomonosov Moscow State University (MSU), which is in the top 200 ranking of the best universities in the world. Other Russian universities have significantly increased their indicators[3] of scientific and educational activities, but are in a position no higher than 201-250. Moreover, competition among Russian universities has intensified over the past 2-3 years. Therefore, for example, the Ural Federal University, despite the increase in absolute indicators in the overall ranking, fell from the position 201-250 in 2021-2022 to 1201-1500 in 2023.

As for the universities of the Republic of Belarus, there are only seven universities in the 1501+ position in the ranking, among which the Belarusian State University is the leader.

In the context of the digitalization of educational institutions, new ratings are also emerging. For example, in 2024, an Autonomous Non-profit Organization "Digital Economy", with the support of the Association of Computer and Information Technology Enterprises (ACITE) and the Ministry of Finance of Russia, published a rating of universities in the digital economy (Table 4).

Table 4. Rating of regional universities of the digital economy[4].

No	Name of the University
1	Ural Federal University named after the first President of Russia, B.N. Yeltsin
2	Novosibirsk State Technical University
3	Novosibirsk National Research State University
4	National Research Tomsk Polytechnic University
5	Kazan (Volga Region) Federal University
6	Lobachevsky National Research Nizhny Novgorod State University
7	Southern Federal University
8	Tomsk State University of Control Systems and Radioelectronics
9	Perm National Research Polytechnic University
10	Voronezh State University

2 Source: World University Rankings 2023. – [Electronic resource]. URL: https://www.timeshighereducation.com/world-university-rankings/2023/world-ranking (accessed: 25.05.2024).

3 The main indicators of comparison are: forms of education (including distance learning), student and teacher mobility, international cooperation, the use of electronic educational technologies, multi–channel financing (primarily extra–budgetary), R & D volumes, citation indexes, the number of publications in Scopus and Web of Science journals Q1 and Q2, *etc.*

4 Source: Ranking of universities in the digital economy. 2023. – [Electronic resource]. URL: https://d-economy.ru/project/rejting-vuzov-cifrovoj-jekonomiki / (accessed 01.07.2024). (In Russ.).

Table **4** showcases that the leader among Russian universities in the digital economy is the Ural Federal University named after the first President of Russia, Boris Yeltsin (hereinafter – UrFU).

This provision is primarily due to the fact that, in the context of digitalization, higher education is undergoing changes, primarily due to the use by all employees of an educational institution of an Electronic Information and Educational Environment (EIEE). Modern EIEE includes information technologies, technical means, and electronic information resources, electronic educational resources that contain electronic educational and methodological materials, as well as state information systems, and ensures that students master educational programs in full, regardless of the location of the students[5]. It is important in the context of our research that the EIEE components can also be tools for compiling various ratings in the HES market. Accordingly, the EIEE in UrFU consists of a set of components that increase the effectiveness of the educational process due to modern information technologies, such as[6]:

- Services for accessing curricula, work programs of disciplines (modules), practices;
- Electronic library systems and electronic educational resources;
- E-learning systems;
- Services for recording the progress of the educational process, the results of intermediate certification, and the results of mastering the basic education.
- Services that ensure the formation of a student's portfolio;
- Services that ensure interaction between participants of the educational process;
- Services that improve the efficiency and quality of the educational process at the University, including the implementation of mechanisms and procedures for monitoring the quality of the educational process.

Also, when compiling indices and ratings of educational institutions, indicators such as the availability of Electronic Educational Resources (EER) are often used. In this regard, we can say that, for example, UrFU actively uses EER, which, according to the completeness of the implemented cycle of educational activities, is divided into electronic educational content and an electronic course (Fig. **1**).

---

5 Source: About education in the Russian Federation: Feder. The law grew. Federal Law No. 273-FZ dated December 29, 2012. – [Electronic resource]. URL: https://docs.cntd.ru/document/902389617 (accessed: 07/01/2024). (In Russ.).

6 Source: Regulations on the electronic information and educational environment of the University. Ural Federal University named after the first President of Russia B.N. Yeltsin. – [Electronic resource]. URL: https://vsalda.urfu.ru/fileadmin/user_upload/site_15357/Raznoe/Polozhenie_ob_ehlektronnoi_informacionno-obrazovatelnoi_srede_universiteta.pdf(accessed 01.07.2024).(InRuss.).

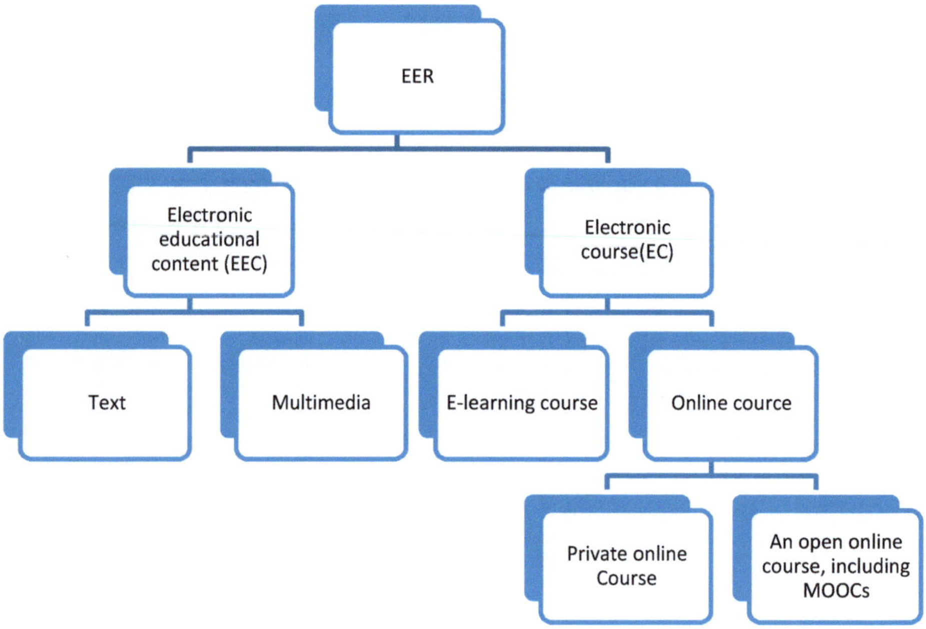

Fig (1). Classification of electronic educational resourcesin UrFU[7].

Also, when compiling indexes and ratings of educational institutions, indicators such as the types of digital educational platforms and courses used are often used (Fig. **1**). For example, in the Republic of Belarus, such platforms include: "All Courses" (vse-kursy. by), "Lerna" (lerna.by), "Leader" (lider.by), and others. In Russia, the range of digital platforms providing access to online educational courses is represented by the following portals: Intuit (intuit.ru), "Lectionary" (lektorium.tv), "Universarium" (universarium.org), "HTML Academy" (htmlacademy.ru), and others (Astratova & Izmailov, 2024; Research Edumarket, 2022; Zhalezko *et al.*, 2022). In relation to individual universities, we can say that the palette of platforms and courses used here is very large (Astratova & Izmailov, 2024; Astratova and Klimuk *et al.*, 2021; Research EdMarket, 2022). This is also illustrated by the data from our survey (Fig. **2**).

---

7 SThe order on the introduction of the Regulation on electronic educational Resources, Version 1. –[Electronic resource]. URL:https://urfu.ru/fileadmin/user_upload/common_files/education/methodological_council/krom/2023/20230303_Prikaz_po_osnovnoi_dejatelnosti_No_0167_03_ot_15.02.2023__O_vvedenii_v_deistvie_Polozhenija_ob___ehlektronnykh_obrazovatelnykh_resurs__.pdf(accessed: 07/01/2024). (In Russ.).

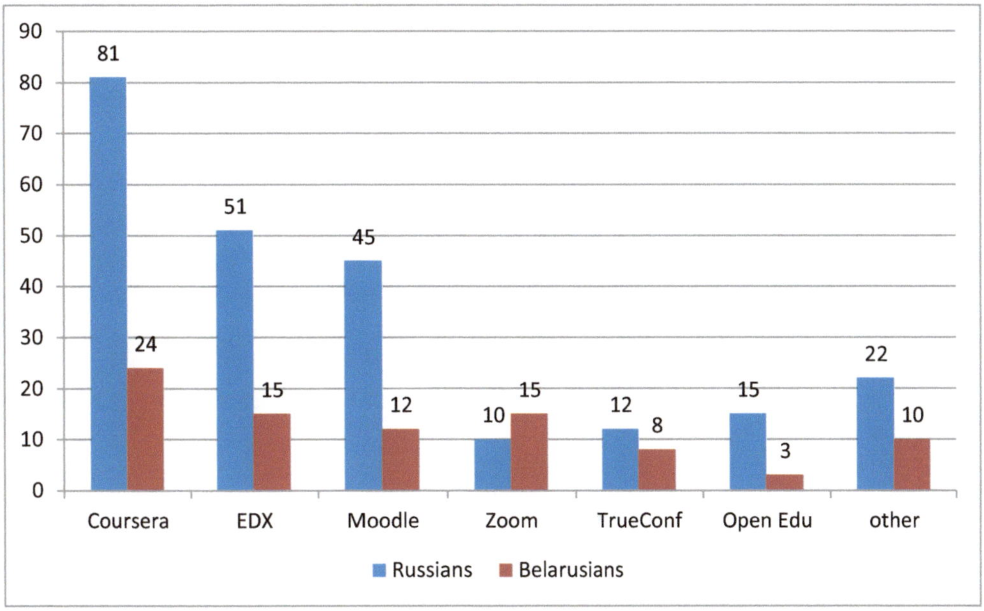

Fig (2). Respondents' answers to the question: "On which platforms are you looking for massive open online courses (MOOCs)?", people, compiled by the authors *(N_1=353; N_2=58; n_1 =349; n_2 = 56; K_k = 0,22; K_c = 0,84)*[8] Source: Survey data in Google Docs and processing in Statistica Note: It was possible to select multiple platforms.

In addition, for example, at the UrFU Online Course Directory for educational Program managers for the 2023-2024 academic year, you can see that it contains 1,139 online courses from 23 educational marketplaces, educational platforms, corporate educational systems with courses, including HTML academy, Skillbox, SkillFactory, SKB Contour, Netology, and Sberbank University[9] (Fig. **2**). The Moodle software tool is most often used for the distance learning system. Today, this tool is used in more than two hundred countries around the world (Research EdMarket, 2022). This also suggests that in the conditions of the digital economy,

---

8 Symbols: N1 – the total number of Russian students interviewed; N2 – the total number of Belarusian students interviewed; n1— the number of responses received from Russian students; n2 – the number of responses received from Belarusian students. The study involved students from a number of universities in Samara and Minsk (Astratova&Izmailov, 2024).

9 SSource: The final report on the results of the implementation of the University development program within the framework of the implementation of the strategic academic leadership program "Priority 2030" in 2023. – [Electronic resource]. URL: https://2030.urfu.ru / (accessed: 07/01/2024). (In Russ.).

the formation of digital competencies is required not only for university students, but also for its employees, since the degree of their formation determines the effectiveness of the organization of the educational process in the conditions of EER, as well as correlation with the demands of the labor market.

Accordingly, in relation to the labor market, various indicators and indices have also been developed at different times, in different countries, and for different purposes. For example, in 2014-2017, the US Federal Reserve calculated the LMCI (Labor Market Conditions Index), which was based on a dynamic factor model of 19 indicators of the US labor market, including unemployment and underemployment, employment, workweek, wages, vacancies, hiring, layoffs, the number of people who quit, as well as consumer perception studies and enterprises (Chung, *et al.*, 2014).

The LMCI index was necessary to assess the maximum level of employment. However, it turned out that this index, firstly, strongly correlates with the unemployment rate, and secondly, it has no significant relationship between labor market conditions and wage growth. In this regard, the US Federal Reserve has stopped updating the index since August 2017. Subsequently, Gallup proposed its own index (standard) for measuring employment based on annually updated and country-comparable labor market indicators statistically related to GDP per capita[10]. There is also a "good job employment indicator" (full-time work of at least 30 hours per week), which includes indicators such as "full-time employment with an employer" and "self-employment"; "part-time employees with an employer, but want to work full-time"; "unemployment" (Orlov& Postnikov, 2022).

In the Russian Federation, the main indicators for assessing the labor market are the number of workers, the number of people employed in tangible and intangible production, the unemployment rate, and the share of unemployed in the total population, as well as wages (Sukhanova, 2024; Yakovleva, 2014; *etc.*).

Also, there is the "Ivanov Consumer Index"[11] (or consumer confidence index, calculated by Sberbank since 2013), which reflects the current needs and expectations of middle-income Russians: it takes into account consumer spending, behavior, savings, and the level of consumer confidence in general.

---

10 Clifton J., Marlar J. Good Jobs: The New Global Standard. – Gallup, Inc. – 2011. – 20 pp. – [Electronic resource]. URL: https://www.gallup.com (accessed: 02.02.2020).

11 Source: Sberbank Investment Research portal. [electronic resource]. URL: http://research.sberbank-cib.com (accessed: 05/25/2024). (In Russ.).

Further, in Russia, the "RIA Rating labor market index" in the regions of Russia[12] is calculated annually, which aggregates the values of eight indicators reflecting employment, salary, conditions, and capacity of the labor market. This rating characterizes the attractiveness of a particular region for the employment of a potential employee.

Finally, the Central Bank of Russia has developed a composite indicator of the contribution of changes in the labor market to inflation growth—LMI (Labor Market Indicator). To do this, in order to take into account the heterogeneity in terms of labor market indicators, the regions are grouped into four clusters, clearly differing in social, demographic, and economic characteristics. At the same time, the impact of unemployment on inflation in Russia can be described as insignificant or moderate. Quarterly LMI values are calculated, which allow assessing the future impact of the labor market on inflation for the quarter ahead using known statistical data, making more informed decisions on monetary policy (Orlov and Postnikov, 2022).

In the context of the digitalization of the economy, experts periodically develop indices that offer not only a systematic view of the state of the labor market, but also a link to the creative nature of work in the knowledge economy.

Many researchers consider creative work in the digital economy through the human development index (Laverov, 2004; Tarasova & Kruchina, 2006; *etc.*). There are also authors' developments of HDI–basic indices, for example, the IID Index of Intellectual Development, which is defined as the arithmetic average of five private indices, respectively characterizing the level of education development, science, innovation, informatization of society, health care, and cultural component. At the same time, the calculation of private indices is carried out in the same way as is used for calculating the HDI (Tretyakova, 2014).

The researchers also propose indicators and indices calculated in the context of human capital development (Soboleva, 2009; Yarushkina & Kobeleva, 2018, *etc.*) and creative/intellectual human capital (Simchenko *et al.*, 2023; Yanovskaya & Simchenko, 2024; Yüksel *et al.*, 2022; *etc.*).

Finally, there are interesting studies where intellectual labor is considered through the prism of "trade—a new measure of labor" in a standardized task for knowledge workers of a new format in the new economic conditions of the

---

12 Source: The index of the labor market in the regions of Russia / The official website of RIA Rating. – [Electronic resource]. URL: https://riarating.ru/infografika/20210906/630207557.html . com (accessed: 05/25/2024). (In Russ.).

modern digital economy both in market conditions and in conditions of partial planning of the development of individual sectors of the economy" (Zbyszko and Stepus, 2022). In a similar position, we can see the research of B.A. Zhelezko with co-authors (2022).

Despite the variety of methods and approaches, we can agree with I.V. Soboleva's statement that each of the indexing methods in the labor market in the context of digitalization "... overlooks certain important aspects, which leads to distortions of the results of empirical research. The largest discrepancies are typical for transformational economies, including Russia, and the data are less contradictory for countries with a developed, competitive labor market. Methodological dead ends and the exhaustion of the possibilities of cost calculations of human capital reserves lead to a change in the perspective of research: from direct measurement of its volumes to the identification of trends and ratios in the analysis of human capital" (Soboleva, 2009, p. 51).

CONCLUSION

The comprehensive analysis of indicators for assessing Complex Socio-Economic Systems (CSES) in the context of digital transformation reveals several important findings. First, the current position of Russia and Belarus in global technological and educational rankings demonstrates significant room for improvement, with both countries lagging behind world leaders across multiple indices. While Russian institutions like Moscow State University have made notable progress in global university rankings, the overall standing of both Russian and Belarusian educational systems requires strategic enhancement to compete internationally.

Second, the digitalization of educational environments through EIEE (Electronic Information and Educational Environments) and EER (Electronic Educational Resources) represents a critical direction for development, as evidenced by successful implementations at institutions like Ural Federal University. These digital transformations not only improve educational effectiveness but also contribute to institutional competitiveness in global rankings.

Third, the labor market indicators in the context of digitalization show a shift from traditional employment metrics toward more nuanced measurements that reflect intellectual development and creative work characteristics. However, the methodological challenges of indexing human capital in digital economies remain substantial, particularly for transformational economies like Russia and Belarus.

Finally, our examination suggests that no single indicator system can fully capture the complexity of CSES development. The most effective approach involves integrating multiple indicator sets to provide a more holistic understanding of technological advancement, educational quality, and labor market dynamics. For policymakers in Russia and Belarus, this implies the need for comprehensive strategies that address not only technological infrastructure and internet penetration but also educational reform, R & D investment, and labor market adaptations to meet the demands of the digital economy. Future research should focus on developing more nuanced indicators that better reflect the unique challenges and opportunities of economies in transition to digital paradigms.

CHAPTER 5

Assessment of the Development Processes of Complex Socio-economic Systems in the Digital Economy of the Union State

Evgeny V. Sinitsyn[1,*], **Viola A. Larionova**[2], **Galina V. Astratova**[3] and **Boris A. Zhalezko**[4]

[1] *Department of Management, Institute of Economics and Management, Ural Federal University (UrFU), Yekaterinburg 620002, Sverdlovsk Region, Russian Federation*

[2] *Department of Economics and Management of Construction and Real Estate Market, Ural Federal University (UrFU), Yekaterinburg 620002, Sverdlovsk Region, Russian Federation*

[3] *Department of Regional Economics, Innovative Entrepreneurship and Economics (REIE&E), Institute of Economics and Management, School of Public Administration and Entrepreneurship (SPAE), Ural Federal University (UrFU), Yekaterinburg 620002, Sverdlovsk Region, Russian Federation*

[4] *Department of Marketing, Belarusian National Technical University, Minsk 220013, Republic of Belarus*

Abstract: This chapter examines the fundamental challenges in assessing Complex Socio-Economic Systems (CSES) within the digital economy of the Union State of Russia and Belarus. The analysis demonstrates that conventional approaches seeking to reduce CSES to a limited set of key indicators inevitably result in incomplete and often inadequate system descriptions. Using a mathematical model of migration between two countries as an illustrative case study, the research reveals how behavioral characteristics significantly influence system dynamics, producing dramatically different equilibrium states depending on migration preferences. The findings clearly establish that proper characterization of CSES requires not discrete numerical indicators but functional dependencies that capture the nonlinear, synergetic nature of these systems. This work contributes to the emerging understanding that complex socio-economic processes must be analyzed through the lens of nonlinear dynamics, accounting for behavioral factors and potential instabilities that can result in unexpected systemic responses to minor perturbations.

Keywords: Behavioral characteristics, Complex socio-economic systems, Digital economy, Functional dependencies, Migration modeling, Nonlinear dynamics, Union State of Russia and Belarus.

[*] **Corresponding author Evgeny V. Sinitsyn:** Department of Management, Institute of Economics and Management, Ural Federal University (UrFU), Yekaterinburg 620002, Sverdlovsk Region, Russian Federation;
E-mail: sinitsyn_ev@mail.ru

Galina V. Astratova, Maxim V. Vlasov, Chigozirim Ndubuisi Onwusiribe & Longinus D.N. Nnadozie (Eds.)

INTRODUCTION

As it is well known, the definition and assessment of the objects' states of an economic system help to identify its level of development and enable operational corrections to shortcomings and the qualitative and quantitative improvement of the state of the object. This corresponds to the information materials of the KOMGOR project, "assessment is a systematic observation of an object and collection of data on it according to predetermined indicators for the purpose of further determining the value or dignity of this object according to certain criteria"[1].

According to the well-known quality management rule of the "lucky seven"[2], the average person controls 7±2 different factors, so the desire to simplify the description of Complex Socio-Economic Systems (CSES) as much as possible by reducing the tremendous set of their parameters to several (or even one) characteristics (indicators) is easy to explain psychologically. Consequently, an analysis and assessment of key indicators of CSES is a completely understandable task, allowing for identifying the key features of the methodology for their calculation and determining their advantages and disadvantages. Ultimately, the goal of such analysis is to establish the patterns of CSES's development.

The contemporary scientific literature available to us presents a set of indicators characterizing the achievement of Sustainable Development Goals (SDGs) of regions and countries. In addition, some consulting companies and rating agencies are developing their own indicators, tools, methods, and techniques for measuring the levels of scientific and technological development and digitalization of countries and individual sectors of national economies (for example, labor markets, HES, and R & D markets).

However, based on the key position of sustainable development as a driving factor of economic growth, social responsibility, and ecological balance[3], sooner or later, an understanding of the following points comes:

---

1 Source: Information materials of the KOMGOR project. Criteria and indicators for assessing the effectiveness of stakeholder participation in the urban governance process using public discussions as an example. – [Electronic resource]. URL: https://ekapraekt.by/wp-content/uploads/2019/12/Infomaterial_Kovalkin1-min.pdf. – (date of access: 15.04.2024). (In Russ.).

2 As it is known, G.V. Miller derived the rule of the "lucky seven" (taking into account individual capabilities 7 ± 2), which suggests that in the learning process, by limiting information to the lower limit (5), the teacher will avoid general fatigue of the audience, but may cause discontent among "excellent students" (gifted listeners).

3 Source: Agenda for Sustainable Development. – [Electronic resource]. URL: https://www.un.org/sustainabledevelopment/ru/about/development-agenda/ (date of access: 18.07.2024). (In Russ.).

Firstly, E.N. Knyazeva notes: "This idea is directly related to the understanding of the world from the standpoint of nonlinear dynamics and synergetic—a complex, nonlinearly developing world, full of instabilities, crises and catastrophes, a world that very often presents us with surprises and whose future is open" (Knyazeva,2009, pp. 108-109). Similar positions on the nonlinear nature of the development of the CSES are also expressed by other authors (Ansoff, 1989; Bengraf *et al.*, 2024; Ermicheva, 2008; Lazimov and Nazarov, 2023; Pasmurtseva, 2020, among others).

Accordingly, for the socio-economic systems considered in this monograph (labor markets, HES, and R & D), *complexity is the essence of these kinds of systems, as CSES*. Therefore, by limiting the variables to only those 'key' factors proposed by a specific model, there is a risk of discarding essential data alongside the irrelevant information. Recent history is replete with cases demonstrating what happens when, for example, purely economic parameters are emphasized while social, cultural, historical, religious, and psychological characteristics of the inhabitants of certain territories are ignored.

Secondly, it is understood that an attempt to reduce the description of a complex system to several characteristics (indicators) is a path to "nowhere", *since the parameters and variables that describe CSES are not numbers, but functions.*

Indeed, from a synergetic position, sustainable development of systems is a self-sustaining and self-organizing development. If we talk about the CSES, then this is a development in which "... humanity as a whole and in each of its representatives shows concern for the future, constructs a desired future in which future generations should have starting conditions of life no worse than those of the current generation" (Knyazeva,2009, p. 109). It becomes obvious that in a synergetic context, the development of the CSEC cannot be described by finite set of "numbers" (indicators), but only by functions. This is very unusual (especially in the context of the economy of the USRB) and quite complex (even mathematically), and requires much more information and consideration of the behavioral aspects of the CSEC.

In connection with this, the authors[4] of a study made an attempt to implement some illustrations of the above-mentioned problems of evaluating key indicators of the development of complex socio-economic systems in the digital economy of the USRB.

---

4 It should be noted that the key role in the development of the idea and content of this section of the monograph belongs to Professor E.V. Sinitsyn.

Apparently, it is necessary to come to terms with the fact that the description of CSES using a limited set of key indicators will always be incomplete and, therefore, not always suitable for describing the processes occurring in them. A complete description of the state of a complex socio-economic system requires the involvement of a large number of variables (proportional to the number of its constituent elements), and the construction of adequate averaged characteristics describing its behavior is a non-trivial mathematical task. It should be borne in mind that the average characteristics of the system may depend on each other; as a result, the equations for determining them are nonlinear. In this regard, the notorious "butterfly effect" can be observed: small external influences on the system can lead to serious transformations of its behavior, and small differences in the functional dependencies of the characteristics of different systems can lead to completely different behavior of externally very similar systems.

To illustrate what has been said, let us turn to the problem of migration between countries.

We will consider migration between two countries, X and Y, but now we will assume that the probabilities of persons' movement between countries *pxy, pyx* depend on the population concentration *x*. For example, we can consider two types of behavior:

1. Migrants prefer a territory with a low population concentration.
2. Preference is given to a country with a high population concentration.

Fig. (**1**) presents the *pxy, pyx* dependencies corresponding to these types of behavior.

Let us denote, by *x,y*– the concentrations of citizens in countries X and Y $(x + y = 1)$. The probability of *x* (or y) distribution –$\Phi\ (x,t)$ is determined, and the solution of it has the form:

$$\Phi(x,t) = \frac{z[W^{-1}(t+W(x)]}{z(x)}\Phi_0[W^{-1}(t+W(x))], \tag{1a}$$

where

$$z(x) = p_+(x - x_S). \tag{1b}$$

$$p_+ = p_{xy} + p_{yx} \tag{1c}$$

$W^{-1}(\ldots)$–inverse function of a function:

$$W(x) = \int \frac{dx}{z(x)} \tag{1d}$$

Φ 0[…]–initial probability distribution function at the moment$t=0$,

In (1b)xS is a singular point corresponding to a stationary state in which $\frac{\partial \Phi(x,t)}{\partial t} = 0$, Solution equation (1a) allows us to analyze the features of Φ (x,t) when transition probabilities *pxy, pyx* depend on x (or y). In this case, the value of x_s turns out to be dependent on x. This, in turn, leads to the fact that Φ (x,t) can have several singularity points that are the solutions of the transcendental equation:

$$x = x_S(x). \tag{2}$$

Consider the case of a uniform initial distribution (all concentrations x are equally probable), so that $\Phi_0(x) = \theta(x)$, where $\theta(x)$ is the Heaviside θ–function. Expanding $z(x)$ in a Taylor series in the neighborhood of any solution x_* of equation (2), we obtain:

$$\Phi(x,t) = e^{\beta t}\{\theta(x - x_{min}) - \theta(x - x_{max})\}. \tag{3a}$$

where

$$\beta = p_+(x_*)[1 - x_S'(x_*)], \tag{3b}$$

and

$$x_{min} = x_*\left(1 - e^{-\beta t}\right),$$
$$x_{max} = x_*\left(1 - e^{-\beta t}\right) + e^{-\beta t}. \tag{3c}$$

Thus, if$x_S'(x_*) = \frac{dx_S}{dx} \leq 1$, then β is positive and, consequently,

$P(x_*,\ t \to \infty,) \to \infty$, while the interval for x $[x_{min}, x_{max}]$ becomes narrower and narrower – that is, a δ-shaped singularity arises. For x'_S $(x_*) > 1$, there is no singularity in the behavior of $P(x_*,\ t)$. The analysis of the Φ (x,t) behavior in the entire interval x requires numerical calculations. We implemented a numerical solution of equations (3a, 3b, and 3c) for the two opposite scenarios of citizen behavior noted above: 1. avoidance of the areas with low population concentration; 2. preferential movement to such areas.

The results are shown in Fig. (**1**).

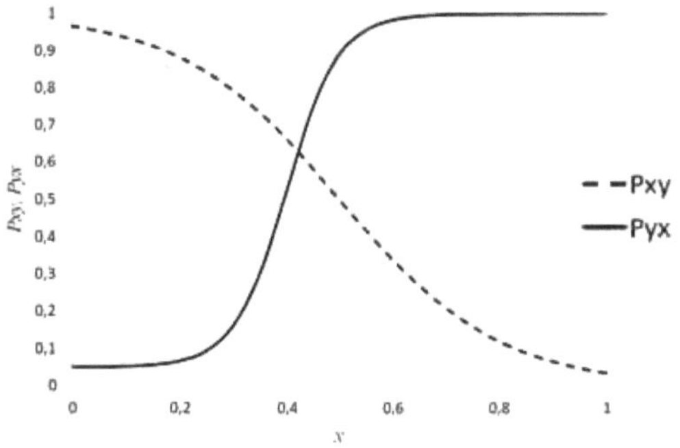

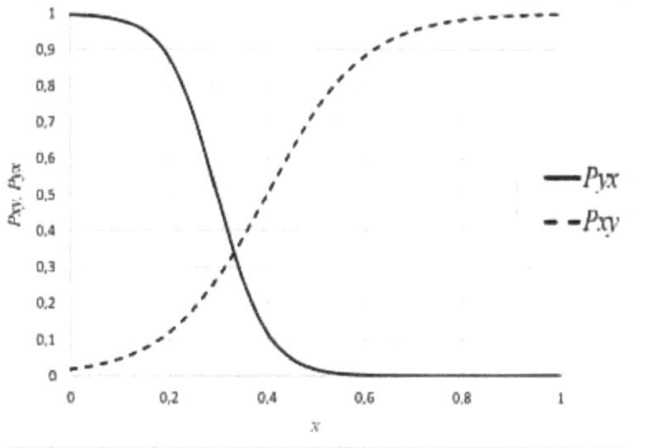

a1 b1

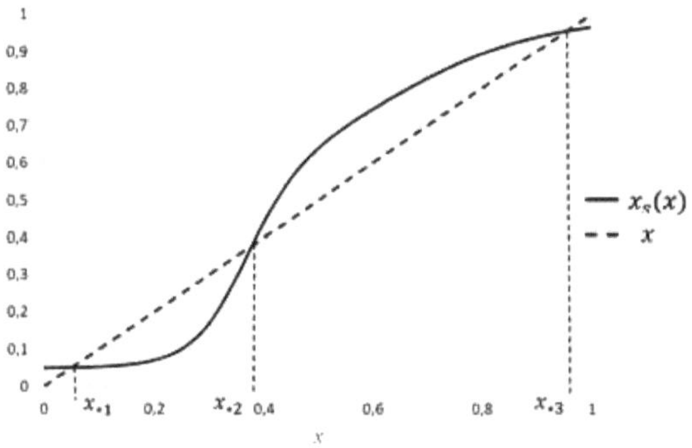

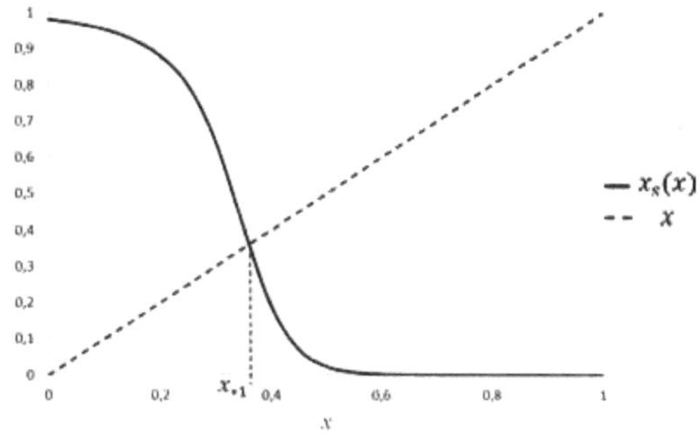

a2 b2

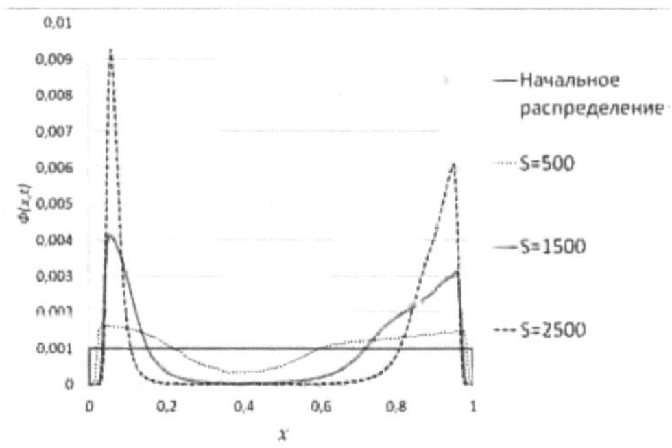

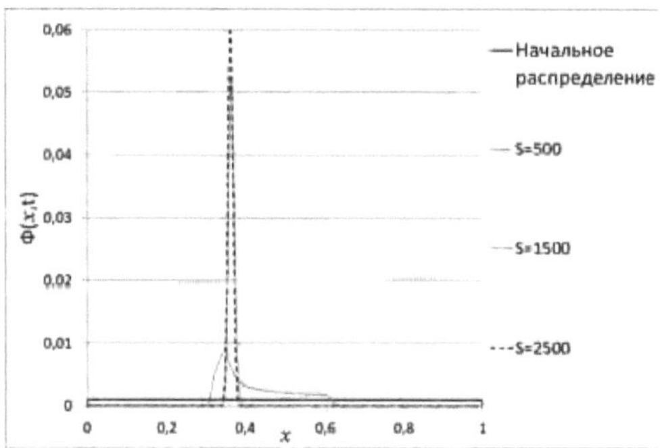

a3 b3

Fig. (1). Probabilities *Pxy, Pyx* of transitions (X→Y, Y→X) and corresponding probability distributions *Φ (x,t)* for different scenarios of citizen behavior:

a. avoidance of places with low concentrations of citizens;
b. tendency to visit places with low concentration;

equation (1a-1d) – probabilities of movements;

(a2, b2) – graphical definition of singularity points – solutions of equation (2) – x_{*i};

(a3, b3) – the results of computer modeling – numerical solution of (2) for Φ (x, t).

Source: author's development

For the numerical solution, we used dimensionless time $S = t/\max\{p+\}$ and normalized probabilities P_{xy}, $P_{yx} = P_{xy}/\max\{p+\}$

It is important to note that the temporal evolution of the probability distribution function has a significantly different character for the population behavior scenarios described above: in the first case (avoidance of territories with low population concentration), we have two stable singular points – (x_{*1}, x_{*3}), corresponding to two equilibrium concentrations; equation for Φ (x,t) have two stable singular points – (x_{*1}, x_{*3}) and one unstable one – x_{*2}, which, in the limit of large times, cannot correspond to any equilibrium concentration.

In the case of the second scenario (the attractiveness of territories with a low population concentration), the dynamics of the population probability distribution – Φ (x,t) is completely different, and there is only one stable point – x_{*1}.

These results clearly demonstrate the significant influence on the migration processes of such an essentially behavioral, intangible characteristic, as the standpoint of migrants on the attractiveness (or, on the contrary, unattractiveness) of a territory. At the same time, the attractiveness itself is a function of the average parameter—the concentration of population in the territory.

Note that estimation of the migration probabilities on the basis of the classical definition of probability (equation 1b), one neglects the considered behavioral features and, hence, the dependences of the probabilities p_{xy}, p_{yx} on x. Therefore, nothing similar to Figs. (**1**, **2** and **3**) will be discovered. It should be emphasized that this example demonstrates that not the two parameters – *pxy, pyx*, but two functions: *pxy* (*x*) and *pyx* (*x*) are the adequate characteristics for studying migration, only one social-economic process from their variety in CSES. To detect the dependencies of probabilities *pxy* (*x*) and *pyx* (*x*) on *x*, a special treatment should be made (see equation 2, 1a-1d, and 3a -3c).

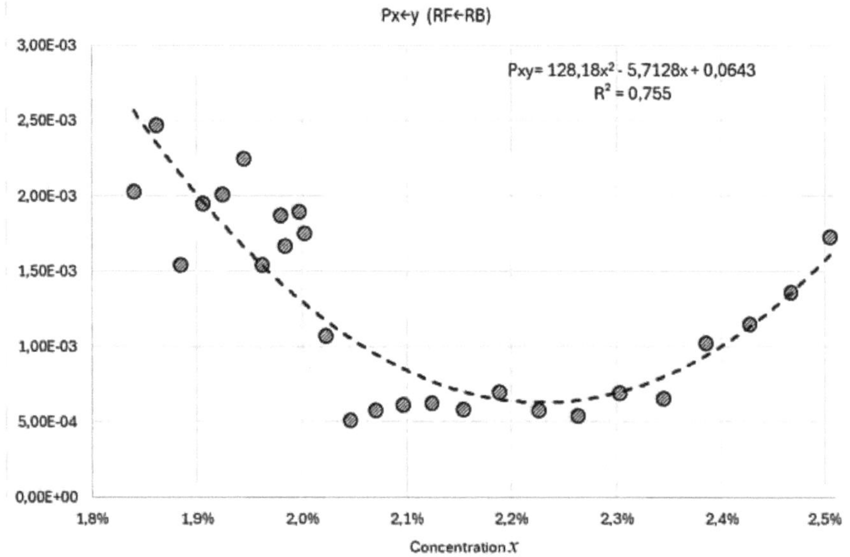

Fig. (2). Dependence *Pxy* (*x*) for the population migration between the Russian Federation and the Republic of Belarus,.
Source: Calculated by the authors on the basis of the model described in Section 1.4.2 and the data from https://rosstat.gov.ru/, https://www.belstat.gov.by/

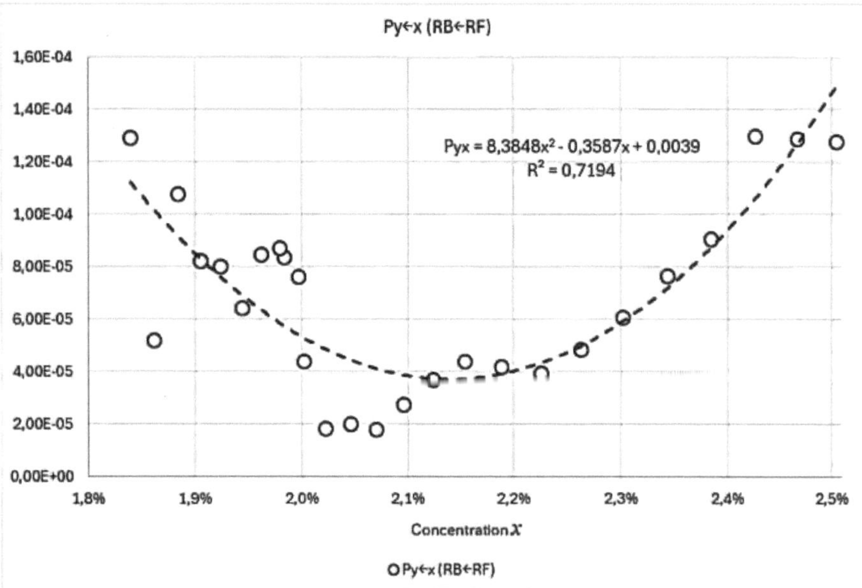

Fig. (3). Dependence P_{yx} (*x*) for the population migration between the Russian Federation and the Republic of Belarus,.
Source: Calculated by the authors on the basis of the model described in Section 1.4.2 and the data from https://rosstat.gov.ru/, https://www.belstat.gov.by/

For example, Figs. (**2** and **3**) show the dependencies *pxy* (*x*) and *pyx* (*x*) for the migration of population between Russia and Belarus. One can see that they are well described by a polynomial dependence on x of degree 2.

Figs. (**2** and **3**) also clearly show the presence of a concentration region in which both probabilities are minimal. If we talk about the behavioral model of migration, then migration processes are most active at minimal and relatively large concentrations of population *x*. It is the functions *pxy* (*x*) and *pyx* (*x*), and not their average values or values at the moment, that are most informative for describing migration processes and the temporal dynamics of the probability of population distribution between countries.

For a more detailed analysis of the impact of behavioral characteristics on migration processes, one needs information on the profiles of the migrating population. For example: an education, age, gender, as well as personal characteristics, *etc*. The obtaining of such data is not a simple task. Its solution can be the subject of an independent study. Summarizing the content of this section, we found it necessary to note that the identification and assessment of the development processes of complex socio-economic systems in the digital economy of the USRB is one of the most difficult problems of our time. This task involves the further study of the dependencies and relationships between a large number of values, parameters, and variables of the CSES. The solution to this problem is the subject of further and independent research in the context of a new scientific direction.

CONCLUSION

The assessment of development processes in Complex Socio-Economic Systems (CSES) within the digital economy of the Union State of Russia and Belarus presents profound theoretical and methodological challenges that demand a paradigm shift in analytical approaches. This chapter has demonstrated conclusively that the conventional practice of reducing CSES to a limited set of numerical indicators, regardless of how carefully these indicators are selected, is fundamentally insufficient for capturing the true nature and behavior of these systems.

Several key insights emerge from our analysis. First, the inherent complexity of socio-economic systems is not merely a complicating factor that can be abstracted away; rather, complexity constitutes the essential character of these systems. By attempting to simplify CSES description through emphasis on selected “key” factors while disregarding social, cultural, historical, religious, and psychological characteristics, analysts risk discarding critical information that determines system behavior.

Second, our mathematical modeling of migration processes between two countries reveals that the adequate characterization of even this single aspect of CSES requires not discrete numerical indicators but functional dependencies. Specifically, the migration probabilities (*p_xy, p_yx*) must be understood as functions of population concentration (x), rather than as static values. The striking differences in system dynamics observed between scenarios where migrants either prefer territories with high population concentration or territories with low population concentration highlight how behavioral factors fundamentally alter system evolution and equilibrium states.

The empirical application of our model to migration data between Russia and Belarus confirms these theoretical insights, showing that migration probabilities follow polynomial dependencies on population concentration. Moreover, the data reveal regions of concentration where both migration probabilities reach minimal values, suggesting that migration processes are most active at minimal and relatively large concentrations of population.

From a methodological perspective, these findings reinforce the synergetic view of sustainable development as a self-organizing process. In this paradigm, the development of CSES cannot be adequately described by a finite set of indicators but requires functional representations that account for nonlinear dynamics, potential instabilities, and behavioral aspects. The notorious "butterfly effect" is not merely a theoretical curiosity but a practical reality in these systems, where small external influences or minor differences in functional dependencies can lead to radically different system behaviors.

Further advancement in understanding and managing CSES will require more sophisticated data collection methods to capture detailed information on migrating populations, including education, age, gender, and personal characteristics. The development of analytical frameworks capable of processing and interpreting such multidimensional data represents a promising direction for future research.

The identification and assessment of development processes in complex socio-economic systems require transcending the limitations of traditional indicator-based approaches. Rather than seeking simplification through reduction, researchers must embrace the inherent complexity of these systems and develop analytical tools that can accommodate functional dependencies, nonlinear dynamics, and behavioral factors. This represents not merely a methodological refinement but a fundamental reconceptualization of how we understand and engage with complex socio-economic systems in the digital economy of the Union State.

CHAPTER 6

Innovative Infrastructure of the Union State of the Russian Federation and the Republic of Belarus as A Key Factor of Import Substitution and Development in new Economic Conditions

Galina V. Astratova[1,*], **Boris A. Zhalezko**[2], **Airat M. Izmailov**[3] and **Lyubov I. Tararyshkina**[4]

[1] *Department of Regional Economics, Innovative Entrepreneurship and Economics (REIE&E), Institute of Economics and Management, School of Public Administration and Entrepreneurship (SPAE), Ural Federal University (UrFU), Yekaterinburg 620002, Sverdlovsk Region, Russian Federation*

[2] *Department of Marketing, Belarusian National Technical University, Minsk 220013, Republic of Belarus*

[3] *Department of Digital Economics, Volga State University of Telecommunications and Informatics, Samara 443090, Middle Volga region, Russian Federation*

[4] *Department of Eurasian Studies, Belarusian State University, Minsk 220030, Republic of Belarus*

Abstract: This chapter examines the innovative infrastructure of the Union State of the Russian Federation and the Republic of Belarus as a critical factor for import substitution and economic development under new economic conditions. The research provides a comprehensive analysis of the concept of "Innovative Infrastructure" (InIn), from broad to narrow interpretations, and presents the authors' definition as "a system that includes the totality of all participants, relationships, products, resources, and types of innovative activities at the level of the world, countries, regions, and firms." The study traces the development of innovative infrastructure in both countries, highlighting the concentration of InIn elements in Russia's Central and Ural Federal Districts and the significant growth of technology parks from 101 in 2014 to 269 in 2019. Similarly, in Belarus, the authors note the successful implementation of the State Program of Innovative Development, which has established an effective network of science and technology parks, technology transfer centers, and other innovation subjects. Particular attention is given to universities as crucial elements of the innovation ecosystem in both countries. The chapter identifies key challenges for university-based InIn business entities, including short-term planning, sanctions

* **Corresponding author Galina V. Astratova:** Department of Regional Economics, Innovative Entrepreneurship and Economics (REIE&E), Institute of Economics and Management, School of Public Administration and Entrepreneurship (SPAE), Ural Federal University (UrFU), Yekaterinburg 620002, Sverdlovsk Region, Russian Federation; E-mail: galina_28@mail.ru

Galina V. Astratova, Maxim V. Vlasov, Chigozirim Ndubuisi Onwusiribe & Longinus D.N. Nnadozie (Eds.)

pressure, and dependence on foreign investments, while also highlighting promising development forms such as business incubators and technology transfer centers. The research emphasizes the critical role of innovative infrastructure in import substitution efforts initiated since 2014 in Russia and recently intensified in Belarus. It outlines state mechanisms implemented in both countries to reduce dependence on foreign technologies and create domestic innovative enterprises. The chapter also identifies nine key factors hampering import substitution policies, with expert surveys revealing the most significant challenges as a lack of domestic investment, low management efficiency, and a shortage of qualified engineers. The authors conclude by proposing six strategic directions to enhance the effectiveness of import substitution policies for high-tech innovative products and services, including technology development, cluster organization for accelerated technology transfer, personnel training, targeted financing, improved public administration, and regulatory framework development.

Keywords: Innovative infrastructure, Import substitution, Industrial clusters, Technological sovereignty, Technology parks, Union State, University innovation.

INTRODUCTION

In modern scientific literature, there are different approaches to the definition of "Innovative Infrastructure" (InIn): from a "broad approach" (it is a conglomerate of all structures, buildings, bridges, transport systems, roads, logistics services, information networks and other systems necessary for the functioning and development of a set of innovative structures of companies and start-ups that promote the development of innovative activities in the country and/or in the region)[1] up to a "narrow approach" or a system consisting of a set of objects that contribute to the implementation of either the entire innovation chain (innovation cycle) at the level of regions or the country as a whole, or its separate stage—commercialization of developments (Kuznetsova, 2015, p. 222).

It is also important that the regulatory framework of the Russian Federation[2] and the Republic of Belarus[3] contains strategic documents, which present such

1 Sources: Bengraf, *et al.*, 2024; KorolevaandYermoshina (2014); Kuznetsova, 2015.; *etc.*

2 The strategy of innovative development of the Russian Federation for the period up to 2023. Approved by the Decree of the Government of the Russian Federation dated December 8, 2011 No. 2227-R. URL: https://z-motiv.ru/strategiya-innovatsionnogo-razvitiya-rf-do-2023-goda / (accessed: 14.12.2023). (In Russ.).

The concept of long-term socio-economic development of the Russian Federation for the period up to 2020 (approved by the decree of the Government of the Russian Federation dated November 17, 2008 No. 1662-r). URL: https://www.garant.ru/products/ipo/prime/doc/94365 / (accessed: 14.12.2023). (In Russ.).

Federal Law on Science and State Scientific and Technical Policy. dated 08/23/1996 N 127-FZ (last revision) on August 23, 1996 N 127-FZ. Adopted by the State Duma on July 12, 1996. Approved by the Federation Council on August 7, 1996. URL: https://www.consultant.ru/document/cons_doc_LAW_11507(accessed: 14.12.2023). (In Russ.).

The draft Strategy for Scientific and Technological Development of the Russian Federation until 2035 was prepared by the Center for Strategic Research Foundation on the instructions of the Ministry of Education and Science of the Russian Federation on May 5, 2016. URL https://strategy24.ru/files/uploads/cd2a43226e0ec13b325e4ff331e428c7.pdf (accessed: 14.12.2023). (In Russ.).

definitions as: “innovation”, “innovative product”, “Innovative Infrastructure”, *etc*., as well as identify priority areas for the development of InIn and RandD in the USRB.

After analysing various Russian, Belarusian, and foreign sources, we came to the conclusion that the “*Innovation Infrastructure*” is a system that includes the totality of all participants, relationships, products, resources, and types of innovative activities at the level of the world, countries, regions, and firms (author's interpretation) (Astratova *et al*., 2024). It can also be said that the innovation infrastructure consists of an interconnected set of innovation systems, implying networks of interaction between business units (firms), universities, and development institutes, research centers, support infrastructure, and other contractors within the framework of the innovation process.

It should be noted that there is not enough information in the public domain about the development of innovation infrastructure in both Russia and Belarus. Thus, in a continuous study of the subjects of the Russian Federation, it was revealed that at the beginning of 2016, the number of active InIn elements in the subjects of the Russian Federation amounted to 1,693, about two hundred more were at the stage of formation (Eferina *et al*., 2017). By 2016, the maximum concentration of InIn elements was observed in the Central Federal District, where a significant part of industrial production and scientific complex is located (548 units), as well as in the Ural Federal District, where 88 units of InIn are localized (Eferina *et al*., 2017, p. 195). The following types of economic activity are most in demand in the current economy (Feringa *et al*., 2017, pp. 197-198):

- Information and communication technologies, business incubators, educational centres; these areas are usually combined with the sphere of consulting services.
- Techno parks, territorial clusters, technology transfer centres, industrial parks, engineering centres, territories of innovative development; these areas are implemented in projects of the manufacturing industry and mechanical engineering.

---

3 Decree of the President of the Republic of Belarus dated January 31, 2017 No. 31 "On the State Program of Innovative Development of the Republic of Belarus for 2016-2020" // ETALON Information Search system [Electronic resource] / National Center for Legal Information of the Republic of Belarus. (accessed: 19.02.2024). (In Russ.).

Decree of the President of the Republic of Belarus No. 1 dated 03.01.2007 (with amendments and additions dated 08/01/2022 No. 265) "On approval of the Regulations on the procedure for the creation of innovative infrastructure entities." URL: https://president.gov.by/bucket/assets/uploads/documents/2022/265uk.pdf (accessed: 14.12.2023). (In Russ.).

The National Strategy for Sustainable Socio-economic Development of the Republic of Belarus until 2030. – Approved by the Presidium of the Council of Ministers of the Republic of Belarus No. 10 dated 05/02/2017. URL: https://economy.gov.by/uploads/files/NSUR2030/Natsionalnaja-strategija-ustojchivogo-sotsialno-ekonomicheskogo-razvitija-Respubliki-Belarus-na-period-do-2030-goda.pdf (accessed: 14.12.2023). (In Russian).

- Technology parks, technology platforms, engineering centres, and technology transfer centres; these areas are used in the field of pharmaceuticals, medical technologies, medical equipment, and biomedicine.

Since 2015, InIn has been consolidating and agglomerating, which was a new stage in its formation and development in Russia. In 2015, the Association of Clusters and Techno Parks of Russia[4] was established, and an industry-specific National standard[5] was developed, which defined the mechanism for the development of the innovation infrastructure in the Russian Federation, the procedure for its financing with the involvement of private resident partners and foreign investments (Dobrova, 2021). The coronavirus pandemic has had a significant impact on the InIn of the Russian Federation, since by 2021 there was an active demand from project teams and applicants of innovative projects for alternative forms of InIn, functioning in a virtual format and allowing projects to be implemented remotely. This makes a realistic assumption about the formation of a new stage of InIn development in the Russian Federation in the post-bubble world (Dobrova, 2021) and the dynamic development of the InIn of the Russian Federation in 2014-2019 (Table **1**).

Table 1. The main indicators of the development of the innovation infrastructure in Russia for 2014-2019 (using the example of technology parks).

Indicators		Analysis Period (year)					
		2014	**2015**	**2016**	**2017**	**2018**	**2019**
1	The number of technoparks, total units. Including:	101	120	146	166	227	269
	1.1 Green-field parks	75	87	102	109	144	171
	1.2 Brownfield parks	26	33	44	57	83	98
	1.3 The number of techno parks in the field of high technologies, units.	3	5	7	9	12	14
2	Total area of techno parks, ha	760	920	1058	1489,2	1592,6	1712,4
3	The number of residents of techno parks, units. Including:	3200	4100	4317	4833	5087	5243
	3.1 Subjects of SMEs, units.	2560	3280	4058	4478	4868	5011
4	The number of employees of the techno park residents.	54900	71200	73546	81607	91561	102108
5	Revenue from sales of products/services, billion rubles.	138.5	188.6	203.5	240.9	270.3	283.5
6	The share of occupied areas of techno parks, %	53.0	50.0	53.0	53.4	58.4	60.0

Source:(Dobrova, 2021, p. 496)

It should be noted that the Republic of Belarus also pays significant attention to the development of InIn and its scientific and technical potential, as well as mechanisms for the development and sale of high-tech products and the creation of innovation-oriented organizations. In accordance with the State Program of Innovative Development of the Republic of Belarus[6], the task was to increase InIn indicators, including: to ensure the activities of 19 InIn entities by 2020, to increase the number of residents in techno parks to 300, and create 1,536 new jobs in them in 2016-2020 (Table **2**).

Table 2. The main forecast indicators in the framework of the implementation of measures for the development of the innovation infrastructure of the republic of Belarus.

Indicators	Values of Indicators by Year				
	2016	2017	2018	2019	2020
The number of subjects of the innovation infrastructure, units.	15	16	17	18	19
The number of residents of science and technology parks, units.	126	168	210	252	300
The number of jobs created (annual growth), units.	336	288	128	80	704
Number of engineering centers, units	3	5	8	11	15
Number of venture capital organizations, units	1	1	1	2	2
The volume of output in value terms, million rubles.	29.4	39.2	49	58.9	70.2
Output of products produced for 1 rub of invested budget funds, RUB.	0.68	1.2	2	4.5	5

Source: (Kosovsky *et al.*, 2017)

By now, it is obvious that the planned targets have been met, and an effective, constantly developing InIn has been created in the Republic of Belarus, including science and technology parks and technology transfer centers. In total, there are 24 subjects of innovation in the country: 16 science and technology parks, 2 subjects of innovation infrastructure, and 6 technology transfer centers[7]. Moreover, the revenue of residents of the market for knowledge–intensive and high-tech goods in the Republic of Belarus in 2020 amounted to 299.46 million BEL. Rubles, and the number of jobs is 3098 for 149 residents of the market (Klimuk, 2023).

---

4 Association for the Development of Clusters and Technoparks in Russia. URL: https://akitrf.ru/about_association/description / (accessed: 14.12.2023). (In Russian).

5 GOST R 56425-2015 Technoparks. Requirements (with Change N 1). URL: https://minprom.gov39.ru/%D0%93%D0%9E%D0%A1%D0%A2%20%D0%A2%D0%B5%D1%85%D0%BD%D0%BE%D0%BF%D0%B0%D1%80%D0%BA%D0%B8.pdf (accessed: 14.12.2023). (InRussian).

6 Decree of the President of the Republic of Belarus dated January 31, 2017 No. 31 "On the State Program of Innovative Development of the Republic of Belarus for 2016-2020" // ETALON Information Search system [Electronic resource] / National Center for Legal Information of the Republic of Belarus. (accessed: 02/19/2024). (InRussian).

7 Decree of the President of the Republic of Belarus No. 1 dated 03.01.2007 (with amendments and additions dated 08/01/2022 No. 265) "On approval of the Regulations on the procedure for the creation of innovative infrastructure entities." - [Electronic resource].URL: https://president.gov.by/bucket/assets/uploads/documents/2022/265uk.pdf (accessed: 14.12.2023). (In Russ.).

It is also important in the context of our research that since the source of innovation is traditionally the four main sectors of science: academic, university, industry, and technology (Panikarova *et al.*, 2020, p. 573), it is not surprising that a significant part of the InIn elements in both Russia and Belarus are represented by universities. However, the peculiarities of the work of educational institutions in general and in the country aspect, in particular, are clearly insufficiently and asymmetrically reflected in the literature available to us. There are only individual works on a number of research areas, for example: the essence and mechanism of formation of the InIn of a Russian university (Doroshenko and Malykhina, 2014), analysis of the development of the national InIn of the Republic of Belarus (Klimuk and Unsovich, 2021; Zhalezko *et al.*, 2020), the role of InIn in ensuring the formation of the digital economy of Russia (Dobrova, 2021), *etc*. Moreover, we did not find a comparative analysis of the innovative infrastructure of the Russian and Belarusian universities.

Having analyzed the types of innovative economic activities of economic entities of the innovation infrastructure of the Russian Federation operating on the basis of higher educational institutions, we can draw a number of conclusions:

- InIn business units at universities are science and technology parks, technology transfer centers, business support centers, educational and scientific laboratories, *etc*.
- InIn business entities at universities face problems of their existence and development, including: short-term planning, sanctions pressure, dependence on foreign investments, *etc*. (Dobrova, 2021, p. 501);
- Promising forms of development of InIn universities are the following types of InIn business entities: business incubators, technology transfer centers, laboratories and test platforms, techno parks, *etc*., as well as formation of financial and technological endowment funds through contributions from mega businesses (Dobrova, 2021, p. 501);
- Universities in Russia become leading by increasing the level of innovation activity, and the leading universities of the country determine its future (Lavrinenko, 2023, p. 1694).

The analysis of the types of innovative economic activity of the economic entities of the InIn of the Republic of Belarus, operating on the basis of higher education institutions, allowed us to draw the following conclusions:

- In the Republic of Belarus, there is a wide network of InIn business units operating very effectively on the basis of higher education institutions, namely:

science and technology parks, technology transfer centers, business support centers, educational, scientific, and production laboratories, *etc.*;
- The expansion of the infrastructure network of universities is aimed at regional specifics, the development of youth entrepreneurial initiatives (innovative entrepreneurship), the maximum full use of available resources, the creation of own and transfer of successful foreign innovative technologies adapted to the conditions of functioning and trend vectors of the country's development (Klimuk and Unsovich, 2021, p. 939-940);
- The accumulation of scientific and innovative potential in higher education institutions, as well as creative and initiative-driven youth, allows for the generation of scientific, technical, and innovative products, as well as socially oriented ideas, and their introduction into the practices of entities within the real economy and social sphere.

It should be noted that, in the new economic conditions, the innovative infrastructure of the Union State of Russia and Belarus (USRB) is not only the foundation for the further development of both countries but also a key factor in import substitution.

Import substitution has become especially relevant for the Russian Federation since 2014, due to restrictions on the supply of imported components to Russian industrial enterprises and the threat of a reduction in production volumes up to the shutdown of production. In order to stabilize the situation, support the development of Russian industrial business, and reduce the share of imports in the market, the Russian Government has focused on the development of large industrial sectors such as Rosatom, Rostec, Rusnano, Rosneft, and Gazprom[8].

Moreover, in 2014, a state program was approved to support the development of industry[9], and later, National Projects were created to support entrepreneurship[10] and increase labor productivity[11]. In 2022, the State Duma of the Russian Federa-

---

8 Moscow Fund for Industry and Entrepreneurship Support. The official website. URL: https://mfppp.ru/news/fond/gosudarstvennaya-podderzhk--importozameshcheniya-v-novykh-usloviyakh / (accessed: 05/12/2024). (In Russian).

9 The state program "Development of industry and improvement of its competitiveness". Approved by Government Decree No. 328 dated April 15, 2014. The current version of the state program "Development of industry and improvement of its competitiveness". URL: http://government.ru/rugovclassifier/862/events /(accessed: 05/12/2024). (In Russian).

10 The national project "Small and medium-sized entrepreneurship and support for entrepreneurial initiative" . URL: https://xn--80aapampemcchfmo7a3c9ehj.xn--p1ai/projects/msp (accessed: 05/12/2024). (In Russian).

The national project "LaborProductivity". URL: https://xn--80aapampemcchfmo7a3c9ehj.xn--p1ai/projects/msp (accessed: 05/12/2024). (In Russian).

11 The national project "Labor Productivity".URL: https://xn--80aapampemcchfmo7a3c9ehj.xn--p1ai/projects/proizvoditelnost-truda (accessed: 05/12/2024). (In Russian).

tion adopted a Government program for financing industrial production for state support of import substitution[12], as well as an impressive list of draft laws, each of which is aimed in one way or another at stimulating the domestic market, and other measures to support import substitution[13]. The following instruments are among the specific legislative acts of this format:

- Establishing the priority of domestic software included in the special register for public procurement;
- The need to purchase Russian products through competitive and auction procedures.
- A full-format request for the purchase of foreign goods for certain sectors of industry.
- The obligation of customers to purchase products manufactured in the territory of the Russian Federation in the established minimum proportions.
- Introduction of a simplified scheme of interaction with products from the field of medicine and pharmaceuticals[14].

As for the Republic of Belarus, according to the Resolution of the Council of Ministers of the Republic of Belarus, technological sovereignty is the ability of the Republic of Belarus to have critical technologies (goods) important for ensuring the welfare of the population and competitiveness, as well as the ability to independently develop or receive them from the economies of other countries without unilateral structural dependence[15]. One of the strategies to ensure the technological sovereignty of the country is import substitution.

In this regard, it should be noted that, first of all, import substitution efforts in the Republic of Belarus are aimed at covering the so-called "critical imports", which include: 1) those groups of goods and services that are not only not produced in the country, but which cannot be dispensed with; 2) those types of raw materials that the country does not possess or possesses in a very limited volume.

---

12 Moscow Fund for Industry and Entrepreneurship Support. The official website. URL: https://mfppp.ru/news/fond/gosudarstvennaya-podderzhk--importozameshcheniya-v-novykh-usloviyakh/ (accessed: 05/12/2024). (In Russian).

13 Import substitution support. URL: https://www.economy.gov.ru/material/directions/sanctions_measures/podderzhka_importozameshcheniya/ (accessed: 05/12/.2024). (In Russian).

14 Government support for import substitution: programs, subsidies and tools to help industrial companies. December 27, 2022. URL: https://delprof.ru/press-center/open-analytics/gosudarstvennaya-podderzhka-importozameshcheniya-programmy-subsidii-i-ins-rumenty-pomoshchi-promyshl/ (accessed: 05/12/.2024). (In Russ.).

15 The list of products classified as import-substituting. Appendix to Resolution No. 9 of the Ministry of Economy of the Republic of Belarus dated May 10, 2022 (as amended by Resolution No. 14 of the Ministry of Economy of the Republic of Belarus dated October 20, 2022). URL: https://economy.gov.by/uploads/files/importozames4enie/Perechen-produktsii-otnosimoj-k-importozameschajuschej.pdf (accessed: 05/12/.2024). (In Russ.).

The annex to the Resolution of the Ministry of Economy of the Republic of Belarus contains a list of products classified as import-substituting[16]. The approved list consists of more than 2,800 products, structured by industry. In addition, large organizations in the country have a list of goods of critical import. One of such enterprises is JSC BMZ, the management company of the BMK holding and the Belneftekhim concern. The list of critical import goods of this organization contains not only the positions of the necessary goods, but also proposals for the enterprise and body (ministries, concerns, executive committees) in the Republic of Belarus to work out the issue of mastering the production of analogues[17].

Thanks to these regulations, Belarusian enterprises aim to use goods produced within the country. This business management strategy will not only help to circumvent sanctions and reduce logistics costs, but should also contribute to strengthening economic sovereignty and developing innovative activities in the country. As mentioned earlier, the conduct of foreign economic activity in the Republic of Belarus with an import-substituting orientation became more pronounced after 2022 due to the economic barriers put forward by Western countries.

Innovative infrastructure contributes to the development of innovative activities with an import-substituting bias. Accordingly, the State Program of Innovative Development of the Republic of Belarus for 2021-2025 presents activities that contribute to the further development of innovative infrastructure, increase the competitiveness of the national economy, achieve the level of RB innovative development of the leading countries, as well as, in particular, it stimulates the protection of the domestic market of scientific and technical products and the creation of import-substituting innovative industries by improving the mechanism for the implementation of public procurement procedures in the fields of scientific, technical and innovative activities[18].

In addition to approving the regulatory framework of the Republic of Belarus in order to stimulate the development of the country's innovative potential, investment projects are being carried out, the implementation of which contributes

---

16 The draft Strategy for Scientific and Technological Development of the Russian Federation until 2035 was prepared by the Center for Strategic Research Foundation on the instructions of the Ministry of Education and Science of the Russian Federation on May 5, 2016. URL https://strategy24.ru/files/uploads/cd2a43226e0ec13b325e4ff331e428c7.pdf (accessed: 14.12.2023). (In Russ.).

17 The list of goods of critical import of Belneftekhim concern organizations for development in the Republic of Belarus.URL: https://fezmogilev.by/upload/iblock/eb9/eb9f61c9ebcce71efad68a44041d54ea.pdf (accessed: 05/12/.2024). (In Russ.).

18 About the State program of innovative development of the Republic of Belarus for 2021-2025.URL: https://pravo.by/document/?guid=3871andp0=P32100348 (accessed: 05/12/.2024). (In Russ.).

to ensuring the technological security of the country. For example, in 2023, the organizations of the Ministry of Industry of the Republic of Belarus implemented 26 import-substituting projects with a total amount of 2.47 billion rubles, and according to the results of work in 2023, another 194.46 million rubles were allocated to this group of projects, and 60 jobs were created (Fig. **1**)[19].

In 2024, financial support will also be provided for innovative projects that solve the problems of import substitution[20].

Thus, the financial assistance of the state, as well as the measures elaborated to develop innovative activities of the Republic of Belarus, contribute to the implementation of import substitution in various sectors of the country's economy, which has a beneficial effect on strengthening the country's sovereignty in the world market.

Summarizing the above, it can be concluded that import substitution is considered both in the Russian Federation and in the Republic of Belarus as a *state mechanism* necessary for the holistic functioning of all sectors of the economy and allowing for reducing dependence on foreign raw materials, developing domestic technologies, and creating innovative enterprises and new jobs. We also find similar positions in the works of other researchers[21] (Bengraf *et al.*, 2024; Popova and Sergeeva, 2022; Zhalezko *et al.*, 2020, *etc.*)

Speaking about integration processes, it should be noted that by 2022, the Russian Federation and the Republic of Belarus have completed about 70% of the 28 integration programs. Moreover, Russia has allocated about $ 1.7 billion in ruble equivalent to Belarus for the implementation of joint import substitution projects (Malashenkov, 2023).

In the wake of import substitution and even "import saving", the heads of Russian regions are actively overseeing the signing of joint production agreements, as well as implementing ambitious plans to create an effective innovation infrastructure. For example, such plans as: to create an assembly plant of Chelyabinsk tracked tractors in Belarus, and Belarusian wheeled tractors in the Russian region; at the

19 Technological security: how much money does the Ministry of Industry plan to spend on innovation in the near future. April 05, 2024.URL: https://www.sb.by/articles/stimul-dlya-rosta.html(accessed: 05/12/.2024). (In Russ.).

20 Import substitution and innovation – The Ministry of Industry announced plans for investment activities in 2024. March 01, 2024.URL: https://www.sb.by/articles/importozameshchenie-i-innovatsii-minprom-ozvuchil-plany-v-investitsionnoy-deyatelnosti-na-2024-god.html (accessed: 05/13/.2024). (In Russ.).

21 Moscow Fund for Industry and Entrepreneurship Support. The official website. URL: https://mfppp.ru/news/fond/gosudarstvennaya-podderzhk--importozameshcheniya-v-novykh-usloviyakh / (accessed: 05/12/2024). (In Russ.).

same time, a serious exchange of competencies will begin; or: to organize a class of the Minsk Tractor Plant in one of the Chelyabinsk universities (Malashenkov, 2023).

It should be noted that the implementation of the state policy of import substitution in both Russia and Belarus, at the same time, is accompanied by certain problems of both an objective and subjective nature. An analysis of the literature[22] available to us has allowed us to identify nine of these most relevant factors that aggravate the implementation of import substitution policies in both countries:

- Possible deterioration of product quality due to reduced competition.
- Rising prices for products with reduced quality.
- Reducing access to technologies, especially innovative ones.
- High level of government corruption: federal, regional, and local.
- Low management efficiency at all levels of government and industrial business.
- Lack of domestic investment, lack of domestic investment mechanisms.
- Not enough highly qualified personnel, especially engineers.
- Weak industrial potential, especially in the engineering industry.
- The threat of monopolies in the absence of external competition.

Our expert survey (using the example of Russia) showed that of these ten factors, three are the most significant, in descending order:

- lack of domestic investment (10 points, 20 responses or 76.9% of respondents);
- low management efficiency (9 points, 18 responses, or 69.2% of respondents);
- lack of highly qualified engineers (8 points, 19 answers, or 73.1% of respondents); Fig. (**1**).

---

22 For example, Problems of import substitution in Russia in 2024. – [Electronic resource].URL: https://digitalved.ru/knowledge-base/problem--importozameshcheniya-v-rossii-2024-godu/(accessed: 05/12/2024).(InRuss.).

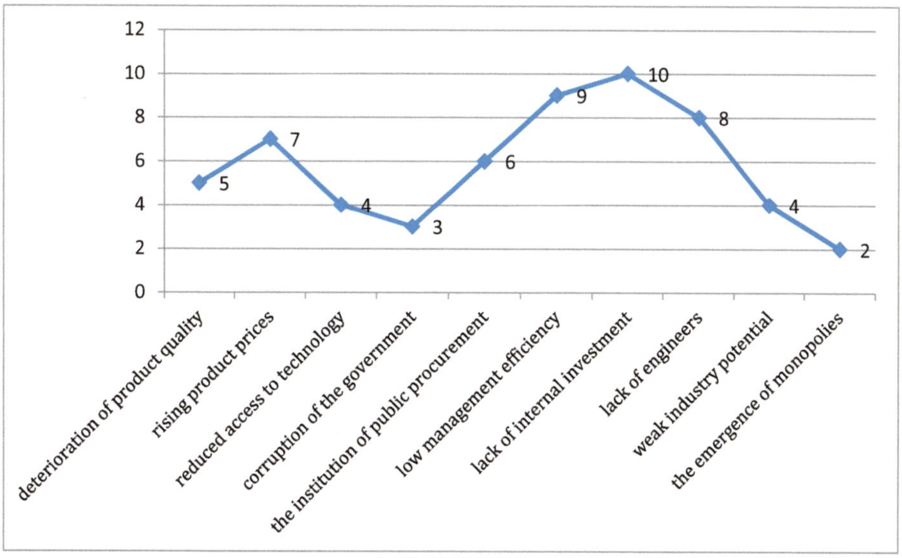

Fig. 1. Factors aggravating the implementation of the import substitution policy in Russia, in points, where 10 is the maximum value, and 1 is the minimum value; compiled by the authors on the basis of an expert survey[23], where each expert rated each factor in points. ($N=27$; $n = 26$; $K_k = 0.21$; $K_c = 0.84$)[24]. *Source: online survey and processing data in Excel.*

The results in Fig. (**1**) also indicate the need for further development of innovation infrastructure, since investing in the creation and production of innovations leads to the development of RandD in conjunction with higher education and the labor market.

In our opinion, the following areas of activity can improve the effectiveness of the implementation of the policy of import substitution of high-tech innovative products and services in Russia:

- Development of new technologies and technical capabilities that allow the design and production of high-tech import-substituting products;

---

23 The survey was organized on November 19, 2022 among university professors and representatives of science and business during the international round table "Strategic vectors of territorial development and a new quality of life in the first quarter of the XXI century: economic models, new technologies and management practices".

24 Here and further: Symbols: N is the total number of respondents, n is the number of respondents' responses received; Kk is the Kramer correlation coefficient (average value); Kc is the concordance coefficient (consistency of respondents' opinions; average value).

- Creating conditions for reducing production time by using a cluster-type organization[25], which allows accelerating technology transfer;
- Training of competent scientific and industrial personnel, both in the system of basic and additional professional education;
- Targeted financing, including through government programs (budget financing), venture funds, private investments, *etc.*;
- The use of NPA ("New Public Management") methods in the public administration system (Astratova, 2023), as well as the realization of the possibility of public-private partnership;
- Development of the regulatory framework in order to specify and ensure control over the implementation of programs, projects, and roadmaps.

We also find similar positions on this issue among other authors (Bengraf *et al.*, 2024; Malashenkov, 2023; Popova and Sergeeva, 2022, *etc.*).

CONCLUSION

The study of the innovative infrastructure of the Union State of the Russian Federation and the Republic of Belarus has demonstrated that it serves as a fundamental platform for economic development and a key factor in import substitution under current geopolitical and economic conditions.

Our research reveals that both Russia and Belarus have made significant progress in developing their innovation infrastructures, with Russia showing substantial growth in technology parks (from 101 units in 2014 to 269 in 2019) and Belarus successfully meeting the targets set in its State Program of Innovative Development. The integration of university-based innovation entities has proven to be particularly effective in both countries, with science and technology parks, technology transfer centers, business support centers, and educational laboratories becoming critical nodes in the innovation ecosystem.

The implementation of import substitution policies has gained strategic importance for both countries, especially since 2014 for Russia and more intensively since 2022 for Belarus. Both governments have established comprehensive regulatory frameworks and financial support mechanisms aimed at reducing dependence on foreign technologies and strengthening economic sovereignty. By 2022, approximately 70% of the 28 integration programs between

---

25 For example, how it is done in such Russian production clusters as: Kamsky Innovative territorial production cluster (Republic of Tatarstan), Petrochemical territorial cluster (Republic of Bashkortostan), Innovative territorial cluster "Phystech XXI" (Moscow region), *etc.*

Russia and Belarus had been completed, with significant financial resources allocated to joint import substitution projects.

However, our analysis has identified several challenges hindering the effective implementation of import substitution policies. An expert survey conducted in Russia highlighted three primary concerns: lack of domestic investment, low management efficiency, and shortage of highly qualified engineers. These findings underscore the need for targeted interventions in these areas.

Based on our research, we propose six strategic directions to enhance the effectiveness of import substitution policies for high-tech innovative products and services:

- Development of new technologies and technical capabilities for the design and production of high-tech import-substituting products.
- Implementation of cluster-type organizational structures to accelerate technology transfer and reduce production times.
- Training of competent scientific and industrial personnel through both basic and additional professional education.
- Establishment of targeted financing mechanisms, including government programs, venture funds, and private investments.
- Application of New Public Management methods in public administration and utilization of public-private partnerships.
- Development of a comprehensive regulatory framework to specify and ensure control over the implementation of programs, projects, and roadmaps.

The continued development of a robust, innovative infrastructure within the Union State will be essential for both countries to maintain technological sovereignty, reduce dependence on foreign imports, and foster sustainable economic growth in an increasingly complex global environment. The collaborative approach between Russia and Belarus offers a model for how integrated innovation systems can provide mutual benefits and strengthen resilience against external economic pressures.

Future research should focus on monitoring the implementation of joint projects, evaluating the effectiveness of proposed measures, and identifying new opportunities for synergy between the innovation ecosystems of both countries. Additionally, comparative analysis with other successful models of innovation infrastructure development worldwide could provide valuable insights for further enhancement of the Union State's innovation capabilities.

CHAPTER 7

Public Management of the USRB Innovation Infrastructure in the Digital Economy

Galina V. Astratova[1,*], **Boris A. Zhalezko**[2], **Airat M. Izmailov**[3], **Natalia A. Simchenko**[4] and **Irina A. Shamardina**[2]

[1] *Department of Regional Economics, Innovative Entrepreneurship and Economics (REIE&E), Institute of Economics and Management, School of Public Administration and Entrepreneurship (SPAE), Ural Federal University (UrFU), Yekaterinburg 620002, Sverdlovsk Region, Russian Federation*

[2] *Department of Marketing, Belarusian National Technical University, Minsk 220013, Republic of Belarus*

[3] *Department of Digital Economics, Volga State University of Telecommunications and Informatics, Samara 443090, Middle Volga region, Russian Federation*

[4] *Department of Economic Theory and Economic Policy, St. Petersburg State University, St. Petersburg 199034, Russian Federation*

Abstract: This chapter examines the public management of innovation infrastructure in the Union State of the Russian Federation and the Republic of Belarus (USRB) within the context of the digital economy. Through comparative analysis of R & D and higher education sectors in both countries, the research identifies key challenges and opportunities for enhancing scientific and technological development. The study reveals that despite significant investment in R & D (1.1% of GDP in Russia and 0.8% in Belarus), both countries face declining effectiveness of research outputs, with patent applications decreasing by approximately 41% in Russia and 50% in Belarus from 2015 to 2022. Survey data from experts, government officials, and students highlight three critical factors for transforming university research into practical innovations: cooperation with enterprises, adequate compensation for scientists, and creation of coordinated R & D market databases. The chapter also analyzes the impact of digitalization on higher education, noting a positive trend in student interest in technology-related programs, with enrollment increasing from 25,000 to 68,000 in Russia and from 12,000 to 30,000 in Belarus between 2020 and 2023. The findings underscore the need for strategic reforms in taxation policies for businesses implementing R & D results, improved financial support for scientific laboratories, and stronger synergy between higher education, R & D, and labor markets to unlock the full potential of digital innovation in the USRB.

[*] **Corresponding author Galina V. Astratova:** Department of Regional Economics, Innovative Entrepreneurship and Economics (REIE&E), Institute of Economics and Management, School of Public Administration and Entrepreneurship (SPAE), Ural Federal University (UrFU), Yekaterinburg 620002, Sverdlovsk Region, Russian Federation; E-mail: galina_28@mail.ru

Galina V. Astratova, Maxim V. Vlasov, Chigozirim Ndubuisi Onwusiribe & Longinus D.N. Nnadozie (Eds.)

Keywords: Digitalization, Higher education transformation, Innovation infrastructure, Public policy, R & D management, Technological development, USRB.

INTRODUCTION

In recent years, the Union State of the Russian Federation and the Republic of Belarus (USRB) has increasingly acknowledged the important role of the state in governing R & D and higher education in the context of the restructuring of the labor market relating to digitalization, as well as economic purposes of stimulating economic growth and gaining international competitiveness for the country (Astratova *et al.*, 2024; Bogdan *et al/.*, 2020). While the research sector of the Union state contributes meaningfully to supporting various sectors of industry (Petrov, *et al/*, 2022), it also imposes a pressing need to develop and implement sectoral policy instruments in the state sector that promote greater research collaboration, increased research funding, and better commercialization of researchers based results for optimal impact in relation to economics (Astratova, 2023b; Ferile, *et al/*, 2008; Smith and Jones, 2020; Znamensky, 2012).

As we already mentioned, the Russian Federation is keen to turn its attention to the area of innovation, which is evidenced by a series of regulatory documents. For example, the Strategy of Innovative Development of the Russian Federation for the period up to 2023 (hereinafter referred to as the Strategy) [1] is developed on the basis of the provisions of the Concept of Long-term Socio-economic Development of the Russian Federation for the period up to 2023[2] and takes account of the Federal Law "On Science and State Scientific and Technical Policy"[3] stipulating that the Strategy is developed to respond to challenges confronting Russia in the area of innovative development, to specify the aims, priorities, and mechanisms of state innovation policy. The Strategy also establishes guidelines for long-term development for subjects of innovation activity, guidelines for financing the area of fundamental science and applied science, and support for the commercialisation of developments. Moreover, the

1 The strategy of innovative development of the Russian Federation for the period up to 2023. Approved by the Decree of the Government of the Russian Federation dated December 8, 2011 No. 2227-R. URL: https://z-motiv.ru/strategiya-innovatsionnogo-razvitiya-rf-do-2023-goda/ (accessed: 12/14/2023). (In Russ.).

2 The concept of long-term socio-economic development of the Russian Federation for the period up to 2020 (approved by the decree of the Government of the Russian Federation dated November 17, 2008 No. 1662-r). URL: https://www.garant.ru/products/ipo/prime/doc/94365/ (accessed: 12/14/2023). (In Russ.).

3 Federal Law on Science and State Scientific and Technical Policy. dated 08/23/1996 N 127-FZ (last revision) on August 23, 1996 N 127-FZ. Adopted by the State Duma on July 12, 1996. Approved by the Federation Council on August 7, 1996. URL: https://www.consultant.ru/document/cons_doc_LAW_11507/(accessed: 12/14/2023). (In Russ.).

Strategy is based on the results of a total assessment of a nation's innovation potential coupled with a long-term scientific and technological forecast. The provisions of the Strategy are to be acknowledged whenever concepts and programs for the socio-economic development of Russia are developed.

A draft Strategy for Scientific and Technological Development of the Russian Federation[4] until 2035 has also been developed, providing scenarios and mechanisms for innovative development, as well as the choice of priority areas of economic activity in the Russian Federation, including:

- Focus on global, "big challenges" facing the country and society, and enshrined in regulatory documents.
- Finding opportunities for both large-scale socio-economic development and potential threats and risks of a systemic nature.
- Obtaining new results with scientific novelty and based on the development of radically innovative technologies.
- Striving for long-term planning, development, and implementation of large-scale projects based on cross-country cooperation, interdepartmental, and interdisciplinary research.

Therefore, the main directions of development of the Russian Federation in R & D focus on both the thematic focus of research and development and on including an indicator of the mission and purpose of that research and development in terms of solving the most important social and state problems or of enabling an opportunity for social and economic development.

With respect to the Republic of Belarus, it is a country that has presently chosen the intellectual route of development as a path. The Scientific Strategy of the Republic of Belarus, for instance, defines the period that will last until 2040. The main predictions of the future intellectual economy, the main objectives of state policy on science and innovation, the tools to stimulate the scientific and technological development of the national economy and the predicted results of the implementation of the Strategy, will allow the country to reach a global level of competitiveness in a number of areas on the base of the development of innovative technologies, intellectualisation and digital industrial revolution.

---

4 The draft Strategy for Scientific and Technological Development of the Russian Federation until 2035 was prepared by the Center for Strategic Research Foundation on the instructions of the Ministry of Education and Science of the Russian Federation on May 5, 2016.URL https://strategy24.ru/files/uploads/cd2a43226e0ec13b325e4ff331e428c7.pdf(accessed: 12/14/2023). (In Russ.).

In addition, the state innovation Program[1] aims to achieve a leading level of innovative development in Eastern Europe based on the realization of the intellectual potential of the Republic of Belarus. To achieve this goal, it is planned to solve a number of tasks, among which it is envisaged to accelerate the development of the innovation infrastructure of the Republic of Belarus, to increase the role of the "creative class" (*i.e.*, persons forming creative human capital), as well as the digital transformation of traditional sectors of the national economy.

Since the formation of the state scientific, technical, innovation and educational policy determines the future vector of innovative development of the country, as well as the formation of scientific, technological and innovative potential, and as a result the growth of the welfare of the country and the nation, it is not surprising that many Russian, Belarusian and foreign scientists are involved in the studying of issues in the field of state scientific, technical, innovation policy and the development of innovative potential of the country.

According to Dorina & Kadovba, (2019), conceptual line of increasing the innovative potential of the regions of the Republic of Belarus and the efficiency of its use, which includes: a) increasing human and scientific potential and preventing specialists from emigrating abroad; b) decreasing financial potential - diversifying the sources of financing and improving its mechanisms; c) improving organizational conditions for innovation; d) increasing demand for innovative products and technologies; and e) activate and improve mechanisms of technology transfer and procedure of commercialization. Through the implementation of these measures, it is possible to improve the state of the regions of the Republic of Belarus in the area of innovation, according to Dorina and Kadovba (2019). Similar positions can also be found in Klimuk and Unsovich *et al.* (2021).

In the case of Russia, there is a perspective that the innovation process in the country as a whole hasn't developed much during the last 30 years, and the innovative activity of domestic industrial enterprises leaves much to be desired (Silakova and Grigoriev, 2021). In particular, following the completion of the strategic innovation project, there is a lag in a number of planned domestic indicators and some global indices (*e.g.*, GII, BII, GCI, *etc.*). At the same time, the practice of Ural industrial enterprise in general, and related to successful cooperation with enterprises of the Republic of Belarus, in particular, can be

1 About the State program of innovative development of the Republic of Belarus for 2021-2025.URL: https://pravo.by/document/?guid=3871&p0=P32100348. (accessed: 12/14/2023). (InRuss.).

screenshot (Petrov *et al.*, 2022). Most positive dynamics are reported in the level of human capital, handling intellectual property, and the formation of the business environment.

According to Dvoretskaya (2018), a new ("fourth") industrial revolution is ushering in the modern day, with fundamentally technological aspects, including digital transformation, intellectualization, and platform solutions (fintech). Nonetheless, the industries leading the innovation ecosystem are companies producing breakthrough technologies and innovations (Dvoretskaya, 2018). In summary, according to the World Economic Forum 2018a, Russia is part of a cluster of countries with an old technological structure based on mostly commodity economies, and there has been little change since (Rostislavsky, 2022).

Following an analysis of data from Rosstat reports, reports on innovative development index results from countries, the Russian Federation's strategy for development, and the strategies of RF subjects for development, A.A. Rostislavsky defines barriers to the nation's scientific and technological advancement and suggests there is a need to strengthen the innovative activity of the enterprises and regions (Rostislavsky, 2022). According to Silakova and Grigoriev (2021), addressing the barriers noted above will require building institutions for innovative development and improving the conditions for business implementation.

The findings of foreign researchers also suggest that R & D and innovation are a driving force of economic development and competitive performance internationally. Brown & White (2018) conducted a comparative analysis of the Russian Federation and the Republic of Belarus and noted that the research sector is a critical part of their economic development. Brown and White recommended that these nations need to make strategic investments in research capacity and human capital. They suggest that countries have to intensify joint research and development beyond national borders in order to solve complex social problems and stimulate sustainable economic performance.

Further, Johnson and Smith (2019) highlight the role of research institutions as a catalyst for innovative ecosystems and the processes of knowledge transfer, commercializing technologies, and collaborating with industry. The scholars commend aligning research priorities with national direction so that the results of research can provide real socio-economic benefits to the populace.

Similar positions are set out in the works of Russian and Belarusian researchers (Klimuk, 2023; Klimuk and Unsovich, 2021; Lvov, 1990; Petrov *et al.*, 2022; Tatarkin and Pilipenko, 2007; Vlasov and Shardina, 2022).

It should be noted that the indicators of R & D development in the Union State Table **1** demonstrate the commitment of the Russian Federation and the Republic of Belarus to the development of a knowledge-based economy.

Table 1. Performance indicators of the research sectorin the Union State of the Russian Federation and the Republic of Belarus in 2023.

Indicators	Russia	Belarus
Research and development expenditures (% of GDP)	1.1	0.8
Number of joint studies	580	320
Patents granted	2500	620

Sources: The official website of the Federal State Statistics Service. URL: https://rosstat.gov.ru / (accessed: 04/26/2024).
Official website of the National Statistical Committee of the Republic of Belarus. URL: https://www.belstat.gov.by /(accessed: 04/26/2024).

From Table **1**, it can be seen that the number of joint research and the number of patents granted in both countries are very significant, which indicates significant research results and indicates the potential for commercialization and economic effect.

Next, it is advisable to analyze the main indicators of organizations that performed R & D in both countries. Table **2** shows the dynamics of the indicators of organizations that performed R & D in the Republic of Belarus.

Table 2. Indicators of organizations that performed R & D in the Republic of Belarus are compiled on the basis of official data (Statistical Yearbook, 2023).

Indicators	2015	2016	2017	2018	2019	2020	2021	2022	Trend, % 2022/2015
1. The number of organizations that performed R & D	439	431	454	455	460	451	445	448	102.1
Sector of activity:									
state	87	90	93	90	89	88	90	93	107.0
commercial	286	277	286	287	296	285	283	281	98.3
higher education	64	61	72	76	74	78	71	74	115.6
2. The number of personnel engaged in R & D, thousand people	26.15	25.94	26.48	27.41	27.74	25.62	25.64	25.2	96.4
Sector of activity:									
researchers	16.95	16.88	17.09	17.80	17.86	16.70	16.32	16.43	97.0
technicians	1.74	1.62	1.69	1.71	1.96	1.66	1.78	1.91	110.0
support staff	7.46	7.45	7.70	7.89	7.91	7.27	7.54	6.89	92.4

(Table 2) cont.....

Indicators	2015	2016	2017	2018	2019	2020	2021	2022	Trend, % 2022/2015
3. Internal R & D costs in current prices, million rubles.	4495.4*	475.3	617.7	739.3	777.8	807.0	813.3	919.8	205.0
4. Domestic R & D expenditures as a percentage of GDP	0.50	0.50	0.58	0.60	0.58	0.54	0.46	0.48	96.0

*The denomination in the Republic of Belarus occurred in 2016, so prices in 2015 are indicated in billions of rubles.

In general, we can say that the situation regarding R & D development in Belarus is positive; it is focused on creating high-level products and technologies to meet the needs of the real sector of the economy in replacing critical imports. Among the negative factors affecting the development of R & D in the Republic of Belarus is a shortage of highly qualified personnel, as evidenced by the dynamics of the number of personnel engaged in R & D, which has decreased by 3.6% or 950 people since 2015. R & D costs by type of work are presented in Table **3**.

The analysis of internal R & D costs by type of work in the Republic of Belarus shows the dynamics of growth in all types of research, a significant increase (almost 2.5 times) in applied research, which is confirmed by the implemented state policy regarding financing for R & D development.

Table 3. Internal R & D costs by type of work in the Republic of Belarus, compiled on the basis of official data (StatisticalYearbook, 2023).

Indicators	2015	2016	2017	2018	2019	2020	2021	2022	Trend, % 2022/2015
Basic research, million rubles.	659.9*	67.6	78.9	83.8	97.1	105.9	117.4	130.6	198.0
Applied research, million rubles.	1271.9*	145.2	160.2	188.6	186.6	230.1	232.8	294.2	231.0
Developments, million rubles.	2367.8*	245.6	348.0	416.4	420.0	398.6	398.0	443.6	187.2

*The denomination in the Republic of Belarus occurred in 2016, so prices in 2015 are indicated in billions of rubles.

However, despite the high R & D costs, the effectiveness of research and development in the Republic of Belarus is unstable, which is manifested in a decrease in R & D performance indicators (Table **4**).

Table 4. The effectiveness of research and development in the Republic of Belarus is based on official data (StatisticalYearbook, 2023).

Indicators	2015	2016	2017	2018	2019	2020	2021	2022	Trend,% 2022/2015

(Table 4) cont.....

Indicators	2015	2016	2017	2018	2019	2020	2021	2022	Trend,% 2022/2015
Applications for patenting inventions have been filed	691	521	524	547	39	394	386	342	50.0
Patents for inventions have been issued	902	941	850	625	461	447	316	302	33.5
Patents are valid	2858	2735	2414	2135	1813	1752	1555	1490	52.0

The dynamics of the indicators that show the effectiveness of R & D in the Republic of Belarus Table **5** tend to decline and deteriorate. For all the indicators presented, the decline rate is close to 50%, and in particular, the rate of patenting inventions has declined by nearly 64.5%, or 600 patents in 2022 compared to 2015. The reasons for this situation stem from the following factors, in our opinion: the vacancies of qualified staff; a low effectiveness of management of higher education institutions and graduate schools; low effectiveness of management of the nation's innovation system, *etc.* (Bengraf *et al.*, 2024). Another important problem is the low availability of knowledge-intensive GDP (Table **2**), and domestic R & D expenditures to GDP in the Republic of Belarus are declining year-on-year and stand at an average of 0.5% of GDP, which is a very low indicator for the fact that it requires the knowledge intensity of GDP (for an average level of scientific, technical and innovation development) at 1% of GDP, at least. We will do a similar analysis of the main indicators of organizations that performed R & D in the Russian Federation. Table **5** presents the dynamics of the indicators of organizations that performed R & D in the Russian Federation.

Table 5. Indicators of organizations that have performed R & D in the Russian Federation, compiled on the basis of official data.

Indicators	**2015**	**2016**	**2017**	**2018**	**2019**	**2020**	**2021**	**2022**	**Trend, % 2022/2015**
1. The number of organizations that performed R & D	4175	4032	3944	3950	4051	4175	4175	4195	100.5
Sector of activity:									
State	1560	1546	1493	1511	1479	1501	1462	1522	97.6
Commercial	1400	1326	1292	1304	1374	1426	1437	1394	99.6
higher education	1124	1064	1038	998	1057	1080	1096	1088	96.8
2. The number of personnel engaged in R & D, thousand people	738.85	722.29	707.89	682.58	682.46	679.33	662.70	669.87	90.7
Sector of activity:									

(Table 5) cont.....

Indicators	2015	2016	2017	2018	2019	2020	2021	2022	Trend, % 2022/2015
Researchers	379.41	370.38	359.79	347.85	348.22	346.50	340.14	340.67	89.8
Technicians	62.81	60.44	59.69	57.72	58.68	59.56	60.47	61.37	97.7
support staff	174.06	171.92	170.35	160.59	160.86	158.30	152.07	154.75	88.9
3. Internal R & D costs in current prices, million rubles.	914.7	943.82	1019.2	1028.3	1134.8	1174.5	1301.5	1435.9	157.0
4. Domestic R & D expenditures as a percentage of GDP	1.10	1.10	1.11	0.99	1.04	1.09	0.99	0.94	85.5

The trends in the development of R & D in Russia are the cooperation of science and business, within the framework of import substitution and technological modernization of the economy (Petrov *et al.*, 2022). During the study, there was a slight growth of R & D organizations in the Russian Federation, but still a decreasing number of qualified personnel. In total, from 2015 to 2022, the number of researchers in Russia decreased by 10.2%, or 38.74 thousand people.

"The reasons for this have been presented before - as you will see, the low salaries of scientific personnel, weak modernization of scientific organizations, ineffective governance, *etc.* Domestic R & D costs by type of work in Russia, despite growth, also reflect a low level of efficiency. " This is again evident from the analysis of the indicators set forth in Table **6** and **7**.

Table 6. Internal R & D costs by type of work in the Russian Federation. (Russian Statistical Yearbook, 2022).

Indicators	2015	2016	2017	2018	2019	2020	2021	2022	Trend, % 2022/2015
Basic research, million rubles.	132.1	132.6	141.3	169.7	181.4	205.3	223.1	236.3	179.0
Applied research, million rubles.	169.7	181.2	172.5	197.2	213.4	218.5	233.5	260.0	153.2
Developments, million rubles.	552.6	560.1	636.4	594.3	665.9	667.6	737.0	826.3	150.0

Table 7. The effectiveness of research and development in the Russian Federation (Russian Statistical Yearbook, 2022).

Indicators	2015	2016	2017	2018	2019	2020	2021	2022	Trend, % 2022/ 2015
Applications for patenting inventions have been filed	45517	41587	36454	37957	35511	34984	30977	26924	59.0

(Table 7) cont.....

Indicators	2015	2016	2017	2018	2019	2020	2021	2022	Trend, % 2022/ 2015
Patents for inventions have been issued	34706	33536	34254	35774	34008	28788	23662	23315	67.2
The number of patents	218974	230870	244321	256419	263688	266189	264587	259020	118.3

According to the Institute of National Economic Forecasting of the Russian Academy of Sciences report about the development of Russia (Belousova & Frolova, 2022), the losses of the Russian Federation associated with the low efficiency of the R & D sector are about $58 billion—four times more than the current volume of exports of high-tech products and weapons (Galcheva, 2022). The next reason for the inefficiency of the R & D sector is, in our opinion, too many priorities for the development of R & D with limited funding and the effect of international sanctions, because prior to the political crisis in the Russian Federation, there was active import of R & D. There is also a trend in reducing the science intensity of GDP, which has decreased by 0.16 percentage points from 2015 to 2022. Therefore, to preserve the technological sovereignty of the country, it is necessary to increase funding, not only to the R & D sector but also to higher education in general. Moreover, analyzing the array of statistical data demonstrated a stark gap in terms of availability of highly qualified personnel in the Russian Federation, and there is a surplus of population with higher education (Bengraf *et al.*, 2024). This fact is proof that confirms the thesis about the low efficiency in realizing strategic management, and the need to modify their respective management systems whilst accounting for current trends in the labor market.

Accordingly, we considered it necessary to ask experts and government officials[1] what factors significantly contribute to the transformation of the results of university science of the USRB into experimental developments, samples, prototypes of products and technologies (Fig. **1**).

---

1 In January-April 2024, a survey of experts (university professors, research institute employees and heads of innovative enterprises) and government officials using Google docs, WhatsApp and Vkontakte was conducted.

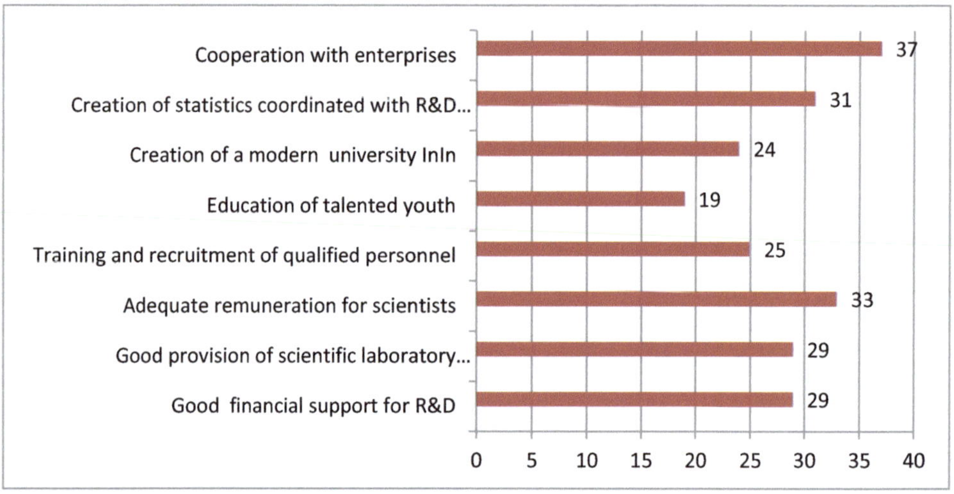

Fig. (1). Respondents' answers to the question: "What factors significantly contribute to the transformation of the results of university science of the Union State of the Russian Federation and the Republic of Belarus into experimental developments, samples, prototypes of products and technologies?", people[1].
($N=83$; $n = 83$; $K_k = 0.22$; $K_c = 0.88$)
Source: data from a survey of experts and government officials in Google Docs, WhatsApp, Vkontakte, and processing in Statistica

Fig. (1) shows that there are at least eight factors that significantly contribute to the transformation of the results of university science of the USRB into experimental developments, samples, prototypes of products and technologies, namely:

- Good financial support for research and development.
- Proper equipment of scientific laboratories.
- Decent pay for scientists, engineers, and researchers.
- Training and recruitment of qualified personnel.
- Education of talented youth.
- Creation of a modern, innovative university.
- Creation of a database of statistical data coordinated with all participants in the R & D market.
- Cooperation with enterprises.

At the same time, three factors turned out to be the most significant, in descending order:

1 Multiple responses from respondents were allowed.

1. Cooperation with enterprises[2] – 37 positive responses;
2. Decent pay for scientists, engineers, and researchers – 33 positive responses;
3. Creation of a database of statistical data was agreed with all participants of the R & D market – 31 positive responses.

The results obtained indicate the need for state reform in terms of changing the taxation of business entities implementing R & D results, as well as stimulating wages and material support for scientific laboratories of the Russian Federation and the Republic of Belarus.

It is important to note that the innovative development of the country today is not possible only without the digital technology industry, but also without the growth of the industries that comprise the knowledge economy: R & D services, along with the Higher Education Services (HES) sector.

Currently, the HES sector is an area where the final stage of formal learning is being delivered, including post-secondary education and research work in specialized educational establishments (*i.e.* universities, academies, institutes, colleges, technology or research institutes, clinics, experimental stations, business schools, *etc.*), which may be of higher education status, or have a higher education, statutory or financial variety (Astratova, *et al.*, 2024; Astratova, *et al.*, 2021; Bengraf, *et al.*, 2024; GlobalEdEc, 2022; GlobalHESRep, 2022).

Moreover, the key element of the HES system—the modern university—is turning from an educational institution into a center of scientific, technical, innovative, and educational policy, where qualitatively new indicators characterizing its activities are being formed, namely:

- The division of education into local (national) and global (supranational).
- Educational programs are in demand at the international level.
- Globally demanded curriculum.
- Extraterritorial teaching staff (faculty).
- Virtual university, institute, laboratory department.
- An international educational standard.
- Certification and accreditation of universities and educational programs in accordance with international standards.
- International mobility of students and teaching staff;
- Using English as an international teaching language, *etc.* (Astratova *et al.*, 2024; Astratova *et al.*, 2022; Astratova *et al.*, 2021; Bengraf *et al.*, 2024; GlobalEdEc, 2022; GlobalHESRep, 2022; *etc.*).

2 This implies, among other things, tax benefits for entrepreneurs who introduce R & D results into production activities..

Thus, the modern HES system serves as a highly dynamic object of study and, as it evolves, it is an important area of development for the global economy, impacting the increase in the intellectual component of labor (exemplified by digitization), and modification of both structure (the modern HES services market has a plethora of public and private companies in both non-profit and commercial segments) and employment structure (offline, online, and blended) (Astratova *et al.*, 2024; Bengraf *et al.*, 2024; Panikarova, *et al.*, 2020).

This allows us to identify four key trends in the development of the HES sector, applicable to both the Russian Federation and the Republic of Belarus:

First, in the 21st century, higher education (along with the R & D sector) has become the largest segment of the global services market (GlobalEdEc, 2022; Global HES Rep, 2022). In fact, at the end of 2022, 2,500 of the world's largest companies spent approximately €1.25 trillion on R & D, which was a record for the world. At the same time, in terms of investments in R & D, China bypassed the EU and came in second place in the global ranking, behind the United States[1].

Additionally, colleges and universities (12% in 2019) and the federal government (9%) accounted for the second[2] and third largest amounts of R & D services in the U.S., also accounting for the majority of fundamental research (Boroush & Guci,2022; Crespi & Antonelli, 2011).

Next, with the rise of globalization and cross-cultural integration, there has been an explosion of different higher education opportunities, some of which are broadly based on more active use of digital technologies, openness to applicants from countries, *etc.* (Astratova & Beleeva, 2021; GlobalEdEc, 2022; GlobalHESRep, 2022) - and an especially interesting recent idea is the "global diploma" based on the notion of "one world, one diploma, and unlimited opportunities"[1].

Also, we should not forget the impact of the global COVID-19 pandemic on the evolution of higher education. Certainly, in the HES system, the most heavily impacted sources of effects by the pandemic were: 1) education delivery organisation; 2) educational internationalization; 3) scientific research; 4) legislation; 5) funding (Astratova *et al.*, 2022; Astratova *et al.*, 2021).

---

1 Research and development, R & D (global market). – 2024. – February 12th. – [Electronic resource]. URL: https://www.tadviser.ru/index.php (accessed: 02/18/2024).

2 After industrial enterprises.

1 Kuveliotis Kiriakos. The proposal to introduce a Global Diploma is a new institutional model of higher education. – June 04, 2021. – [Electronic resource]. URL: https://www.un.org/ru/142812 (accessed: 05/16/2024).

Fourth, digitalization has significantly transformed the higher education system as a whole. Digitalization, or the incorporation of digital technologies in all areas of human activity, has engendered (1) digital educational technologies (EdTech), made possible by classes at universities, in remote format, during the late XX-VIXX centuries (Astratova *et al.*, 2022; Astratova *et al.*, 2021) [2].

It's important to note that the HES system is preparing specialists to enter the labor market, including in the field of information technology, which has great importance in the digital economy. Although in 2023, the IT industry was experiencing an increase in employees (857 thousand people in the Russian Federation in 2023, which was 12.7% more than in 2022), the shortage of personnel in this industry was, according to the Ministry of Finance of Russia, 500-700 thousand in 2023[3].

The lack of specialists in the field of information technology leads to the necessity of the creation of support measures, primarily from the state. So, in Russia, since 2019, more than 343 thousand people have been admitted to universities for educational programs in the field of information technology at the expense of the federal budget; by 2024, this figure is planned to be increased to 500 thousand people[1]. In addition to the increase in the number of budget places in IT specialties for university applicants, there are a number of federal projects in the Russian Federation aimed at obtaining IT education or additional IT competencies at various levels of education: for school education there is a project "Lesson numbers" and "Code of the Future", for additional education - projects "Digital professions", CDO (Chief Data Officer), "Training in digital transformation of public administration", "Ready for digital", for university students – the project "Digital Departments"[2].

---

2 Gorbis Marina. The Future of Education Eliminates the Classroom, because the World is your Class. – 03.04.2013. – [Electronic resource]. URL: https://www.fastcompany.com/2681507/the-future-of-education- eliminates-the- classroom-because-the-world-is-your-class (accessed: 24.05.2024). Kuveliotis Kiriakos. The proposal to introduce a Global Diploma is a new institutional model of higher education. June 04, 2021. – [Electronic resource]. URL: https://www.un.org/ru/142812 (accessed: 05/16/2024).

3 The Internet in Russia in 2022-2023: the state, trends and prospects of development. Industry report. 2023. – [Electronic resource]. URL: https://digital.gov.ru/uploaded/files/internet-v-rossii-v-2022-2023-godah.pdf (accessed 01.07.2024). (In Russ.).

1 Source: Personnel for the Digital Economy. 2024. – [Electronic resource]. URL: https://digital.gov.ru/ru/activity/directions/866 / (accessed 01.07.2024). (In Russ.).

2 Digital Departments" is a joint project of the Ministry of Education and Science and the Ministry of Finance launched in 2022 under the federal project "Development of human resources in the IT industry" within the framework of the national program "Digital Economy of the Russian Federation". During their studies in one of the professional retraining programs of the digital Department, students have the opportunity to receive a second qualification in the field of information technology in parallel with their studies in the main educational program; the main educational program does not necessarily have to be related to information technology. Students of bachelor's degree (after the 1st year), specialty (after the 2nd year) and master's degree can become participants of the program. The key goal of the project is 900 thousand students by 2030 who have mastered digital competencies while studying at a university. Source: Digital Departments. Sociocenter. – [Electronic resource]. URL: https://sociocenter.info/projects/tsifrovye-kafedry/#project (accessed 01.07.2024). (In Russ.).

The importance of using digital technologies in the HES system is also confirmed by the results of our online research. In particular, it was revealed that Russian and Belarusian students are very positive about the use of digital technologies in the higher education system (Fig. 2).

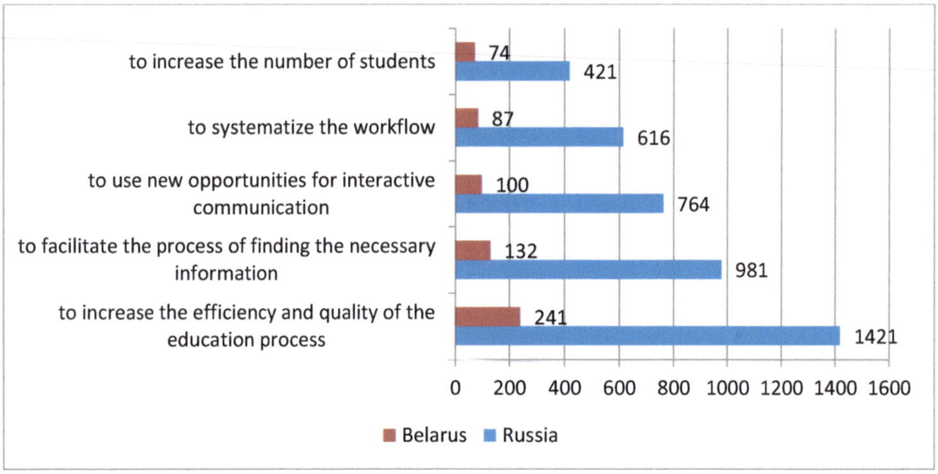

Fig. (2). Respondents' answers to the question: "The use of digital technologies in higher education allows ...", people[1].
($N_{РФ}$=1520; $n_{РФ}$ = 1519; $N_{РБ}$=246; $n_{РБ}$ = 244; K_k = 0.24; K_c = 0.87)[2]
Source: Survey data in Google Docs and processing in Statistica

Fig. (2) states that both Russian and Belarusian students believe that digital technologies allow, in descending order, to achieve the following key effects:

- To improve the efficiency and quality of the education process (93.55% of respondents from the Russian Federation and 98.77% of respondents from the Republic of Belarus);
- To facilitate the process of searching for the necessary information (64.58% and 54.10%, respectively);
- To use new interactive communication opportunities (50.30% and 40.98%, respectively);
- To systematize document flow (40.55% and 35.66%, respectively);
- To increase the number of students (27.72% and 30.33%).

---

1 Multiple responses from respondents were allowed.

2 Here and further: Symbols: N is the total number of respondents, n is the number of responses received; RF is the index , related to the Russian Federation; RB – index related to the Republic of Belarus; Kk– Kramer correlation coefficient (average value); Kc – concordance coefficient (consistency of respondents' opinions; average value).

We also found no significant differences in the opinions of both groups of the studied youth.

The importance of digital technologies is also evidenced by data on the number of university students studying at the USRB in technology-related programs Table **8**.

Table 8. The number of students of higher educational institutions of the USRB studying in programs related to digital technologies (2020-2023)[1].

Years	Russian Federation	Republic of Belarus
2020	25.000	12.000
2021	45.000	18.000
2022	60.000	25.000
2023	68.000	30.000

Sources: The official website of the Federal State Statistics Service. URL: https://rosstat.gov.ru/ (accessed: 04/26/2024).
Official website of the National Statistical Committee of the Republic of Belarus. URL: https://www.belstat.gov.by/(accessed: 04/26/2024).

Table **8** shows an obvious trend towards an increasing interest of students in digital technologies.

It is necessary to draw attention to the fact that in the educational process, and throughout the academic world in general, a number of fundamentally new trends appeared in the global educational system as a result of the adaptation of digital technologies for the academic environment, and these trends—*e.g.*, the phenomenon of online learning, the concept of lifetime educational markets for the global economy—are actually relevant for the Russian Federation, and the Republic of Belarus as well. We offer a summary of the following trends that affirm the benefits of collaboration in higher education:

- It puts universities in a position to be aware of even the most recent developments in the international market.
- Universities establish long (three to five) year plans of development and partnerships with key stakeholders of the HES market.

1 Data for 2023 are presented for the first 9 months of the year.

- Higher education institutions demonstrate a greater level of collaboration in global student markets to develop cross-cultural communications, provide bespoke services for international students, personalized learning pathways, *etc.*
- Universities develop promotional programs in global markets, including calls for the best programmers in the world. Many such positions are articulated in the previous authors' research works (Astratova *et al.*, 2021; Bengraf *et al.*, 2024; Global Ed Ec, 2022; Global HES Rep, 2022; Panikarova *et al.*, 2020; Vlasov and Shardina, 2022).

It should be emphasized that the above trends in the HES system require serious investments. According to research by various authors (Drapkin *et al.*, 2019; Zaytsev,2021), developing countries do not always have enough of their own resources to invest in the implementation of scientific, technical, innovation, and educational policies.

Accordingly, in addition to increasing the tax base of their own population, many countries often resort to external assistance as one of the key factors in increasing the effectiveness of the economic management of the country's sustainable development. Accordingly, the Russian Federation is very actively providing external assistance to developing countries (Astratova & Toshpulotov, 2023; Drapkin *et al.*, 2019; Zaytsev, 2021), providing assistance to CIS countries, including the Republic of Belarus (Astratova & Toshpulotov, 2023, p. 97).

In this regard, we believe that the most relevant area for future research should be the problem of:

A. Financial management in the public administration of developing countries (primarily the Russian Federation and the Republic of Belarus) and the problems of the effectiveness of foreign aid from the Russian Federation and the Republic of Belarus;
B. The sectoral specifics of public administration in the system of R & D and higher education of the Russian Federation and the Republic of Belarus in the context of digitalization.

This is also evidenced by the research of Ignatieva *et al.* (2019): the problems of developing innovative infrastructure in the regions should be solved comprehensively, since infrastructure development affects all socio-economic processes. Consequently, both in the Russian Federation and the Republic of Belarus, it is necessary to create conditions for the innovative development of the real sector and the optimal use of its material and labor resources.

As noted in our earlier study (Astratova, 2023b), there are currently two main approaches to the study of sectoral public administration policy in the higher education system: 1) reform of public policy and decision-making processes; 2) identification of political regimes implementing this policy. Although both approaches consider the HES system as a special branch of management, there are opinions that the changes that have occurred in the field of HES are similar to transformations in other branches of public administration and signal a new understanding of the role of the national state in society. New models of public and municipal management also lead to a rethinking of the mechanisms of sectoral public financing, including in the field of HES. Without questioning the need for state participation in the formation of the knowledge economy, we believe that further research needs to explore issues related to determining the most effective share of state participation in the management of the higher education system (Astratova, 2023b). This is especially relevant in the context of digital transformation, as the digital economy poses new challenges and opportunities for higher education institutions to teach students the skills and knowledge necessary to thrive in a rapidly changing environment.

For example, the Garcia & Patel (2020) study explores the role of HES in increasing digital literacy and cultivating a culture of innovation among students. The authors emphasize the importance of integrating new technologies into the curriculum to ensure that graduates are well prepared to navigate the complexities of the digital economy.

In addition, a comparative analysis conducted by Kim *et al.* (2019) sheds light on the strategies used by leading universities to adapt their programs to the demands of the digital age. The study highlights the importance of industry partnerships, hands-on learning opportunities, and ongoing professional development initiatives to bridge the skills gap and expand graduate employment opportunities in a digital-centric economy.

The advent of the digital economy has accelerated profound transformations in labor markets, requiring a reassessment of traditional employment models and skill requirements. The seminal work of Li and Wang (2018) explores the impact of automation and artificial intelligence on the movement of jobs and the emergence of new job categories in the digital age. These authors emphasize the need for an active labor market policy that promotes retraining and lifelong learning in order to mitigate the negative effects of technological failures.

Moreover, a study by Chen and Wu (2020) is devoted to the economics of concerts and the implications for the dynamics of the labor movement in the digital age. These authors emphasize the growing prevalence of freelance work and the need for a regulatory framework that protects the rights and interests of concert workers. They also emphasize the importance of creating a supportive ecosystem that allows individuals to use digital platforms to generate income and develop skills.

In fundamental research by Russian scientists (Ivanova and Vasilevskaya, 2019; Petrov *et al.*, 2022; Vasilevskaya, 2019) also notes that in the context of the implementation of the strategy for the formation of a unified scientific and technological space of Russia and Belarus, based on the introduction of digital technologies, not only the issues of mastering new professions and obsolescence of previous types of employment, but also the problems, structure and scale of labor migration in the Union State, as well as the phenomena of discrimination caused by such negative factors as: precarization of employment, polarization of the labor market, gender and age inequality. Similar positions are noted in our previous studies (Astratova *et al.*, 2022; Astratova *et al.*, 2021; Bengraf *et al.*, 2024).

Summarizing the conclusions of these key studies, it becomes obvious that higher education institutions, the R & D sector, and labor market stakeholders play a crucial role in shaping the profession of the future in the digital economy. Joint efforts to improve digital literacy, promote lifelong learning, and adapt the regulatory framework to changing working conditions are necessary to ensure that the population can thrive in the digital age and make a meaningful contribution to economic development.

In the context of public management of innovation infrastructure, the formation of a knowledge society and the change of technological structure (Astratova 2023b; Bengraf *et al.*, 2024; Klimuk, 2023; Klimuk and Unsovich, 2021; Lvov, 1990; Panikarova *et al.*, 2020; Petrov *et al.*, 2022; Tatarkin and Pilipenko 2007; Vlasov and Shardina, 2022), the processes of interconnection of the elements forming the innovation infrastructure in general, and in the Union State of Russia and Belarus, in particular, have especially importance.

Summarizing the conclusions from the mentioned studies, we can conclude that the interaction between such socio-economic systems as HES, the R & D sector, and the labor market, in the context of public management of the innovation infrastructure of the Union State, plays an important role in overcoming the difficulties of the digital economy and stimulating sustainable economic development. Accordingly, future research should focus on strengthening the synergy between these key components in order to unlock the full potential of digital innovation and propel the USRB towards a prosperous and inclusive future.

CONCLUSION

This chapter has examined the public management of innovation infrastructure in the Union State of the Russian Federation and the Republic of Belarus (USRB) in the context of the digital economy, focusing particularly on the R & D sector and higher education system. Our analysis reveals several important findings with significant implications for policy development and strategic planning.

The comparative assessment of R & D indicators in both countries demonstrates a commitment to knowledge-based economic development, yet also highlights concerning trends. Despite increased financial investment in R & D activities (with internal R & D costs growing by 157% in Russia and 205% in Belarus from 2015 to 2022), both countries face declining research effectiveness as evidenced by the decreasing number of patent applications and grants. This paradox suggests that financial resources alone are insufficient to stimulate innovation without corresponding structural reforms.

A critical challenge identified in both countries is the shortage of qualified personnel in the R & D sector. The number of researchers decreased by 10.2% in Russia and 3.6% in Belarus during the study period, indicating issues with talent retention and development. This human capital deficit represents a significant barrier to innovation and technological sovereignty, especially in the context of international sanctions and the need for import substitution in critical technologies.

Our survey of experts and government officials revealed that effective transformation of university research into practical innovations requires three key factors: meaningful cooperation between academia and industry, competitive compensation for scientists and researchers, and integrated information systems that facilitate knowledge exchange among all R & D market participants. These findings underscore the importance of a systemic approach to innovation policy that addresses not only funding but also institutional connections, incentive structures, and information flows.

In the higher education sphere, digitalization has emerged as a transformative force, with both Russian and Belarusian students recognizing its potential to improve educational quality, facilitate information access, and enable new interactive communication channels. The significant increase in students pursuing technology-related programs (growing from 25,000 to 68,000 in Russia and from 12,000 to 30,000 in Belarus between 2020 and 2023) reflects growing awareness of the importance of digital skills in the modern economy.

Looking forward, the USRB faces both challenges and opportunities in managing its innovation infrastructure. To address the identified issues, we recommend several strategic interventions: reforming taxation policies to incentivize businesses implementing R & D results; enhancing financial support and equipment for scientific laboratories; implementing targeted measures to attract and retain scientific talent; strengthening university-industry partnerships; creating integrated databases for R & D stakeholders; and developing coordinated educational policies that align with labor market needs in the digital economy.

The successful management of innovation infrastructure in the USRB will depend on the ability to foster synergy between higher education institutions, the R & D sector, and industry while adapting regulatory frameworks to the rapidly changing technological environment. Future research should focus on optimizing the role of state participation in the knowledge economy, addressing financial management challenges in public administration, and exploring the sectoral specifics of public management in R & D and higher education in the context of ongoing digital transformation.

In conclusion, as the USRB continues to navigate the complexities of the digital economy, strategic public management of innovation infrastructure will be essential for maintaining technological sovereignty, stimulating economic growth, and ensuring international competitiveness in the global knowledge economy.

CHAPTER 8

Identification of Bottlenecks Limiting The Effectiveness of Public Administration in HES and R & D Sectors in Russia and Belarus

Galina V. Astratova[1,*], **Chigozirim N. Onwusiribe**[2] and **Maxim V. Vlasov**[1]

[1] *Department of Regional Economics, Innovative Entrepreneurship and Economics (REIE&E), Institute of Economics and Management, School of Public Administration and Entrepreneurship (SPAE), Ural Federal University (UrFU), Yekaterinburg 620002, Sverdlovsk Region, Russian Federation*

[2] *School of Public Administration and Entrepreneurship (SPAE), Ural Federal University (UrFU), Yekaterinburg 620002, Sverdlovsk Region, Russian Federation*

Abstract: This chapter investigates the key challenges and "bottlenecks" limiting the effectiveness of public administration in Higher Education Services (HES) and Research and Development (R & D) sectors in Russia and Belarus. Through a comprehensive analysis of World Bank and United Nations data on e-government development, corruption control, public administration effectiveness, and educational expenditures, the research identifies systemic inefficiencies affecting these knowledge economy sectors. The study employs correlation analysis and expert surveys (N=83 for Russia; N=25 for Belarus) to evaluate the impact of global trends—scientific-technological progress, budget sequestration, and decision-making optimization—on sectoral governance. Findings reveal that while both countries demonstrate positive attitudes toward digital transformation in public administration, Belarus significantly lags behind Russia in harmonizing with global trends in HES governance. The research identifies bureaucratic inefficiency, corruption, and insufficient digital competencies among civil servants as primary bottlenecks hindering effective public administration. Despite fluctuating government expenditures on HES and R & D in both countries, the e-Government Development Index (eGDI) shows gradual improvement, indicating positive trends toward digital governance. The study concludes that priority reforms should focus on enhancing transparency, accountability, and citizen representation in government bodies to improve management efficiency and institutional development in the knowledge economy sectors.

* **Corresponding author Galina V. Astratova:** Department of Regional Economics, Innovative Entrepreneurship and Economics (REIE&E), Institute of Economics and Management, School of Public Administration and Entrepreneurship (SPAE), Ural Federal University (UrFU), Yekaterinburg 620002, Sverdlovsk Region, Russian Federation;
E-mail: galina_28@mail.ru

Keywords: Bureaucratic bottlenecks, Digital transformation, E-government, Higher education services, Knowledge economy, Public administration, Research and development.

INTRODUCTION

The "knowledge economy" as a special branch of the national economy, which is formed by the R & D services sector and the higher education services sector, is one of the most difficult objects of implementing the sectoral principle in public administration (Astratova, 2023b). Sector HES plays a very special role in the knowledge economy, since the final stage of formal education is being implemented in the HES system (Astratova *et al.*, 2022; Astratova *et al.*, 2021; Panikarova *et al.*, 2020; Tatarkin and Pilipenko, 2007), and also because HES has a dual content, being at the same time a socially significant good and the totality of the competencies of professional development, both of an individual and of the whole society (Astratova, 2023b, p. 3).

From the point of view of systems theory, the public sector is a complexly integrated organizational structure and has interrelated components that interact both internally and externally (Economics in Context Initiative, 2021; Eucken, 1990; Felício *et al.*, 2021). Consequently, the "knowledge economy" industry and its main elements (higher education and R & D) are the basis for analyzing the complex relationships between key stakeholders, policies, resources, and processes.

It should be noted that in the HES sector, systems theory is one of the tools used to understand the problems existing at the university, including insufficient funding, differentiated teaching levels, poor-quality infrastructure, *etc.* A systematic approach is especially relevant in the implementation of innovative technologies and the creation of innovative infrastructure, where universities play a crucial role (Abiona and Sodeinde, 2022; Vasiliev *et al.*, 2020). At first glance, it seems that these problems are not interconnected, but in fact, they are interconnected and hinder effective public administration in providing high-quality education. The main task of systems theory is to ensure the integrated and systematic provision of educational services that eliminate structural gaps, collaboration of participants, and policy coherence to achieve better results, which applies to HES as well. We find similar positions on this issue in the works of other researchers (Vasiliev *et al.*, 2020; Helbing, 2012).

It should also be noted that in addition to systemic approaches to public administration at the end of the 20th century, the scientific literature began to talk about the need to reform the public sector, in connection with which such terms as "new public administration" appeared, as well as new models of this management: "Public Administration", "New Public Management", "NPM" and "Good Governance", *etc.* (Barabashev, 2016; Dolgikh, 2017; Maratova, 2022; Pollitt and Bouckaert, 2000). This led to the consistent reform of the public sector in the OECD countries, starting in the 90s of the XX century (Pollitt and Bouckaert, 2000). In order to improve the efficiency of work in public institutions, focus on results and strengthen public sector accountability (Hood, 1995).

The popularity of the concept of "New Public Management" (NPM) has led to the industry application of this public administration tool, including in the HES system. This led to the emergence of the term: "new public administration of higher education" (Shibanova, 2023). Moreover, the role of higher education in society has increased so much that by now they are talking about its new positioning ("repositioning" or "repositioning") (Broucker, 2022).

Despite the generally recognized importance of the HES and R & D sectors, public administration in these branches faces serious challenges in the Russian Federation and the Republic of Belarus. It is known from the practice of other countries that inefficiency of bureaucracy, corruption, and political interference are the main obstacles to effective governance, constraining innovation in research initiatives (Agbazuere, 2020; Inakefe *et al.*, 2021; Olojede and Ann, 2023). Similarly, the problems of Russian public administration include issues of legitimacy, corruption, efficiency of bureaucracy, and digitalization, which focus on the difficulties faced in the process of transforming social institutions and achieving economic results under global pressure (Avdeev D.A., 2021; Borenstein and Pozdnyakova, 2022; Nemeryuk *et al.*, 2020). In the Republic of Belarus, the problems facing public administration cover a number of issues, including digital development in the knowledge economy[1], as well as corruption, the effectiveness of administrative and tort policies[2], the dynamics of relations with the Russian Federation and the transition to the principles of sustainable development, the implementation of which requires comprehensive strategies for managing political dynamics and promoting effective development (Gavrikov, 2022; Palchik *et al.*, 2020; Pilgun and Leshenyuk, 2021).

Accordingly, our research is aimed at identifying "bottlenecks" that limit the effectiveness of public administration in the Russian Federation and the Republic

---

1 The concept of digital transformation of processes in the education system of the Republic of Belarus for 2019-2025. Approved by the Minister of Education of the Republic of Belarus I.V. Karpenko on March 15, 2019. (Electronic resource). URL: https://crit.bspu.by/wp-content/uploads/2021/08/concept.pdf (accessed 03/25/2024). (In Russ.).

2 Tort policy is a system of concepts, ideas and views on legal and organizational and tactical issues of combating administrative offenses.

of Belarus in the sectors of higher education, research, and development. For the analysis, data on development indicators from the Knowledge Base of the World Bank and the United Nations on e-government, presented in Table **1**, were used.

Table 1. Methodology of obtaining research data, in the author's interpretation.

Variables	Source	The Nature of the Data
The fight against corruption: a number of sources	The World Bank World Development Indicators	Numeric, graphical
The effectiveness of public administration: Assessment	The World Bank World Development Indicators	Numerical, estimated
Research and development expenditure (% of GDP)	The World Bank World Development Indicators	Percentage (%)
Government discrepancies in education, all (% of GDP)	The World Bank World Development Indicators	Percentage (%)
Human capital index (HCI), upper bound (scale 0-1)	The World Bank World Development Indicators	Numeric scale, (0-1)
The Electronic Law Development Index (E-Government Development Index, EGDI)	United Nations E-government Knowledge base	Numericscale

The web databases listed in Table **1** provide a comprehensive overview and reliable information on various socio-economic parameters and their development in the field of e-government at the country level.

A correlation analysis was performed to study the relationships between different variables. Pearson correlation coefficients were calculated to determine the strength and direction of the connections between pairs of variables.

Fig. (**1**) presents the dynamics of government spending on higher education as a percentage of GDP from 1996 to 2023 in the Russian Federation and the Republic of Belarus.

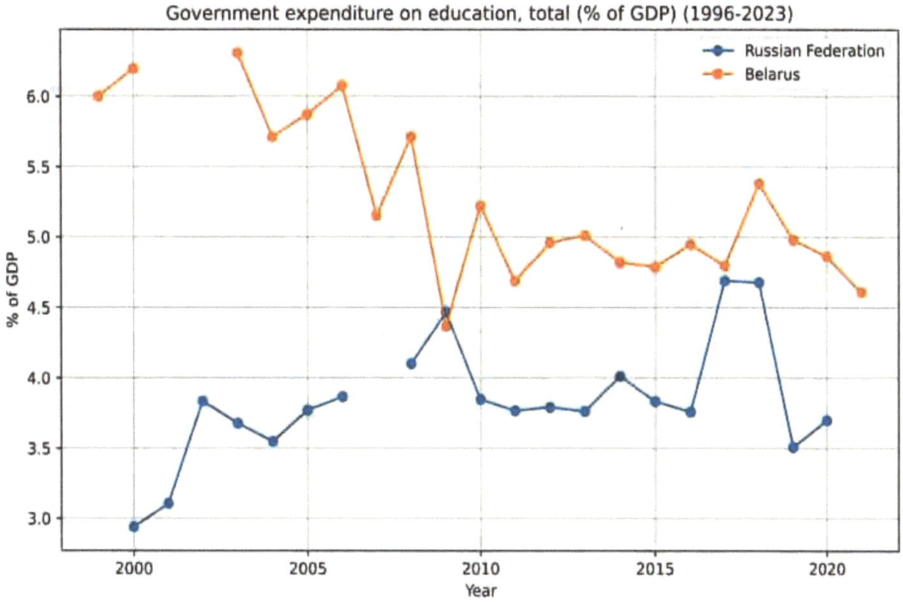

Fig. (1). Government spending on higher education, total (% of GDP) from 1996 to 2023 in the Russian Federation and the Republic of Belarus, compiled by the authors.

The graph in Fig. (**1**) shows that the dynamics of HES expenditures (% of GDP) in Russia are somewhat unstable, which indicates fluctuations over the years. Since the late 1990s and mid-2000s, public investment in HES has undergone various growth trends, followed by small fluctuations in subsequent years. Nevertheless, it is obvious that education occupies a very worthy place in the budget, and despite the protracted economic sanctions of the West, education spending in the Russian Federation tends to increase rather than fall.

This trend in spending fluctuations is consistent with the situation in Belarus, where HES spending (% of GDP) varies from year to year. As Fig. (**1**) shows, from the early 2000s to the mid-2010s, there was a significant increase in investment in education, and then in subsequent years, there was some instability. Despite frequent fluctuations, consistent efforts can be noted to allocate significant budgetary funds for higher education, which reflects the Government's priority attention to human capital problems.

At the same time, many researchers note (Astratova, 2023b; Astratova *et al.*, 2022; Panikarova *et al.*, 2020; Tatarkin and Pilipenko, 2007; Zemrani, 2019) that the available public investments to achieve the global goals of sustainable development and quality education are insufficient. This is primarily due to the fact that by the beginning of 2020, the deficit of government spending on HES in Russia and Belarus, together with countries with lower income levels, totaled about $148 billion per year (Policy Brief, 2020).

Analyzing government spending on HES and the repositioning of public administration in this industry, it should be noted that the current situation is largely due to a number of factors, which has been discussed in more detail in our previous study (Astratova, 2023b): scientific and technological progress, sequestration of state budgets for the HES sector, optimization of decision-making processes (Table 2).

Table 2. The degree of influence of key global trends on the sectoral public administration of the HES system in Russia and Belarus, compiled by the authors based on the results of an expert survey[3] ***(N=83; n = 82; K_k = 0,25; K_c = 0,87)***[4]**.**

Name of the Trend	**Trend Characteristics, Compiled from the Source** (Astratova, 2023b)	The Degree of Influence of the Trend	
		Russia	**Belorus**
1. Scientific and technological progress.	It leads to a global expansion of the knowledge economy sector, where universities turn into economic entities that turn human and financial capital into an intellectual product; it stimulates the development and implementation of new teaching methods and technologies in educational activities, including EdTech.	78.4	50.2
2. Sequestration of government budgets for the HES sector.	It leads to the transition to a multi-channel system of sources of financing for universities.	75.6	44.8
3. Optimization of decision-making processes.	It improves the survival of universities in an aggressive, competitive environment and improves the motivation and effectiveness of teaching at universities.	89.8	32.1

Source: data from a survey of experts and government officials in Google Docs, WhatsApp, and VKontakte, and processing in Statistica.

3 In January-April 2024, a survey of experts (university professors, research institute employees and heads of innovative enterprises) and government officials using Google docs, WhatsApp and Vkontakte was conducted..

4 Here and further:
Symbols: N is the total number of respondents, n is the number of responses received; Kk is the Kramer correlation coefficient (average value);Kc is the concordance coefficient (consistency of respondents' opinions; average value).

Table **2** showcases that, according to expert estimates, Belarus lags significantly behind Russia in terms of harmonization with global trends in sectoral public administration of the HES system. Fig. (**2**) shows the dynamics of government spending on Research and Development (R & D) as a percentage of GDP from 1996 to 2023 in Russia and Belarus.

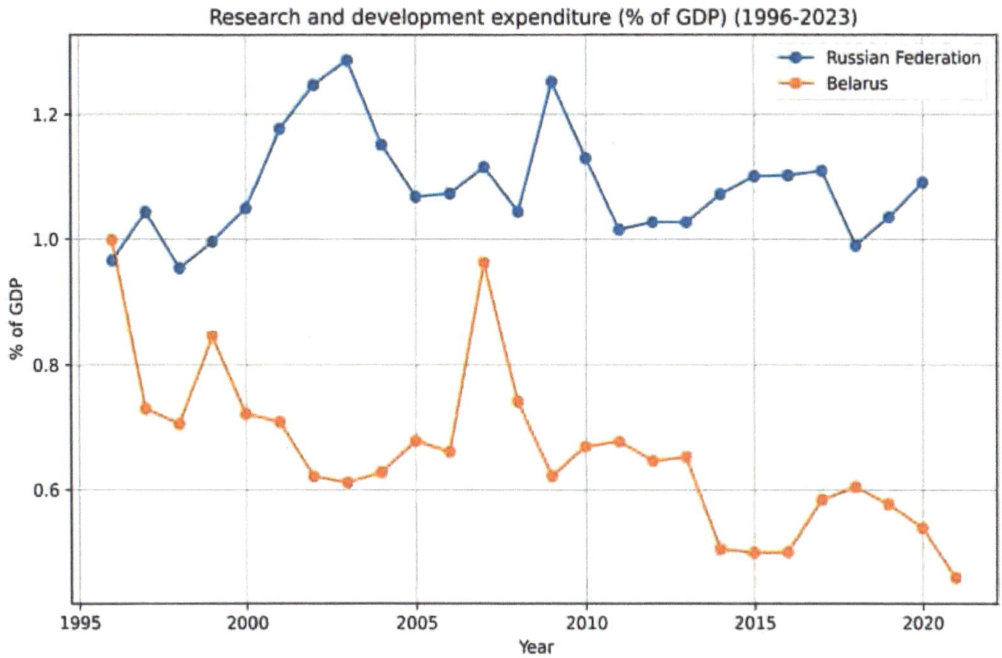

Fig. (2). Government spending on research and development, total (% of GDP) from 1996 to 2023 in Russia and Belarus, compiled by the authors.

The share of research and development expenditures in Belarus' GDP, shown in Fig. (**2**), illustrates some volatility over the years. R & D expenditures are cyclical in nature, as they increase or decrease slightly in certain periods. Nevertheless, the level of R & D expenditures in the USRB as a percentage of GDP, as noted in the previous section of the monograph, is quite low compared to the indicators of other countries, which indicates the risk of not achieving innovative development and technological progress.

As showcased in Fig. (**2**), the share of the Russian Federation's R & D expenditures (as % of GDP) has fluctuated over the years. Around the mid-1990s and early 2010s, there was a significant increase in R & D investment, with some fluctuations in recent years. Despite the fluctuations, the Government of the Russian Federation is still ready to allocate funds for R & D, which indicates that innovation and technology are considered as priority measures.

It should be noted that in the context of the digital transformation of society, the issues of effective sectoral policy in the field of higher education and R & D are becoming even more relevant, as we noted in the previous section.

The importance of using digital technologies is also confirmed by the results of our online research. It was revealed that the student youth in the Russian Federation and the Republic of Belarus have a positive attitude towards the use of digital technologies both in the higher education system of the previous section and in public administration (Figs. **3** and **4**). Civil servants in both countries are also positive about the use of digital technologies (Fig. **5** and **6**).

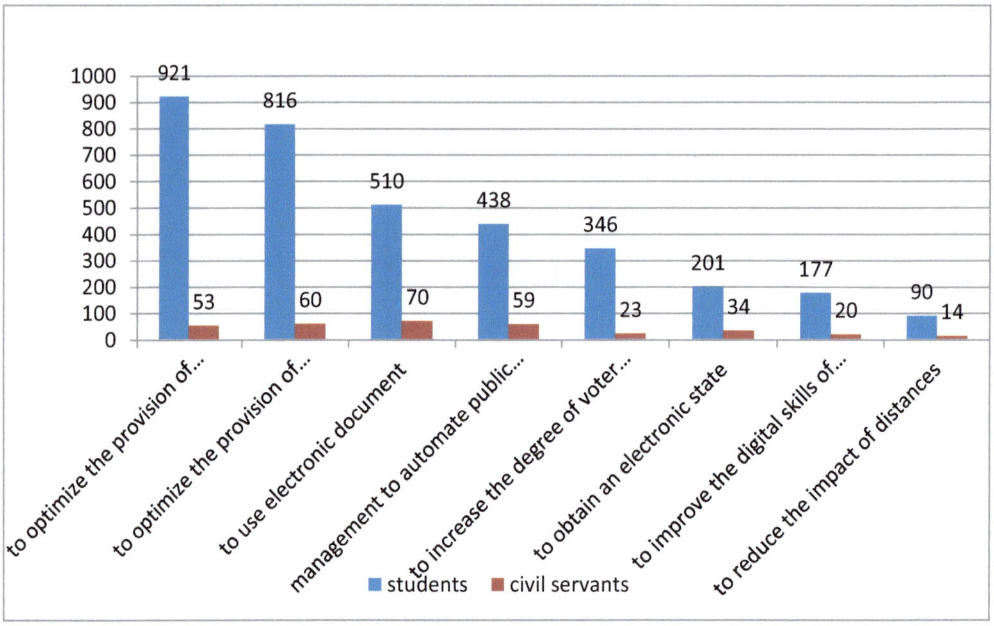

Fig. (3). Answers of students and civil servants of the Russian Federation to the question: "The use of digital technologies in public administration allows ...", people; multiple choice is possible in the answers of respondents.

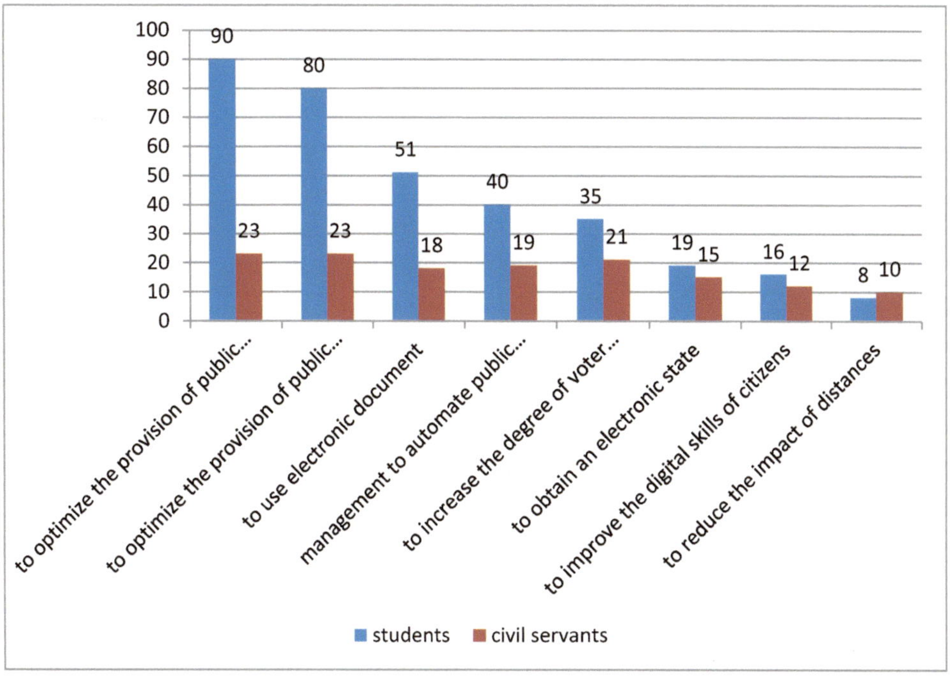

Fig. (4). Answers of students and civil servants of the Republic of Belarus to the question: "The use of digital technologies in public administration allows ...", people; multiple choice is possible in the answers of respondents ($N_{stud}=114$; $n_{stud} = 109$; $N_{CivServ} = 25$; $n_{CivServ} = 23$; $K_k = 0.20$; $K_c = 0.88$ Source: the data of the responses for Belarus were obtained based on the distribution of questionnaires on social networks in Google Docs and processed in Statistica.

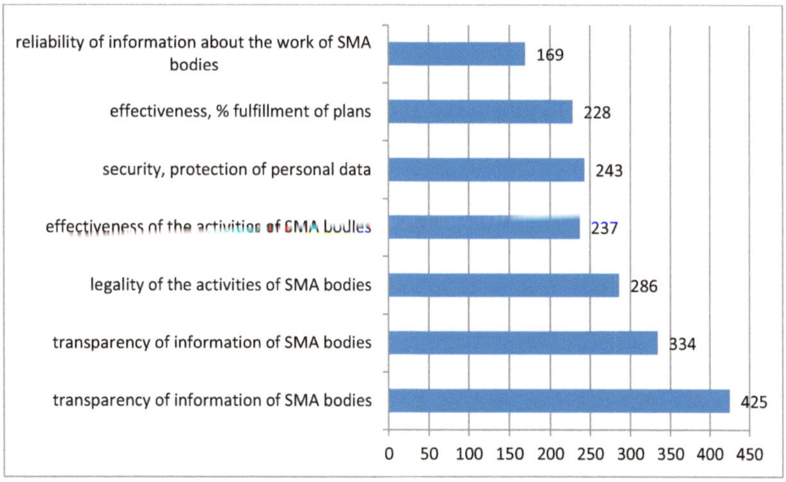

Fig. (5). The answers of Russian students to the question: "Assess the level of characteristics inherent in electronic state and municipal management", people ($N=1042$; $n = 778$; $K_k = 0.27$; $K_c = 0.76$) Source: Survey data in Google Docs and processing in Microsoft Excel and Statistica.

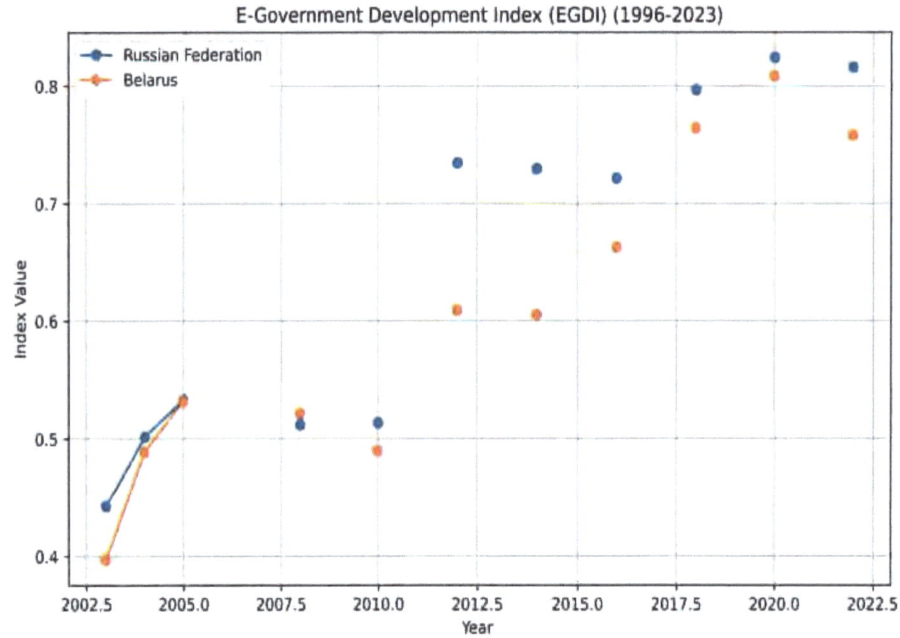

Fig. (6). Dynamics of the e-Government Development Index (EGDI) in the Russian Federation and in the Republic of Belarus from 2002 to 2022, compiled by the authors Source: Survey data in Google Docs and processing in Statistica (N_{stud}=1520; n_{stud} = 1519; $N_{CivServ}$ =72; $n_{CivServ}$ = 70; K_k = 0.21; K_c = 0.84)[5] .

It follows from (Fig. **5** and **6**) that, in general, both in the Russia and in the Belarus, students believe that the use of digital technologies in public administration is useful, first of all, for business and the public, and civil servants in both countries argue that digitalization is necessary for the use of electronic document management, automation of public administration, and increasing the degree of the participation of voters in the governance of the country and the transition to e-government.

It should also be noted that the state and municipal administration (hereinafter referred to as SMA), based on the use of digital technologies, or Digital Public Administration (DPA) represents one of the stages in the creation of the so-called "e-government" (Coursey and Norris, 2008) or "electronic state", which is a system that includes e-democracy, e-government and e-justice and which is not only able to solve many of the above problems, but also ensure the economic productivity of e-government (Kiselev, 2018, p. 32).

---

5 Here and further: Symbols: index "stud" - students; index "CivServ" - civil servants.

It is also important that state structures are invariably characterized by the routine of the bureaucratic process, which negatively affects the work of government agencies not only with the population and business, but also in their interactions with each other. The work of many researchers in Russia and Belarus is devoted to this issue (Astratova, 2023b; Barabashev, 2016; Kiselev, 2018; Klimenko and Klishch, 2013; Obolonsky, 2014), as well as abroad (Caprar *et al.*, 2022; Monteiro and Adler, 2022; Pirannejad and Ingrams, 2022). At the same time, the use of electronic services makes it possible to increase the efficiency of SMA bodies both in Russia and in Belarus, by reducing the time required to provide information, unifying document flow, reducing corruption, *etc.*, as stated in the works of many authors (Coursey and Norris, 2008; Dobrolyubova *et al.*, 2019; Lindgren and Veenstra, 2018; Luzgina, 2017; Marushko *et al.*, 2017).

At the same time, it should be borne in mind that the productivity/effectiveness of SMA digital modernization also depends on the digital competence of government civil servants and other factors, which a number of researchers draw attention to (Kosovsky *et al.*, 2017; Kovalev and Avdonin, 2020; Marushko *et al.*, 2017; Merkulov and Malakhova, 2020).

In the context of the prospects for the development of e-government, the implementation of the principles of "Good governance" (Alekseeva, 2016) will make it possible in practice to involve a large number of civilians in public administration (Dolgikh, 2017, p. 26). In this regard, it is important that the student youth is very positive about the electronic state, as they highly appreciate its main characteristics[6] (Fig. **5**).

Fig. (**5**) shows that in e-government, students approve, first of all, of such characteristics as:

- Openness of information from SMA authorities (74.67% of respondents).
- Transparency of information from SMA authorities (32.25% of respondents).
- The legality of the activities of SMA bodies (27.45% of respondents).

At the same time, it is alarming that only 16.22% of respondents highly appreciate the reliability of information about the work of SMA bodies. Obviously, this should serve as a subject for further research.

6 Here Based on the list of tasks of e-government specified by A.S. Kiselev (Kiselev, 2018, p. 36), we formulated a list of characteristics of e-government, which was used in the preparation of the questionnaire for the survey.

Fig. (**6**) shows the dynamics of the e-government Development Index (EGDI) in the Russian Federation and in the Republic of Belarus from 2002 to 2022.

Fig. (**6**) shows that there has been a gradual increase in the EGDI index in the Republic of Belarus over the past twenty years, which indicates achievements in the field of e-government formation. As it is well known, the EGDI index is an indicator of the quality of public administration, openness, and the possibility of citizens' access to public information. With an upward trend, he declares his desire to increase digital governance and achieve success in the provision of public services in Belarus.

According to Fig. (7), Russia has lower indicators of the e-government development index than Belarus. The general trend in the dynamics of the EGDI index reflects the gradual progress that has been observed from 2002 to 2022, and indicates attempts to modernize public administration, increase the convenience of citizens' access to digital services, as well as the fact that the country has opportunities for further improvement.

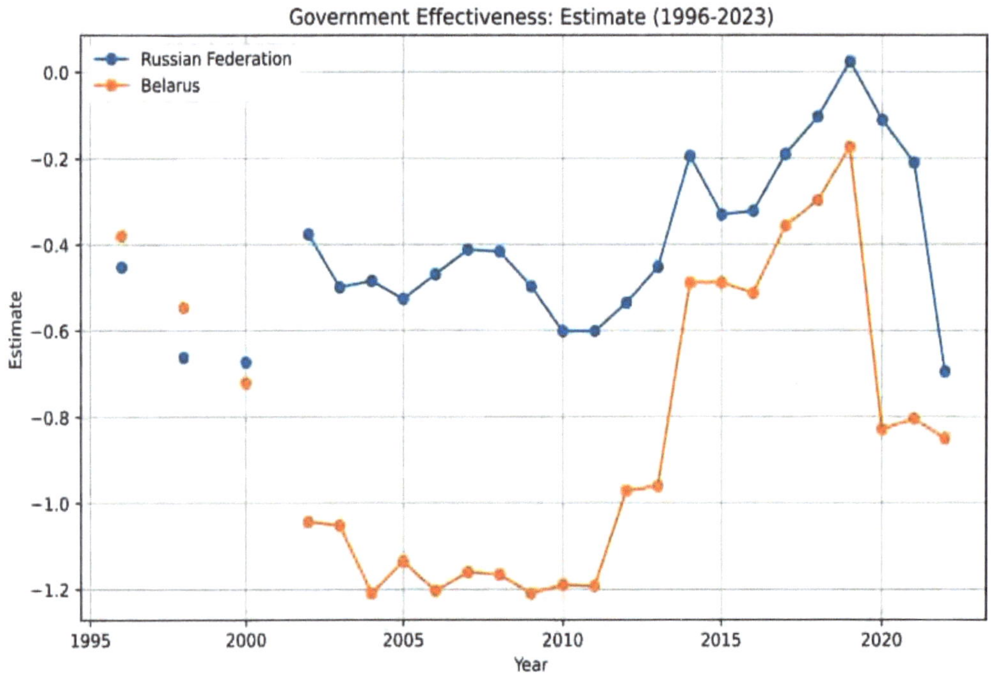

Fig. (7). The effectiveness of public administration in the Russian Federation and in the republic of Belarus from 2002 to 2022, compiled by the authors.

It was also considered necessary to assess the effectiveness of public administration in the Russian Federation and in the Republic of Belarus (Fig. 7).

Fig. (7) showcases that the dynamics of the effectiveness of public administration in both countries have the form of ups and downs. It is obvious that at first the efficiency indicator is negative, which indicates that there are problems with the effectiveness of public administration. On the other hand, we see that there are points at which efficiency increases to a neutral value, and then tends to increase again. Despite the fluctuations, the overall movement towards solving public problems and improving the efficiency of public administration in both countries until 2020 was positive, and after 2020, there was a decrease, obviously due to the coronavirus pandemic (Astratova *et al.*, 2022).

In general, the results of the assessment of the effectiveness of public administration in the Russian Federation and in the Republic of Belarus demonstrate a number of problems that affect the implementation of public administration in the assessed countries. The lack of consistency between performance indicators points to problems of bureaucracy, corruption, and insufficient quality of public services. These difficulties can hinder the work of relevant government agencies and hinder their development. We find similar positions on this issue in the works of other researchers (Barabashev, 2016; Klimenko and Klishch, 2013; Kovalev and Avdonin, 2020; Lvov, 1990; Obolonsky, 2014; Monteiro and Adler, 2022, *etc.*).

Increasing transparency, accountability, and representation of citizens in government bodies of the Russian Federation and the Republic of Belarus will help to improve management efficiency and allow citizens to trust public sector organizations more. Moreover, it is the ability to act in accordance with the strategic interests of society and the most influential classes and social groups that determines the quality of public economic management (Smirnov, 2019).

Our research shows that it is necessary to take priority measures to implement reforms in order to improve the government's work in the field of education, digitalization, and R & D. Government responses, such as simplifying routine procedures, fighting corruption, and improving the quality of services, can only be a small part of solving the problems of public administration and institutionalization of development. In addition, through the creation of alliances with international partners and the use of technological advances, the Government's activities will become more efficient, and socio-economic results will improve.

CONCLUSION

This research has identified several critical "bottlenecks" that limit the effectiveness of public administration in the Higher Education Services (HES) and Research and Development (R & D) sectors in Russia and Belarus. The analysis of comprehensive data from the World Bank and United Nations databases, along with expert surveys, reveals systemic challenges that require strategic intervention.

The study demonstrates that despite varying levels of government expenditure on HES and R & D in both countries over the past two decades, these investments remain insufficient to achieve global sustainable development goals for quality education. Our findings indicate that while both countries show positive trends in e-government development, significant discrepancies exist in their adaptation to global trends in sectoral public administration. Notably, Belarus lags considerably behind Russia in harmonizing with international developments in higher education governance, particularly in the areas of scientific-technological progress implementation, multi-channel financing systems, and decision-making optimization. The research identifies bureaucratic inefficiency, corruption, and inadequate digital competencies among civil servants as fundamental obstacles hindering effective public administration in both countries. These challenges are compounded by the routine nature of bureaucratic processes that negatively impact not only government interactions with citizens and businesses but also inter-agency cooperation.

Our analysis of the e-Government Development Index (eGDI) reveals a gradual improvement in both countries, with Belarus demonstrating stronger performance in this area than Russia. This positive trend indicates ongoing efforts to modernize public administration and enhance digital service provision. However, the fluctuating effectiveness of public administration in both countries, particularly the decline observed after 2020 due to the coronavirus pandemic, highlights the vulnerability of these systems to external shocks. Student surveys in both countries revealed a strong positive attitude toward digital technologies in public administration, with particular emphasis on the openness and transparency of information from state and municipal administration bodies. However, the relatively low assessment of information reliability raises concerns that merit further investigation.

To address these bottlenecks and enhance the effectiveness of public administration in the HES and R & D sectors, priority measures should focus on implementing comprehensive reforms aimed at increasing transparency, accountability, and citizen representation in government bodies. The development of digital competencies among civil servants, simplification of bureaucratic procedures, stronger anti-corruption measures, and improved service quality represent essential components of these reforms. Furthermore, the creation of strategic international partnerships and the more effective utilization of technological advancements will contribute to improved government efficiency and enhanced socio-economic outcomes. As the knowledge economy continues to evolve as a critical branch of national economies in both Russia and Belarus, addressing these bottlenecks becomes increasingly urgent to ensure sustainable development and global competitiveness.

CHAPTER 9

Economic Mechanisms for Stimulating the Scientific and Innovative Activity of the USRB

Galina V. Astratova[1,*], **Natalia A. Simchenko**[2] and **Airat M. Izmailov**[3]

[1] *Department of Regional Economics, Innovative Entrepreneurship and Economics (REIE&E), Institute of Economics and Management, School of Public Administration and Entrepreneurship (SPAE), Ural Federal University (UrFU), Yekaterinburg 620002, Sverdlovsk Region, Russian Federation*

[2] *Department of Economic Theory and Economic Policy, St. Petersburg State University, St. Petersburg 199034, Russian Federation*

[3] *Department of Digital Economics, Volga State University of Telecommunications and Informatics, Samara 443090, Middle Volga region, Russian Federation*

Abstract: This chapter examines the economic mechanisms for stimulating scientific and innovative activity within the Union State of Russia and Belarus (USRB). The authors analyze three primary theoretical frameworks for understanding economic mechanisms: mechanistic, process-based, and institutional approaches. Through expert surveys conducted in early 2024, the study reveals that experts from both countries overwhelmingly support building the economic mechanism on mutually beneficial relations (89.81% of Russian and 96.43% of Belarusian respondents). The research identifies four key development scenarios for the USRB economy: socio-economic integration, diversification of foreign economic activity, creation of a unified scientific-educational space, and constitutional reform. The majority of experts (48.15% Russian, 39.62% Belarusian) view socio-economic integration as the most likely development path, with significant support for unified scientific space formation (25% Russian, 26.42% Belarusian). The study extensively analyzes the evolution of innovation models from the original "Triple Helix" (university-government-business) to expanded models incorporating society ("Quadruple Helix") and environmental factors ("Quintuple Helix"). These models are examined as frameworks for innovation policy and regional development strategies, with particular attention to their applicability in developing countries like Russia and Belarus. Expert survey results indicate strong consensus (89.81% Russian, 96.43% Belarusian) that the innovative infrastructure management mechanism for USRB universities should integrate four key elements: government, universities, industrial enterprises, and student youth. International cooperation between the fraternal countries is identified as the crucial catalyst for creating synergistic effects in this integrated system. The chapter emphasizes the

* **Corresponding author Galina V. Astratova:** Department of Regional Economics, Innovative Entrepreneurship and Economics (REIE&E), Institute of Economics and Management, School of Public Administration and Entrepreneurship (SPAE), Ural Federal University (UrFU), Yekaterinburg 620002, Sverdlovsk Region, Russian Federation; E-mail: galina_28@mail.ru

Galina V. Astratova, Maxim V. Vlasov, Chigozirim Ndubuisi Onwusiribe & Longinus D.N. Nnadozie (Eds.)

critical role of higher education institutions in driving innovation and economic development, proposing a comprehensive economic mechanism that aligns scientific and innovative activities with sustainable regional development goals.

Keywords: Economic mechanism, Innovation management, Regional economic integration, Scientific development strategy, Triple Helix model, Union State of Russia and Belarus, University innovation infrastructure.

INTRODUCTION

The essential content and development of the economic mechanism for the development of national economy facilities is one of the key and actively controversial issues, the relevance of the study of which does not weaken over time.

This is due, in our opinion, to two reasons: 1) the relative novelty of the use of the term "economic mechanism" and 2) the ambiguity of the interpretation of its content, based on mechanistic concepts, process, and institutional approaches. This allows us to imagine the evolution of the category of "economic mechanism" as a sequence of "mechanistic", "process", and "institutional" concepts (Table **1**).

Table 1. Analysis of the concepts of "economic mechanisms" proposed by various researchers, in the author's interpretation (Bengraf *et al.*, 2024, p. 189).

Name of the concept	Description of the concept
1. The mechanical concept	The possibility of obtaining a positive effect from the use of various resources is described. The technical analogue is movement, a gain in effort when using mechanical tools.
2. Process approach.	The "mechanism" (the 1st element of the process) is considered, which allows using "control" (the 2nd element of the process) to implement the function of the process (the 3rd element of the process), that is, to convert the "input" into "output". The essence of an economic mechanism is defined as a set of economic resources and ways of their interaction for the implementation of a specific economic process.
3. Institutional approach.	When developing an economic mechanism, the focus is not on purely economic issues, but on the interrelation of economic problems together with non-economic factors: social, political, ethical, and legal problems.

From Table **1**, it can be concluded that the Economic Mechanism (EM) is an instrument of the economic laws of social reproduction, that is, production, exchange, distribution, and consumption. There are other ideas about the essence of EM in the literature, which were discussed in more detail in our earlier study (Bengraf *et al.*, 2024).

The results of our expert survey[1] show that the economic mechanism for the development of the Union State of Russia and Belarus should be based primarily on building mutually beneficial relations with a fraternal country—89.81% of respondents from the Russian Federation and 96.43% of respondents from the Republic of Belarus answered in the affirmative (Fig. **1**).

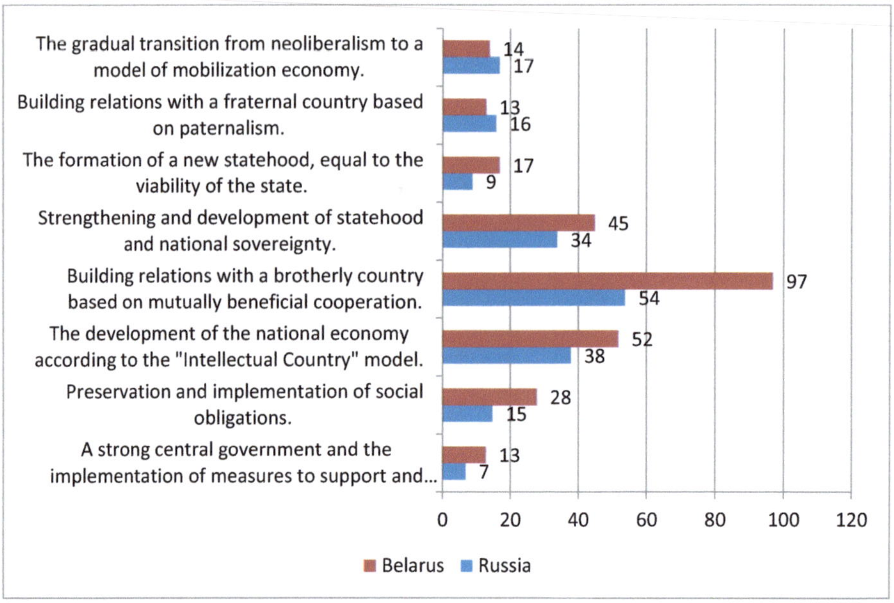

Fig. (1). Experts' answers to the question: "The mechanism of development of the Union State of the Russian Federation and the Republic of Belarus should be based on such tools as ... ", people; multiple choice is possible in the answers of respondents.
($N_{RF}=111$; $n_{RF} = 108$; $N_{RB}=58$; $n_{RB}= 56$; $K_k = 0.21$; $K_c = 0.86$)

At the same time, the development of the national economy according to the "Intellectual Country" model also took very high positions: second place in the rating of responses, or 48.15% of respondents from the Russian Federation who answered in the affirmative, and 67.86% of respondents from the Republic of Belarus. Finally, the third position in the respondents' responses belongs to the strengthening and development of statehood and national sovereignty, respectively, 41, 67% and 60.71%.

---

1 In January-April 2024, a survey of experts (university professors, research institute employees and heads of innovative enterprises) and government officials using Google docs, WhatsApp and Vkontakte was conducted.
The data of the Belarus responses were obtained based on the distribution of links to questionnaires in Google docs by e-mail and social networks and processing in Statistica.

In our previous studies (Astratova, 2023a; Bengraf *et al.*, 2024), it was found that in the new economic conditions, the development of the union economy of the Russian Federation and the Republic of Belarus can occur according to at least four main scenarios:

1. Economic (socio-economic) integration of the Republic of Belarus and the Russian Federation.
2. Diversification of foreign economic activity of the Republic of Belarus and the Russian Federation.
3. The formation of a unified scientific and educational space in the SRB.
4. Constitutional reform.

In this regard, the experts were asked what the most likely scenario for the economic development strategy of the Union State of the Russian Federation and the Republic of Belarus was (Fig. **2**).

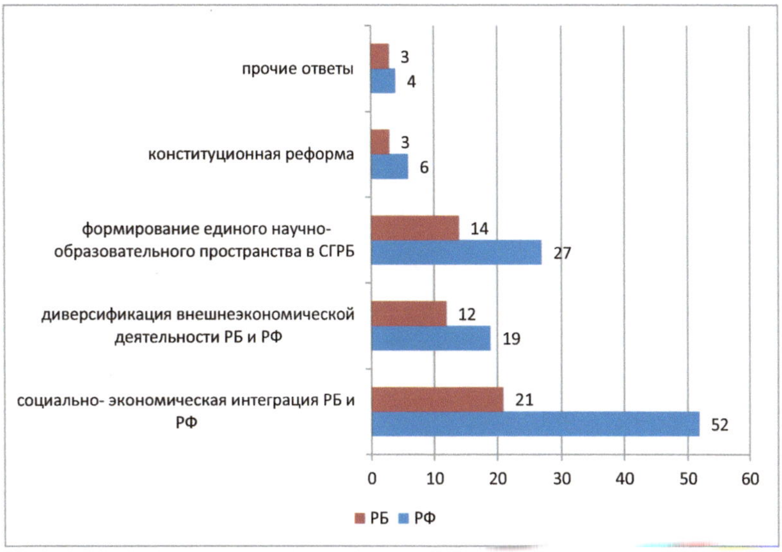

Fig. (2). Experts' answers[2] to the question: "What is the most likely scenario for the economic development strategy of the Union State of the Russian Federation and the Republic of Belarus (SRB), in your opinion?" are: the only choice is possible in the answers of respondents.
(N_{RF}=111; n_{RF} = 108; N_{RB}=58; n_{RB}= 53; K_k = 0.20; K_c = 0.83)

2 In January-April 2024, a survey of experts (university professors, research institute employees and heads of innovative enterprises) and government officials using Google docs, WhatsApp and Vkontakte was conducted.
The data of the Belarus responses were obtained based on the distribution of links to questionnaires in Google docs by e-mail and social networks and processing in Statistica.

Fig. (**2**) shows that the majority (48.15% of respondents from the Russian Federation who answered in the affirmative and 39.62% of respondents from the Republic of Belarus) believe that the most likely scenario for the economic development strategy of the Union State of the Russian Federation and the Republic of Belarus is the socio–economic integration of fraternal countries. It is also important that the proportion of responses is high, as the formation of a unified scientific space in the USRB is also a likely scenario for the economic development strategy of the Union State: 25.00% of respondents from the Russian Federation answered in the affirmative, and 26.42% of respondents from the Republic of Belarus.

As for the economic mechanism of innovation management in general and the innovation infrastructure of universities, in particular, and the InIn of the USRB, especially, we have not found a clearly deterministic term in the literature available to us. Based on the previously available literature we studied, we presented the author's interpretation of the EM InIn of universities: "*The economic mechanism for the development of the innovative infrastructure of universities is a documented, purposeful process for solving strategic and operational tasks of the functioning of the university as an integrated system of organizational, institutional and effective impact on the subjects of this socio–economic system to achieve an equilibrium state between production and consumption products and services of intellectual activity*"(Bengraf, *et al.*,2024, p. 190-191).

In our opinion, many researchers quite rightly point out that the EM of innovative development can be considered as a variant of the practical implementation of the theory of the "triple helix" (Triple Helix model), which reconciles innovations and initiatives at three levels: 1) the state, 2) universities and research institutes, 3) business (Abd *et al.*, 2016, p. 49; Doroshenko and Malykhina, 2014, p. 87;)

This is due to the fact that the theory of the "triple helix"(«Triple Helix model»), which was developed by Etzkowitz (2008) and emerged from regional innovative practices, has now received many interpretations, connotations, upgrades, and continuations.

This situation is caused by two provisions: the change of roles and the continuity of movement. Indeed, firstly, this model has "blurred" the boundaries of the basic roles and models of functioning of universities, industry and government, both individually and together, while creating a new model of the EM knowledge economy, where all elements of the EM are equivalent leaders, and emerging innovations contribute to new innovations ("innovations in innovation") and the emergence of many hybrid forms (Etzkowitz, 2008; Etzkowitz&Leydesdorff, 1995). For example, these may be hybrid forms such as university technology transfer/transfer offices; business and/or financial support institutions (business angel networks, venture capital funds, *etc.*) (Etzkowitz, 2008, p. 30).

Secondly, the triple helix theory not only reveals the content of ongoing regional knowledge-based innovations, but also initiates the study of new innovative models and EM growth in regions and countries around the world, while providing "... a new paradigm for the joint development of innovation and entrepreneurship education by government, enterprises, universities and other subjects" (Zhang, 2021, p. 246).

Thus, the theory of the "triple helix" considers EM as a spiraling, interconnected, and interdependent interaction between the elements of innovation infrastructure—innovative agents of government, universities, and enterprises – for the production, transformation, and transfer of knowledge Table **2**.

Table 2. The main provisions of the theory of the "triple helix" in the context of "levels of meaning", compiled by the authors based on the study of various sources (Bengraf *et al.*, 2024; Broström,2011; Etzkowitz, 2008; Zhang, 2021, *etc.*).

Levels of theory meaning.	Characteristics of semantic levels
1. Movement in a spiral.	The government, universities, and enterprises are independent of each other and interact with each other in the process of spiraling.
2. Transformation within the framework of the spiral.	The roles of government, universities, and enterprises are both integrated and transformed. In other words, the functions on each spiral can be integrated, both completely and partially.
3. Interpenetration within the framework of the spiral.	Government, universities, and enterprises interact through three spiral chains to create interpenetrating organizational structures and networks, providing a new platform for creative collaboration between government, industry, and the scientific community.

It should also be noted that in the process of developing the theory of the "triple helix," there was a transition from models in 1, 2, 3 links to four and five links (Fig. **3**).

For example, the concept of four links (the "Quadruple Helix" model or the "quadruple helix model") includes society: civil society and the media (Fig. **4**).

This model aims to bridge the gap between innovation and society. The inclusion of new elements is due to the fact that in the basic model ("Triple Helix model"), new technologies do not always meet public needs, which limits their potential (Carayannis and Campbell, 2009).

The concept of five links (the "Quintuple Helix" model or the five-fold spiral model) also includes such factors as the environment, the natural environment, and ecology (Fig. **5**).

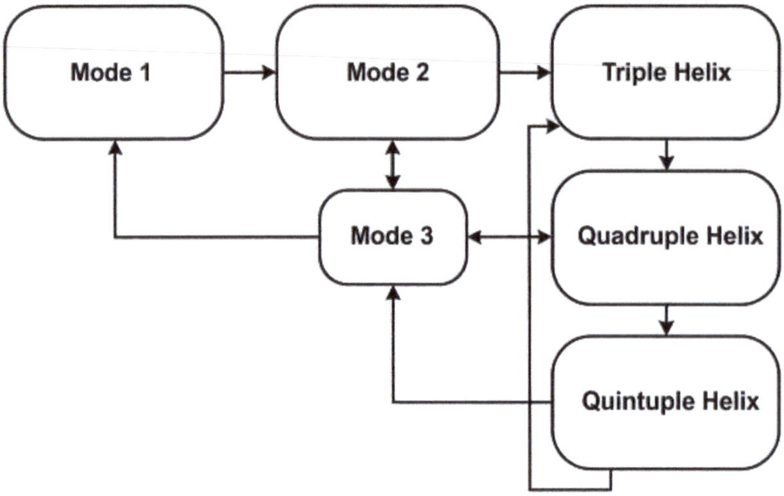

Fig. (3). The evolution of knowledge creation models from 1, 2, 3, 4, 5 links (Carayannis *et al.*, 2012).

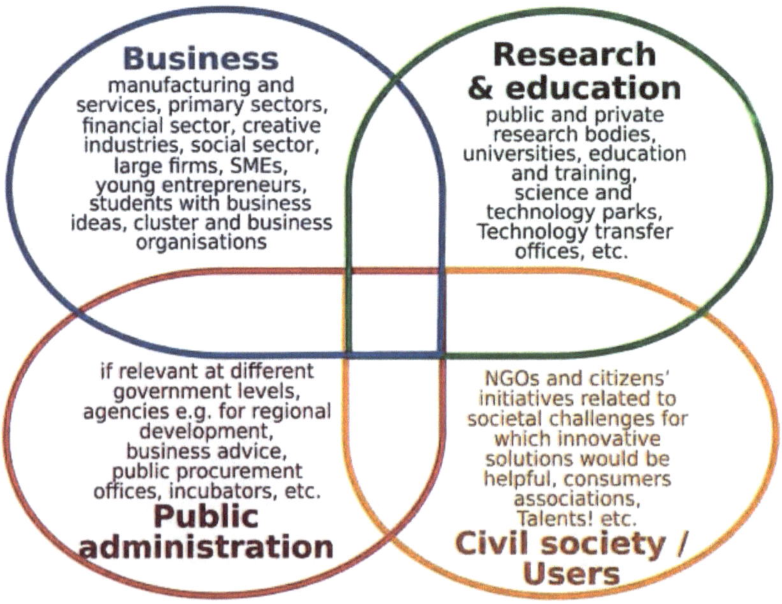

Fig. (4). A four-link concept model (the "Quadruple Helix" model or the "quadruple helix model" (Edwards, 2013).

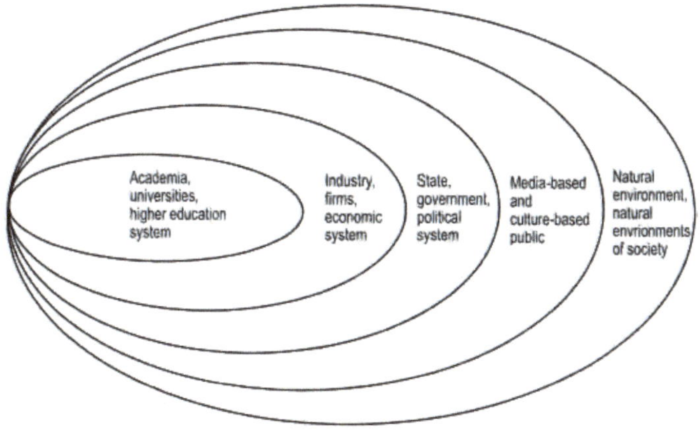

Fig. (5). A five-link concept model (the "Quintuple Helix" model or the "five-fold helix model") (Carayannis *et al.*, 2012).

Indeed, the focus of the international community today is on the environmental agenda, since forecasts of the state of ecology and human habitat in the strategic period are very optimistic (for example, the problem of global warming). Accordingly, the "Quintuple Helix" model, which contributes to the formation of a mutually beneficial balance between ecology, knowledge and innovation, creating a synergistic effect from the interaction of the economy, society and democracy, has great potential, since it ensures the effectiveness of investments in education for sustainable development (Carayannis, *et al.*, 2012) (Fig. **6**).

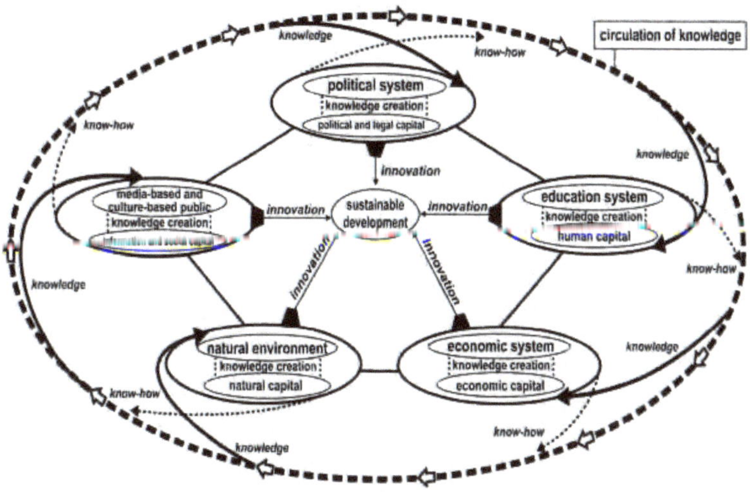

Fig. (6). The effectiveness of investments in education for sustainable development as a consequence of the five-link concept model ("Quintuple Helix" model) (Carayannis *et al.*, 2012).

It is important that the role of universities in the development of environmental strategies and practices in innovation supply chains is extremely important for the public sector (Abd, *et al.*, 2016; Smorodinskaya, 2011; Zhang, 2021; *etc.*) since higher education institutions shape the environmental and innovative thinking of students, allow them form potential mechanisms for integration and structuring joint improvements, developments and innovative initiatives in further.

For example, as noted in the study by Pakhomova (2012), research universities, together with the state and business, play a huge role in the development of the region's economy, which allows developing strategies for cooperation, joint work in the field of creation and improvement of regional innovation infrastructure. In particular, this researcher proposed a very non-trivial algorithm for the relationship of a research university with a regional economy (Pakhomova, 2012, p. 4).

It should be noted that the triple helix model, as well as versions of this model expanded to 4...5 links, have been repeatedly criticized by many researchers as "... *a tool for creation of policies for economic growth and regional development*" (Galvao, *et al.*, 2019), that is, precisely, to our mind, as a special economic mechanism.

One of the most important arguments of criticism was that the model of H. Itzkowitz was developed on the example of the countries of the developed West and, accordingly, can be fair only with a certain set of economic indicators, adequate policies, and constant environmental factors, and is not applicable to developing countries (Yuzhuo, 2013 and 2014).

At the same time, there are opinions that the "triple helix" model (in any expansion variant) is applicable, firstly, to describe the economic situation in developing countries, for example, for China (Yuzhuo Cai, 2013 and 2014; Zhang, 2021), for Russia (Efremova, 2019; Smorodinskaya, 2011; Udaltsova & Krutskikh, 2021), and for Belarus (Razuvanova, 2016; Yunchits, 2016; *etc.*). Secondly, it is very useful for planning state innovation and sectoral policy (Smorodinskaya, 2011; Saad and Zavdi, 2011), which is especially relevant in the context of the economy and society's digitalization (Pakhomova, 2012; Smorodinskaya, 2011; Zimina, 2016).

For example, in Zhang Chunlei's study, based on the use of the "Triple Helix model" theory, in the context of the digitalization of the economy, *"... a new way of deep integration of education in the field of innovation and entrepreneurship with vocational education" based on several modes, such as: ... conceptual integration, integration of curricula and interdisciplinary integration*" (Zhang, 2021, p. 246). At the same time, students should become the "personnel base" of innovation and entrepreneurship in universities. To implement this thesis, it is necessary to introduce "... an innovative model of entrepreneurship in universities based on the needs of the digital age" (Zhang, 2021, p. 247). Similar positions are set out in the works of both Russian and Belarusian authors (Andryushkevich and Denisova, 2014; Dezhina and Kiseleva, 2007; Pakhomova, 2012; Smorodinskaya, 2011; Smirnov, 2019; Zimina, 2016, *etc.*).

The results of our expert survey show that the majority of experts (89.81% of respondents from the Russian Federation who answered in the affirmative and 96.43% of respondents from the Republic of Belarus) believe that the mechanism for managing the innovative infrastructure of universities in the USRB should include the following four elements (Fig. 7):

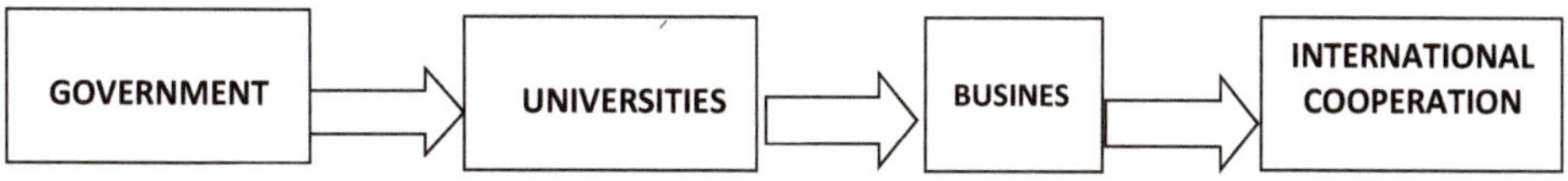

Fig. (7). The model of the mechanism for managing the innovative infrastructure of universities in the USRB, obtained as a result of experts' answers[3] to the question: "Do you think the mechanism for managing the innovative infrastructure of universities in the USRB should include the following elements ..." people; the only choice is possible in the answers of respondents.
(N_{RF}=111; n_{RF} = 101; N_{RB}=58; n_{RB}= 51; K_k = 0.23; K_c = 0.81)

The result suggests that international cooperation between fraternal countries should be exactly the element that will cause a synergistic effect from integral interaction in the society of universities, the state, and industrial enterprises.

Moreover, student youth as a "personnel basis" will allow the formation and development of such a system of relationships, "... in which innovations serve as the basis for effective socio-economic development, and the evolution trends of this society determine the most important areas of innovation" (Doroshenko and Malykhina, 2014, p. 86). At the same time, the driver of the innovative sphere should be as shown in our earlier studies (Panikarova *et al.*, 2020, p. 573), the higher education system.

Such a mechanism will be an essential tool for improving scientific, technical, and innovative activity in countries such as the Russian Federation and the Republic of Belarus.

---

3 In January-April 2024, a survey of experts (university professors, research institute employees and heads of innovative enterprises) and government officials using Google docs, WhatsApp and Vkontakte was conducted.
The data of the Belarus responses were obtained based on the distribution of links to questionnaires in Google docs by e-mail and social networks and processing in Statistica.

CONCLUSION

This chapter has comprehensively examined the economic mechanisms for stimulating scientific and innovative activity within the Union State of Russia and Belarus (USRB), revealing several critical findings that shape our understanding of innovation development pathways.

The research establishes that economic mechanisms have evolved from simple mechanistic concepts to sophisticated institutional approaches that incorporate social, political, ethical, and legal dimensions. The expert survey data demonstrates overwhelming consensus that the USRB's economic mechanism should be fundamentally grounded in mutually beneficial relations between the fraternal countries, with 89.81% of Russian and 96.43% of Belarusian respondents supporting this approach. The analysis of potential development scenarios confirms that socio-economic integration represents the most likely path forward, supported by nearly half of Russian experts and 40% of Belarusian experts. Significantly, the formation of a unified scientific space emerged as the second most viable scenario, indicating strong support for deepening academic and research collaboration between the two nations.

The examination of innovation models, from the original "Triple Helix" to the expanded "Quadruple" and "Quintuple Helix" frameworks, demonstrates the increasing complexity and sophistication of innovation ecosystems. These models provide valuable theoretical foundations for policy development, particularly when adapted to the specific contexts of developing countries like Russia and Belarus. The incorporation of societal and environmental factors in the expanded models reflects the growing importance of sustainable and socially responsible innovation. The proposed innovation infrastructure management mechanism for USRB universities, validated by expert consensus, provides a practical framework for implementing these theoretical insights. By integrating government, universities, industrial enterprises, and student youth within a system of international cooperation, this mechanism offers a pathway to catalyze synergistic effects and drive technological advancement.

Ultimately, this chapter establishes that successful economic mechanisms for stimulating scientific and innovative activity in the USRB must balance theoretical rigor with practical applicability, institutional integration with flexible adaptation, and national interests with international cooperation. The findings presented here provide a robust foundation for policymakers and academic leaders to develop and implement effective strategies for fostering innovation and scientific advancement within the Union State. The higher education system emerges as a crucial driver of innovation, positioned to shape not only technological development but also the environmental and innovative thinking of future generations. This underscores the strategic importance of investing in and carefully managing university innovation infrastructure as a key component of the USRB's economic development strategy.

CHAPTER 10

Indicative Planning in the Process of SMA's Management of Innovation Activity at the USRB

Maxim V. Vlasov[1,*]

[1] *Department of Regional Economics, Innovative Entrepreneurship and Economics (REIE&E), Institute of Economics and Management, School of Public Administration and Entrepreneurship (SPAE), Ural Federal University (UrFU), Yekaterinburg 620002, Sverdlovsk Region, Russian Federation*

Abstract: This chapter examines the role of indicative planning in managing innovation activities within the Union State of the Russian Federation and the Republic of Belarus (USRB). The research investigates how scientific activity and knowledge generation influence innovation systems' effectiveness. Through comprehensive analysis of economic indicators and econometric modeling, the study identifies significant correlations between scientific performance indicators (capital expenditures on R & D, internal R & D costs, patents for inventions, and utility model patents) and innovation activity metrics (costs of innovative activities, advanced manufacturing technologies used, volume of innovative goods and services, and developed advanced technologies). The findings confirm that scientific activity has a strong, sustainable impact on business entities' innovation performance, providing a solid foundation for indicative planning by state and municipal administration bodies. The developed econometric models offer practical tools for forecasting and strategic management of innovation infrastructure within the USRB.

Keywords: Econometric modeling, Indicative planning, Innovation management, Innovation systems, Knowledge economy, Scientific activity indicators, Union State of Russia and Belarus.

INTRODUCTION

One of the most important tasks facing the SMA management of the Union State of the Russian Federation and the Republic of Belarus is to achieve long-term development goals of ensuring a high standard of living for the population and the dynamic progressive development of all sectors of the economy. This vector of

* **Corresponding author Maxim V. Vlasov:** Department of Regional Economics, Innovative Entrepreneurship and Economics (REIE&E), Institute of Economics and Management, School of Public Administration and Entrepreneurship (SPAE), Ural Federal University (UrFU), Yekaterinburg 620002, Sverdlovsk Region, Russian Federation;
E-mail: m.v.vlasov@urfu.ru

Galina V. Astratova, Maxim V. Vlasov, Chigozirim Ndubuisi Onwusiribe & Longinus D.N. Nnadozie (Eds.)

development is impossible without switching to an innovative type of development.

In this regard, the most important task facing the SMA management at the USRB, as we have already noted earlier[1], is the creation and effective functioning of an innovative infrastructure consisting of a set of innovative systems. The effective functioning of innovative systems is possible provided that innovative projects are implemented in a timely manner that meet the requirements of the external and internal environment and contribute to building up their own potential with the orientation of the company's activities for a long-term development perspective. The realization of the scientific potential of economic entities contributes to increasing the importance and role of R & D in their innovative activities. The results of scientific activity are becoming a decisive factor for obtaining long-term profits and productivity of an economic entity in a knowledge-based economy, as more and more organizations define their core competencies in the field of intangible assets.

In these conditions, the use of indicative planning tools becomes especially important—that is, the activities of SMA bodies to make forecasts and targets for output based on the use of a system of economic indicators (Andryushkevich, 2012; Nielsen, 2008; Nove, 1987, *etc.*). It should be noted that indicative planning is carried out by the state in an attempt to solve the problem of asymmetric information in a market economy through the coordination of investments by the state and private investors, based on forecasts and output targets. The final plans are aimed at obtaining valuable information from an economic point of view. As a result, this information acts as a public good, which is especially important for those cases when: a) the market cannot independently disseminate this information, and b) viable markets have yet to emerge. Accordingly, indicative plans will complement market information and serve to expand the market, but do not replace the market mechanism. That is why indicative plans are widely used in both market and mixed economies (Nielsen, 2008). When using indicative planning to influence the economy, the state uses such basic tools of "influence" as subsidies, grants, and taxes, but does not use tools of "coercion" in relation to economic entities (Nove, 1987). Moreover, indicative planning contrasts with directive or mandatory planning, when SMA bodies set quotas and mandatory requirements for production volume.

---

1 See section 1.4.1. of this monograph.

It should be emphasized that in modern conditions, due to the strengthening of the position of private business and increasing the stability of market mechanisms, the method of indicative planning has become less frequently used. At the same time, targeted programs (strategies) and forecasts for the development of certain strategically important industries are used by SMA bodies as a very effective management tool.

Since the development of the knowledge economy and the creation of a unified scientific and technological space of the SRB is a pressing task of our time, it is therefore relevant to use indicative planning tools by SMA bodies to identify and assess the impact of the intensity of scientific activity in terms of generating fundamental knowledge on the effectiveness of innovative systems.

As we have already noted in previous sections[2], as a result of numerous scientific studies, it has been proven that innovations currently play an important role in the competitiveness of economic agents at all levels of management. The importance of innovations focused on the sustainable development of economic agents increases every year. However, the costs of innovative projects can pay off and contribute to economic development only if these projects are based on the results of serious scientific research (Siegel *et al.*, 2004).

According to Noack and Jacobsen (2021), in recent years, there has been an increasing relevance of scientific knowledge for production, requiring new tools to establish closer relations between the academic community and industry.

Also, in a study by Fayyaz *et al.* (2021), it was proven that the processes of knowledge generation and exchange between employees of an organization lead to faster innovation in organizations. As a result of the research conducted by these researchers, it was proven that the processes of knowledge generation and exchange are strongly related to the effectiveness of innovation in an organization (Fayyaz *et al.*, 2021).

Thus, we can conclude that, despite the importance of knowledge generation processes for the development of innovative systems, which has been repeatedly shown in numerous scientific publications (Kaihua and Mingting, 2014; Rajnoha, *et al.*, 2019; Secundo, *et al.*, 2016), the assessment of the impact of scientific results on innovation The activity of economic entities today is beyond the achievements of modern economics. Moreover, the assessment of the impact of the results of scientific activity on the innovative activity of business entities is

2 See Chapter 1.4 of this monograph.

beyond the field of view of SMA bodies and beyond the limits of public indicative planning.

In connection with the above, it was considered appropriate:

- To develop an author's methodology that allows identifying key indicators and evaluating the impact of the intensity of scientific activity in terms of generating fundamental knowledge on the effectiveness of innovative systems;
- Identify indicators of innovation activity and indicators of scientific performance as economic indicators.

Indicators of Innovation Activity

Innovative activity has been studied by various authors. Thus, the cost of innovation activity, as the most important indicator of innovation activity, was highlighted by such authors as E.R Gold (Gold, 2021), M.J. Thompson and M. Woerter (Thompson & Woerter, 2020). According to N. AlQershi and co-authors (Al Qershi *et al.*, 2021), as well as P.F. Borowski (Borowski, 2021), the main indicator of innovation activity is the developed and used advanced manufacturing technologies. According to M. Marčeta and S. Bojnec, the main indicators of innovation are "R & D expenditures" and "volumes of innovative products" (Marčeta & Bojnec, 2021).

In a fundamental study by P.M. Bikan and A. Brem, the most significant indicators of innovation were recognized as "expenses for innovative activities", "volume of innovative goods", "development and use of new technologies by business entities" (Bican & Brem, 2020).

Among Russian researchers, the work of M.R. Efimova and colleagues (Efimova *et al.*, 2021) can be distinguished, where the following indicators are named as indicators characterizing innovative activity: the cost of innovative activities of organizations, advanced production technologies developed and used, and the volume of innovative goods, works, and services.

Among Belarusian scientists, the research of N.I. Bogdan and co-authors (Bogdan *et al.*, 2020), V.V. Klimuk (Klimuk, 2023), A.N. Unsovich (Klimuk and Unsovich, 2021), and other scientists, who also point out that among the indicators of innovative activity of business entities, such indicators should be taken into account as: internal and external R & D costs, the cost of developing a digital technology system, the share of shipped innovative products in the total volume of shipped products, *etc.*

Thus, based on the analysis of the literature available to us, we come to the conclusion that the following indicators can be named as the key results of the functioning of innovative systems:

- Costs of Innovative Activity of Organizations (CIAO)
- Advanced Manufacturing Technologies Used (AMTU)
- The Volume of Innovative Goods, Works, Services (VIGWS)
- Developed Advanced Manufacturing Technologies (DAMT)

Performance Indicators of Scientific Activity

A number of Russian, Belarusian, and foreign scientists call the financing of scientific activities, the number of patents, and the number of trained graduate students the main indicators of the development of science (Astratova *et al.*, 2024; Astratova and Klimuk, 2022; Bican and Brem, 2020; Dobrotă *et al.*, 2019; Efimova *et al.*, 2021; Klimuk and Astratova, 2022; Marčeta and Bojnec, 2021; *etc.*).

In particular, to analyze the development of the R & D sector in the Union State of the Russian Federation and the Republic of Belarus, Vladimir V. Klimuk and Galina V. Astratova (Astratova *et al.*, 2022; Astratova and Klimuk, 2022; Klimuk and Astratova, 2022)proposed the following system of indicators for evaluating the effectiveness of using scientific potential:

- The share of research expenditures in the total volume of expenditures of the republican/federal budget.
- The share of research expenditures in the country's GDP.
- The share of internal research expenditures in the country's GDP.
- The coefficient of return of internal research expenditures (the ratio of the volume of research to the internal costs of its implementation).
- Labour productivity in the R & D sector (the ratio of the volume of research and development to the average number of employees employed in the R & D sector).
- The amount of financing for research and development costs per 1 employee employed in the R & D sector (per capita financing of research and development).

Also, G. Mutanov and colleagues (Mutanov *et al.*, 2020) determine the costs of scientific activity and the number of patents granted as the main indicators of the effectiveness of knowledge generation processes.

A study by G. Sadykzhanova and colleagues (Sadykhanova *et al.*, 2019) proved that the amount of funding for scientific research by innovatively active business entities is the most important indicator of the level of development of the knowledge economy.

The results of the study by S. Barkhordari and colleagues (Barkhordari *et al.*, 2019) identified the main indicators of the knowledge economy—financing of scientific research, as well as registered inventions.

M. Smol and J. Kulczycka (Smol & Kulczycka, 2019) in their study identified such indicators as: financing of science, the number of inventions, and the percentage of scientists with scientific degrees.

Thus, based on the analysis of the literature available to us, we come to the conclusion that the main indicators of knowledge generation of scientific institutions that determine the increase in innovative activity of business entities are the following:

- Capital expenditures on research and development
- Internal research and development costs
- The number of patents granted for inventions
- The number of utility model patents granted

Research Methodology

The regional innovation system of the Union state of Russia and Belarus was chosen as the object of the study. The choice of the research object is determined by the fact that official statistics data make it possible to assess the relationship between the effectiveness of scientific activity and the effectiveness of the development of innovative systems at the level of the Union state of Russia and Belarus.

Correlation analysis was used to analyze the data, which shows the relationship between two or more values. The value of the correlation coefficient reflects the strength of the relationship between the data series. We will interpret the data of the correlation analysis using the Cheddock scale (Ishkhanyan and Karpenko, 2016, p. 10).

The Results of the Study

First of all, the analysis of the impact of the dynamics of financing scientific activities on the indicators of innovative activity of business entities was carried out (Tables **1** and **2**) from equation 1.

From the analysis of the data presented in Table **1**, we can draw the following conclusions. The results of the study indicate the steady influence of the indicator "Capital expenditures on research and development" on the effectiveness of innovative activity of business entities. In particular, this indicator of scientific activity has the most significant impact on such indicators of innovation activity as "Developed advanced production technologies" and "Costs of innovative activities of organizations".

Table 1. The relationship between the indicator "Capital expenditures on research and development" (CERD) and the effectiveness of innovation activities, according to the author's methodology.

	Advanced Manufacturing Technologies Used (AMTU)	The Volume of Innovative Goods, Works, and Services (VIGWS)	Developed Advanced Production Technologies (DAPT)	The Costs of Innovative Activities of Organizations (CIAO)
Correlation coefficient	0.767	0.903	0.843	0.95
The relationship formula	AMTU=0.0002* CERDP^2-1.3612* CERD+1364.3	VIGWS=-0.0008* CERD^2-41.674* CERD +18303	DAPT=0.0117* CERD+10.982	CIAO=21.136* CERD+5901.8
R^2	0.8492	0.835	0.8842	0.9025

Table 2. The relationship between the indicator "Internal costs of research and development" (ICRD) and indicators of the effectiveness of innovative development, according to the author's methodology.

	Advanced Manufacturing Technologies Used (AMTU)	The Volume of Innovative Goods, Works, and Services (VIGWS)	Developed Advanced Production Technologies (DAPT)	The Costs of Innovative Activities of Organizations (CIAO)
Correlation coefficient	0.75	0.872	0.911	0.98
The relationship formula	AMTU=0.0865* ICRD^2+1273.9* ICRD+1364.3	VIGWS=1.6304* ICRD+18303	DAPT=0.0006* ICRD+10.678	CIAO =1.2553* ICRD+4516
R^2	0.7667	0.762	0.8303	0.9614

The results of the study presented in Table **2**, estimated from equation 2, indicate a stable, strong influence of such an indicator of scientific activity as "internal costs of research and development" on the effectiveness of innovative activity of economic entities, because all correlation coefficients are greater than 0.75.

At the next stage of the study, the influence of such an indicator of scientific performance as the number of patents granted for inventions was analyzed, along with the indicators of innovative activity of economic entities (Table **3**), estimated from equation 3.

Table 3. The relationship between the indicator "Patents granted for inventions" (PGI) and indicators of the effectiveness of innovative development, according to the author's methodology.

	Advanced Manufacturing Technologies Used (AMTU)	The Volume of Innovative Goods, Works, and Services (VIGWS)	Developed Advanced Production Technologies (DAPT)	The Costs of Innovative Activities of Organizations (CIAO)
Correlation coefficient	0.762	0.86	0.903	0.952
The relationship formula	AMTU=2.1824* GPI+1847.73	VIGWS=120.72* GPI+13266	DAPT=0.0486* GPI+7.6008	CIAO=95.463* GPI-140.31
R^2	0.7531	0.7949	0.8157	0.9077

The analysis of the obtained data presented in Table **3**, which was estimated from equation 3, allows us to conclude that such a result of scientific activity as "the number of patents granted" has a strong, stable effect on the innovative activity of business entities, because the minimum value of the correlation coefficient is 0.762.

The last hypothesis of this study is the following: "The number of patents obtained for new utility models affects the performance indicators of innovative activity of business entities." The results of the verification of this hypothesis are presented in Table **4**.

Table 4. The relationship of the indicator "Patents for utility models have been issued" (PUMI) and indicators of the effectiveness of innovative development, according to the author's methodology

	Advanced Manufacturing Technologies Used (AMTU)	The volume of Innovative Goods, Works, and Services (VIGWS)	Developed Advanced Production Technologies (DAPT)	The Costs of Innovative Activities of Organizations (CIAO)
Correlation coefficient	0.783	0.858	0.9148	0.9402
The relationship formula	AMTU=6.0879* PUMI+1719.8	VIGWS=333.99* PUMI 6913.3	DAPT=0.1312* PUMI+6.6988	CIAO=250,94* PUMI-1988.6

(Table 4) cont.....

	Advanced Manufacturing Technologies Used (AMTU)	The volume of Innovative Goods, Works, and Services (VIGWS)	Developed Advanced Production Technologies (DAPT)	The Costs of Innovative Activities of Organizations (CIAO)
R^2	0.7605	0.8598	0.837	0.8842

It follows from Table **4** that all correlation coefficients between such an indicator of scientific activity as the number of patents granted for utility models and indicators of innovative development are more than 0.76. This allows us to conclude that the development of activities for the development of utility models has a strong, stable impact on the innovative activity of business entities (equation 4).

From the analysis of the data presented in Tables **1** - **4**, we can conclude that the results of the scientific activity of academic institutions on the generation of new fundamental knowledge:

- Have a strong, sustainable impact on the innovative activities of business entities;
- They are the main factor in the development of innovative activity of business entities.

The obtained conclusions determine the need to formalize the patterns of influence of scientific activity on the development of innovative systems. Accordingly, it is possible to present a model for the development of innovative activity of economic entities of regional innovation systems as follows:

$$AMTU = \begin{cases} 0.0002 * CERD^2 - 1.3612 * CERD + 1364.3 \\ 0.0865 * ICRD^2 + 1273.9 * ICRD + 1364.3 \\ 2.1824 * PGI + 1847.73 \\ 6.0879 * PUMI + 1719.8 \end{cases} \quad (1)$$

$$VIGWS = \begin{cases} -0.0008 * CERD^2 - 41.674 * CERD + 18303 \\ 1.6304 * ICRD + 18303 \\ 120.72 * PGI + 13266 \\ 333.99 * PUMI + 6913.3 \end{cases} \quad (2)$$

$$DAPT = \begin{cases} 0.0117 * CERD + 10.982 \\ 0.0006 * ICRD + 10.678 \\ 0.0486 * PGI + 7.6008 \\ 0.1312 * PUMI + 6.6988 \end{cases} \quad (3)$$

$$CIAO = \begin{cases} 21.136 * CERD + 5901.8 \\ 1.2553 * ICRD + 4516 \\ 95.63 * PGI - 140.31 \\ 25.94 * PUMI - 1988.6 \end{cases} \quad (4)$$

Where,

CERD - Capital expenditures for research and development.

ICRD - Internal research and development costs.

PGI - Patents for inventions have been issued.

PUMI - Patents for utility models have been issued.

AMTU - Advanced manufacturing technologies used.

VIGWS - The volume of innovative goods, works, and services.

DAPT - Developed advanced production technologies.

CIAO - is the cost of innovative activities of organizations.

Summarizing the Above, it is Necessary to Draw the Following Conclusions

- On the basis of econometric modeling, the positive impact of the results of scientific activity of the academic sector on the development of innovative systems of the Union State of the Russian Federation and the Republic of Belarus has been proved.
- The econometric model of the development of regional innovation systems developed by the authors, based on the application of the results of scientific activity, allows for indicative planning of innovation infrastructure and improving management processes in the state and municipal administration of the USRB.

CONCLUSION

The comprehensive analysis conducted in this chapter yields several significant conclusions regarding the relationship between scientific activity and innovation development within the Union State of Russia and Belarus.

First, the research definitively establishes that scientific performance indicators have a strong and consistent impact on innovation metrics across all examined parameters. The correlation coefficients between scientific activity indicators (capital expenditures for R & D, internal R & D costs, patents for inventions, and utility model patents) and innovation performance metrics consistently range between 0.75 and 0.98, demonstrating robust relationships according to the Cheddock scale. This confirms our initial hypothesis that the generation of fundamental knowledge serves as a critical foundation for innovation systems' development.

Second, the econometric models developed through this research provide a formal framework for understanding how specific scientific activities influence various dimensions of innovation. These models allow for quantitative prediction of how changes in research funding or patent activity will affect innovation costs, technology development, and production of innovative goods and services. The high R^2 values (ranging from 0.76 to 0.96) validate the reliability of these mathematical relationships.

Third, the findings underscore the strategic importance of indicative planning as a policy tool for SMA (state and municipal administration) bodies in the USRB. While traditional directive planning approaches have become less relevant in modern market economies, targeted indicative planning that focuses on knowledge generation processes represents an effective mechanism for coordinating public and private investments in innovation infrastructure.

Fourth, the results highlight the necessity of coordinated policy approaches that recognize the interconnectedness of academic research and commercial innovation. Policies that enhance capital expenditures for research and development, stimulate internal R & D investments, and encourage patent activity will yield measurable improvements in innovation metrics.

Finally, this research establishes a foundation for evidence-based decision-making in innovation policy by providing specific mathematical formulations that can be used for forecasting and planning. These tools enable more effective allocation of resources and targeted interventions to strengthen the innovation ecosystem of the Union State. The econometric modeling presented in this chapter represents a significant contribution to both theoretical understanding and practical management of innovation systems. By quantifying the relationships between scientific activity and innovation outcomes, we provide SMA bodies with concrete tools for indicative planning that can drive the transition toward a knowledge-based economy in the USRB. Future research should focus on refining these models with additional variables and extending the analysis to specific sectors and regions within the Union State.

CHAPTER 11

The Challenges of Creative Human Capital in the Digital Economy

Natalia A. Simchenko[1,*] and **Maxim V. Vlasov**[2]

[1] *Department of Economic Theory and Economic Policy, St. Petersburg State University, St. Petersburg 199034, Russian Federation*

[2] *Department of Regional Economics, Innovative Entrepreneurship and Economics (REIE&E), Institute of Economics and Management, School of Public Administration and Entrepreneurship (SPAE), Ural Federal University (UrFU), Yekaterinburg 620002, Sverdlovsk Region, Russian Federation*

Abstract: This chapter examines the evolving concept of creative human capital in the context of the digital economy and the fourth industrial revolution. As technological breakthroughs in artificial intelligence, robotics, and other digital technologies transform the labor market, there is a growing demand for workers with cognitive skills and creative thinking. The study explores how creative human capital becomes a strategic resource for social development, with particular focus on the health sector in the Russian Federation and the Republic of Crimea. The research analyzes the socio-technological infrastructure that supports creative human capital formation, identifies the challenges in the health sector workforce, and proposes strategies for enhancing productivity through creative human capital management. Special attention is given to the integration of the sanatorium-resort complex with the healthcare system in Crimea, highlighting its role in regional economic development and public health improvement.

Keywords: Creative human capital, Digital economy, Fourth industrial revolution, Healthcare workforce, Regional development, Socio-technological infrastructure, Sanatorium-resort complex.

INTRODUCTION

As it is well known, in the conditions of socio-economic development based on creation and application of digital technologies, society has defined trends of development of such technological breakthroughs as: artificial intelligence, the Internet of things, fully automated production, robotics, virtual and augmented reality, information storage and storage technologies, nanotechnology, and biotechnology *etc*. (Astratova, *et al*., 2022; Bengraf, *et al*., 2024).

* **Corresponding author Natalia A. Simchenko:** Department of Economic Theory and Economic Policy, St. Petersburg State University, St. Petersburg 199034, Russian Federation; E-mail: natalysimchenko@yandex.ru

Galina V. Astratova, Maxim V. Vlasov, Chigozirim Ndubuisi Onwusiribe & Longinus D.N. Nnadozie (Eds.)

So, there is a gradual transition of the economy and society into the fourth industrial revolution. One of the features of the fourth industrial revolution is the appearance of supercomputers and robots, which allow the replacement of human labor by complex work performed by automated intelligent machines, and can further lead to job reductions while creating new ones. It's going to be targeted at people with cognitive skills and creative thinking. Thus, the concept of «creative human capital» is being introduced into the digital economy. The fact is that sectors such as industry, medicine (*e.g.*, nanotechnology), financial and economic systems that use blockchain technologies are adopting digital currencies (cryptocurrencies) among the first to adopt new digital technologies (Yanovskaya and Simchenko, 2024).

At the same time, the digital economy is contributing to all positive factors and negative ones that need to be regulated at the state level (Astratova and Bekshaev, 2024; Astratova, 2023b; Bogdan *et al.*, 2020; *etc.*). For example, the increased role of cybersecurity involves collecting and storing a huge amount of information, both personal and public. In addition, digital technologies and tools directly influence the transformation of labor markets and social-labor relations.

Let's note that the global world community is living an amazing time; a time of digitalization, in which innovations are being formed and implemented, inventions based on digital technologies and, therefore, in the future, the usual social life and activities will change radically: new methods and technologies applied in the management of organizations will appear, human capital, people's health, education, industry, information transmission and perception *etc.* In other words, for society, we are entering a new era of creative human capital formation and development based on digital content.

In the conditions of digital society, it is human capital that becomes a strategic resource for social development, where the development vector is directed towards the intellectual and creative activities of employees. At the same time, in the Russian Federation, the process of formation and management of creative human capital is the basis of many state-directed programs and national projects. However, in these programs, the region-wide component of the socio-spatial development of human capital and its potential comes to the fore. This fact is confirmed by the results of research conducted by L.S. Mazelis, *et al.* (2018), which investigated the question of the interrelation and interconditioning of development of creative human capital and trajectories of socio-spatial development of regions, because human capital forms the conditions for improvement, innovation, acceleration and efficiency in all spheres of economic development, in other words, human capital creates the prerequisites for increasing production volumes, increasing the quality of life of the population, filling federal and regional budgets of the country» (Mazelis, *et al.*, 2018).

Given the rapid spread of socio-technological infrastructure, the basis for the development of an innovative and digital economy is modern knowledge that allows for the creation, development, and expansion of human capital. In the digital economy, creative human capital is of particular importance.

Such human capital factors as intelligence, health, knowledge, and quality of life, as a result of the synergistic effect, generate creative innovation and entrepreneurial activity necessary for the growth of the digital economy. The complex and distributed mechanism of interaction of factors of development of creative human capital of the region ensures the functioning of its socio-technological infrastructure. The elements of socio-technological infrastructure are the first and second-level economic spheres in the mechanism of human capital formation of the region (Ganieva, 2022).

So, the first layer of socio-technological infrastructure includes areas directly involved in human capital creation and development. The funds invested in them by the multiplier effect are reflected in the growth of human capital:

- Education and science – includes the structure of the regional educational system, staffing, and support system for scientific activities.
- Health – competence of medical workers, quality of medical services, level of preventive and diagnostic provision, and technological component.
- IT-sphere – includes availability and sufficiency of information resources, level of digitalization of the branches of economy, innovation, and progressiveness of software (Ganieva, 2022).

The second level of socio-technological infrastructure is the spheres indirectly involved in the formation of human capital, but certainly playing a significant role in its creation, namely:

- Industry.
- Agriculture and agro-technological system.
- Transport and logistics technologies.
- Recreation, tourism, and sanatorium-resort complex (Ganieva, 2022).

At the same time, the assessment of the contribution of creative human capital is characterized by objective methodological limitations in the ecosystem of the region's development. Creative human capital is capable of accumulation and reproduction; that is, it has all the characteristics of a productive factor to be evaluated. For example, the economist G. Becker conducted a neoclassical analysis of discrimination issues in the labor market and defined areas of use of the theory of investment in "human factor." In his theory, G. Becker calculated the return on investment in education as a 12-14% annual increase (Becker, 1964). Also, he proved that the costs of education, medical care, and other social programs are equivalent to investments in the creation of new technologies. Moreover, for this scientific study, G. Becker was awarded the Nobel Prize in 1992 (Yanovskaya and Simchenko, 2024). However, it is worth noting that the return on investment in human capital is inertial; the time lag increases significantly if it is necessary to evaluate the investments in the institutional components of creative capital, such as social institutions—education, formation of creative elite, economic freedom and security, *etc*.

It should be noted that one of the advantages of human capital formation and development is to ensure productivity growth in all areas of economic activity. It is human capital elements, such as the knowledge and skills of specialists, that underlie competitive advantages in the digital economy.

Analysis of literary sources allows for the formation of the author's interpretation of the concept "creative human capital." The ability of an employee to strategically assess the current situation while using their accumulated knowledge and skills to develop and create innovative methods and technologies, and apply advanced tools in their professional activities.

Human capital contributes to the creation and development of high-technology and knowledge-intensive industries in the region. By using the latest advances in science and technology in all sectors of the economy of the region, human capital contributes to the increase of productivity, which will ensure the efficiency of the regional economy as a whole (Mukhametova, 2019; Shirinkina, 2019).

At the same time, the formation and development of creative human capital strengthen competitive positions among workers in different spheres of activity, namely:

- High creative potential of the worker and its importance in a certain kind of activity are accompanied by high employment and economic activity in the organization.
- The employee's creative abilities help to reduce the risk of becoming unemployed and increase their competitiveness.
- The expression of creative potential increases the employee's earnings and provides easy access to jobs in his or her line of work, the most attractive in terms of office and salary.

- Creativity of the worker in skills and abilities contributes to their high territorial and professional mobility (Popikov, 2016).

Thus, an employee with a high creative potential quickly adapts to changes, seeks to acquire new skills and knowledge, and quickly assimilates and implements in their professional activity the achievement of scientific and technological progress.

In the conditions of digitalization of the economy and transformation of socio-technological infrastructure, creative human capital is formed, that is, the action of the synergistic effect of health, knowledge, and quality of life, which, as a result, generates creative innovation and entrepreneurial activity necessary for the economic growth of the digital economy. In this process, the health sector is quite capacious in structure and composition of creative human capital, which is the basis for the formation and development of the industry. Of course, the primary role is played by skilled health workers—doctors and medical professionals—but without effective management and administration, IT staff implementing advanced technologies cannot build a modern health care system. Digital technologies and tools are equally important to the high-tech medical services of physicians as well as their highly professional competencies.

To evaluate the quality of creative human capital, it is necessary to monitor the productivity of health care workers; it depends not only on economic performance, but also on the social dimension. The implementation of a policy of economic production plays an important role in increasing the productivity of health service workers. The concept is based on the management of health care organizations, with a focus on ensuring high-quality services and eliminating all types of costs and losses.

Based on the concept of a scientist, R. Florida, who introduced into scientific circulation the concept of «creative class», which is understood as a community of people working in the field of science and technology, as well as in other sectors of the economy, where priority is given to creating new ideas and technological solutions that determine the future directions of development (Florida, 2011). We note the need to form and develop creative human capital in the health sector. After all, the health sector is the basis of development not only for society and individual people, but also for the state. That is, the health of the population is a crucial factor in the sustainable social and economic development of society.

---

1 Source:[Electronic resource]. URL: https://www.hse.ru/mirror/pubs/share/218427645 (accessed: 07/31/2024). (In Russ.).

The special report of the Higher School of Economics (Russia) "Health: necessary answers to the challenges of time[1]" describes key solutions in the field of health for human resource development, which are divided into three areas:

- Updating the professional competences of medical workers.
- Increase the motivation of health workers.
- Reorganization of medical education.

In summary, we note that the priority place in the formation and development of creative human capital in the field of health, in our view, is the implementation of principles of frugal production. The United Nations system is a global health system that works to ensure the quality of services provided. But we need to develop a model of patient-centricity in modern health care; in this case, the formation of an effective system for managing interaction with patients and its role in increasing the productivity of organizations in the field becomes important. The health care system is a social model of spatial human capital development in the region.

For example, the development of medical services in the Republic of Crimea is inextricably linked to the state of the sanatorium and resort industry in the region. The Republic of Crimea is a unique region. The National Health Institute, which has been a centre for health and rehabilitation services for large numbers of people for decades, is due to its natural factors. Develop and maximize the health potential with emphasis on innovative technologies and traditional factors, with maximum interaction with practical health, is the main task of the development program of the medical biological cluster of the Republic of Crimea.

The development of sanatorium and resort complexes is a priority direction of economic development of the Crimea. According to the Strategy for tourism development in Russia, tourism is considered as a source of financial income for the budget, a means of increasing employment and quality of life of the population, a way to maintain the health of citizens, a basis for the development of a socio-cultural environment and education of patriotism, as well as a powerful tool for education and formation of an ethical platform for civil society development[2].

---

2 Here Source: Strategy for the development of tourism in the Russian Federation up to 2035. Approved by the Government of the Russian Federation Order dated 20.09.2019 2129-p. – [Electronic resource]. URL: http://government.ru/docs/37906/ (accessed:07/31/2024). (In Russ.).

3 Source: `State program of development of resorts and tourism in the Republic of Crimea. Approved by the Resolution of the Council of Ministers of the Republic of Crimea of 29 December 2016. No 650. – [Electronic resource]. URL:https://mtur.rk.gov.ru/ru/structure/245 (accessed:07/31/2024). (In Russ.).

In the relevant State Program of resorts and tourism development in Crimea, the government of the Republic of Crimea has defined the strategic goal of development of Crimea, which is the formation of a modern tourist-recreational complex, characterized by competitiveness, demand, variety of offered tourist and health care services, and high quality of service[3].

Sustainable development of sanatorium and resort in Crimea allows increasing investment flows into the region; increasing the level of infrastructure provision of territories, the Russian economy is currently experiencing a decline in its exports of goods and services. However, the sanatorium-resort sector and all related industries provide a huge number of jobs, thereby reducing unemployment in the region (Pavlenko and Bukreev, 2020; Pavlenko and Bezukladov, 2019).

The health sector is sufficiently capacious in structure and composition of workers taking part in the formation and development of the industry. Undoubtedly, the main role is assigned to medical personnel—doctors and secondary medical personnel, but, for example, without employees of a health organization or technical workers who maintain expensive equipment, the industry will not be able to exist. At the same time, the sanatorium-resort complex is integrated into the health care system, which also employs a large number of medical personnel, including doctors, nurses, and support staff.

Let's highlight the trends in the health sector, for example, in Crimea:

- The reduction of medical personnel, regardless of categories, is caused by many objective reasons; from the policy of regulating the industry in the field of accreditation of medical staff, optimization of budget expenditures to increase the burden on health care workers for various reasons, for example, at the time of the spread of a virus COVID-19, there was an enormous burden on medical personnel, There is also a tendency to release jobs by employees of retirement and pre-retirement age, as well as insufficient number of young professionals (due to the demographic crisis of the 1990s) who enter Russia's labor market for the first time;
- The reduction in the number of medical personnel with higher and first qualification categories is due to:
    - Older health workers (they are more difficult to learn and adapt to rapidly changing conditions, digital skills, *etc*.).
    - High requirements for the employee to meet the qualification category.
    - The system of remuneration for health workers, including basic salary, compensatory and incentive payments, made it unfeasible for doctors to have a role in supplementing the qualification category compared with incentive payments, the size of which depends on more complex and high-quality

health services being delivered, rather than documented criteria for professionalism.

- Some employees are moving to the private health sector, where an effective system of motivation is devised, and the calculation of wages is carried out with reference to individual indicators, and there is no obligation to fill in redundant medical documentation.

The problem then is that the provision of high-tech medical care has the right to be performed by a medical worker of a qualified category not lower than the first. To offset this trend, the current public health regulatory policy in the area of simplification of documentation should be reviewed and amended, that is, reduce the burden on doctors, for example, to fill out various documents, replacing them with digital technologies that allow for automation of this process.

Thus, in the process of creating creative human capital to achieve effective productivity growth in health services, it is necessary, first, to provide quality health care personnel; second, to increase coverage for preventive and clinical examinations; third, to increase the use of economical technologies; and fourth, to increase the number of leaders in lean manufacturing.

In summing up the present study, we note that despite the strict regulation of the health sector, the creative human capital in this field should be understood as the responsibility of the medical and nursing staff to ensure that the quality of health services is improved. The management of creative human capital is long-term and is a systemic change, including the formation of key strategic goals and objectives, forecasting of key indicators, organization, regulation, and control of the increase of intellectual and creative potential of the region's labor force, and the assessment of the contribution of investment in human capital development to the socio-economic growth strategy.

We also want to note that the problems we have noted in the medical industry are typical for most areas of non-material production, including science and education. Moreover, the problems of Russian creative human capital in general and Crimea in particular are typical for Belarus as a post-Soviet state.

CONCLUSION

The development of creative human capital represents a fundamental strategic priority in the era of digital transformation. This study has demonstrated that in the conditions of digitalization and the fourth industrial revolution, traditional labor markets are undergoing profound changes that necessitate a new approach to human capital development focused on creativity, innovation, and intellectual capacity.

The socio-technological infrastructure that supports creative human capital formation operates on two levels: the first level is directly involved in human capital creation (education, healthcare, and IT), and the second level indirectly contributes to its development (industry, agriculture, transport, and recreation). This multilayered infrastructure creates the ecosystem necessary for the accumulation and reproduction of creative human capital, which has been shown to yield significant returns on investment, as demonstrated by G. Becker's pioneering work in this field.

In the healthcare sector specifically, our analysis reveals several concerning trends, particularly in the Republic of Crimea: a reduction in medical personnel across all categories, and a decline in the number of medical staff with higher and first qualification categories. These trends are attributed to multiple factors, including regulatory policies, demographic shifts, optimization of budget expenditures, and increased workloads. The situation is especially problematic given that high-tech medical care requires practitioners with first-category qualifications or higher.

To address these challenges and enhance productivity in health services through creative human capital, several strategic priorities emerge:

- Ensuring the provision of quality healthcare personnel through improved recruitment, retention, and professional development strategies.
- Increasing coverage for preventive and clinical examinations to improve population health outcomes.
- Implementing lean production technologies to maximize efficiency and reduce unnecessary costs.
- Developing effective leadership in lean management practices.
- Reducing administrative burdens on medical professionals through automation and digital technologies.
- Creating patient-centered models of healthcare delivery that enhance service quality.
- Integrating the sanatorium-resort complex more effectively with the broader healthcare system to leverage Crimea's unique natural healing factors.

The management of creative human capital must be approached as a long-term, systemic undertaking that encompasses the formation of strategic goals, forecasting of key indicators, organization, regulation, and control of the intellectual and creative potential of the regional workforce. Furthermore, it requires a rigorous assessment of the contribution of investments in human capital development to the overall socio-economic growth strategy.

It is worth noting that the challenges identified in the healthcare sector mirror those found in other areas of non-material production, including science and education. Moreover, the issues facing Russian creative human capital, in Crimea and elsewhere, share similarities with those in other post-Soviet states such as Belarus. As society transitions into the era of the fourth industrial revolution, the formation and development of creative human capital based on digital content will become increasingly crucial. Those regions and nations that successfully cultivate their creative human capital, particularly in strategic sectors like healthcare, will be better positioned to achieve sustainable economic growth, improved quality of life, and competitive advantage in the global digital economy.

CHAPTER 12

Sectoral State Regulation of the Higher Education System in Russia and Belarus in the Context of Digitalization

Galina V. Astratova[1,*], **Chigozirim N. Onwusiribe**[2] and **Maxim V. Vlasov**[1]

[1] *Department of Regional Economics, Innovative Entrepreneurship and Economics (REIE&E), Institute of Economics and Management, School of Public Administration and Entrepreneurship (SPAE), Ural Federal University (UrFU), Yekaterinburg 620002, Sverdlovsk Region, Russian Federation*

[2] *School of Public Administration and Entrepreneurship (SPAE), Ural Federal University (UrFU), Yekaterinburg 620002, Sverdlovsk Region, Russian Federation*

Abstract: This chapter examines the sectoral state regulation of higher education systems in Russia and Belarus within the context of digitalization. It analyzes the organizational principles of public management with a focus on sectoral, intersectoral, and territorial management approaches as applied to Higher Education Services (HES). The study explores how the knowledge economy, particularly the HES sector, functions as a critical component of socio-economic development in both countries. The research identifies three key mechanisms of public policy in higher education management—financing, restructuring, and autonomy management—and presents expert opinions on their effectiveness in Russia and Belarus. The chapter further discusses challenges and opportunities in the digital transformation of educational governance, highlighting the need for innovative approaches to civil servant training and the development of digital competencies. The findings indicate that while the sectoral principle remains foundational in both countries' governance structures, the autonomy management model appears most promising for future development of higher education systems in the Union State of Russia and Belarus.

Keywords: Autonomy management, Digitalization, Higher education system, Knowledge economy, Public management, Sectoral state regulation, Union State of Russia and Belarus.

[*] **Corresponding author Galina V. Astratova:** Department of Regional Economics, Innovative Entrepreneurship and Economics (REIE&E), Institute of Economics and Management, School of Public Administration and Entrepreneurship (SPAE), Ural Federal University (UrFU), Yekaterinburg 620002, Sverdlovsk Region, Russian Federation; E-mail: galina_28@mail.ru

Galina V. Astratova, Maxim V. Vlasov, Chigozirim Ndubuisi Onwusiribe & Longinus D.N. Nnadozie (Eds.)

INTRODUCTION

The specifics and essence of management processes in the public sector are reflected, as is well known, in scientific principles, which are, on the one hand, the "guiding idea" and, on the other hand, express the internal consistency of the structural elements of the public sector as a system (Bratanovsky & Demenchuk, 2018, p. 20-21).

Among the organizational principles of public management, industry affiliation plays an important role:

- The principle of sectoral management.
- The principle of intersectoral management.
- The principle of territorial sectoral management (Bratanovsky and Demenchuk, 2018, p. 25-26) (Table **1**).

Table 1. Description of the principles of public administration related to sectoral affiliation, compiled by the authors on the basis of various sources (Bratanovsky & Demenchuk, 2018; Manokhin, 2012; Yusupov, 2013, *etc.*)

Name of the Principal	Characteristics of the Principle	The Opportunities Provided to SMA Bodies by the Implementation of the Principle
1. The principle of sectoral management	It is implemented as a special system for building SMA bodies, where the SMA body and its structural divisions are assigned such management objects that are homogeneous and organically related to the nature of industry activities.	It allows you to focus the resources of SMA bodies on management facilities, as well as on the selection and placement of highly qualified personnel in public administration who know the theory and practice of working in the industry.
2. The principle of intersectoral management	It is carried out by interdepartmental (supranational) management bodies and is implemented as one management function applicable to certain areas of public administration (planning, organization, standardization, certification, *etc.*).	It provides an opportunity to strengthen coordination, regulation, and control between several industries and areas of management of a group of organizations.

(Table 1) cont.....

Name of the Principal	Characteristics of the Principle	The Opportunities Provided to SMA Bodies by the Implementation of the Principle
3. The principle of territorial sectoral management	It is implemented as an organic combination of sectoral and territorial principles in the construction of the activities of SMA bodies.	It allows you to consolidate the territorial competencies of SMA bodies in management sectors. For example, in the subjects of the Russian Federation, territorial bodies of federal executive authorities are being created in federal districts, taking into account the industry, the specifics of the region, the climatic and geographical and socio-economic characteristics of the region, *etc.*

It should be noted that the sector is "not only a complex of homogeneous structures with a common activity profile that meet the material and spiritual needs of society" (Astratova, 2023b). In the system of Russian statehood, the sectoral principle was initially laid down: "... at the stage of public administration of the affairs of society, the concept of an industry as a branch of public administration was formed, which entered into sectoral legislation, including constitutional legislation" (Manokhin, 2012, p. 82). In other words, the entire Russian SMA system is based on the sectoral principle, and this is not accidental, since for the Russian Federation, the largest state in the world (17,098,246 km2)[1], only "... thanks to the sectoral principle, it is possible to ensure effective communication and production links between organizations hundreds and thousands of kilometers apart as well as qualified management from one center" (Astratova, 2023b).

As for the Republic of Belarus, in fact and geographically, it belongs to the small states, despite very active discussions on this issue in the scientific literature (Browning, 2006; Mukhametov, 2020; Novikova, 2022; Potreba, 2019) (Table **2**).

1 Source: [Electronic resource]. URL: https://rosreestr.gov.ru / (accessed: 06/07/2024). (In Russ.).

2 Source: [Electronic resource]. URL: https://gtmarket.ru/ratings/world-population (accessed: 06/07/2024). (In Russ.).

3 According to the World Bank PPP data for 2018

Table 2. The Republic of Belarus is a small state, comparative aspect, compiled by the authors on the basis of various sources (Mukhametov, 2020; StatBul, 2024)[2].

Criteria	Republic Belarus	The Arithmetic Mean for the Countries of the World	Share of Global Importance, %
Population, people, as of 01.01.2024	9 155 978	31 160 000	0.12
The area of the territory, thousand km^2	207.6	545.50	1.39
The volume of GDP, $ billion[3]	189.0	690.50	0.14

At the same time, the sectoral principle of public administration, laid down in Soviet times, continues to operate in the Republic of Belarus even now. However, it needs a modern understanding and an adequate change in the role, functions, and forms of public administration in order to increase the efficiency of industries in close relationship with regional and territorial management in the new economic conditions (Medvedeva, 2006).

It should be noted that one of the most difficult aspects of the sectoral principle in public administration is the branch of the "knowledge economy", which, as we noted earlier, forms the R & D services sector and the higher education services sector, or HES (Astratova, 2023b; Tatarkin and Pilipenko, 2007; Vlasov and Shardina, 2022).

The HES sector plays a special role in the knowledge economy due to the following factors:

- In the higher education system, the final stage of formal education is being implemented, including post-secondary education and research activities in various educational institutions (Astratova *et al.*, 2024; Astratova *et al.*, 2022; Astratova *et al.*, 2021; Bengraf *et al.*, 2024; *etc.*);
- As a branch of the economy, higher education services are simultaneously:

  a. A socially significant benefit due to the implementation of traditional and basic functions: "socialization, personality formation, education of civic feelings" (Mamedov, 2011, p. 29);
  b. The set of competencies for the professional development of an individual and the whole society (Global RES Req, 2022; Nelson and Strohl, 2014);

- High-quality higher education is a key factor in the country's innovative development (Astratova *et al.*, 2024; Bengraf *et al.*, 2024; Mamedov, 2011).

In connection with the most important socio-economic role of the education sector, governments of all countries are developing the so–called "state educational policy," which entails "... guiding and regulating the activities of the state in the field of education, carried out by it to achieve relevant strategic goals and objectives of national and even global importance" (Mironov, 2002). Accordingly, the state policy in the field of higher education in the Russian Federation and in the Republic of Belarus is based on well-known key principles inherited from the Soviet era:

- the humanistic nature of education.
- unity of the federal cultural and educational space.
- accessibility of education.
- secular nature of education.
- freedom and pluralism in education.
- democratic public-public nature of education management» (Mamedov, 2011, p. 29).

The main instruments for the implementation of state policy in the field of education are the sectoral State Program of the Russian Federation[4], as well as the relevant state programs for the development of education adopted by the subjects of the Russian Federation: a) the Federal Target Program for the Development of Education; b) the Federal Targeted Investment Program; *etc*. The main directions of the development of the education system of the Republic of Belarus are defined, as we noted earlier, by the Program of socio-economic development of the Republic of Belarus for 2016-2020; The State program "Education and Youth Policy" for 2016-2020; The Concept and Program of continuous education of children and students for 2016-2020.

Thus, the state sectoral policy for the development of scientific and educational potential in the Russian Federation and the Republic of Belarus is not only significant, but in many ways decisive, since in the end it is the state that determines the conditions for the functioning of the economy and the development of all sectors, including higher education (Znamensky, 2012).

It should be emphasized that in the context of the digitalization of the economy of the Russian Federation and the Republic of Belarus, the effectiveness of sectoral

---

4 The State program of the Russian Federation "Development of education". Approved by Decree of the Government of the Russian Federation No. 1642 dated December 26, 2017. – [Electronic resource]. URL: https://www.consultant.ru/document/cons_doc_LAW_286474/cf742885 e783e08d9387d7364e34f26f87ec138f/ (accessed: 03/04/2023). (In Russ.).

government policy in general, and in the field of HES, in particular, is becoming even more relevant. This is due both to the need to introduce innovations into production (Tatarkin and Pilipenko, 2007) and to ensure qualified public administration in a number of areas (Znamensky, 2012). However, the theoretical and methodological basis of the above-mentioned problems is still being developed both in Russia and abroad.

As we noted above, due to the emergence of the concepts of "new public management" (NPM) (Hood, 1995), as well as Digital Public Administration (DPA) (Kiselev, 2018), models of public administration in general began to be considered in a new way (Coursey and Norris, 2008; Pirannejad & Ingrams, 2022) and sectors, in particular, including the management of the HES sector.

For example, Van Vught's research notes that public administration today is a special branch of knowledge that requires revision and revision, as there is a discussion where different points of view, theories, and concepts that explore the organizations, functions, and activities of SMA bodies collide (Van Vught, 1991, p. 58-59). In this regard, Van Vught, based on a review of the literature on economic theory, identifies at least six new concepts of public administration, which further contributed to eclecticism ("eclecticism") and conceptual pluralism in public administration as a scientific discipline in general (Van Vught, 1991), and in relation to separate industries, in particular (Astratova, *et al.*, 2024).

It should be noted that the focus of public administration of the HES sector appeared only in the second half of the 70s of the XX century. That is why we can say that the sectoral state regulation of higher education as a special branch of knowledge is very young. An analysis of the literature available to us allows us to say that the HES sector has come into the range of attention of public administration due to a number of reasons:

- The HES system and its universities imply the presence of "multi–way" coordination of interests and complex communication processes, including with SMA bodies;
- Decision-making processes in the HES system take place collectively and require the development of special coordination mechanisms, which are in many ways similar to decision-making processes in SMA bodies;
- The HES system and its universities are managed by highly educated and talented managers who, unlike businesses in the real sector, are guided not only by commercial interests, but also by needs of the highest order, directly or indirectly related to the social policy of the state, which greatly simplifies the coordination of the interests of managers in the SMA and HES system (Astratova, *et al.*, 2024).

Therefore, it is not surprising that, as a result, the attention of political systems to higher education turned out to be "very fruitful" (Van Vught & Boer, 2015).

It is expected that in the future, sectoral government regulation by the HES sector will be based on the study of "coordination mechanisms in collective decision-making processes" and "a comparative analysis of external functions and government performance" (Van Vught and Boer, 2015).

It should be noted that, in addition to the models of public management of the HES sector, the financial side of the issue is also an important issue. Indeed, at the moment, the sectoral contribution of national governments is traditionally the highest (World DepRep, 2022) among other investors in the industry (Agasisti *et al.*, 2022; Agasisti *et al.*, 2021; Astratova *et al.*, 2022; Astratova *et al.*, 2021; Bengraf *et al.*, 2024). However, there is no consensus on the share of government participation in the management of the HES sector.

In the study by Shibanova (2023), it is noted that in the context of the application of the NPM model, the main tools of public management of the HES sector have now become three key mechanisms of public policy: 1) financing; 2) restructuring; 3) autonomy management. In this regard, we considered it appropriate to characterize these three control mechanisms (Table **3**), as well as to find out from experts which of these tools are most effective in modern conditions for the Russian Federation and the Republic of Belarus (Fig. **1**).

Table 3. Characteristics of the main tools of the new model of public administration of the higher education system, compiled on the basis of the work of Shibanova (Shibanova, 2023).

Government Policy		
Financing	**Restructuring**	**Autonomy Management**
Provides for strengthening top-down control over the expenditure of public funds by universities, based on the principle of an optimal price-quality ratio of educational services, as well as through the introduction of standardized performance indicators of educational institutions. There is a stimulation of market competition and the desire of universities for leadership on the basis of "quasi-market" instruments.	The institutional diversity and diversification of the HES sphere are being carried out in order to increase the effectiveness and competitiveness of both individual universities and the entire HES system. There is a concentration of resources at the most successful universities, which increases their competitiveness in international markets due to increased productivity of R & D services and HES.	It implies the need to implement an autonomous (*i.e.*, decentralized) model of managerial decision-making by university rectors without any restrictions on the part of the public administration apparatus. In other words, the independence of universities in such matters as financial management, recruitment policy, operational management, *etc.*, is recognized.

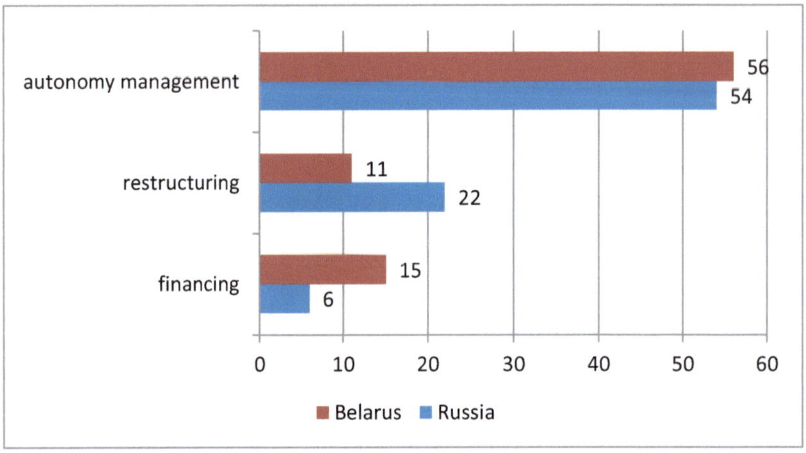

Fig. (1). Respondents' answers to the question: "What tools of the new model of public administration of the higher education system do you consider the most optimal for Russia and Belarus?", people. (*N=83; n = 82;* K_k *= 0.25;* K_c *= 0.87). Source: data from a survey of experts and government officials in google docs, whatsapp, and vkontakte, and processing in statistica.*

It follows from Fig. (**1**) that the majority chose autonomy management as the optimal model of university management for both countries. This suggests, in our opinion, that at the moment there are no optimal mechanisms for state management of the HES sector in Russia and Belarus.

It should also be noted that the role and effectiveness of public administration of the HES sector are also highly debatable. Thus, there are opinions that the effectiveness of public management of the higher education system is insufficient (Bolgova & Kalashnikova, 2015; Koryttsev, 2009; Kostyuchenko, 2009, *etc.*). Also, some authors believe that reducing government spending on the HES sector and increasing market competition contribute to improving the productivity of educational organizations (Gunter *et al.*, 2016; Schubert, 2009; Shibanova, 2023, *etc.*). At the same time, there are approaches claiming that sequestering public financing of the higher education system can lead to a reduction in both the operational efficiency/productivity of universities and the opportunities of the population to receive quality education (Sav, 2016; Sav, 2017).

Without questioning the need for state participation in the formation of the knowledge economy, we believe that further research needs to explore issues

5 The Union State: 25 years of integration – results and new tasks. June 06, 2024. – [Electronic resource]. URL: https://forumspb.com/programme/business-programme/131433/#broadcast (accessed: 06.06.2024). (In Russ.).

related to determining the most effective share of state participation in the management of the higher education system.

It should also be noted that the Russian Federation and the Republic of Belarus pay considerable attention to the development of digital technologies and their application in the education system in general and higher education in particular. However, the level of digitalization, as we noted earlier, varies significantly in fraternal countries. This cannot help but affect both the development of the HES sector and the development of sectoral public management of this sector.

Moreover, in the context of the digital transformation of the USRB economy, the issues of effective sectoral policy in the HES sector are becoming more and more in demand, due to the following main factors:

Firstly, in the context of the 25th anniversary of the Union State[5], the task of building an "innovative economy" is being actualized (Petrov *et al.*, 2022) in order to form a unified scientific and technological space and an innovation system designed to ensure the implementation of R & D results in the real sector of the economy (Bengraf *et al.*, 2024; Petrov *et al.*, 2022; Tararyshkina, 2019). Secondly, it is necessary to ensure qualified public administration in the USRB in a number of key areas of activity:

- Creation and support of the functionality of integrated scientific and educational structures, university and interuniversity complexes, scientific, educational and production centers (including innovative ones) to consolidate efforts and resources, develop international cooperation and international cooperation in the interests of training qualified personnel in scientific, scientific, technical and innovative fields (Astratova, *et al.*, 2024; Bengraf, *et al.* 2024);
- The development of modern information and telecommunications and other high-tech technologies and their implementation in R & D, scientific and technical activities, and the educational process (Astratova *et al.*, 2022; Astratova *et al.*, 2021; Bengraf *et al.*, 2024; Klimuk, 2023; Klimuk and Unsovich, 2021);
- Joint use of scientific, experimental, and instrument-based academic, university, and industry sectors of science in research and educational processes (Astratova, 2023b; Klimuk, 2023; Klimuk and Unsovich, 2021; Znamensky, 2012).

Thirdly, as we have repeatedly noted earlier, in connection with the emergence of the concepts of "New Public Management" (NPM) (Hood, 1995), as well as Digital Public Administration (DPA) (Kiselyov, 2018), it is necessary to develop models of "electronic government", the use of digital management or electronic administration technologies (Alekseeva, 2016; Coursey and Norris, 2008;

Merkulov and Malakhova, 2020; *etc.*).

One of the ways to solve the problem of effective sectoral policy in the HES sector in the context of digitalization may be to intensify the introduction of distance learning technologies for training civil servants (Hinkley, 2023).

At the same time, it should be understood that the digitalization of SMA bodies is not only the reengineering of technical and technological processes and/or their transfer to a remote format, but also the total digitalization of all workplaces based on the integration of DT into services and decision–making processes (Williamson and Hague,2009).

In this regard, it is necessary to prepare civil servants in the HES system for the full implementation of DT based on the operational network model. In the future, this will create new jobs for both civil servants and citizens and enterprises, as well as increase the efficiency of their activities (Casalino *et al.*, 2020, p. 316). In addition, this leads to the need to further conduct research on at least three main aspects:

- The relationship of DT—new information technologies—digital competencies;
- Development of new, innovative curricula, teaching methods, and training courses;
- Accessibility of open and distance learning platforms (Casalino *et al.*, 2020, p. 316).

Since the topic of the introduction of distance learning technologies for training civil servants is new and has not been sufficiently studied, it was considered advisable to consider issues related to the formation of digital competencies, the development of new training courses, and the availability of digital platforms for students in more detail in the following sections of this monograph.

Summarizing the content of this section, we can say that despite the controversial concepts of NPM and DPA, there is no doubt that the strategic goal of the state policy in the field of education was, is and will be to increase the availability of high-quality education that meets the requirements of the innovative development of the USRB economy, the modern needs of society and every citizen of the Russian Federation and the Republic of Belarus.

CONCLUSION

The sectoral state regulation of higher education systems in Russia and Belarus continues to evolve in response to the challenges of digitalization and the demands of the knowledge economy. Despite the geographical, economic, and demographic differences between these countries, both maintain the sectoral principle of public administration established during the Soviet era, while adapting it to modern conditions. The research reveals that among the three key mechanisms of public policy in higher education management—financing, restructuring, and autonomy management—experts favor the autonomy management model for both Russia and Belarus. This suggests a growing recognition of the benefits of decentralized decision-making in university administration, though optimal mechanisms for state management of the HES sector are still developing in both countries.

As the Union State of Russia and Belarus approaches its 25th anniversary, the formation of a unified scientific and technological space becomes increasingly critical. The digital transformation of the economy necessitates effective sectoral policy in higher education to support innovation, develop qualified personnel, and implement modern information technologies in research and educational processes. Future research should focus on determining the most effective share of state participation in higher education management, developing models for "electronic government" in educational administration, and enhancing digital competencies among civil servants. Additionally, attention must be paid to creating innovative curricula and ensuring the accessibility of digital learning platforms. Ultimately, the strategic goal of state policy in education remains constant: to increase the availability of high-quality education that meets the requirements of innovative economic development and serves the needs of society and citizens in both Russia and Belarus. The challenge lies in balancing traditional sectoral governance principles with the flexibility and innovation demanded by digital transformation.

CHAPTER 13

Consumer Behavior in the Digital Educational Environment: Main Characteristics, Motives, and Impact Factors

Galina V. Astratova[1,*]

[1] *Department of Regional Economics, Innovative Entrepreneurship and Economics (REIE&E), Institute of Economics and Management, School of Public Administration and Entrepreneurship (SPAE), Ural Federal University (UrFU), Yekaterinburg 620002, Sverdlovsk Region, Russian Federation*

Abstract: This study explores consumer behavior in the digital educational environment, focusing on its characteristics, motivations, and influential factors. Through surveys of Russian and Belarusian students, the research examines the shift from traditional to digital educational consumer behavior in higher education. The study reveals significant differences between Russian and Belarusian students' perceptions of higher education as a guarantee of success, with Russians being more skeptical. Both groups demonstrate similar preferences in additional education programs, course content expectations, and value assessments. The research identifies the challenges students face in distance learning, including excessive materials, inconsistent teaching, and technological difficulties. Marketing strategies targeting "Generation C" and "Generation Z" are analyzed, with findings suggesting that personalized educational offerings, online reviews, university ratings, and social media advertising significantly influence consumer choices in both countries. The study contributes to the understanding of digital educational consumer behavior as a complex social and digital phenomenon currently in the formative stage of theoretical and practical study.

Keywords: Consumer behavior, Digital educational environment, Distance learning, EdTech, Generation C, Higher education services, Marketing strategies.

INTRODUCTION

One of the key mainstreams of our time is the active introduction of Digital Technologies (DT) into both business and daily human life. This determines the

* **Corresponding author Galina V. Astratova:** Department of Regional Economics, Innovative Entrepreneurship and Economics (REIE&E), Institute of Economics and Management, School of Public Administration and Entrepreneurship (SPAE), Ural Federal University (UrFU), Yekaterinburg 620002, Sverdlovsk Region, Russian Federation;
E-mail: galina_28@mail.ru

Galina V. Astratova, Maxim V. Vlasov, Chigozirim Ndubuisi Onwusiribe & Longinus D.N. Nnadozie (Eds.)

prioritization of digitalization in the economic development of the Union State of the Russian Federation and the Republic of Belarus. In the realities of the digital economy, there is also a significant change in marketing tools and the relationship between consumers/buyers and producers/sellers in all markets, including in the markets of educational services.

Speaking about the changing relations between an educational institution and its client, a consumer of educational and intellectual services, it is necessary to highlight the three main trends, in our opinion.

Firstly, due to the strengthening of market mechanisms in the global HES system, students have been "conceptualized" as consumers (or customers) of higher education services (Naidoo and Whitty, 2014).

Secondly, if earlier universities offered clients "standard sets" of educational services[1], by now it is becoming almost impossible. In the context of widespread "commodification[2] of higher education" and increased competition, both in local and global educational markets, universities are forced to continuously develop new types of educational and intellectual products/services targeted at specific consumer groups: schoolchildren, applicants, college and university graduates, adult audiences, as well as those who want to improve their skills, change the direction of activity, learn foreign languages, as well as take up hobbies and master personal growth programs, *etc*. This trend is described in our earlier publications (Astratova and Izmailov, 2024; Astratova *et al.*, 2023; Astratova *et al.*, 2022; Astratova and Klimuk *et al.*, 2021; Astratova *et al.*, 2021; Astratova *et al.*, 2019a; Astratova *et al.*, 2019b; Larionova *et al.*, 2019; *etc.*), as well as in the works of other authors (Abrami *et al.*, 2011; Belenova and Arenkov, 2021; Ermakova and Bagrova, 2016; Research EdMarket, 2022; *etc.*).

Thirdly, the development of e–learning technologies (EdTech) using the Internet significantly contributes to the process of "commodification of higher education", which is especially important in the context of the current growth in the number of MOOCs offering mass online educational courses (Naidoo and Whitty, 2014). Indeed, the galloping development of the digital economy provides easy and fast access for individuals to various services *via* the Internet, including intellectual–intensive products and educational services (MOOCs, among others). This trend is described in the articles of a number of authors (Aguaded, 2013; Ainslee, 2018; Astratova & Izmailov, 2024; Research EdMarket, 2022, *etc.*).

---

1 For example, in the pre-digital era, a student had the opportunity to receive only one basic educational program, and additional training programs took the form of electives, or were mastered after completing the basic program. In the digital age, a student can simultaneously master several educational programs, both basic and additional directions.

2 "Commodification" (from "commodity", i.e., "product") is a process in which an increasing number of different types of human activity acquires monetary value and becomes a commodity bought and sold on the market.

Thus, the above trends emphasize the increasing importance of knowledge of consumer behavior in the digital educational environment: the main characteristics and motives for choosing intellectual-intensive products and educational services, as well as marketing tools to influence consumer choice.

Moreover, as we have repeatedly noted earlier (Astratova & Izmailov, 2024; Astratova, 2023b; Astratova *et al.*, 2023; Astratova *et al.*, 2022; Astratova *et al.*, 2021; Astratova *et al.*, 2019a; Astratova *et al.*, 2019b; Larionova *et al.*, 2019; *etc.*), knowledge of the characteristics of consumer behavior in the digital educational environment, it is also important for universities that are exists in conditions of limited budgets and the need to optimize them in the process of choosing priority vectors of digital educational technologies and software, as well as the most cost-effective educational programs and courses.

At the same time, many questions on the stated issues are very debatable, and the theoretical and methodological basis of "digital behaviorism" in general, and in the educational services market, in particular, and in the sector HES, especially, is still being formed, both in the Russian Federation and the Republic of Belarus, and abroad. For example, as noted in a fundamental study by Güngör and Cadirci (2022), combining machine learning algorithms and bibliometric analysis, the key topics of journal articles in 5-year intervals and their evolution over time were identified. The results of the study of these authors show that digitalization has become an integral aspect of the main consumption patterns. Moreover, the study identifies three key areas of consumer behavior research in the digital environment, or "digital consumers."

- The use of well-known classical theories of marketing and consumption, as well as their application in the context of digitalization;
- Analysis of consumer behavior individually and in a group (transactional analysis) in a digital environment;
- The impact of marketing on the consumption of certain types and groups of digital goods and services (Güngör and Cadirci, 2022).

In this regard, we will consider some of the most important positions in our opinion concerning area number 3: "the impact of digital marketing on the consumption of certain product groups" (Güngör and Cadirci, 2022, p. 1829), namely: features of consumer behavior in a digital educational environment.

We will conduct the author's research according to the following plan: 1) portrait of the consumer of digital educational services (EdTech); 2) features of consumer behavior of EdTech; 3) effective marketing tools in the EdTech market that affect the consumer.

Portrait of a Consumer of Digital Educational Services (EdTech)

According to the theory of generations by N. Howe and V. Strauss (1997), a set of people born in the same time period (20-25 years) have common beliefs and behaviors, as well as a sense of belonging to their "group". These "groups" of generations were identified by N. Howe and V. Strauss:

- "Baby Boomers": people born in 1943-1960, whose age in 2024 is 81 years – 64 years;
- "Generation X": They were born in 1961-1981, and are now 63-43 years old;
- "Millennials" ("Millennials" or "Generation Y"): They were born in 1982-2005, and are now 42 years old – 19 years old;
- "Generation Z" (Generation of "Homebodies"): They were born in 2006 and beyond, and are now 18 or less years old (Strauss and Howe, 1997).

Despite the heated discussions around this theory (Zhavoronkova, 2023), it is relevant to this day, because on its basis it is not only possible to track current trends and make forecasts of the development of society, but also "... teach representatives of different generations to better understand and interact with each other, track and understand what employees and managers in the coming decades, and, consequently, what the business environment as a whole will be like" (Ozhiganova, 2015, p. 4). Moreover, the theory of generations by N. Howe and V. Strauss (1997) is used in their research by many scientists in Russia, Belarus, and abroad, as it provides an opportunity to explain consumer behavior in various industries and fields of activity in the digital environment (Astratova *et al.*, 2019a; Piatrov and Kusá, 2019; Zhavoronkova, 2023; *etc.*).

In the context of our research, "Generation Z" and "Generation C" are interesting

"Generation Z" (Generation of "Homebodies") – this is the one who "lives with a smartphone in his hands", understands technical innovations, and gadgets. The main sources of information for this generation are photos, audio/video (music, songs, movies); they perceive text information poorly, therefore, they do not like to read. At the same time, they pay great attention to their appearance, as well as " ... fight for ultra-popular values: gender equality, care for nature and animals, privacy, freedom of expression. They are influenced by fashion bloggers and youth influencers. They are interested in popular science, art, and creativity[1]." The

1 Theory of generations (X, Y, Z) in Internet marketing // Marketing. – 07/13/2021. – [Electronic resource]. URL: https://vc.ru/marketing/266386-teoriya-pokolenii-x-y-z-v-internet-marketinge?EA2872EC-68C7-C646-AD91-2DE2A664DE58_kfa_cup_C6FA3ED5_6D17_47D1_B6E2_F4B02CC905E0_(accessed 06/19/2024). (In Russ.).

values of this generation are: material security, freedom, comfort and safety, science and art, a healthy lifestyle, home and family, and friends.

"Generation C" (from the words "connected users" or connected clients), allocated in 2012, unlike the "groups" of the generations of N. Howe and V. Strauss (1997), is not a demographic, but, above all, a psychographic group, not limited by age, but connected by values, interests, personal qualities, views and lifestyle, and not by the time of their birth (Grishaeva, *et al.*, 2022; Hurdey, 2011; Piatrov and Kusá, 2019; Solis, 2015; Solis, 2018; *etc.*).

It is important that "Generation C" is a "digital natives" who have "integrated technology into all aspects of their daily lives[1]." In this regard, we can say that "Generation C" and "Generation Z" are close, but differ only in age: "Generation C" has no age restrictions, but "Generation Z" does. Accordingly, in the context of our study, it is more convenient to use the term "Generation C", since educational services can be used by people without age restrictions and study throughout their whole lives.

To get answers to the questions: 1) "Who is the consumer of digital educational services (EdTech)? and 2) "What are the main characteristics and motives of consumer behavior in the digital environment?" We conducted an online survey[2] of students in the Russian Federation and the Republic of Belarus. The survey data was processed using Google Docs, Microsoft Excel, Statistica, and taking into account the recommendations of N.K. Malhotra on methods of economic and statistical analysis (Malhotra, 2002).

It was revealed that the ratio of men and women among respondents was approximately equal for the Republic of Belarus, and about 45:55 for the Russian Federation, which corresponds to the gender ratio in the system of Russian and Belarusian higher education (Bengraf *et al.* 2024; Education in numbers, 2023; Women and men, 2022) (Fig. **1**).

---

1 Bosley-Plump Charlotte. 6 things you need to know about Generation C. – February 10. – 2021. – [Electronic resource]. URL: https://www.airswift.com/blog/generation-c (accessed: 19.06.2024).

2 The authors developed a questionnaire using standard measurement and scaling procedures using nominal, ordinal, interval and relative scales. The questionnaire consisted of three blocks: 1) Introduction; 2) Main content (34 questions); 3) Personal questions (7 questions). By using e-mail mailing lists and posting links to the questionnaire in Google docs on social networks (VKontakte, WhatsApp), university students from various Russian cities from Vladivostok to Kaliningrad took part in the survey, which was conducted from May 2023 to June 2024 – 1,520 people.

A similar study was conducted in the Republic of Belarus, which took place in two stages: 1) from May 2023 to June 2024, by link in Google docs and as a result of using the e-mail mailing list – 114 people; 2) from March 2024 to May 15, 2024, by address questionnaire of students of the Faculty of International Relations of the Belarusian State University, Minsk – 132 people; total – 246 people.

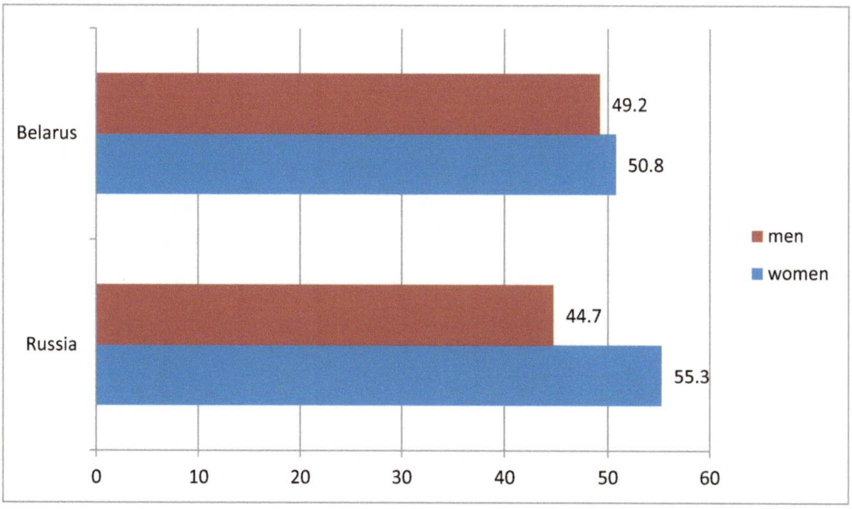

Fig. (1). Gender distribution of student youth in Russia and Belarus, %.
(N_{studRF}=1520; n_{studRF} = 1520; N_{studRB}= 246; n_{studRB} = 246; K_k = 0.20; K_c = 0.88).
Source: Survey data in google docs and processing in microsoft excel and statistica.

The age of the respondents was also determined: the majority of students, both in the Russian Federation and in the Republic of Belarus, were between the ages of 16 and 22. *i.e.*, 87.4% of Russians and 74.4% of Belarusians. The data obtained also correlate with data on the main composition of students enrolled in bachelor's and master's degrees in the Russian Federation and the Republic of Belarus (Bengraf *et al.* 2024; Education in numbers, 2023) (Fig. **2**).

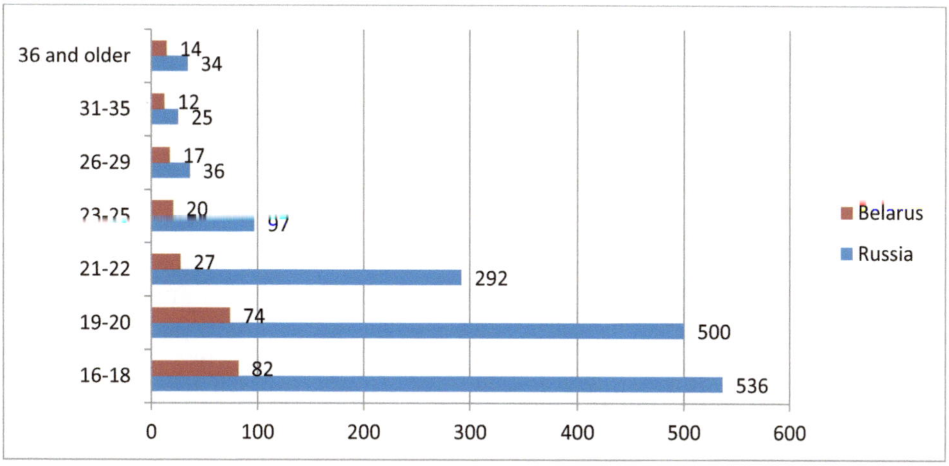

Fig. (2). Distribution of student youth in Russia and Belarusby age, people.
(N_{studRF}=1520; n_{studRF} = 1520; N_{studRB}= 246; n_{studRB} = 246; K_k = 0.21; K_c = 0.86).
Source: Survey data in google docs and processing in microsoft excel and statistica.

It was also interesting in the context of our research to understand who pays for university tuition, as well as what sources of income students have.

Fig. (**3**) shows that about half of the respondents study on a budget (48.3% of Russians and 45.5% of Belarusians) and about the same amount is paid, where parents pay for education from 32.0% of Russian students and 26.8% of Belarusian students; at the same time, 10.7% of Russians surveyed and 16.7% of Belarusians pay their own tuition.

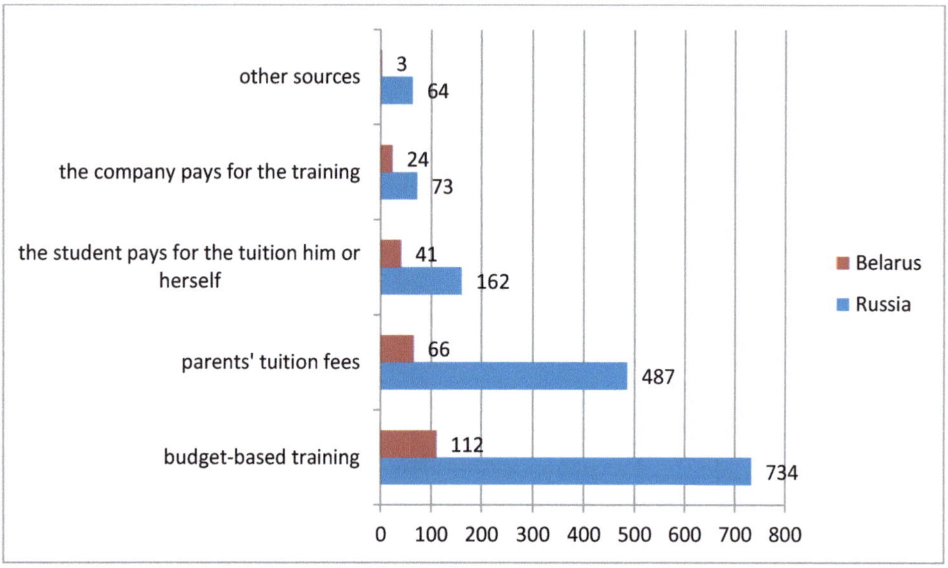

Fig. (3). Distribution of student youth in Russia and Belarus on tuition fees at the university, people. (N_{studRF}=1520; n_{studRF} = 1520; N_{studRB}= 246; n_{studRB} = 246; K_k = 0.21; K_c = 0.87).
Source: Survey data in google docs and processing in microsoft excel and statistica.

Fig. (**3**) shows that almost all respondents have several sources of income, including:

- Parents'/friends' money is in the first place (62.6% of Russians and 51.2% of Belarusians answered).
- Scholarship (43.4% and 51.2%, respectively) and salary (42.9% of the responses from Russians and 40.2% of Belarusians) are in second place.
- Savings are in third place (31.4% and 23.4%, respectively).

It was also considered necessary to determine the income level of consumers in the digital educational environment, so we used segmentation based on five groups, in the author's interpretation (Astratova, 2024, p. 79).

The results of the study show that both Russian and Belarusian students are generally approximately equally distributed by income level in Fig. (**4**): the majority of respondents (80.1% of Russians and 82.5% of Belarusians) It can be attributed to the middle class in terms of material security in the range from "middle class +" to "middle class – "(Table **1**).

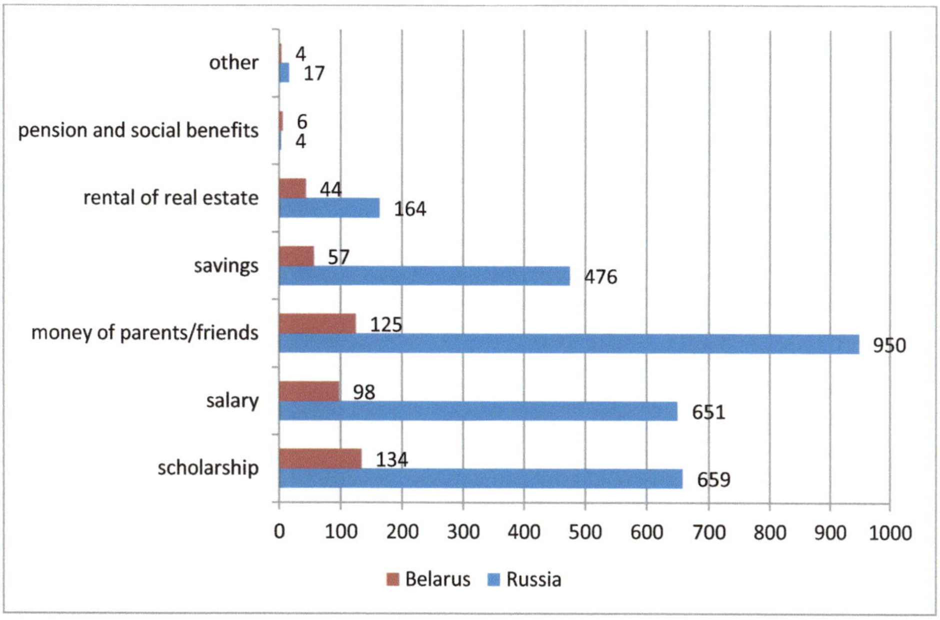

Fig. (4). Distribution of student youth in Russia and Belarusby sources of income during university studies, people; multiple choices of answers were allowed.
(N_{studRF}=1520; n_{studRF} = 1518; N_{studRB}= 246; n_{studRB} = 244; K_k = 0.21; K_c = 0.75)
Source: Survey data in Google Docs and processing in Microsoft Excel and Statistica.

Table 1. Gradation of consumers by income, in the author's interpretation (Astratova, 2024, p. 79), and calculation of the response rates of students in Russia and Belarus, % (N_{studRF}=1520, n_{studRF} = 1516; N_{studRB}= 246; n_{studRB} = 242; K_k = 0.20; K_c = 0.73)

Name of Consumer Groups	Descriptive Characteristics of Consumer Groups	Russians	Belarusians
1 level — «unsecured»	These are those citizens whose share of food expenses is more than 75% of the household budget and who answered in the affirmative to the following statement: "We live from paycheck to paycheck, there is not enough money even for food, we often have to borrow money for the most necessary things, savings are out of the question."	9.4	9.9

(Table 1) cont.....

Name of Consumer Groups	Descriptive Characteristics of Consumer Groups	Russians	Belarusians
2 level — «low-income»	These are those citizens whose share of food costs is high, but not more than 75% of the household budget, and who agreed with the assessment of their well-being as: "There is enough money for daily expenses and meals, but already buying clothes is difficult, we have to borrow or save money on purpose."	16.5	12.6
3 level — «medium-income»	These are those citizens whose share of food expenses does not exceed 50% of the household budget and for whom a statement like: "There is enough money for proper nutrition and good clothes, we can save something, but there is not enough savings for the purchase of durable goods (refrigerator, TV, furniture, *etc.*)."	36.7	44.5
4 level — «wealthy»	These are those citizens whose food costs do not exceed 25% of the household budget and who answered in the affirmative to the following statement: "There is enough money for proper nutrition and high-quality clothing, as well as durable goods, but buying an apartment, car, or cottage is not yet available."	26.9	25.4
5 level — «rich»	These are those citizens whose food expenses amount to no more than 15% of the household budget, and who agreed with the assessment of their well-being, as: "We practically do not deny ourselves anything: we can afford to buy almost everything: from expensive food and luxury goods to real estate."	10.5	7.6

Source: Survey data in google docs and processing in microsoft excel and statistica.

The data obtained also generally correspond to the distribution of poverty and wealth levels in the higher education system (Bengraf, *et al.* 2024; Education in Numbers, 2023; Women and Men, 2022).

Features of EdTech Consumer Behavior

As it is well known, in the traditional economy, the consumer behavior model can be expressed in a simple five-step linear scheme: 1) awareness of the problem; 2) search for information; 3) evaluation of options; 4) purchase decision; 5) reaction to the purchase (Kotler, 1991, p. 219).

This model is also applicable to consumer behavior in the educational services market, which in the traditional marketing system is a set of interrelated and interdependent actions, including awareness of the problem as "formation of the need for education", as well as "search for information about relevant educational service providers, evaluation of options, purchase decision and its subsequent assessment during direct consumption of educational services"; in this case, it is either getting an education, or using the acquired knowledge, skills and abilities to "... achieve professional or status goals" (Belenova & Arenkov, 2021, pp. 2924-2925).

Consumer Behavior has changed significantly in the Digital Economy

First of all, digital behavior is not synonymous with simply "using the Internet"; it becomes "need-personified[6]."As noted in the study by Flerov and Kutaitseva (2023), this is due to the fact that digital behavior "... includes not only technical and spatio-temporal characteristics of being online, but also meaningful personality-driven aspects of digital life," namely: "... *value-semantic, ideological, cognitive, motivational, and target components. They represent a complex of interrelated manifestations of human existence in the digital space in terms of their personal attitudes and motives for certain specific actions*" on the web (Flerov and Kutaitseva, 2023, p. 59). Other authors also note similar positions in their research (Belenova and Arenkov, 2021; Ermakova and Bagrova, 2016; Larionova *et al.*, 2019; Roy and Datta, 2022).

Secondly, the consumer's digital behavior model looks like a set of multiple transformations of information, namely: 1) information retrieval; 2) information consumption; 3) information production; 4) information exchange. This model is very close, in our opinion, to the theoretical model of information processing by James R. Bettman, based on cognitive assumptions and descriptions of the process of processing information about a product/service (Bettman 1979). However, as O.V. Flerova and O.N. Kutaitseva emphasize, "... the structure of digital behavior is the unity of all network actions" performed with information. Moreover, information consumption "... is a key information aspect of personal development in the digital environment" (Flerov and Kutaitseva, 2023, p. 59).

The consumer of digital educational services (EdTech) is in the conditions of "modification of consumer behavior", which can be described by the following main characteristics:

- "The growth of consumer competencies.
- Strengthening the influence of the information component when making a purchase decision.
- The consumer's perception of the product is primarily as a set of certain value characteristics.
- Personalization of needs.

6 The author's definition.

- Complications of the decision-making mechanism and standards.
- The leading role of the media in the formation of stereotypes of consumer behavior" (Belenova and Arenkov, 2021, p. 2925).

Based on theoretical approaches to the consumer behavior model in the online education market, it was considered advisable to obtain the necessary information on the stated issues through a survey of student youth in Russia and Belarus (Table **2**).

Table 2. Comparative analysis of the main attributes of consumer behavior in the online education market based on surveys of student youth in Russia and Belarus, % (*N_{studRF}=1520; n_{studRF} = 1518; N_{studRB}= 246; n_{studRB} = 243; K_k = 0.20; K_c = 0.73*).

Name of the Questions	Russians	Belarusians
1. Awareness of the need for higher education		
1) *Is higher education a guarantee of success in life today?* (There is no alternative choice of the answer)		
No	44.7	12.5
Yes, if you make an effort	25.2	22.4
Yes	29.1	64.6
I don't know	1	0.5
2) *What is the most important thing in your life?* (Multiple choices were allowed)		
peaceful sky overhead	57.2	58.3
health	56.6	54.3
family and children	52.3	53.4
true love	49.8	50.0
financial well-being	40.6	42.3
friendship	36.8	37.3
interesting work	30.7	32.4
freedom in different ways	23.9	19.5
to help people	15.7	12.4
3) *How do you feel about distance learning? (There is no alternative choice of the answer)*		
I am for online learning, and I really like this format	35.7	23.0
I prefer the traditional form of education	14.5	65.0
I am in favor of the hybrid format	49.8	12.0
3) *On which platform does distance learning take place at your university?* (Multiple choices were allowed)		
Zoom	38.4	23.7
Microsoft Teams	36.7	9.6
Moodle	21.2	7.4

(Table 2) cont.....

Name of the Questions	Russians	Belarusians
Big Blue Button	17.8	4.1
Puzzle English	9.2	1.3
Yandex Teleconference	4.3	0.1
Opendu.ru	5.6	0.2
Google Meet	3.2	1.3
Electronic Information and Educational Environment (EIOS)	2.3	0.6
To-Study	1.2	5.9
Viber	1.1	15.3
Skype	1.1	14.1
others	1.1	0.3
4) In which areas of additional professional education would you like to study remotely? (Multiple choices were allowed)		
foreign languages	52.6	54.8
psychology	51.3	50.6
IT sphere (programming)	46.9	47.1
marketing, management	31.3	32.4
design	28.8	26.3
economics and finance	27.5	28.4
advertising	19.5	20.1
law	19.3	18.9
sports and fitness	16.2	16.6
beauty services	14.3	12.7
other	1.2	1.3
5) What should a good online course include? (Multiple choices were allowed)		
Presentations with videos and films	51.6	51.9
Guides for easy memorization of the material	52.2	50.3
Webinars	51.4	49.8
Practical cases	47.6	44.8
Tests	46.3	44.5
Video recording of the course	38.4	38.8
Control points	34.3	33.8
The list of recommended literature	27.7	29.9
Audio recording of the course	20.7	19.3
Titles/comments in Russian	20.2	18.9

(Table 2) cont.....

Name of the Questions	Russians	Belarusians
6) What is important for you when choosing an online course? (multiplechoiceswereallowed)		
Completeness of the material	58.3	57.9
Professionalism and experience of the teacher	55.7	59.8
Feedback	50.8	54.4
User-friendly interface	48.4	50.6
Open discussions	35.6	38.8
Availability of homework	30.9	25.4
Forms of control	27.9	28.0
Connection with practice	13.7	15.4

Source: Survey data in google docs and processing in microsoft excel and statistica.

Table **2** shows that the awareness of the need for higher education differs significantly in fraternal countries: almost 45% of Russians believe that higher education is not a guarantee of success in life, and among Belarusians, the absolute majority (almost 65%) consider education to be a guarantee of success. The result shows, in our opinion, the gaps in the upbringing of the younger generation in the Russian Federation. As noted in our earlier research, we are deeply convinced that "education is a way of thinking for a person. Accordingly, the more multifaceted this way of thinking is, the brighter a person's personal and professional life develops. In other words, our author's position is that a good higher education is the guarantor of a person's success in life" (Astratova *et al.*, 2023, p. 14). Therefore, it is necessary to develop measures to eliminate the noted gap in education in order to comply with Russian legislative norms: "*Higher education aims to ensure the training of highly qualified personnel in all major areas of socially useful activities in accordance with the needs of society and the state, meeting the needs of the individual in intellectual, cultural and moral development, deepening and expanding education, scientific and pedagogical qualifications*"[7].

Table **2** also shows that the value choice (answers to the question of what is the most important thing in life for young people) for Russians and Belarusians is very close, since the main vectors are: a peaceful sky above your head (57.2-58.3%, respectively); health (56.6% and 54.3%); family and children (52.3% and 52.4%); love (49.8% and 50.0%) are the prevailing values. At the same time,

---

7 Article 69. Higher education. Federal Law No. 273-FZ of 12/29/2012 (as amended on 02/17/2023) "On Education in the Russian Federation" (with amendments and additions, intro. effective from 02/28/2023). [electronic resource]. URL: https://www.consultant.ru/document/cons_doc_LAW_140174/779e21e98202dcc3c9d0dd5994c7d061e7ab1f5f / (date of access: 05/27/2023).

40.6% of Russians and 42.3% of Belarusians also note financial independence as an indicator of success in life. It is important that the answers received by almost 98.8% fall into the range of values when answering the question: "What is life success?", since the answers of both Russians and Belarusians are distributed as follows, in descending order:

- Be healthy
- Be safe
- Have a good family
- To love and be loved
- Be financially independent
- To do an interesting/favorite thing

From the data in Table **2**, it can be concluded that Russians are more inclined to a hybrid learning format (49.8%), although the share of those who prefer online learning is also large (35.7%). Belarusians have a slightly different picture: the majority votes for the traditional form of education (65.0%), which can be explained by the insufficient development of digital technologies in the Republic of Belarus. At the same time, although respondents indicated that distance learning takes place on a wide range of digital platforms, in most Russian and Belarusian universities, the following four platforms are used, in descending order: Zoom, Microsoft Teams, Moodle, and Big Blue Button.

As for the choice of additional education programs, both Russian and Belarusian students turned out to be surprisingly similar in their preferences: foreign languages come first; psychology comes second, and in third place is the IT sphere (programming), since over 45% of respondents chose these directions (Table **2**).

As for the content of a good online course, according to students, the opinions of Russians and Belarusians also converge here, since they were named. In descending order, the following characteristics:

- Presentations with videos and movies
- Guides for easy memorization of the material
- Webinars
- Practical cases
- Tests
- Video recording of the course
- Control points
- List of recommended literature

- Audio recording of the course
- Titles/comments in Russian

When choosing an online course, both Russians and Belarusians are also unanimous in assessing the characteristics, since the following attributes were named in descending order:

- Completeness of the material
- Professionalism (teaching experience)
- Teacher feedback
- User-friendly interface
- Open discussions of the subject being studied in the classroom
- Availability of homework
- Forms of control
- Connection with practice

It was also important to know what types of devices students use for distance learning. It is expected that the majority of Russians and Belarusians use a mobile phone (Fig. **5**).

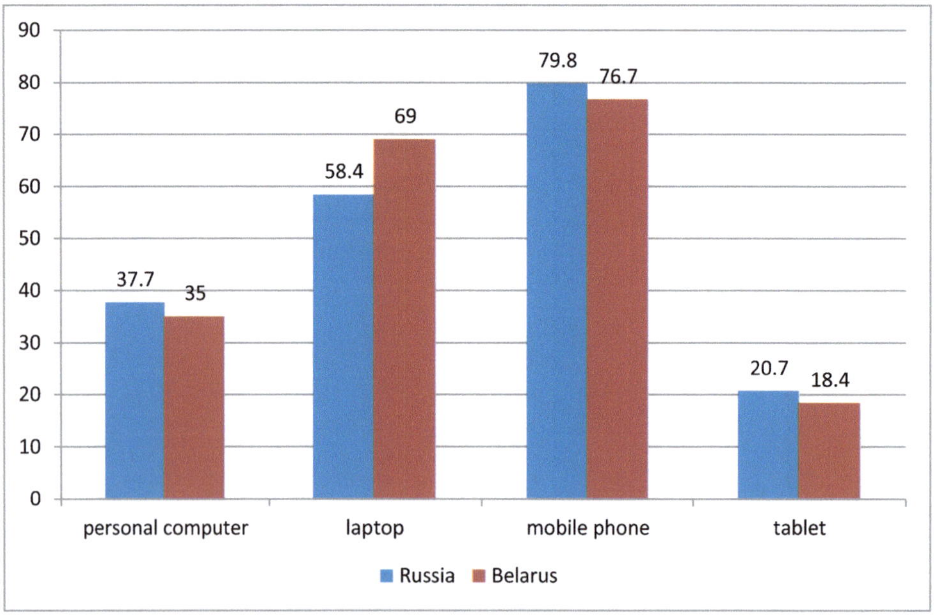

Fig. (5). Distribution of students in Russia and Belarus by types of devices used for distance learning, %; multiple-choice answers were acceptable.
(N_{studRF}=*1520;* n_{studRF} = *1520;* N_{studRB}= *246;* n_{studRB} = *246;* $K_k = 0.20$; $K_c = 0.88$).
Source: Survey data in google docs and processing in microsoft excel and statistica.

It is also important to consider what difficulties students face in the process of distance learning (Fig. **6**).

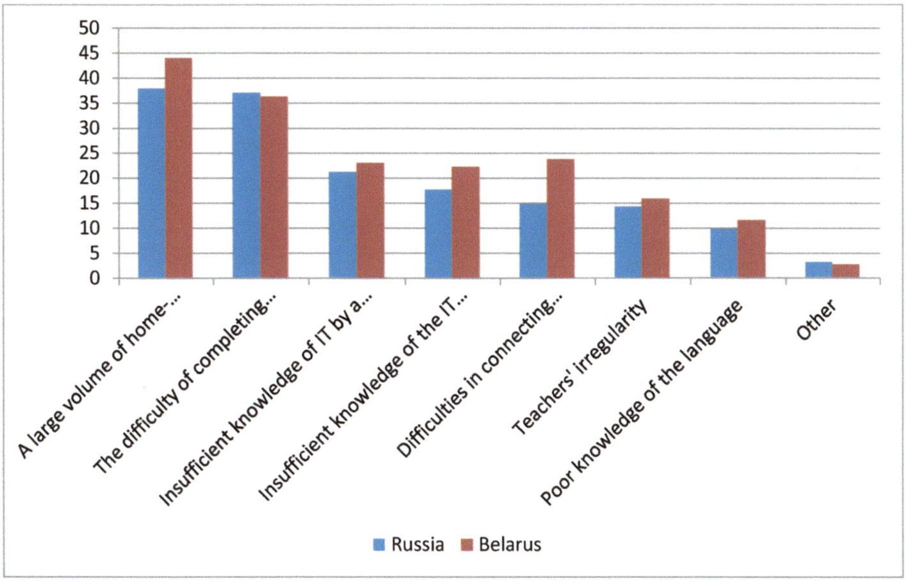

Fig. (6). Distribution of the student youth of Russia and Belarus according to the answer to the question: "What difficulties have you encountered in the process of distance learning?", %; multiple-choice answers were allowed.
(N_{studRF}=1520; n_{studRF} = 1517; N_{studRB}= 246; n_{studRB} = 243;K_k = 0.18; K_c = 0.86).
Source: Survey data in google docs and processing in microsoft excel and statistica.

Fig. (**6**) states that the large volume of materials given at home, together with the irregularity of teaching staff (*i.e.*, the untimely presentation of materials and homework by teachers), as well as difficulties in mastering technology on the part of teaching staff and the student, expectedly lead to the difficulty of completing practical tasks without explanations from the teacher. The linguistic problem also draws attention to itself: not all students understand the language of instruction, which is typical for English-language programs.

Although our survey data show that over 67% of students, both Russians and Belarusians, rate the work of teaching staff in the distance format as "excellent" and "good", it is obvious, in our opinion, that the problems indicated in Fig. (**6**) should become a field for active activity to improve the educational process at the university in the distance the format.

The most difficult question turned out to be the question of how much money students are willing to pay for their studies. It is expected that over 30% of both Russians and Belarusians would like to receive any kind of education free of charge (Figs. **7** and **8**).

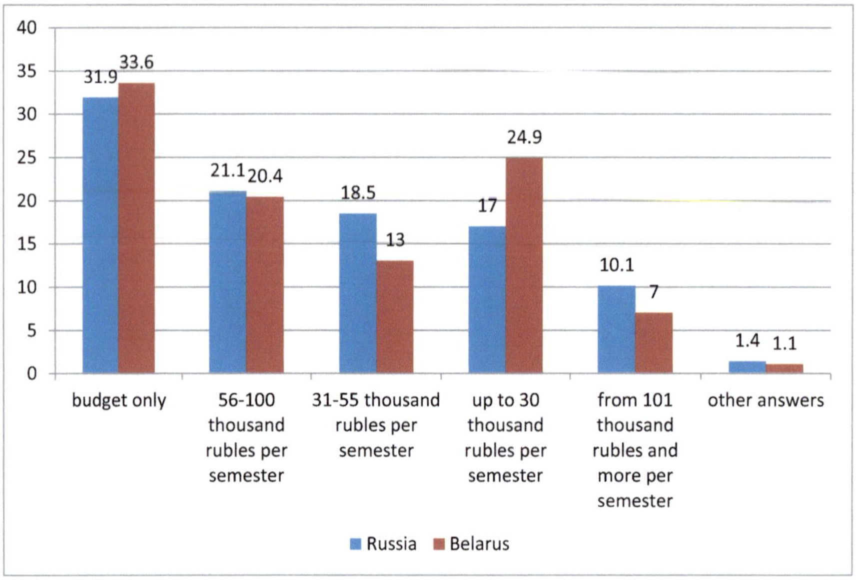

Fig. (7). Distribution of student youth in Russia and Belarus according to the survey responses: "How much money are you willing to pay for a basic higher education program?".
(N_{studRF}=1520; n_{studRF} = 1518; N_{studRB}= 246; n_{studRB} = 245; K_k = 0.21; K_c = 0.87)
Source: Survey data in Google Docs and processing in Microsoft Excel and Statistica.

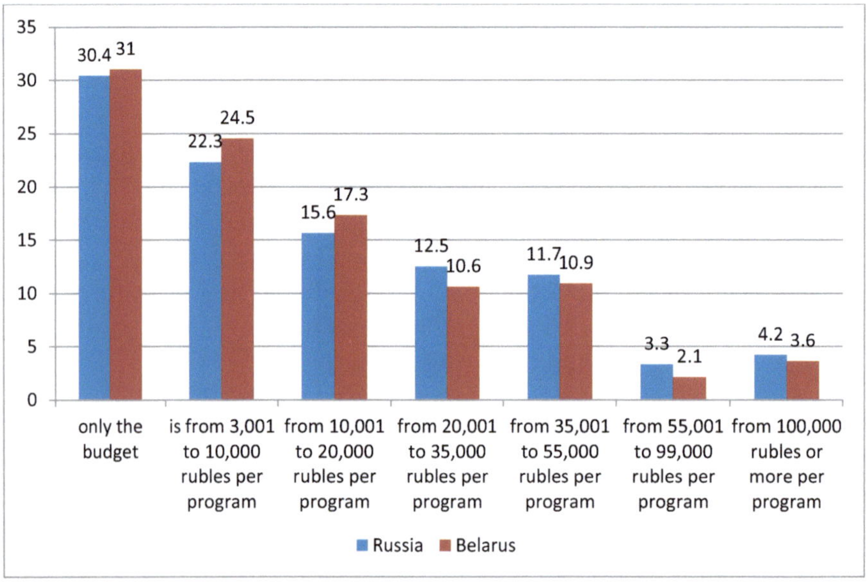

Fig. (8). The distribution of the student youth of Russia and Belarus according to the survey responses: "How much money are you willing to pay for an additional vocational training program?".
(N_{studRF}=1520; n_{studRF} = 1516; N_{studRB}= 246; n_{studRB} = 242; K_k = 0.23; K_c = 0.84).
Source: Survey data in google docs and processing in microsoft excel and statistica.

The data obtained as a result of a survey of student youth in Russiaand Belarus are consistent with the results of our earlier studiesof consumer behavior on different markets (Astratova and Izmailov, 2024; Astratova *et al.*, 2023; Astratova *et al.*, 2022; Astratova and Klimuk *et al.*, 2021; Astratova *et al.*, 2021; Astratova *et al.*, 2019a; Astratova *et al.*, 2019b; Astratova, 2018a; Astratova, 2018b; *etc.*), as well as with the results of research by other authors on the stated issues (Fitzpatrick *et al.*, 2017; Grishaeva *et al.*, 2022; Güngör and Cadirci, 2022; Noor *et al.*, 2022; Roy and Datta, 2022; *etc.*).

Effective Marketing Tools in the EdTech Market that Affect the Consumer

For "Generation C" and "Generation Z" (the Generation of "Homebodies"), the following advertising strategies on the Internet may be working:

- "Advertising on social networks: TikTok, YouTube, Likee, Instagram
- Minimum text, the basis of advertising—photos, videos
- Recommendations through popular bloggers for this target audience
- Tracking trends and using them in advertising
- Emphasis on freedom of expression and tolerance
- Interactivity, the shortest way to the target action[8].

In this regard, we asked students about what they are guided by when choosing additional professional online education programs (Fig. **9**).

Fig. (**9**) states that, on the one hand, the consumer of HES is competent and tries to meet their own educational needs in a personalized way (about 50% of respondents' responses). On the other hand, we see that reviews on the Internet, the university's rating, and advertising on social networks have a significant impact on consumer choice in Russia and Belarus, and for over half of Belarusians, the advice of acquaintances is also important.

8 Theory of generations (X, Y, Z) in Internet marketing // Marketing. – 07/13/2021. – [Electronic resource]. URL: https://vc.ru/marketing/266386-teoriya-pokolenii-x-y-z-v-internet-marketinge?EA2872EC-68C7-

C646-AD91-2DE2A664DE58_kfa_cup_C6FA3ED5_6D17_47D1_B6E2_F4B02CC905E0_(accessed 06/19/2024). (In Russ.).

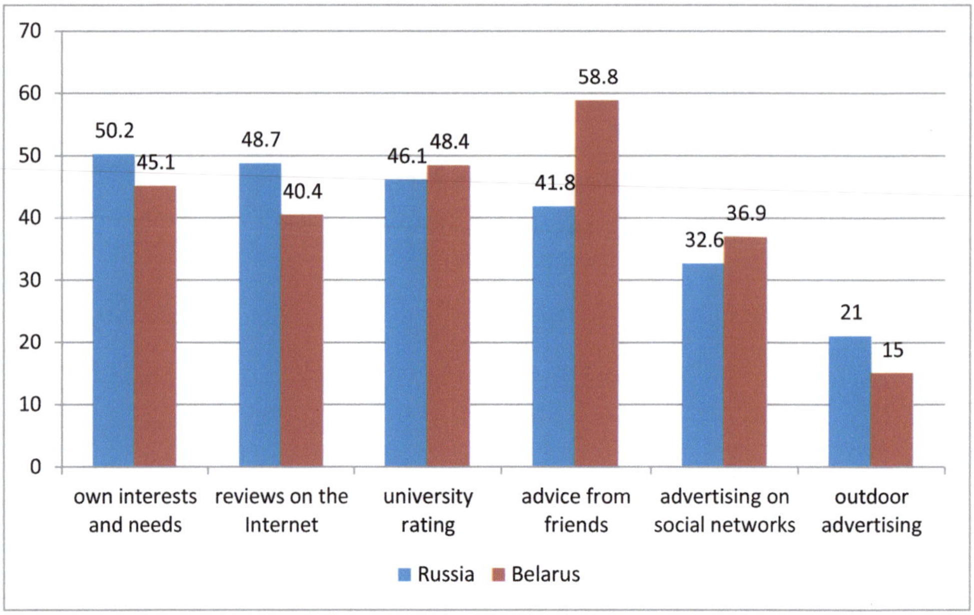

Fig. (9). The distribution of the student youth of Russia and Belarus according to the survey responses: "What do you focus on when choosing a program of additional professional online education?" Multiple-choice answers were allowed.
(N_{studRF}=1520; n_{studRF} = 1519; N_{studRB}= 246; n_{studRB} = 241; K_k = 0.22; K_c = 0.86).
Source: Survey data in google docs and processing in microsoft excel and statistica.

It should be noted that, as the results of our earlier studies have shown (using the example of voters of political parties in the city of Yekaterinburg), that the best tools for promoting political parties on the Internet, giving the greatest feedback, are, in descending order: 1) Social networks – 59.2% of respondents' responses; 2) Internet sites – 43.5%; 3) Blogs – 32.5% (Astratova and Bekshaev, 2024). Accordingly, since we have already noted above in this monograph that the coordination mechanisms in the HES and public administration systems have a number of similar points, we believe that the data we have obtained may well be used in the development of marketing strategies for promoting the educational services of universities in the digital environment.

Moreover, we believe that marketing tools that influence consumers in the digital environment should become a field for further research and activities to promote educational programs of Russian and Belarusian universities in a remote format.

Summarizing the content of this section, we consider it necessary to note that in modern conditions consumer behavior in the digital educational environment is a complex social and digital phenomenon, where the theory and practice of studying the main characteristics, motives and factors of influence on the consumer are in the stage of active formation both in the Russian Federation and the Republic of Belarus, and beyond.

CONCLUSION

This research presents a comprehensive analysis of consumer behavior in the digital educational environment, revealing several important findings and implications for educational institutions in Russia and Belarus. The study demonstrates that consumer behavior in the digital educational environment represents a complex social and digital phenomenon that extends beyond mere internet usage, encompassing value-semantic, ideological, cognitive, motivational, and target components. The digital behavior model manifests as multiple transformations of information through retrieval, consumption, production, and exchange processes.

Our findings reveal distinct differences in how Russian and Belarusian students perceive higher education's value. While 64.6% of Belarusian students consider higher education a guarantee of success in life, only 29.1% of Russian students share this view. This significant disparity signals a concerning gap in educational values among Russian youth that requires attention from educational policymakers to realign with legislative norms emphasizing higher education's role in intellectual, cultural, and moral development. Despite these differences, both Russian and Belarusian students exhibit remarkably similar value orientations, prioritizing peace, health, family, love, and financial independence. These shared values transcend national boundaries and provide important insights for developing educational marketing strategies. The research identifies a notable difference in learning format preferences, with Russians favoring hybrid (49.8%) and online formats (35.7%), while Belarusians predominantly prefer traditional education (65.0%). This distinction likely reflects varying levels of digital technology adoption between the two countries.

Regarding additional education program preferences, both nationalities show striking similarities, with foreign languages, psychology, and IT/programming ranking as the top three desired fields. Similarly, expectations for online course content converge around presentations with multimedia elements, study guides, webinars, practical cases, and assessment tools. When selecting online courses, students from both countries prioritize content completeness, instructor expertise, feedback mechanisms, and user-friendly interfaces. The study identifies several challenges in distance learning, including excessive materials, irregular teaching staff engagement, technological difficulties, and problems completing practical tasks without direct instructor guidance. These issues, despite generally positive ratings for teaching staff performance, represent critical areas for improvement in distance education delivery.

Consumer behavior in the digital educational environment is characterized by increased competencies, stronger influence of information on decision-making, perception of educational products as value sets, personalized needs, complex decision mechanisms, and media influence on behavioral stereotypes. Marketing strategies targeting “Generation C” and “Generation Z” should focus on social media advertising, visual content, influencer recommendations, trend awareness, emphasis on expression freedom, and interactive approaches. Student responses regarding factors influencing their choice of additional online education reveal a dual nature of the modern educational consumer: independently meeting personalized educational needs while being significantly influenced by online reviews, university rankings, and social media advertising. For Belarusian students, recommendations from acquaintances hold particular importance. The research suggests that social networks, internet sites, and blogs represent the most effective tools for promoting educational services in the digital environment, aligning with previous findings on promotion mechanisms in related fields. These digital marketing channels should be further developed as part of comprehensive strategies for promoting educational programs at Russian and Belarusian universities.

In conclusion, consumer behavior in the digital educational environment remains in an active formative stage both theoretically and practically. Educational institutions must adapt their approaches to address the evolving characteristics, motives, and influential factors affecting student consumers in the digital age. Future research should focus on developing effective marketing tools tailored to the digital educational environment and exploring how technological advancements continue to reshape consumer behavior patterns in higher education. Additionally, investigating the long-term implications of varied educational format preferences between Russian and Belarusian students could provide valuable insights for institutional planning and international educational collaboration initiatives.

CHAPTER 14

Artificial Intelligence and Data Analytics in the Organization of the Educational Process and Quality Assessment of Higher Education

Evgeny V. Sinitsyn[1,*] and **Viola A. Larionova**[2]

[1] *Department of Management, Institute of Economics and Management, Ural Federal University (UrFU), Yekaterinburg 620002, Sverdlovsk Region, Russian Federation*

[2] *Department of Economics and Management of Construction and Real Estate Market, Ural Federal University (UrFU), Yekaterinburg 620002, Sverdlovsk Region, Russian Federation*

Abstract: This paper examines the integration of Artificial Intelligence (AI) and data analytics in higher education, with particular focus on their applications in educational process organization and quality assessment. The research explores how generative AI technologies like ChatGPT and YandexGPT are transforming educational methodologies, student-teacher interactions, and assessment practices. Through theoretical analysis and application of information theory, the study presents mathematical models for evaluating Control and Measurement Materials (CMM) in educational settings. A framework for analyzing individual digital profiles of students is proposed, incorporating state vectors and Markov processes to predict learning outcomes and assess educational quality. The findings suggest that while AI presents challenges to traditional educational paradigms, its strategic implementation can enhance student engagement, support personalized learning trajectories, develop critical thinking skills, and improve overall educational quality when integrated with appropriate analytics tools and pedagogical approaches.

Keywords: Artificial intelligence, Educational quality assessment, Generative AI, Individual digital profiles, Information theory, Learning analytics, Markov processes.

INTRODUCTION

The advent of the 21st century was characterized by the rapid evolution of Artificial Intelligence (AI), which was introduced to a multitude of economic activities: medicine, banking, retail, security, science, education, *etc*. Today, the

* **Corresponding author Evgeny V. Sinitsyn:** Department of Management, Institute of Economics and Management, Ural Federal University (UrFU), Yekaterinburg 620002, Sverdlovsk Region, Russian Federation;
E-mail: sinitsyn_ev@mail.ru

Galina V. Astratova, Maxim V. Vlasov, Chigozirim Ndubuisi Onwusiribe & Longinus D.N. Nnadozie (Eds.)

implementation of AI as a core tenet of business processes and its application as a decision-making tool is essential for sustaining market position and serves as a transformational force for entire industries. Further, the emergence of advanced generative models represents another revolution in the maturation of intellectual technologies (Lutsenko and Golovin, 2024), and a new stage in the transformation of the division of labor system that will produce inevitable changes in social and economic relations on a global scale.

Generative AI generates conditions to interact with machines on a natural language basis, allowing virtually any person, including people without specialized programming language proficiency, to extract useful information from the vast expanse of data at their disposal by leveraging the Internet. With a high enough level of computing power of modern computers, GPT almost becomes an accessible working tool for specialists regardless of their background or field of work. This prescribes its widespread application across a number of professional fields and the requirement of appropriate training to utilize this technology in the resolution of practical tasks.

ChatGPT, DALL-E, and the Russian YandexGPT are examples of knowingly accepted tools based on machine learning. According to statistics, more than 1.8 million visitors accessed ChatGPT[1] in April 2023. Of these, about 60 percent were aged 18 to 34. This apparatus does not just analyze and classify information, but also generates written or visual material. Yandex has announced the launch of the third generation of language models, which is more efficient in working with requests that have multiple conditions and is capable of providing a more extensive and accurate response to the user's task[2]. The Russian neural network YandexGPT, unlike ChatGPT, allows the user to ask a question by voice, but unfortunately, it has not come close to creating poems and translating texts like their foreign counterpart. New neural networks are excellent in customer service, online sales, digital communications, marketing, advertising, and personal management, and can even write in any programming language you ask for. However, you must always be mindful to recognize that a neural network can simply fabricate an illusion or a fake answer that has no relation to reality. This requires the user to be sufficiently immersed in the topic and to think critically to recognize and understand the mistake.

---

1 Source: [Electronic resource]. URL: https://www.similarweb.com/website/chat.openai.com/#traffic (accessed 06/28/2024)

2 Source: [Electronic resource]. URL:https://yandex.ru/company/news/02-28-03-2024 (accessed: 06/ 28/2024).

Generative AI is yet another challenge for the education system. There is a heated debate in the international academic community regarding whether it is a threat (for example, to the traditional grading system) or whether it opens up new educational opportunities for students and can become an indispensable teaching assistant. Either way, generative AI is already disrupting the education system, introducing changes in the design of pedagogy and management of educational processes, the development of test materials, as well as student-teacher interaction (Walczak and Cellary, 2023). It is essential to think about how systemically higher education with GPT can co-exist and be utilized to enhance students' education engagement and development of professional competencies and soft skills, individualize educational trajectories, and overall increase the quality of learning.

This technology is most frequently applied to assess and provide feedback on student work in the higher education sector, including student essays and written work (Escalante *et al.*, 2023), a variety of graphics, design, and other work (Almasre, 2024), and coding and programming work (Richards *et al.*, 2024). For example, S.S. Biswas in his study illustrates how ChatGPT can be used for mediation of models, data analysis and interpretation, scenario and model assessment (Biswas, 2023). H..Marzuki and colleagues observed a positive effect of ChatGPT on the quality of students' writing work, mostly on the aspects of its content and structure of the writing (Marzuki, *et al.*, 2023). Lastly, J. Qadir sees ChatGPT as a superior modern tool to create realistic in-action virtual simulations (Qadir, 2023). However, for the scholar, although a high level of engagement is provided through the technology, it is not necessarily an effective means of engaging in the strong possibility of developing realistic virtual simulations. In addition, it is doubly problematic that not only will it provide fictitious information and tailor the way in which learners engage, but it also provides defective information and a false sense of reality for students. A similar view regarding the possible conclusions regarding ChatGPT is that of R.W. Although not based on an extensive quantitative study, McGee (2023) argues that the actual intelligence displayed by AI during statistical analysis is virtually non-existent at this time.

AI is being used as a pedagogical design field by teachers to build educational programs/course content (Sridhar *et al.*, 2023). For example, with neural networks, we can generate images such as Sberbank's Kandinsky neural network (https://fusionbrain.ai). Not only can we get high-quality and unique images, but we can do it without issues of copyright. Another way to use AI is to take a text file and convert it to a voice file for posting on a variety of platforms, a voice-over of a presentation, or collaborating on a project together. A good neural network for voicing text would allow you to set accents, add voice effects in a simple visual editor, and voice text in multiple languages. Freetts (https://freetts.ru) is such a free service for voice-over text, and adding an audio track with more than one male or female voice can alter speech speed and pitch. Even more advanced services, such as Apihost (https://apihost.ru), could support more than forty languages; more than 30 male and female voices; and have additional settings that may include things like pitch, style, and tone of voice. There are also specialized services to produce musical accompaniment and for educational games.

Nevertheless, the chatbot feature on the learning management platform gives students the possibility of receiving spontaneous responses to any questions they might have during their studies. It improves learning and helps to support students' anxiety levels. P.P. Ray, in his study, suggested that ChatGPT has the potential to help students' well-being while studying in a university education context, in particular, online or blended learning environments, when they could be isolated geographically (Ray, 2023). ChatGPT enables a sense of presence and social engagement by offering customized support based on the unique academic and emotional needs of each student.

Moreover, GPT can act as a virtual consultant, and by analysing students' messages, it will signal, by any disorderly conduct in the style and language, the first signs of psychological disorders to the tutor or course leader in a timely manner. Fitzpatrick *et al.* (2017) would also agree with this viewpoint because they recommended applying AI to develop a self-help program for anxiety and stress symptoms in students. There is no fear of judgment from others if students can freely discuss issues with ChatGPT. Support for this viewpoint is found in T. Kolenik and M. Gams' view that ChatGPT is an intelligent cognitive assistant that imitates the behaviours of humans (Kolenik and Gams, 2021).

Thus, ChatGPT has great potential for use in the educational process. While there are prospects for the implementation of ChatGPT in education, there are ethical policies from the university that need to be taken into consideration in order to ensure confidentiality and protection of personal information and data, and also to ensure that the dependence upon s technology is regulated. As this technology is new and with no prevailing opinion upon the effectiveness of interventions in the educational process, the potential, practical implementation, and pedagogical methods, impacts, and limitations of this technology require more research studies to be conducted. That said, we can be definite about the following:

- Generative AI can be embedded for use in the educational process from the first year of study in relation to various educational tasks with the mandatory engagement of students with the teacher, and in this context, the teacher's role takes on more of an expert context and the teacher has a more valuable role: he should teach the student to critically reflect on the results of interactions with the neural network.

- Generative AI is an intellectual tool similar to other intellectual tools and generative AI represents another category of tools, as do calculation programs, CAD-systems, software environments and others, therefore using generative AI results in the development of thinking in students, and the context in which students use generative AI represents the kind of results that can speak to their sophistication of their conceptual development.
- Generative AI is also a tool that can enable you to get a temporal sweep of the thinking process by reflecting on the prompts initiated by students and also the responses generated by the neural networks, which is relatively difficult to obtain using many other tools, where even in using that other tools, you can comment on some of the characteristics of student thinking such as, logical, coherence, systematic, outcome-driven, critical.
- Despite the low "entry threshold" when working with generative AI, preliminary training of students in the basics of prompt-engineering is required, which will allow students to acquire additional competencies and more consciously approach the work with the neural network, and the instructor to assess the development of their thinking in dynamics based on the results of the student's interaction with the neural network.

Learning Analytics Tools for Assessing the Quality of Education

The introduction of AI into educational activities, as well as other digital technologies that increase the flexibility and accessibility of learning, ensure the personalization of the educational trajectory, and achieve higher learning outcomes by students, should be accompanied by systematic research in the field of education quality. One of the main aspects of education quality is the level of competency formation in students by the time they graduate from university. This is directly related to the learning outcomes they achieve in various subjects and modules of the educational program.

During training, students of an educational program pass several mandatory checkpoints, in which the current level of mastery of the program is assessed. For an educational program, such checkpoints can be individual disciplines or modules included in it, interdisciplinary projects, results of the final state certification, and results of the defense of the graduation qualification work. Within individual disciplines, such checkpoints can be theoretical tests, homework, or projects on the discipline. Individual questions in theoretical tests or tasksin homework can also be considered as checkpoints.

In this case, the students' progress cannot serve as an objective criterion of the quality of training, because it is subjective on the part of teachers and depends on many factors. Even if we eliminate the subjective factor in the form of face-to-face exams and credits and replace them with an independent automated control of learning outcomes, the question remains the extent to which the database of test materials created by teachers meets the quality requirements based on known approaches of psychometrics (Crocker and Algina, 2010).

The problem is becoming more acute with the introduction of Massive Open Online Courses (MOOCs) in both higher education and continuing professional education. The relatively low cost of online learning, its high availability, and a wide range of opportunities for independent learning make this technology in demand despite several disadvantages arising from the lack of contact with the teacher and the low level of self-motivation of students.

The success of online course participants is certainly influenced by their individual perceptions of new information and the level of support they receive during the learning process. However, the degree of confidence in the results of online learning and the possibility of re-crediting them in the mainstream higher education program directly depends on the quality of course content and assessment materials. This is where learning analytics comes in, based on digital data that is accumulated in various university systems, on internal and external platforms, and contains information on all student learning activities and achievements.

Data analysis tools of open education platforms allow for a comprehensive assessment of the quality of course content and control and measurement materials based on the analysis of the digital footprint left on the open education platform, and to decide on the use of an online course in an educational program.

State Vectors and Individual Digital Profiles

To describe the results of a series of N checkpoints passed by a student, we will use a vector of dimension N, the components of which correspond to the passed checkpoints. In this case, we will distinguish between the checkpoints characterizing the current state of the learning process (*e.g.*, current tests, homework, *etc.*) and its result (final testing in the form of an exam or credit). This division is justified due to the importance of learning outcomes that confirm the achievement of the set goals. It can also be useful in solving problems related to predicting learning outcomes based on data on the current academic performance of students.

We will use a vector to describe the current state:

$$X = \{x_1, x_2, \dots, x_N\} \quad (1)$$

The components of the vector X can be both real numbers from the range [0.0,1.0], showing the number of points received for the checkpoint, and categoricalvariables taking values according to Table **1**.

Table 1. Values of nominal variables of students' performance, in the author's interpretation.

x_i	Assessment	Range of Received Points
2	Checkpointnotpassed – "unsatisfactory".	[0.0, 0.4]
3	The checkpoint is passed – "satisfactory". The student demonstrates knowledge and understanding of the basic provisions of the educational material, but makes inaccuracies in completing the tasks provided by the program.	[0.4, 0.6]
4	Checkpointpassed – "successful".	[0.6, 1.0]

We will use a vector to describe the learning outcome:

$$Y = \{y_1, y_2, \dots, y_K\}, \quad (2)$$

where,

y_j is the resulting score on one of the summative tests j. The number of summative tests can be K ($j \epsilon$ [1, K]).

The set of grades characterizing the current academic performance and the result of training will be called an individual digital profile of a student, for the description of which we will use a vector:

$$Y' = \{x_1, x_2, \dots, x_N | y_1, y_2, \dots, y_K\}, \quad (3)$$

The variables x_i are conditionally independent (independent of y_i), and y_i are conditionally dependent. For simplicity of calculations, we will often assume $K = 1$, which is a rather common situation when considering checkpoints in the framework of different disciplines.

The main goal of the project is to improve the quality of education. If it is necessary to use additional information about the listener, the vector (see equations 1, 2 and 3) can be extended with additional L conditionally independent variables z_l ($l \epsilon$ [1, L]), characterizing, for example, psycho-physiological features of the listener, the degree of attention during the passage of online course, peculiarities of the individual style of working with the computer while taking the online course, the number of attempts at passing tests, the listener's participation in extracurricular activities of the university, *etc*. By analogy with the reasoning above, a vector can be defined on these variables:

$$\boldsymbol{Z} = \{z_1, z_2, \dots, z_L\}. \quad \textbf{(4)}$$

The complete vector describing the individual digital profile of a listener can generally be represented as follows:

$$\boldsymbol{Z'} = \{x_1, x_2, \dots, x_N, z_1, z_2, \dots, z_L | y_1, y_2, \dots, y_K\}, \quad \textbf{(5)}$$

The vectors in equations 4 and 5 are named vectors conventionally, due to tradition, since they do not form a vector space (*e.g.*, the sum of any such vectors characterizing different listeners is an object that has no meaning). It is more correct to call the objects under consideration sets; however, due to the habitual use of the term "feature vector" in the tasks of data mining and machine learning, the vector terminology will be retained.

For any pair of vectors, we can introduce the notion of distance. In the case where the vector components are real variables, it can be Euclidean distance, Chebyshev distance, *etc*. For categorical variables as vector components, it can be the Hamming distance, the Jacques-Karas measure, *etc*.

If the components of vectors (1-5) are categorical variables according to Table **1**, it is possible to represent them as text strings obtained by "chaining" the components of vectors in text format:

$$\boldsymbol{X} = \{2, 2, 4, 4, 3, 4\} = 224434. \quad \textbf{(6)}$$

This way of representation can be useful for visualizing vectors, and opensa wide range of possibilities for applying text analytics techniques well developed in machine learning.

Information Theory Methods in Learning Analytics

Using equations 1-6 and assuming K = 1, the set of individual digital profiles S of the course attendees can be represented as Table **2**.

Table 2. Individual digital profiles of trainees, in the author's interpretation.

Listener ID	x_1	x_2	...	x_N	y
ID_1	x_{11}	x_{21}	...	x_N1	y_1
ID_2	x_{12}	x_{22}	...	x_N2	y_2
...	...	...	...	...	...
ID_S	x_{1S}	x_{2S}	-	x_{NS}	y_S

Using the notations introduced in Table **1** and the categorical conversions of trainees' performance according to Table **2**, we can assess the qualityof the Control and Measurement Materials (CMM) on the basis of the information theory (Wentzel, 2002).

Information Coefficient of the Checkpoint

Let us define for the checkpoint *x* the information entropy:

$$H(x_i) = -\sum_{j=2,3,4} P_{x_i(j)} log_3 P_{x_i(j)}, \quad \textbf{(7)}$$

where $P(_{xi\ (j)})$ is the probability of obtaining grade *j* at the end of the checkpoint x_i, which in practice will be calculated through the frequency ratio (Equation 7) (statistical probability of obtaining grade *j*):

$$P_{x_i(j)} = \frac{N_{x_i(j)}}{\sum_{j=2,3,4} N_{x_i(j)}} \quad \textbf{(8)}$$

Due to the fact that the base of the logarithm can be any number a > 1 and determines the entropy measurement units, let us choose a = 3 as the base and measure entropy in "ternary units" or "trites", since in the system under consideration, there are three possible states corresponding to equation 4 at the end of the checkpoint.

The change in information entropy can be used to estimate (Equation 8) the information contained in the message about the results of passing the checkpoint. After passing the checkpoint, the state of the system becomes known exactly, and its information entropy (a measure of uncertainty) becomes zero. In this case, information equals entropy:

$$Inf(x_i) = H(x_i) - 0 = H(x_i). \quad \textbf{(9)}$$

The information (in equation 9) is maximized when all three states are equally probable $P_{(2)} = P_{(3)} = P_{(4)} = 1/3$ and is thus equal to *Inf*(*max*) = 1 *trit*.

The information coefficient of the checkpoint in the general case can be defined as the ratio of information (equation 8) to the maximum information value, which in the chosen units of measurement will be a dimensionless value normalized by one:

$$I(x_i) = \frac{Inf(x_i)}{Inf(max)} \quad \mathbf{(10)}$$

The informativeness coefficient (equation 10) can be used to evaluate the CMM of an individual checkpoint, as well as to make recommendations to CMM developers for improvement.

Distribution of Individual Digital Profiles

In the process of mastering course materials and passing checkpoints between performance groups, for example, as in Table **2**, there are moves of students, which can be described as random wanderings of the studied subjects on the nodes of the oriented graph using the mathematical apparatus of the theory of Markov processes (Wentzel & Ovcharov, 1991).

In the following, we will denote the number of performance groups: $N_{(2)}$, $N_{(3)}$, $N_{(4)}$, and the relative shares of the group are: $n_{(2)}$, $n_{(3)}$, $n_{(4)}$:

$$N_{(2)} + N_{(3)} + N_{(4)} = N_{students}\text{или}n_{(2)} + n_{(3)} + n_{(4)} = 1 \quad \mathbf{(11)}$$

We will also assume that during the course, trainees do not drop out of the course, but only transfer between performance groups. In practice, this condition can be realized by excluding such trainees in equation 11 from the calculations.

The process of transitions between performance groups when passing the CMM checkpoint can be described using a matrix:

$$\widehat{\boldsymbol{P}} = \begin{Vmatrix} P_{22} & P_{23} & P_{24} \\ P_{32} & P_{33} & P_{34} \\ P_{42} & P_{43} & P_{44} \end{Vmatrix} \quad \mathbf{(12)}$$

The indices of the matrix P correspond to the designations of achievement groups. The matrix itself is non-symmetric and for indices $i = 2,3,4$ is $\sum_{j=2,3,4} P_{ij} = 1$.

Schematically, such transitions in equation 2 can be depicted as the directed graph shown in Fig. (**1**).

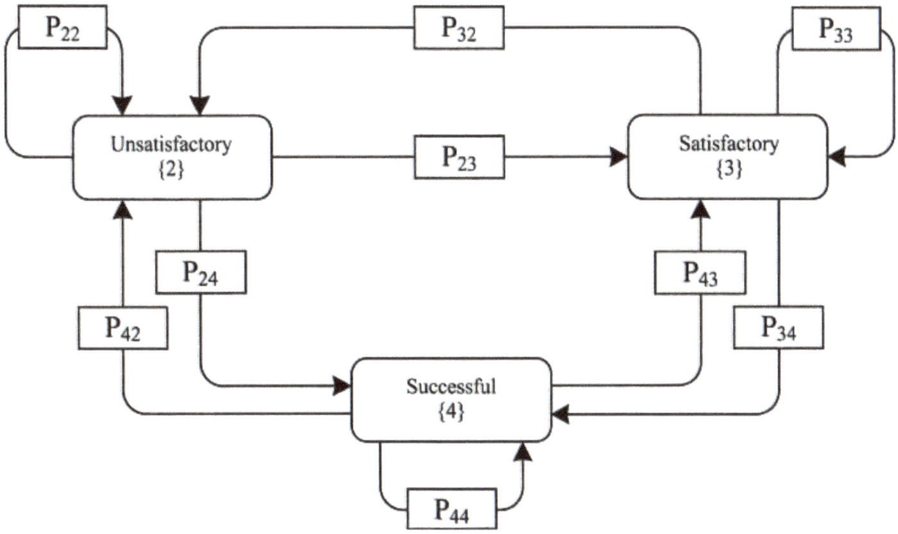

Fig. (1). Graph of transitions of trainees between performance groups, in the author's interpretation.

Considering transitions as a Markovian random process with discrete states and continuous time, we can formulate the following general case of the equation for probability:

$$P \equiv P(\vec{X}|t) \equiv P(N_{(2)}, N_{(3)}, N_{(4)}|t), \quad \mathbf{(13)}$$

that in the performance groups *(2)–(3)–(4)*at time *t* will be $N_{(2)}$, $N_{(3)}$, $N_{(4)}$ trainees. Components of the vector $\vec{X} = \{N_{(2)}, N_{(3)}, N_{(4)}\}$ are equal to the number of groups.

Taking into account equations 11, 12, and 13, this equation will have the following form:

$$\frac{\partial P}{\partial t} = -\lambda \cdot P \cdot N_{students} + \lambda \cdot \sum_{\substack{i=2,3,4 \\ j=2,3,4 \\ j \neq i}} (N_i + 1) \cdot P(\dots, N_i + 1, \dots, N_j - 1, \dots |t) \cdot P_{ij}\ , \quad \mathbf{(14)}$$

where P_{ij} – are the components of the matrix (Equation 12), which are computed from learning analytics data, and λ is the transition probability between performance groups perunit time.

The solution of equation (14), which in general can be done by numerical methods, will allow us to study various aspects of the behavior of probability (equation 13), in particular, to predict group distributions at arbitrary moments of time and to estimate confidence intervals. However, in the applied purposes, we will proceed to the mathematical expectations of values. For this purpose, let us proceed to the mathematical expectations of values $_{(2)}$, $n_{(3)}$, $n_{(4)}$ from (11) and transform (14) to a discrete form:

$$n_{(2)}(t+1) = n_{(2)}(t) - n_{(2)}(t) \cdot P_{23} - n_{(2)}(t) \cdot P_{24} + n_{(3)}(t) \cdot P_{32} + n_{(4)}(t) \cdot P_{42} \quad \textbf{(15)}$$

$$n_{(3)}(t+1) = n_{(3)}(t) - n_{(3)}(t) \cdot P_{32} - n_{(3)}(t) \cdot P_{34} + n_{(2)}(t) \cdot P_{23} + n_{(4)}(t) \cdot P_{43} \quad \textbf{(16)}$$

$$n_{(4)}(t+1) = n_{(4)}(t) - n_{(4)}(t) \cdot P_{42} - n_{(4)}(t) \cdot P_{43} + n_{(2)}(t) \cdot P_{24} + n_{(3)}(t) \cdot P_{34} \quad \textbf{(17)}$$

Due to the fact that a random process with continuous time and a finite number of states, as in the considered case, always possesses the ergodic property, then after a sufficiently large time interval, the system enters the steady-state regime, which does not depend on the initial state of the system (equation 13). This means the existence of a vector $\vec{X} = \{N_{(2)}, N_{(3)}, N_{(4)}\}$ and vector $\vec{\alpha} = \{n_{(2)}, n_{(3)}, n_{(4)}\}$, which defines a fixed distribution of studentsinto performance groups. This distribution can be seen as a characteristic of the test materials used, independent of the specifics of the particular group of students who take the test point in question. This corresponds to the hypothetical situation of multiple use of the CMM at a checkpoint by groups of trainees with statistically similar learning achievements.

The vector $\vec{\alpha}$ can be found directly from (equations 15-17) when $t \to \infty$. Also, the vector $\vec{\alpha}$ can be found as the marginal distribution after multiple transitions in the graph (Fig. **1**) defined by the species matrix (equation 12):

$$\vec{\alpha}(t+1) = \widehat{\boldsymbol{P}} \cdot \vec{\alpha}(t), \quad \textbf{(18)}$$

or as an eigenvector P with eigenvalue 1, which follows from the previous expression when $t \to \infty$: $\vec{\alpha} = \widehat{\boldsymbol{P}} \cdot \vec{\alpha}$. Obviously, the result of finding the vector $\vec{\alpha}$ does not depend on the method of calculation.

As shown above, the matrix (12) unambiguously determines the influence of the endpoint on the distribution of students into performance groups and indirectly serves as an indicator of the quality of the control task, but its direct use for CMM evaluation is inconvenient due to the rather large number of parameters (nine transition probabilities using three performance groups) and their complex, though unambiguous, relationship with traditional and understandable characteristics of learning success. Against this background, the vector $\vec{\alpha}$ is a more visual and practical use of a characteristic for CMM evaluation. Relationships like (equations 15-17) or (equation 18), if the matrix (equation 12) is known, can also be used to predict the group results of passing a checkpoint.

Thus, the systematic introduction of AI into educational activities, accompanied by mandatory monitoring of the quality of learning based on educational analytics, will allow us to identify the possibilities and limitations of this technology as a tool to improve learning effectiveness. Generative AI can be incorporated into the educational process from the first year onwards for a range of educational tasks, with the necessary activity being distinctively student work with a teacher. The teacher becomes more of an expert and significant figure. The technological benefit of the neural network is that it is an educational technology for fostering critical and entrepreneurial thinking in students, underpinned by the important criterion of mastering the fundamentals of industrial engineering as a new competency in the digital age.

CONCLUSION

The systematic integration of artificial intelligence into higher education represents a transformative force that is reshaping traditional educational paradigms. This research has demonstrated that AI applications, particularly generative models, offer substantial opportunities for enhancing educational processes while simultaneously necessitating new approaches to quality assessment and pedagogical design.

Our analysis of current AI implementations in education reveals several significant insights:

First, generative AI technologies such as ChatGPT and YandexGPT have proven to be more than mere productivity tools; they represent a new category of intellectual instruments that can contribute meaningfully to the development of critical thinking and conceptual sophistication in students. When properly implemented, these tools provide unique opportunities to capture and analyze the temporal progression of student thinking processes through the examination of prompt-response interactions.

Second, the application of learning analytics based on information theory offers a robust framework for assessing the quality of educational content and control materials. By defining information coefficients for checkpoints and modeling the distribution of individual digital profiles, educators and administrators can gain objective insights into the effectiveness of their assessment approaches, independent of subjective factors that often influence traditional grading systems.

Third, the mathematical modeling of student performance using state vectors and Markov processes provides a powerful predictive capability that can inform pedagogical interventions and curriculum design. The ergodic properties of these processes enable the identification of steady-state distributions that characterize the inherent quality of assessment materials, regardless of specific student cohorts.

Fourth, despite the apparent low threshold for entry when working with generative AI, our findings underscore the importance of preliminary training in prompt engineering for students. This training not only equips students with valuable digital competencies but also enables more conscious and effective engagement with neural networks, while providing instructors with a framework for assessing the development of student thinking based on AI interactions.

The integration of AI into education must be approached with careful consideration of ethical implications, particularly regarding data privacy and dependency concerns. As highlighted in our research, AI tools should complement rather than replace traditional teaching roles, with educators taking on more expert and facilitative positions in guiding students through critical reflection on AI-generated content.

Looking forward, the potential of AI in education extends beyond current applications to include enhanced personalization of learning pathways, improved accessibility, and more nuanced assessment of complex competencies. However, realizing this potential requires ongoing research into effective implementation strategies and pedagogical methodologies that leverage AI capabilities while addressing their limitations.

The successful incorporation of AI and data analytics into higher education represents a delicate balance between technological innovation and pedagogical wisdom. By viewing AI not as a replacement for human expertise but as a sophisticated tool for enhancing the educational experience, institutions can harness these technologies to foster critical thinking, entrepreneurial mindsets, and digital competencies essential for success in the 21st century. The systematic monitoring of educational quality through advanced analytics will remain crucial in refining our understanding of AI's impact and optimizing its integration into the educational ecosystem.

CHAPTER 15

Evaluating Digital Educational Technologies: A Comprehensive Semantic and Sentiment Analysis in Russian Universities

Chigozirim N. Onwusiribe[1,*]

[1] *School of Public Administration and Entrepreneurship (SPAE), Ural Federal University (UrFU), Yekaterinburg 620002, Sverdlovsk Region, Russian Federation*

Abstract: This chapter examines the implementation and effectiveness of digital educational technologies in Russian universities through the lens of semantic and sentiment analysis. The digital transformation of Russian higher education represents a complex journey marked by significant progress alongside persistent challenges. While 88% of universities have implemented learning management systems, only 45% effectively utilize these resources for educational activities, revealing a considerable gap between infrastructure availability and practical implementation. Through a comprehensive analysis of theoretical frameworks, user experiences, and learning outcomes, this chapter explores how digital technologies are reshaping educational practices across Russia. The research reveals that student perspectives generally demonstrate positive attitudes toward digital innovation, while faculty members express greater ambivalence and a preference for traditional teaching methods. Online educational platforms show varied effectiveness depending on implementation quality, student preparation, and institutional support structures. The chapter identifies key challenges, including infrastructure limitations, pedagogical integration barriers, and digital literacy gaps, while highlighting opportunities for enhancement through strategic infrastructure development, comprehensive faculty training, student-centered design, and continuous improvement processes. Moving forward, Russian universities should pursue balanced digital transformation strategies that leverage technological affordances while preserving valuable educational traditions, ultimately enhancing learning experiences and preparing students for an increasingly digital future.

Keywords: Digital Educational Technologies, Higher Education Transformation, Learning Management Systems, Online Learning Platforms, Russian Universities, Semantic Analysis, Sentiment Analysis.

* **Corresponding author Chigozirim N. Onwusiribe:** School of Public Administration and Entrepreneurship (SPAE), Ural Federal University (UrFU), Yekaterinburg 620002, Sverdlovsk Region, Russian Federation; E-mail: ndubuisichigo@gmail.com

Galina V. Astratova, Maxim V. Vlasov, Chigozirim Ndubuisi Onwusiribe & Longinus D.N. Nnadozie (Eds.)

INTRODUCTION

The landscape of higher education has undergone a profound transformation with the integration of digital technologies. Russian universities, following global trends, have increasingly embraced various digital educational tools to revolutionize their pedagogical approaches and enhance the learning experience for students (Schurig *et al.*, 2022; Grimalt-Álvaro and Usart, 2023). This shift toward digitalization stems primarily from institutional desires to create more adaptable, accessible, and engaging educational opportunities. Yet, amidst this digital revolution, a critical question emerges: How effectively do these technological innovations serve their intended purpose?

The digital transformation of Russian higher education represents a significant yet uneven journey. While substantial progress has been made in establishing digital infrastructure with data indicating that 88.51% of student residences provide internet connectivity and 88% of universities have implemented Learning Management Systems (LMS) the effective utilization of these resources remains a challenge (Statista, 2024). Only 45% of these institutions successfully employ LMS for educational activities, revealing a considerable gap between infrastructure availability and practical implementation.

Furthermore, the digital landscape across Russian universities exhibits notable disparities. Only 44% of institutions possess licenses for collaborative software platforms like Zoom, while 13% lack fundamental digital infrastructure components such as high-speed internet or specialized data storage systems (Statista, 2024). Perhaps most concerning is that only 11% of universities maintain digital infrastructure adequate for delivering comprehensive online education through their own resources (Peskova *et al.*, 2022). These statistics underscore the necessity for focused strategies to enhance both digital infrastructure quality and effective utilization.

The growing popularity of online coursework further emphasizes the importance of evaluating digital educational technologies. During 2019, the predominant online learning platforms in Russia included Coursera (15%), GeekBrains (8%), and National Open University INTUIT (7%), among others (Grimalt-Álvaro and Usart, 2023). The number of online education users has expanded dramatically, rising from 4.12 million in 2018 to 9.9 million by 2023. This substantial growth represents a broader shift toward digital learning approaches, necessitating robust assessment methodologies for these technologies.

This essay explores the complex landscape of digital educational technologies in Russian universities, examining their implementation, effectiveness, and impact on learning outcomes. Through a comprehensive analysis of semantic and sentiment aspects of user experiences, we seek to understand how these technologies are perceived by students and educators, identifying both successes and challenges in their deployment. By exploring these dimensions, we aim to contribute to the ongoing dialogue about effective integration of digital technologies in higher education and provide insights for future development.

THE EVOLUTION OF DIGITAL EDUCATIONAL TECHNOLOGIES IN RUSSIAN HIGHER EDUCATION

Historical Context and Current Landscape

The integration of digital technologies in Russian higher education has followed a trajectory shaped by both global technological advances and local educational traditions. Historically, Russian universities maintained a strong emphasis on traditional face-to-face instruction, with technological integration occurring gradually throughout the early 2000s. The initial phase primarily focused on basic computerization equipping classrooms with computers and establishing internet connectivity rather than comprehensive digital transformation of pedagogical approaches.

The pace of digital adoption accelerated significantly after 2010, with Russian higher education institutions recognizing the potential of digital technologies to enhance educational quality and accessibility. This period saw the emergence of various digital initiatives, including the development of national educational platforms and the integration of international learning management systems. However, the transformation remained uneven, with leading universities in major urban centers adopting technologies more rapidly than regional institutions (Peskova *et al.*, 2022).

The COVID-19 pandemic served as a catalyst for unprecedented acceleration in digital adoption across Russian universities. The sudden necessity for remote education forced institutions to rapidly implement digital solutions, regardless of their previous technological readiness. This emergency transition revealed both the potential of digital educational technologies and significant gaps in infrastructure, skills, and preparedness across the sector.

Theoretical Foundations of Digital Education

The theoretical underpinnings of digital education in Russian universities draw from various pedagogical frameworks, with Constructivist Learning Theory (CLT) emerging as particularly relevant. CLT emphasizes learning as an active process where learners construct knowledge through experience and reflection rather than passive reception of information. Digital technologies, when effectively implemented, can create environments that support constructivist principles by enabling interactive learning experiences, collaborative knowledge construction, and personalized learning pathways.

Within this constructivist framework, digital educational technologies serve multiple functions. Learning Management Systems provide structured environments for content organization and delivery, while also facilitating communication between instructors and students. Collaboration tools enable social learning experiences that align with constructivist principles of knowledge co-creation. Assessment technologies allow for continuous evaluation and feedback, supporting the iterative nature of knowledge construction.

The application of semantic and sentiment analysis to evaluate these technologies represents an innovative approach that aligns with constructivist principles. By analyzing how users express their experiences with digital tools, these analytical methods provide insights into the subjective process of knowledge construction and the emotional dimensions of learning experiences. This approach recognizes that effective learning environments must address both cognitive and affective aspects of the educational experience.

Current Implementation Challenges

Despite the theoretical promise of digital educational technologies, their implementation in Russian universities faces several significant challenges. The disparity between infrastructure availability and effective utilization represents a fundamental issue. While many institutions have acquired digital tools, their integration into pedagogical practice remains limited (Statista, 2024). This gap stems from various factors, including insufficient training for educators, limited digital literacy among students, and organizational resistance to change.

Additionally, regional disparities in digital infrastructure create an uneven landscape for digital education across Russia. Universities in major urban centers like Moscow, St. Petersburg, and Yekaterinburg generally possess more advanced digital capabilities than institutions in smaller cities and rural areas (Peskova *et al.*, 2022). This digital divide threatens to exacerbate existing educational inequalities, with students at technologically advantaged institutions potentially receiving higher-quality educational experiences.

Furthermore, the cultural dimension of technology adoption presents unique challenges in the Russian context. Traditional pedagogical approaches emphasizing the authoritative role of the instructor may conflict with the more collaborative and student-centered models enabled by digital technologies. This cultural tension requires thoughtful navigation to ensure that digital technologies enhance rather than disrupt effective educational practices.

SEMANTIC AND SENTIMENT ANALYSIS: INNOVATIVE APPROACHES TO EDUCATIONAL TECHNOLOGY EVALUATION

Fundamentals of Semantic and Sentiment Analysis

Semantic analysis and sentiment analysis represent powerful methodological approaches for evaluating digital educational technologies. Semantic analysis examines the contextual meanings of words and phrases, enabling researchers to identify patterns and themes in how users describe their experiences with educational technologies. This approach helps uncover the conceptual frameworks that users apply when engaging with digital tools and can reveal insights about how these technologies shape learning experiences.

Sentiment analysis, meanwhile, focuses on the emotional dimensions of user feedback, identifying positive, negative, or neutral attitudes expressed in text. When applied to educational contexts, sentiment analysis can reveal how digital technologies affect student engagement, satisfaction, and motivation crucial factors in learning outcomes. By quantifying emotional responses to specific aspects of educational technologies, sentiment analysis provides valuable insights for targeted improvements.

Combined, these analytical approaches transform qualitative feedback into actionable insights, enabling educational institutions to understand user experiences comprehensively. For example, Aspect-Based Sentiment Analysis (ABSA) delivers nuanced perspectives by evaluating specific components of educational tools alongside their associated sentiment expressions (Kastrati *et al.*, 2020). This granular methodology proves invaluable for pinpointing particular areas requiring refinement, ensuring digital solutions effectively address both student and educator requirements.

Applications in Educational Technology Assessment

The application of semantic and sentiment analysis to educational technology assessment represents an emerging field with significant potential. These techniques have been employed to analyze various forms of user feedback, including forum discussions, course evaluations, and social media comments, providing insights into how students and educators experience digital learning environments.

Semantic analysis has been particularly useful for identifying key themes in educational technology feedback. Research by Nikolić *et al.* (2020) demonstrated how semantic analysis could identify recurring topics in student reviews, revealing patterns in how users conceptualize and evaluate digital learning experiences. This approach helps educational institutions understand which aspects of digital technologies are most salient to users and how these perceptions evolve over time.

Sentiment analysis adds an emotional dimension to this understanding, revealing how users feel about specific aspects of educational technologies. Wan and Tang (2021) illustrated how sentiment analysis could identify emotional responses to ideological and political instruction delivered through digital platforms, demonstrating improved teaching outcomes through multimodal sentiment recognition. Similarly, research by Le *et al.* (2018) developed specialized modules alerting instructors when students expressed negative or distressed sentiments, facilitating timely interventions.

The integration of these analytical approaches provides a comprehensive framework for evaluating educational technologies. By understanding both what users are saying about digital tools and how they feel about them, educational institutions can develop nuanced strategies for improvement that address both functional and emotional aspects of the user experience.

Methodological Innovations and Challenges

The application of semantic and sentiment analysis to educational technology assessment continues to evolve, with researchers developing increasingly sophisticated methodologies. Deep learning approaches have demonstrated particular promise in this domain. Onan (2020) found that deep learning-based architectures surpass conventional sentiment analysis methods when analyzing feedback on Massive Open Online Courses (MOOCs), delivering superior predictive capabilities.

Similarly, Zhai *et al.* (2020) proposed a Multi-Attention Fusion Modeling approach for educational data sentiment analysis, achieving superior classification results by integrating global and local attention mechanisms. These advanced techniques enable more accurate identification of sentiment in complex educational contexts, where traditional methods might miss subtle emotional expressions or contextual nuances.

Despite these advances, significant methodological challenges remain. Cultural and linguistic factors significantly influence how users express sentiment, particularly in educational contexts. Research by Smetanin (2020) identified specific challenges in sentiment analysis for Russian texts, emphasizing the need for specialized datasets and improved analysis methodologies that account for linguistic particularities.

Additionally, integrating semantic and sentiment analysis with existing educational assessment frameworks presents practical challenges. Educational institutions must develop systems that can collect, analyze, and respond to user feedback in ways that meaningfully improve educational experiences. This requires not only technical expertise but also organizational structures that value and act upon user perspectives.

THE DIGITAL INFRASTRUCTURE LANDSCAPE IN RUSSIAN UNIVERSITIES

Current State and Regional Disparities

The digital infrastructure across Russian universities presents a complex landscape characterized by significant progress alongside persistent gaps and regional disparities. While basic digital infrastructure components like internet connectivity have achieved widespread implementation, more advanced elements necessary for comprehensive digital education remain unevenly distributed.

The concentration of digital transformation efforts in major urban centers represents a significant challenge for equitable educational access. Universities in Moscow, St. Petersburg, and Yekaterinburg generally possess more advanced digital capabilities, while institutions in smaller cities and rural areas often struggle with basic infrastructure limitations (Peskova *et al.*, 2022). This geographic disparity creates an uneven foundation for digital education implementation, potentially exacerbating existing educational inequalities.

Additionally, the digital infrastructure landscape is characterized by significant inter-university differentiation, even within the same regions. Some institutions have made substantial investments in digital technologies, establishing comprehensive digital learning environments that support diverse pedagogical approaches. Others maintain only minimal digital infrastructure, limiting their capacity to implement innovative educational practices.

Implementation Gaps and Utilization Challenges

Perhaps the most striking aspect of the digital infrastructure landscape is the gap between availability and utilization. While 88% of universities report having Learning Management Systems (LMS), only 45% effectively utilize these systems for educational purposes (Statista, 2024). This disparity reveals that the mere presence of digital infrastructure does not guarantee its effective educational application.

Several factors contribute to this implementation gap. First, faculty digital literacy varies significantly across institutions, with many educators lacking the skills or confidence to fully utilize available digital tools. Second, pedagogical integration of digital technologies requires thoughtful redesign of courses and teaching approaches, a process that many institutions have not adequately supported. Third, technical support for digital infrastructure often proves insufficient, creating barriers to effective utilization when problems arise.

Collaborative software availability represents another area of concern. Only 44% of universities possess licenses for platforms like Zoom, limiting opportunities for interactive remote learning experiences (Statista, 2024). This deficiency became particularly problematic during the COVID-19 pandemic, when synchronous remote communication tools became essential for educational continuity.

Strategic Implications for Digital Education

The current state of digital infrastructure in Russian universities has significant implications for digital education strategies. First, it highlights the necessity for targeted investments that address specific infrastructure gaps rather than generic technology adoption. Institutions must identify their particular limitations and develop strategic plans to address these deficiencies.

Second, the implementation gap underscores the importance of comprehensive approaches to digital transformation that address not only technological infrastructure but also human factors like skills development and organizational change management. Universities must invest in training programs that enhance digital literacy among faculty and staff, while also developing supportive structures that encourage digital tool adoption.

Third, the regional disparities suggest the need for national-level policies that promote more equitable digital infrastructure development across different regions. Without such interventions, the digital divide between leading urban universities and regional institutions may continue to widen, creating increasingly unequal educational opportunities.

USER EXPERIENCE AND FEEDBACK ON DIGITAL EDUCATIONAL TECHNOLOGIES

Student Perspectives and Engagement

Student perspectives on digital educational technologies in Russian universities reveal complex and nuanced attitudes that significantly influence engagement and learning outcomes. Generally, students demonstrate positive attitudes toward digital technologies, recognizing their potential to enhance educational accessibility and flexibility. Research by Ronzhina *et al.* (2021) found that students assigned higher ratings to the positive impact of digitalization on academic performance compared to their instructors, suggesting particular receptiveness to digital innovation among the student population.

However, student perspectives vary considerably depending on specific technological implementations and contexts. Accessibility issues, both technical and financial, emerge as significant concerns. Students consistently report frustration with platforms that present technical barriers or require expensive subscriptions, highlighting the importance of designing accessible digital educational experiences that minimize these obstacles.

Engagement with digital educational technologies appears strongly influenced by design factors. Students particularly value platforms that offer customization options, allowing them to tailor learning experiences to their preferences and needs. Similarly, interactive and engaging content delivery significantly enhances student satisfaction compared to passive digital experiences. These findings align with constructivist principles that emphasize active learning and personalization as key factors in effective educational experiences.

Faculty Attitudes and Adoption Patterns

Faculty attitudes toward digital educational technologies in Russian universities demonstrate greater complexity and ambivalence compared to student perspectives. Research indicates that 87.8% of professors express a preference for face-to-face teaching formats, suggesting substantial resistance to digital transformation of educational practices (Statista, 2024). This preference likely reflects both pedagogical beliefs about effective teaching methods and concerns about the limitations of digital environments for certain educational activities.

Faculty perspectives on the convenience of digital education further illustrate this ambivalence. Only 5.1% of professors report finding distance education personally convenient, while 67.2% express reservations (Statista, 2024). These attitudes suggest significant concerns about workload implications, technological challenges, and pedagogical limitations associated with digital teaching methods.

Adoption patterns among faculty reflect these attitudes, with significant variation in how instructors integrate digital technologies into their teaching practices. Some embrace digital tools as opportunities to enhance pedagogical approaches, developing innovative methods that leverage technological affordances. Others adopt minimal digital practices, maintaining traditional teaching methods as much as possible within digital contexts. This variation creates inconsistent student experiences across different courses and programs, potentially limiting the overall effectiveness of digital education initiatives.

Feedback Patterns and Improvement Opportunities

Feedback patterns on digital educational technologies reveal several recurring themes that suggest specific improvement opportunities. Technical stability emerges as a fundamental concern across various platforms, with users consistently reporting frustration with system crashes, synchronization issues, and other technical problems that disrupt learning experiences. This feedback highlights the critical importance of robust technical infrastructure and support systems for effective digital education.

User interface design represents another significant theme in feedback. Students and faculty alike express preferences for intuitive, customizable interfaces that facilitate rather than complicate educational activities. Platforms with outdated or confusing interfaces generate substantial negative feedback, underscoring the importance of user-centered design principles in educational technology development.

Cost concerns appear prominently in feedback on commercial platforms, with users questioning whether premium subscription fees deliver corresponding value. This feedback suggests opportunities for developing tiered pricing models, scholarship programs, or alternative funding approaches that enhance accessibility while maintaining quality.

Content quality and engagement factors feature prominently in positive feedback. Users particularly value educational platforms that offer high-quality, engaging, and interactive content from reputable sources. This feedback aligns with research by Grimalt-Álvaro and Usart (2023), who found that sentiment analysis could significantly improve learning through timely and personalized feedback, highlighting the importance of responsive, high-quality content in digital educational environments.

THE IMPACT OF ONLINE EDUCATIONAL PLATFORMS ON LEARNING OUTCOMES

Evaluating Effectiveness Across Different Platforms

The impact of online educational platforms on learning outcomes in Russian higher education demonstrates significant variation across different platforms and contexts. Leading platforms like Coursera (15% market share) appear to derive their effectiveness from extensive course offerings from prestigious institutions, providing high-quality content and valuable credentials (Grimalt-Álvaro & Usart, 2023). These platforms particularly excel in knowledge acquisition and practical skill development, often through structured learning pathways and interactive content.

Platforms with specialized focus, such as GeekBrains (8% market share) and National Open University INTUIT (7%), demonstrate particular effectiveness in technical education domains. Their alignment with industry needs and practical approach to skill development creates significant positive impacts on learning outcomes, particularly for students seeking specific technical competencies (Grimalt-Álvaro & Usart, 2023).

The effectiveness of platforms also varies depending on how they are integrated into broader educational contexts. When used as supplementary resources within traditional educational programs, online platforms can enhance learning outcomes by providing alternative explanations, additional practice opportunities, and expanded content access. However, when employed as primary educational delivery mechanisms without adequate support structures, these platforms may prove less effective, particularly for students requiring more guidance or struggling with self-directed learning.

Measuring Impact Through Multiple Dimensions

Comprehensively evaluating the impact of online educational platforms requires consideration of multiple dimensions beyond traditional academic performance metrics. While academic achievement represents an important outcome measure, engagement, motivation, and skill development provide equally valuable perspectives on platform effectiveness.

Research by Noor *et al.* (2022) demonstrates that educational apps and virtual classrooms can significantly enhance university students' learning behaviors and motivations, leading to improved academic outcomes. These motivational impacts represent crucial intermediate factors that influence longer-term learning success, highlighting the importance of designing digital learning experiences that foster engagement and intrinsic motivation.

Accessibility and flexibility dimensions also significantly influence platform impact. Research by Liu *et al.* (2020) emphasizes that online platforms allow students to learn at their own pace and convenience, potentially resulting in better engagement and improved learning outcomes for students with diverse needs and circumstances. These flexibility benefits prove particularly valuable for working students, those with family responsibilities, or individuals facing mobility challenges.

Long-term skill development and career preparation outcomes provide additional important measures of platform effectiveness. Platforms that successfully develop practical, industry-relevant skills may generate significant positive impacts on employment outcomes and career advancement, even if traditional academic metrics show only modest improvements.

Contextual Factors Affecting Platform Success

The effectiveness of online educational platforms is significantly influenced by various contextual factors that shape how these tools are implemented and experienced. Technological infrastructure quality represents a fundamental contextual factor, with poor internet connectivity and limited device access significantly diminishing potential benefits regardless of platform quality. This factor particularly affects regional institutions outside major urban centers, where infrastructure limitations may create substantial barriers to effective digital education.

Student preparation and digital literacy levels similarly influence platform effectiveness. Students with strong digital skills and self-directed learning capabilities generally derive greater benefits from online platforms compared to those lacking these foundational competencies. This variation suggests the importance of providing digital literacy support alongside platform implementation to maximize learning benefits for all students.

Faculty preparation and support structures also critically affect how effectively online platforms enhance learning outcomes. When faculty receive adequate training, ongoing technical support, and recognition for digital teaching innovations, they can more effectively integrate online platforms into coherent educational experiences. Conversely, insufficient faculty support often results in fragmented or ineffective platform utilization that limits potential learning benefits.

Institutional policies and culture significantly shape platform implementation contexts. Universities with clear digital strategies, supportive policies for innovative teaching approaches, and cultures that value pedagogical experimentation typically achieve more successful platform integration compared to institutions with rigid traditional structures. These organizational factors create environments where the potential benefits of online platforms can be more fully realized through thoughtful implementation.

CHALLENGES AND OPPORTUNITIES IN DIGITAL EDUCATIONAL TECHNOLOGY IMPLEMENTATION

Infrastructure and Resource Limitations

Infrastructure and resource limitations present significant challenges for digital educational technology implementation in Russian universities. Despite progress in basic connectivity, many institutions still lack the comprehensive digital infrastructure necessary for advanced educational applications. The finding that only 11% of universities maintain digital infrastructure adequate for delivering comprehensive online education through their own resources underscores the severity of this challenge (Peskova *et al.*, 2022).

Financial constraints further complicate infrastructure development, particularly for regional institutions with limited budgets. The costs associated with acquiring, maintaining, and updating digital technologies can prove prohibitive, especially when considering comprehensive solutions that include hardware, software, and support services. These financial limitations often force institutions to make difficult choices between different technology investments, potentially resulting in fragmented or incomplete digital ecosystems.

Technical support limitations represent another significant infrastructure challenge. Even when digital technologies are available, insufficient technical support can severely limit their effective utilization. Many Russian universities struggle to maintain adequate technical staff for troubleshooting, training, and system maintenance, creating barriers to consistent technology usage by faculty and students alike.

Despite these challenges, infrastructure development also presents significant opportunities. Strategic investments in shared digital resources and collaborative platforms can maximize impact while minimizing costs for individual institutions. National initiatives to develop digital infrastructure in underserved regions could address geographical disparities while creating more equitable educational opportunities across different areas. Additionally, partnerships with technology companies and international educational institutions offer potential pathways for accelerating infrastructure development through resource sharing and knowledge exchange.

Pedagogical Integration and Faculty Development

The integration of digital technologies into pedagogical practices represents a complex challenge that extends beyond mere technology availability. Many faculty members in Russian universities express a preference for traditional teaching methods and demonstrate limited familiarity with digital pedagogical approaches. Research indicates that 87.8% of professors prefer face-to-face teaching formats, revealing significant resistance to digital transformation of educational practices (Statista, 2024).

Faculty development limitations exacerbate this challenge. Many institutions lack comprehensive training programs that would help educators develop both technical skills for using digital tools and pedagogical approaches for effective digital teaching. Additionally, workload concerns frequently emerge as barriers to digital adoption, with 85.7% of professors reporting no increase in free time due to distance education (Statista, 2024). This perception suggests that digital technologies may initially create additional work rather than reducing burdens, potentially discouraging adoption.

However, pedagogical integration also presents substantial opportunities for educational enhancement. Digital technologies can enable innovative teaching approaches that align with contemporary learning theories like constructivism, creating more interactive, personalized, and engaging educational experiences. Successful integration examples demonstrate how digital tools can enhance rather than replace effective pedagogical practices, combining technological affordances with sound educational principles.

Faculty development initiatives represent a critical opportunity in this area. Comprehensive programs that address both technical skills and pedagogical applications can transform faculty attitudes and capabilities, enabling more effective digital technology integration. Communities of practice that allow educators to share experiences and innovations can accelerate this transformation while creating supportive professional networks that sustain ongoing development.

Student Access and Digital Literacy

Student access challenges create significant barriers to equitable digital education in Russian universities. Financial constraints limit many students' ability to acquire necessary devices and internet connectivity, particularly affecting those from lower-income backgrounds. Geographic disparities in internet infrastructure further complicate access, with students in rural areas often facing connectivity challenges that urban students do not experience. Digital literacy variation among students presents additional challenges for effective technology utilization. While some students possess advanced digital skills, others struggle with basic technological operations, creating disparate experiences with the same digital tools. These literacy gaps can exacerbate existing educational inequalities if not specifically addressed through targeted support programs.

However, these challenges also present opportunities for developing more inclusive educational approaches. Digital literacy initiatives that systematically develop students' technological capabilities can create foundations for more effective learning with digital tools. Universal design principles in digital educational resources can make these tools more accessible to diverse learners, including those with varying technological proficiency levels. Alternative access models represent another promising opportunity area. Shared device programs, campus technology centers, and offline access options for digital materials can address device limitations for students with financial constraints. Mobile-optimized learning resources can leverage widespread smartphone ownership to provide educational access even when computer availability is limited.

Cultural and Institutional Factors

Cultural and institutional factors significantly influence digital educational technology implementation in Russian universities. Traditional educational values emphasizing direct instructor authority and standardized approaches may conflict with digital education models that promote student autonomy and personalized learning pathways. These cultural tensions can create resistance to digital transformation at both individual and institutional levels.

Organizational structures in many Russian universities reflect hierarchical models that may impede agile technology adoption and innovation. Decision-making processes often involve multiple approval levels, potentially slowing technology implementation and limiting responsiveness to emerging educational needs. Additionally, evaluation systems that primarily value traditional teaching methods may insufficiently recognize or reward digital innovation, creating disincentives for faculty experimentation with new approaches. However, cultural evolution also presents opportunities for meaningful educational transformation. Digital technologies can serve as catalysts for broader educational reform, introducing new models that blend valuable traditional approaches with innovative digital practices. Institutional policies that explicitly value and support digital innovation can create environments where technological and pedagogical experimentation flourishes. Leadership development represents a crucial opportunity within this domain. Developing educational leaders who understand both pedagogical principles and technological possibilities can accelerate institutional transformation. These leaders can navigate cultural tensions while creating supportive environments for digital innovation, ultimately fostering more effective educational technology implementation across Russian universities.

FUTURE DIRECTIONS AND RECOMMENDATIONS

Enhancing Digital Infrastructure and Access

Future development of digital educational technologies in Russian universities should prioritize strategic infrastructure enhancement that addresses current limitations while creating foundations for ongoing innovation. National and regional policies should focus on reducing digital disparities between urban and rural areas, ensuring that all universities have access to reliable high-speed internet and essential digital resources. These policies might include targeted funding programs for underserved regions and incentives for technology companies to expand infrastructure in less-developed areas. Universities should develop comprehensive digital infrastructure plans that move beyond basic connectivity to create integrated digital ecosystems supporting diverse educational activities. These plans should include not only hardware and software acquisition but also robust maintenance and support systems that ensure consistent accessibility and functionality. Cloud-based solutions may prove particularly valuable for institutions with limited local infrastructure capabilities, providing access to advanced resources without requiring extensive on-site systems.

To address student access challenges, institutions should develop initiatives that ensure all students have the necessary devices and connectivity for effective digital learning. Device loan programs, subsidized internet access, and technology grants for low-income students represent valuable approaches for enhancing equitable access. Additionally, educational applications should be optimized for diverse devices, including smartphones and tablets, to accommodate students with varying technology resources.

Faculty Development and Pedagogical Innovation

Comprehensive faculty development programs represent essential components of future digital education advancement in Russian universities. These programs should address both technical skills for using digital tools and pedagogical approaches for effective technology integration into teaching practices. Ongoing professional development opportunities, rather than one-time training sessions, can support faculty through continuous learning journeys as technologies and best practices evolve.

Institutional policies should explicitly recognize and reward digital innovation in teaching, creating incentives for faculty to explore new approaches. These policies might include considering digital teaching innovations in promotion decisions, providing financial incentives for course redesign incorporating digital technologies, and celebrating exemplary digital teaching practices through institutional recognition programs. Communities of practice focused on digital pedagogy can accelerate innovation by facilitating knowledge sharing among educators. These communities might include cross-disciplinary faculty groups exploring common digital teaching challenges, partnerships between technical specialists and discipline experts, and networks connecting educators across different institutions. Such collaborative approaches can generate creative solutions to implementation challenges while creating supportive professional environments for ongoing innovation.

Student-Centered Design and Support

Future digital educational technologies should embrace student-centered design principles that prioritize usability, engagement, and personalization. User experience research involving actual students should inform platform development, ensuring that digital tools align with student needs and preferences. Particular attention should focus on creating intuitive interfaces that minimize cognitive load associated with technology use, allowing students to focus primarily on learning content rather than navigating complex systems.

Personalization capabilities represent another important direction for future development. Digital platforms should increasingly provide adaptive learning pathways that respond to individual student progress, preferences, and needs. These personalized approaches can enhance engagement while providing appropriate challenges and support for diverse learners. Comprehensive student support systems should accompany digital educational technologies, ensuring that technical or skill barriers do not impede learning. These support systems might include help desks for technical issues, tutorials for developing digital learning skills, and guidance for effective self-regulated learning in digital environments. Particular attention should focus on supporting students who may have limited prior experience with educational technologies, ensuring that digital approaches enhance rather than hinder their educational opportunities.

Research and Continuous Improvement

Ongoing research represents an essential component of effective digital educational technology development in Russian universities. Educational institutions should establish systematic approaches for gathering and analyzing data about technology implementation, user experiences, and learning outcomes. These research initiatives should employ diverse methodologies, including the semantic and sentiment analysis approaches discussed earlier, to develop a comprehensive understanding of how digital technologies affect educational processes. Continuous improvement processes should build upon this research foundation, creating structured approaches for refining digital educational technologies based on empirical findings. These processes might include regular review cycles that examine implementation data, stakeholder feedback, and learning outcomes to identify improvement opportunities. Cross-functional teams, including educators, technologists, and students, can provide diverse perspectives on potential enhancements.

Collaborative research networks connecting multiple institutions can accelerate knowledge development in this domain. By sharing findings, methodologies, and best practices across different universities, these networks can create collective intelligence that benefits the broader Russian higher education system. International research partnerships can further enhance these efforts by connecting Russian institutions with global expertise and innovation in digital education.

CONCLUSION: TOWARD A BALANCED DIGITAL TRANSFORMATION

The digital transformation of Russian higher education represents a complex and multifaceted process with significant implications for educational quality, accessibility, and effectiveness. This exploration of digital educational technologies in Russian universities reveals both substantial progress and persistent challenges requiring thoughtful navigation. While technological infrastructure has expanded considerably with 88% of universities implementing learning management systems effective utilization remains limited, with only 45% of institutions successfully employing these systems for educational activities (Statista, 2024). The semantic and sentiment analysis approaches examined in this essay offer valuable methodologies for understanding user experiences with digital educational technologies. These analytical techniques transform qualitative feedback into actionable insights by examining both contextual meanings and emotional responses, providing crucial perspectives for enhancing digital education initiatives. Particularly promising applications include aspect-based sentiment analysis (ABSA), which delivers nuanced insights by evaluating specific components of educational tools alongside their associated sentiment expressions (Kastrati *et al.*, 2020).

The impact of online educational platforms on learning outcomes demonstrates significant variation across different contexts and implementations. While research indicates modest positive effects overall (Alshammary and Alhalafawy, 2023), effectiveness depends substantially on implementation quality, student preparation, and support structures. This variation underscores the importance of thoughtful, comprehensive approaches to digital education that address not only technological components but also pedagogical, cultural, and organizational dimensions. Moving forward, Russian universities should pursue balanced digital transformation strategies that leverage technological affordances while preserving valuable educational traditions. These strategies should prioritize equitable access, faculty development, student-centered design, and continuous improvement based on systematic research. By addressing current implementation challenges while establishing foundations for ongoing innovation, Russian higher education can develop digital educational approaches that enhance learning experiences while preparing students for an increasingly digital future. The ultimate measure of success in this digital transformation lies not in technology adoption itself but in how effectively these tools enhance educational quality, accessibility, and outcomes. Digital educational technologies should serve as means for achieving broader educational goals rather than ends in themselves. By maintaining this perspective, Russian universities can navigate digital transformation in ways that genuinely advance their educational missions while addressing the diverse needs of 21st-century learners.

CHAPTER 16

Human Capital Development in the Context of Integrating R & D and Higher Education in the USRB Digital Economy

Galina V. Astratova[1,*], **Natalia A. Simchenko**[2] and **Maxim V. Vlasov**[1]

[1] *Department of Regional Economics, Innovative Entrepreneurship and Economics (REIE&E), Institute of Economics and Management, School of Public Administration and Entrepreneurship (SPAE), Ural Federal University (UrFU), Yekaterinburg 620002, Sverdlovsk Region, Russian Federation*

[2] *Department of Economic Theory and Economic Policy, St. Petersburg State University, St. Petersburg 199034, Russian Federation*

Abstract: This chapter examines the critical role of human capital development in the integration of Research and Development (R & D) and higher education within the digital economy of the Union State of the Russian Federation and Belarus (USRB). The research identifies human capital as the most significant economic category and a key factor in the development of the knowledge economy, innovation, and digital transformation. The chapter analyzes current trends, challenges, and opportunities in human capital formation through a comparative assessment of innovation activity ratings, education spending, and labor market dynamics in both countries. Special attention is given to the regional aspects of human capital development and the structural transformations necessary for adapting to digital economy requirements. The findings reveal a significant potential for enhancing scientific and innovative capabilities in the USRB despite insufficient R & D investments, and highlight the importance of practice-oriented approaches in higher education for developing specialists capable of responding to contemporary economic challenges. The research provides recommendations for improving strategic management of human capital to address the qualitative gaps in the labor market and foster creative human capital necessary for sustainable economic growth in the digital era.

Keywords: Digital economy, Higher education, Human capital, Innovation development, Knowledge economy, R & D integration, Union State of Russia and Belarus.

* **Corresponding author Galina V. Astratova:** Department of Regional Economics, Innovative Entrepreneurship and Economics (REIE&E), Institute of Economics and Management, School of Public Administration and Entrepreneurship (SPAE), Ural Federal University (UrFU), Yekaterinburg 620002, Sverdlovsk Region, Russian Federation;
E-mail: galina_28@mail.ru

Galina V. Astratova, Maxim V. Vlasov, Chigozirim Ndubuisi Onwusiribe & Longinus D.N. Nnadozie (Eds.)

INTRODUCTION

Human capital is the most important economic category, implying a set of intelligence, knowledge, skills, and abilities used to meet the diverse needs of the individual and society. Human Capital (HC) is also an intensive productive factor in the development of the economy and society, including health, education, quality of life, and productive work. Moreover, in any organization, the most important resource is HC, that is, “collective knowledge, qualities, skills, experience, and health of the workforce” (Madgavkar *et al.*, 2022).

Currently, there are several types of classification of human capital, among which the following is the most common:

- Individual or personal HC;
- Human capital of the organization (firm);
- National/regional human capital.

In the context of our research, it is important, firstly, that HC is a key factor in the development of the knowledge economy, innovation, and digital economy. Indeed, the quality of human capital, as well as the level of development of education and science in the country, is able to ensure economic growth and the authority of the state on the world stage. Advanced knowledge, scientific research, innovative developments, and technologies contribute to improving the competitiveness of the national economy. Other authors also present similar positions on this issue (Bengraf *et al.* 2024; Eskindarov *et al.*, 2022; Ishmuratova, 2021; Madgavkar *et al.*, 2022; Panikarova *et al.*, 2020; Simchenko *et al.*, 2023; *etc.*).

Secondly, according to the results of a fundamental study by E. Fedorova and colleagues (2023) and by A. Yanovskaya and N. Simchenko (2024), it was found that HC plays a special role in the digital economy. It is true due to the presence of a number of causal factors:

♦ In the process of developing socio-economic and labor relations, new technologies and approaches to human resource management have been introduced at different periods of time. This led to the formation of theoretical and conceptual changes in the organization of labor, which manifested first in the primary displacement of physical labor[1], and then in the mass displacement of low-skilled mental labor[2] and its subsequent replacement with automated techno-

1 *i.e.*, technology of the period of the 1st Industrial Revolution.
2 *i.e.*, technology of the period of the 4th Industrial Revolution.

logies. This leads to the fact that difficult work dominates the work activity, a person becomes an important resource, the need for intellectual and cultural qualities of an employee increases, and the concept of labor management focuses on HC, that is, on a person and is aimed at managing automated and robotic labor through digital technologies, synchronizing them with highly qualified personnel (Yanovskaya and Simchenko, 2024; p. 135 and p. 150);

♦ There are a number of factors illustrating the special role of human capital in a digital society, namely:

- An increase in publication activity, which indicates "... an exponential increase in scientific interest in the theory of human capital in the international scientific community" (Fedorova *et al.*, 2023, p. 1).
- The manifestation of the universal nature of the integration of digital technologies into the theory and practice of the development of national economies.
- Stimulating R & D in the development of HC management mechanisms by the State and Municipal Administration (SMA) in cooperation with institutions and businesses.

Thirdly, *the regional aspect of HC development is important*. In this regard, it is also relevant that many issues of HC's impact on current innovations, economic growth, and development still remain an incomprehensible "black box", especially in the regional context as a whole (Diebolt and Hippe, 2019; Eskindarov *et al.*, 2022; Fonseca and Pedro, 2019) and at the level of the Union State of the Russian Federation and the Republic of Belarus, in particular (Bengraf *et al.*, 2024; Kozopolyanskaya, 2018; Simchenko *et al.*, 2023; *etc.*). One of the key priorities of the innovative development of the Union State of the Russian Federation and the Republic of Belarus is the formation of a new type of knowledge-based economy. Knowledge is the basis for the development of human and scientific potential and contributes to increasing the knowledge intensity of production processes. During the transformation of the Russian and Belarusian economies to an innovative path of development, the scale of scientific research and technical developments increased, as we noted earlier, and, accordingly, the role of knowledge and its impact on national economies increased (Bengraf *et al.* 2024). Therefore, in the current conditions, special attention should be paid to the process of investing in knowledge in order to form, develop, accumulate, and reproduce it. Accordingly, if more recently the emphasis was on the quantitative component of education, now its qualitative and creative components are coming to the fore. Other authors also present similar positions on this issue (Bengraf *et al.* 2024; Eskindarov *et al.*, 2022; Ishmuratova, 2021; Panikarova *et al.*, 2020;

Simchenko *et al.*, 2023; Vlasov and Shardina, 2022; Yanovskaya and Simchenko, 2024; *etc.*).

According to the research data of the World Intellectual Property Organization (WIPO), which identifies and ranks the innovative activity of over 130 countries of the world, the Russian Federation and the Republic of Belarus occupy positions equal to 80 and 51 in the overall world ranking, respectively (Dutta *et al.*, 2024). At the same time, according to the indicator "human capital and research", the ratings of fraternal countries are in the range of 40-50, and higher education is about 60 (Table **1**).

Table 1. Ratings of innovation activity of the Russian Federation and the Republic of Belarus in 2023 in the global context, compiled by the authors based on the source (Dutta *et al.*, 2024, p. 87 and p. 179).

Name of Indicators	Score	Value Rating
Russian Federation		
1. Human capital and R & D	47.2	26
2. Education sector	57.0	50
Spending on education, % of GDP	3.5	90
3. Higher education	45.9	20
The number of applicants to universities, % of the total number	86.4	16
Graduates of research and engineering specialties, %	32.6	13
Academic mobility, %	5.0	49
University rankings QS, top 3	49.0	21
4. R & D	38.7	27
Republic of Belarus		
1. Human capital and R & D	39.9	37
2. Education sector	61.6	26
Spending on education, % of GDP	4.7	45
3. Higher education	48.1	13
The number of applicants to universities, % of the total number	82.2	22
Graduates of research and engineering specialties, %	34.6	9
Academic mobility, %	6.5	38
University rankings QS, top 3	17.6	56
4. R & D	10.1	59

Table **1** shows that in terms of further development of human capital, both the Russian Federation and the Republic of Belarus have something to work on in the near future.

Indeed, as noted in a fundamental study by Moscow scientists (Eskindarov *et al.*, 2022), in the process of digitalization of the economy, the study of the role of HC is especially relevant due to the need to search for new models and mechanisms for the functioning and further development of the economy of Russia and its regions. In particular, by 2025, it is planned to implement three key areas of activity in the field of HC and HES (Table **2**).

Table 2. The results of building a modern digital economy in the field of "Human capital and education" in 2025 (Eskindarov *et al.*, 2022, p. 1116).

Results	Characteristics
Specialized scientific base	The functioning of a network of alliances for the collective use of digital devices and scientific equipment.
An attractive environment for IT professionals to work in	Improving the regulatory framework and improving the technological socio-economic platform for verifying research results.
Formation of personnel for the digital economy through educational programs	Education based on the principles of a personal approach, a combination of educational and labor development vectors, *etc.*

Therefore, in the context of digitalization and the need to increase human capital, Russian universities should become more active in the areas of training specialists for knowledge-intensive and high-tech sectors of the economy. To achieve this goal, it is necessary to solve the following main tasks:

- Improving the digital literacy of the population;
- Creation of HR forecasting practices focused on knowledge-intensive and high-tech sectors of the economy;
- Organization of the educational process with an emphasis on the formation of skills in the field of ensuring the operation of digital systems (Eskindarov *et al.*, 2022, p. 1117).

According to the conceptual approaches to the development of the education system of the Republic of Belarus by 2030[3], it is planned to transform leading uni-

3 Source: National Strategy for Sustainable Socio-Economic Development of the Republic of Belarus for the period up to 2030. – [Electronic resource]. URL: https://economy.gov.by/uploads/files/NSUR2030/Natsionalnaja-strategija-ustojchivogo-sotsialno-ekonomicheskogo-razvitija-Respubliki-Belarus-na-period-do-2030-goda.pdf. (date of application: 02/08/2024). (In Russ.).

versities into scientific, educational, and industrial clusters aimed at systematically solving issues of innovative development of industries and intersectoral complexes (Klimuk, 2023; Klimuk-Unsovich, 2021). The main goal of the national education system transformation will be to obtain new knowledge that can either be used for practical purposes or form the basis for subsequent fundamental and applied research. Through knowledge and R & D, intelligent products and innovative technologies are created, which are introduced into production, increasing its knowledge intensity. It should be noted that investments in knowledge do not bring instant income, and therefore, it is difficult to immediately assess their effectiveness, especially in relation to intellectual work. As an employee acquires experience and professional skills, the degree of his contribution to improving labor productivity and production efficiency increases (Alekseev and Dudko, 2018).

To assess the costs of R & D in Belarus, it is necessary to understand that after the collapse of the USSR and the implementation of market reforms, many technological chains of the vast majority of industries were broken; the scientific and educational complex functioned in the mode of constant non-payments and low wages of workers, there was a drastic decrease in the social status of a scientist and a higher school employee, the material and technical base science has not been practically modernized; R & D costs have decreased, and this negative trend has not been overcome at the present time (Fig. **1**).

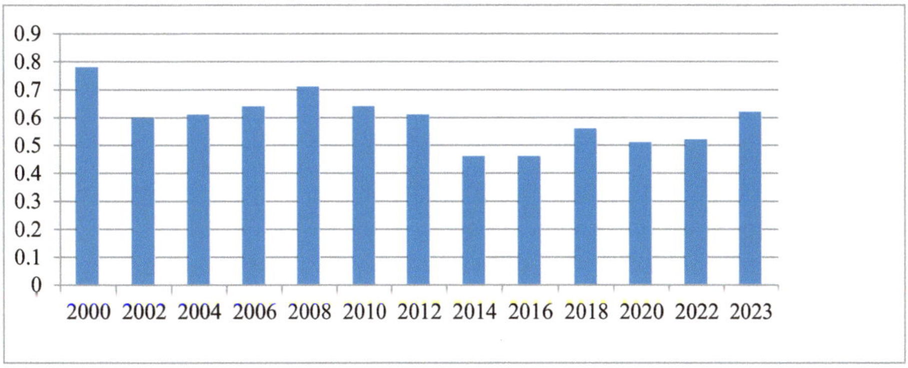

Fig. (1). R & D costs in the Republic of Belarus, as % of GDP[4].

Despite this, the Republic of Belarus, like the Russian Federation, is at a fairly high level in terms of the knowledge intensity of GDP (Astratova *et al.*, 2024).

4 Source: World Data Atlas. Belarus is an education. – [Electronic resource]. URL: knoema.ru/atlas /Belarus / topics / Education /Financing of education/Government spending on education as a percentage of GDP. (accessed: 01/18/2024). (In Russ.).

Based on the above, it can be concluded that USB has a significant resource for the development of scientific and innovative potential, increasing the knowledge intensity of production, despite insufficient investments in R & D.

As noted above, modern achievements and development are impossible without the transformation of the educational process. Today, society is making new demands on the educational process. Education should be adapted to real life as an opportunity to combine various applications of the acquired knowledge (Astratova *et al.*, 2024). In this regard, it should be noted that both the Russian Federation and the Republic of Belarus are very actively supporting education (Table **3**).

Table 3. Government spending on education (% of GDP), compiled by the authors based on various sources (Stat SocEc, 2023) [5].

Country	Years												
	2010	**2011**	**2012**	**2013**	**2014**	**2015**	**2016**	**2017**	**2018**	**2019**	**2020**	**2021**	**2022**
Belarus	5.2	4.7	5.0	5.0	4.8	4.8	5.0	4.8	4.7	4.7	4.7	4.9	4.9
Azerbaijan	2.8	2.4	2.7	2.5	2.6	3.0	2.9	2.5	2.5	2.5	2.6	2.7	2.7
Armenia	2.8	2.8	2.4	2.	2.4	2.4	2.75	2.7	2.7	2.2	2.5	2.7	2.9
Kazakhstan	3.5	3.6	4.0	3.3	3.3	3.3	3.0	2.8	2.8	2.6	2.8	2.8	2.7
Kyrgyzstan	5.4	6.4	7.0	6.1	5.6	6.0	6.1	6.0	5.5	5.4	5.4	5.3	5.3
Moldova	9.1	8.3	8.4	7.0	7.0	6.9	6.71	5.6	5.4	6.1	6.1	6.0	6.0
Russia	4.2	4.0	4.1	4.1	3.9	3.8	3.7	4.7	4.7	4.7	4.9	5.0	5.2
Tadjikistan	3.1	4.8	4.3	5.0	5.1	5.2	5.0	5.1	5.5	5.6	5.7	5.7	5.7

The data in Table **3** illustrate that the Union State is currently developing scientific potential inherent in advanced technological structures, adapting scientific schools to modern financing conditions, and creating a system for training scientific personnel capable of adequately responding to internal needs and external challenges.

Indeed, in the Republic of Belarus, according to the 2019 census, persons with higher education accounted for 17.9% of the total population, with specialized

5 Hasanli A. Forecasts of the state budget of Azerbaijan have been announced. – 2024. – [Electronic resource] / A. Hasanli // TrendNewsAgency. – Access mode: https://www.trend.az/business/economy/2433196.html. (accessed: 02/09/2024. (In Russ.).
RBC research: how much Russia actually spends on its citizens. December 14, 2016. – [Electronic resource]. URL: www.rbc.ru/economics/14/12/2016/584fd32e9a7947c251265ede. (accessed: 02/07/2024). (In Russ.).

secondary education – 25.6%, with vocational – 10.5%, with general secondary – 22.3%, with basic general – 12.6%, with primary education – 11.1%[6]. Meanwhile, in the United States, the proportion of people with higher and secondary specialized education among the adult population reached 60% over the same period. From 2000 to the present, there has been a steady trend in the Republic of Belarus towards restructuring the structure of educational services in favor of higher education.

The increasing role of higher education in the SRB in recent years has contributed to a qualitative change in the labor market and, as a result, an increase in the knowledge intensity of production (Danilchenko & Kharitonovich, 2019). This, in turn, activates the innovative development of the country, the transition of society to the next technological order, and the implementation of the concept of lifelong education (Table **4**).

Table 4. The number of institutions of higher education and the number of students in post-Soviet countries[7].

Country	2014/2015 Academic Year		2015/2016 Academic Year		2016/2017 Academic Year		2017/2018 Academic Year		2018/2019 Academic Year	
	number of Institutions, Units	Number of Students, Thousand	Number of Institutions, Units	Number of Students, Thousand	Number of Institutions, Units	Number of Students, Thousand	Number of Institutions, Units	Number of Students, Thousand	Number of Institutions, Units	Number of Students, Thousand
Belarus	54	363	52	336	51	313	51	284	51	268
Azerbaijan	53	158	54	161	51	184	52	184	52	186
Armenia	65	94	63	97	67	93	58	92	56	95
Moldova	31	90	31	82	30	75	30	71	29	68
Russia	950	5209	896	4766	818	4399	766	4246	741	4162
Ukraine	277	1438	288	1375	287	1369	258	1324	242	1297

Currently, a significant number of young specialists with sufficient knowledge and competencies are being trained for the national economies of post-Soviet countries. In particular, in higher education in Russiaand Belarus, a practice-oriented approach is being implemented in the training of specialists, which contributes to their early adaptation to the workplace. The practical orientation of specialists allows increasing the growth rate in many high-tech areas of the real sector of the economy. This, in turn, enhances the importance of higher education

---

6 Source: Education . // National Statistical Committee of the Republic of Belarus. – [Electronic resource]. URL: https://www.belstat.gov.by/ofitsialnaya-statistika/solialnaya-sfera/obrazovanie/. (accessed: 02/11/2024). (InRuss.).

7 Source: Ranking of countries in the world according to the Human Development Index. [Electronic resource] // Humanitarian portal. – [Electronic resource]. URL: https://gtmarket.ru/ratings/human-development-index (accessed: 02/19/2024). (In Russ.).

and contributes to the development of research potential (Danilchenko & Kharitonovich, 2019).

The analysis of the array of statistical data revealed an acute shortage of highly qualified personnel in the Russian Federation, while the population with higher education is in excess (Bengraf *et al.*, 2024). This fact confirms the thesis about the inefficient implementation of strategic management and the need to transform management systems, taking into account current trends in the labor market.

Results of our long-term researches (Astratova *et al.*, 2024; Astratova and Sinitsyn *et al.*, 2024; Astratova and Klimuk, 2022; Astratova *et al.*, 2022; Astratova *et al.*, 2021; Astratova *et al.*, 2019a; Bengraf *et al.*, 2024; Klimuk and Astratova, 2022; *etc.*) made it possible to identify common trends in the development of the labor market in the Russian Federation and the Republic of Belarus in connection with the development of HC in general and in creative human capital, especially, with link with higher education, R & D and digitalization:

- The analysis of the labor force of the Russian Federation and the Republic of Belarus allows us to conclude that there is a structural imbalance in the labor market, which is expressed in the discrepancy between the supply and demand of labor by territorial, sectoral, qualification, age, educational, and gender characteristics.
- There is an increase in employment in the service sector. This is due to the influence of digital technologies, which are able to replace human resources with automated and robotic ones. At the same time, the released labor force moves into the service sector, for example, acquiring skills in the IT industry, providing computer, telecommunications, and information services, *etc.*
- The structure of the labor market is influenced by factors of labor migration, which decreased during the coronavirus crisis, and its further development slowed down due to factors affecting the stability and structure of the global labor market. In the Russian Federation, the availability of employment for low–skilled personnel, foreign citizens is expressed. At the same time, as a result of the growth of economic activity, the removal of many anti-covert measures, and the restoration of air traffic in the Russian Federation, the demand for foreign highly qualified specialists has increased.
- There are dynamic changes in the level of real wages, the indicators of which are unstable - there is a decrease in the level, then a slight increase, which indicates an increase in the level of inflation, crisis phenomena, *etc.*
- Due to the gradual introduction of innovations and digital technologies into the business processes of enterprises and organizations, there is a gradual increase in

the number of vacancies, and the dynamics of the number of unemployed confirm the thesis that the qualifications of the workforce do not correspond to modern economic realities. There is a qualitative gap in the labor market.

- An analysis of the structure of the employed population and the unemployed by level of education in the Russian Federation shows that women with higher education are more in demand, their share in the employment structure is almost 40%, for men, this indicator stopped at 30%, in the structure of employed men, there is an increase in the level of vocational education.
- There are significant reductions in the main indicators of higher education, which can be associated with the demographic crisis in the 1990s, the government's policy aimed at reducing the number of students on a fee-based basis, low material and technical security, staffing, as well as the presence of certain dissatisfaction (inefficiency) from higher education among young professionals.
- Due to the tightening of the rules for defending dissertations, the requirements for the work of staff with a scientific degree have increased, as well as dissatisfaction with wages, which forces employees to move to more profitable sectors of the economy, or problems of migration of highly qualified scientists and researchers are manifested.
- Due to the reduction in the science intensity of GDP, it is necessary to increase financing not only for R & D, but also for higher education in general, to increase human capital in general and creative human capital in particular.
- The practice of stimulating the use of domestic ICT services and software by government agencies is expanding.

Thus, in order to achieve a high-quality level of economic development in the USRB at the present stage, innovative technologies and research achievements, as well as educated human potential, which acts as an effective tool for these transformations, are necessary.

CONCLUSION

The comprehensive analysis conducted in this chapter demonstrates that human capital is indeed the cornerstone of economic development in the context of the digital transformation occurring in the Union State of the Russian Federation and Belarus. Several important conclusions can be drawn from this research:

First, the study confirms that human capital plays a pivotal role in the development of the knowledge economy, innovation, and digital transformation. Both the Russian Federation and the Republic of Belarus recognize this importance, as evidenced by their relatively high expenditure on education as a percentage of GDP compared to other post-Soviet countries. However, their positions in global innovation rankings, particularly in human capital and research (positions 26 and 37, respectively), indicate substantial room for improvement.

Second, the research reveals a significant structural imbalance in the labor markets of both countries. This imbalance manifests as a discrepancy between labor supply and demand across territorial, sectoral, qualification, age, educational, and gender characteristics. Notably, in Russia, there is a paradoxical situation where an excess of individuals with higher education coexists with an acute shortage of highly qualified personnel, pointing to inefficiencies in strategic human capital management.

Third, the digital transformation of the economy is reshaping employment patterns, with increasing movement toward the service sector, particularly in IT-related fields. This shift underscores the need for educational systems that can rapidly adapt to technological changes and market demands. The emphasis on practice-oriented approaches in higher education in both countries represents a positive step toward better aligning graduate skills with workplace requirements.

Fourth, despite insufficient investments in R & D (as reflected in the declining R & D expenditure as a percentage of GDP in Belarus), both countries maintain a relatively high knowledge intensity of GDP. This suggests significant potential for enhancing scientific and innovative capabilities if more resources were directed toward research and development activities.

Fifth, the reduction in key higher education indicators—including student numbers and academic staff—poses a serious challenge for future human capital development. This decline can be attributed to various factors, including demographic trends, policy changes, dissatisfaction with educational quality, and inadequate remuneration of academic and scientific staff, leading to brain drain issues.

Sixth, the study identifies that in order to achieve high-quality economic development in the USRB, there must be a stronger integration between innovative technologies, research achievements, and educated human potential. This requires systematic approaches to human capital development that encompass not only quantitative aspects (such as education spending) but also qualitative dimensions (such as creative and innovative capabilities).

Finally, to address the identified challenges, both countries need to implement targeted policies that:

- Increase R & D funding and improve its efficiency
- Enhance the quality and relevance of higher education

- Bridge the gap between education outcomes and labor market requirements
- Stimulate the development of creative human capital through appropriate incentives
- Foster closer integration between academic institutions and industry
- Develop effective forecasting mechanisms for future skill requirements in knowledge-intensive sectors
- Improve digital literacy across the population

By addressing these priorities, the Union State can strengthen its position in the global innovation landscape and ensure sustainable economic growth driven by high-quality human capital adapted to the requirements of the digital economy. The transformation of leading universities into scientific, educational, and industrial clusters, as envisioned in Belarus's education system development concept through 2030, represents a promising direction for achieving these goals. Such integration would systematically address innovation challenges across industries and intersectoral complexes, ultimately enhancing the competitive position of the USRB in the global knowledge economy.

CHAPTER 17

The Labour Market as a Complex Socio-economic System: Some Aspects of Mathematical Modelling in the Labour Market of the Union State

Evgeny V. Sinitsyn[1,*] and **Viola A. Larionova**[2]

[1] *Department of Management, Institute of Economics and Management, Ural Federal University (UrFU), Yekaterinburg 620002, Sverdlovsk Region, Russian Federation*

[2] *Department of Economics and Management of Construction and Real Estate Market, Ural Federal University (UrFU), Yekaterinburg 620002, Sverdlovsk Region, Russian Federation*

Abstract: This chapter examines the labor market as a complex socio-economic system, with a particular focus on mathematical modeling of labor migration between the Russian Federation and the Republic of Belarus within the framework of the Union State. The study proposes a stochastic model based on Markov processes to analyze cross-country migration flows, treating population movements as random processes determined by transition probabilities. Using historical data from 1997-2022, the research demonstrates how these migration probabilities have changed over time and identifies similar trends in migration patterns between both countries despite differences in magnitude. The model accounts for the factorization of population and capital movements, allowing for the calculation of equilibrium concentrations and the prediction of long-term population distribution. Special attention is given to working-age migration, which constitutes over 80% of total migration flows. The findings reveal a notable anomaly during 2005-2014 for Russia and 2006-2012 for Belarus, when migration trends would have led to significant increases in population concentration in both countries if maintained long-term. The chapter concludes by suggesting that further research could benefit from a more detailed clustering analysis of labor migrants by demographic and socioeconomic characteristics to enhance the predictive capabilities of the model.

Keywords: Labor market, Markov model, Mathematical modeling, Migration flows, Population equilibrium, Stochastic processes, Union State.

[*] **Corresponding author Evgeny V. Sinitsyn:** Department of Management, Institute of Economics and Management, Ural Federal University (UrFU), Yekaterinburg 620002, Sverdlovsk Region, Russian Federation;
E-mail: sinitsyn_ev@mail.ru

INTRODUCTION

The labour market is a complex system of public economic relations between employers and employees in the processes of the labour services provision, as well as the negotiations about prices and working conditions, *etc*. The emergence and evolution of the labour market is a process of "... the emergence and growth of market potential through the formation of qualitatively new structural relations" (Babenkova, 2008, p. 45). It is well known that the labour market management mechanism is determined by the institutional environment and the structure of relations between the elements of the complexly organized economic system. Labour migration plays a special role in the system of labour market relations. It is not only a force that influences the demographic situation in a country or region and facilitates the influx of specialists lacking in the market, but it also creates the prerequisites for cross-cultural communication between the populations of different countries/regions. Moreover, "... *labour markets in the countries with a high standard of living are developing due to the constant influx of labour from other countries and regions. The labour markets of these countries are much more attractive than the labour markets in countries with an average standard of living, confirming the hypothesis about the economic nature of modern migration*" (Wang and Platonova, 2019, p. 1).

It should be mentioned that the problems of labour migration, mutual investments (capital flows), as well as export-import operations in the post-Soviet space, became relevant after the collapse of the Soviet Union. The problem of labour migration is especially relevant in the post-Soviet republics with a population close in language, religion, mentality, and cultural customs, and most of all, for the Republic of Belarus and the Russian Federation. The Union State Treaty between them will turn 25 years old in December 2024. All of the processes listed above are cross-connected and, anyway, affect all the spheres of economic, socio-political, demographic, and cultural life of the member countries in the interstate Union.

In the contemporary migration relations between Russia and Belarus, Belarus acts primarily as an exporter of labour (Vasilevskaya, 2019). Moreover, Belarusian labour migrants have become a "permanent component of the Russian labour market" (Poletaev, 2021). These trends are obviously illustrated in Fig. (**1**).

Migration flows differ in their structure based on various criteria: geographic location, time, gender, age, education, social status, *etc.*

The mathematical modelling of processes in the labour market as a whole and in relation to labour migration is relevant both for the predictive analysis of socio-political and economic phenomena, and for the reliable planning of the socio-economic development of the USRB.

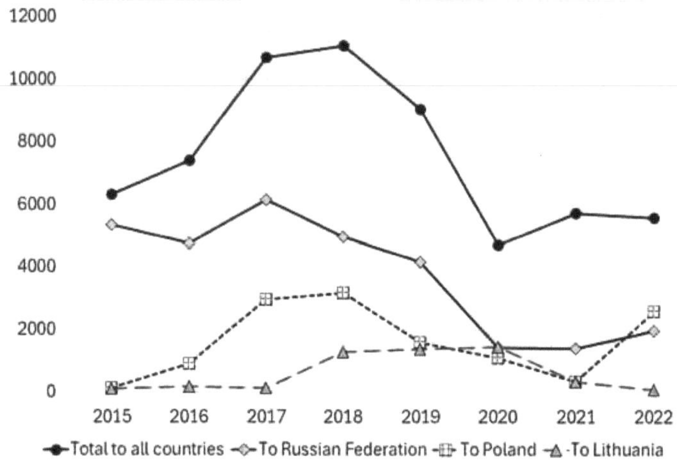

Fig. (1). Number of labour migrants from Belarus outside the country with the official work permissions, in 2015-2022, persons. *Source: authors' results based on the data from the Ministry of Internal Affairs of the Republic of Belarus. Available at: https://mvd.gov.by/ru/page/uchet-trudyashihsya-emigrantov-i-trudy-ashihsya-immigrantov (Accessed: 04/14/2024).*

The authors propose a mathematical model that allows identifying the complex dependencies and forecasting the processes of cross-country migration on the basis of historical data mining. Unfortunately, the authors have not had sufficient data to conduct a full analysis, but they hope that the capabilities of the model itself will be of interest to the economic community. The model is based on the theory of random processes in stochastic systems. The mathematical justification and basic formulas of the model are presented in our work (Astratova and Sinitsyn *et al.*, 2024), which presents a generalization of the model previously used (Sinitsyn *et al.*, 2022; Tolmachev *et al.*, 2019) in the study of intra-urban population migration processes, forecasting the demand for transport services, and a number of other socio-economic problems.

A. Data and Calculation Methods

Data on mutual migration of the population are presented in Figs. (**2** and **3**). As can be seen from Fig. (**1**), the migration from the Russian Federation to the Republic

As can be seen from Fig. (**2**), the migration from the Russian Federation to the Republic of Belarus reached a minimum in 2007-2012, after which it began to increase (although with significant dips in some years).

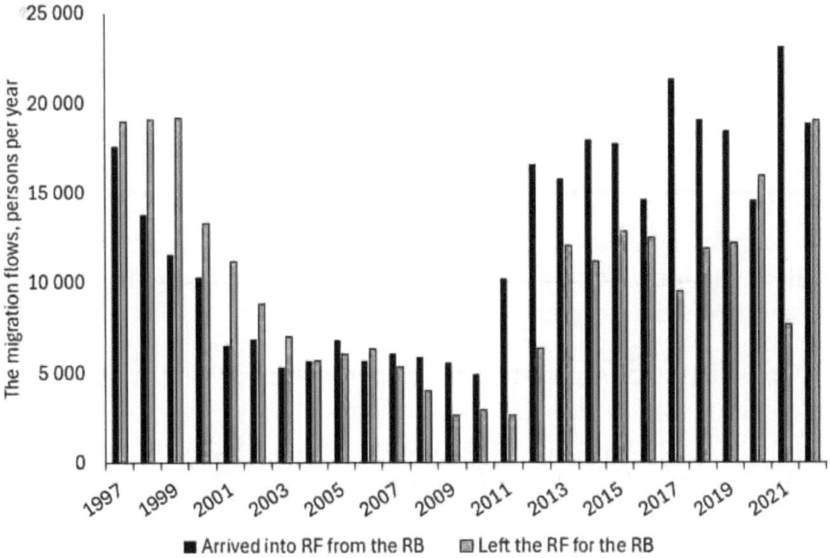

Fig. (2). The Migration flows between the Russian Federation and the Republic of Belarus; the results of the authors' compilation of the data from https://rosstat.gov.ru/.

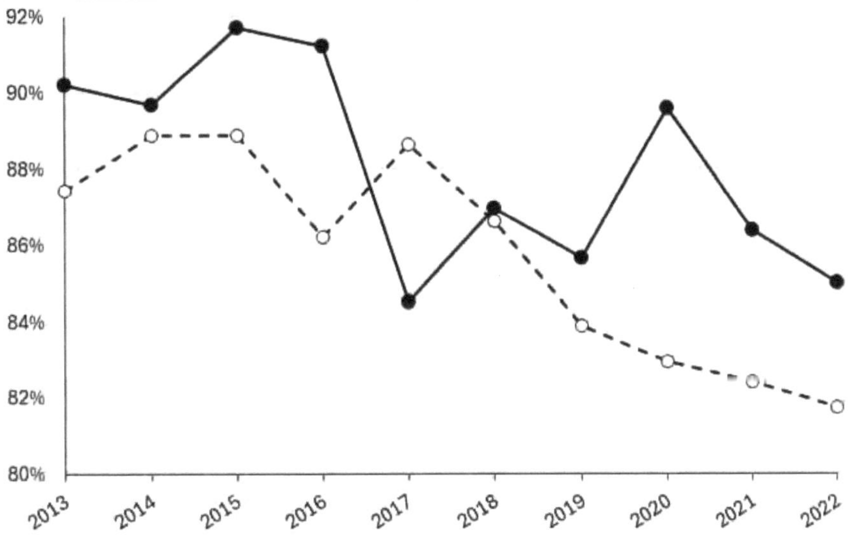

Fig. (3). The share of the working-age population in the migration flows between the Russian Federation and the Republic of Belarus; the results of the authors compiled on the data from https://rosstat.gov.ru/.

Moreover, since 2007, the flow from the Republic of Belarus to the Russian Federation usually exceeds the migration flow in the opposite direction. Before

2007, the opposite trend was observed. At the same time, the working-age population prevails in migration flows (Fig. **3**), and the share of the working-age population among those leaving the Russian Federation (2017 is the exception) exceeds the share of the working-age population among migrants from the Republic of Belarus.

In the models of these processes, we assumed that migration flows and capital movements are influenced by economic reasons. The movement of a working person itself is random. The probability of a person's decision to move from one country to another is determined by the ratio of the countries' economies.

In further considering abstract human communities X and Y, between which movements of population occur, we will keep in mind, first of all, the Russian Federation and the Republic of Belarus. The relations between these countries are least burdened by considerations of a political or ideological nature, rather than economic ones.

We will also introduce a third entity: the union of all countries that do not include the previously considered countries X and Y. The processes of population migration can be considered as walking along a directed graph with three vertices (Fig. **4**). Considering internal migration in the listed countries X, Y, and the group of countries Z, we get the expression presented in equation 1a:

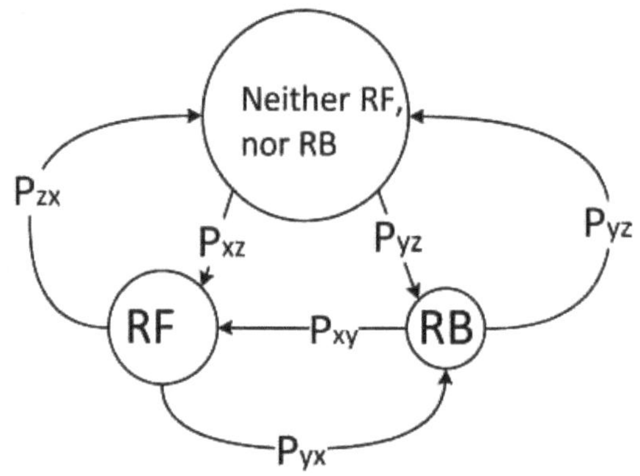

Fig. (4). Schematic representation of the population and capital flows and the corresponding probabilities between countries X, Y, and Z.

$$\sum_i p_{ij} = 1 \qquad \textbf{(1a)}$$

The migration of the population is considered a Markov random process determined by the probability p_{yx} of a single resident moving from country X to country Y (the notations for all other probabilities are analogous). The probabilities of a single person's migration per year are estimated as the expressions presented in equation 1b:

$$p_{xy} = \frac{N_{x \leftarrow y}}{N_y}, \; p_{yx} = \frac{N_{y \leftarrow x}}{N_x} \tag{1b}$$

Here $N(_{i \leftarrow j})$ are migration flows from country *j* to country *i* (persons/year), N_i is the average annual population in country i. The model is suitable for studying an arbitrary number of communities (Sinitsyn *et al.*, 2022), but for simplicity, we will only consider the transitions of population and capital between two countries. Since the processes under consideration are random, the states of countries characterized by certain values of the population and capital will be described by the probability distribution function of random variables N_x, N_y, K_x, K_y at a certain moment of time t-$\Phi(N_x, N_y, K_x, K_y, t)$. This allows determining both the mathematical expectations of these quantities and the possible spread of their values (variance and moments of higher orders).

In our earlier study (Astratova and Sinitsyn *et al.*, 2024), it was shown that the change in the distribution function over time is determined by the gradients of the flows presented in equations 2a and 2b:

$$-\frac{\partial \Phi}{\partial t} = \frac{\partial J_x}{\partial x} + \frac{\partial J_{k_x}}{\partial k_x} + \frac{\partial J_{k_y}}{\partial k_y} \tag{2a}$$

$$J_x = \left(x\left(p_{xy} + p_{yx}\right) - p_{xy}\right)\Phi \tag{2b}$$

Here J_x– is the probability flow of the population migration between countries. In addition, instead of N_x, N_y, K_x, K_y, the concentrations presented in equations 3a and 3b are used:

$$x = \frac{N_x}{N}, \; y = \frac{N_y}{N} \tag{3a}$$

$$k_x = \frac{K_x}{K_0}, \; k_y = \frac{K_y}{K_0}. \tag{3b}$$

K_0 is some initial value of the total capital in economies X and Y at the base moment of time from which the report was started. Note that the sum $k_x + k_y$ is not constant, while $x + y = 1$[1]. The distribution function Φ in these notations depends

1 In this case, changes of the population value due to natural processes of growth and decline are not taken into account

on x, k_x, k_y and time. The parameters included in equations (3a and 3b) are determined by socio-economic processes in each of the countries. In the general case, they depend simultaneouslyon their population concentration and the capital concentration. To test the model's correctness, let's consider some situations.

B. Independent Migration of Population and Capital

If the probabilities of migration p_{ij} do not depend on the concentrations of capital in countries, and the probabilities of capital movement, generation, and depreciation, nor do they depend on the concentrations of the population in them, then the distribution function $\Phi(x, k_x, k_y, t)$ is factorized, splitting into two independent functions characterizing the probability distribution of population concentrations $P(x, t)$ and capitals $Q(k_x, k_y, t)$:

The general solution of the equation for population migration has the form presented below in the equations 4a-4d (Sinitsyn *et al.*, 2022):

$$P(x,t) = e^{p_+ t} P_0\big((x - x_s)e^{p_+ t} + x_s\big) \quad \textbf{(4a)}$$

where:

$$P_0(x) = P(x, t = 0) \quad \textbf{(4b)}$$

initial distribution of population concentration,

$$p_+ = (p_{xy} + p_{yx}), \quad \textbf{(4c)}$$

$$x_s = \frac{p_{xy}}{p_{xy} + p_{yx}} \quad \textbf{(4d)}$$

x_s– stationary point of the equation for $P(x, t)$.

The average value and standard deviation of population concentration are given by the expressions presented in equations 5a & 5b:

$$\overline{x}(t) = x_s - e^{-p_+ t}(x_s - x_0), \quad \textbf{(5a)}$$

$$\sigma^2(t) = e^{-2p_+ t}{\sigma_0}^2. \quad \textbf{(5b)}$$

Here x_0 is the initial concentration – $\overline{x}(t = 0)$, a${\sigma_0}^2 = \sigma^2(t = 0)$ – is is the initial error in determining population concentrations in countries. Note that the stationary concentration x_s– (equation 7d) has a clear meaning. When the concentration of the summary population of countries in country X is x_s and in the country Y is y_s = 1- x_s, the mutual migration flows between these countries are balanced (J_x = 0), as is shown by equation 6:

$$j_{x\leftarrow y} = p_{xy}y_s = p_{yx}x_s = j_{y\leftarrow x} \quad \textbf{(6)}$$

Note that if, for example, country X introduces some migration restrictions: a ban on immigration while emigration is permitted ($p_{xy} = p_{xz} = 0$) or ban on emigration with permitted immigration ($p_{yx} = p_{zy} = 0$), one gets in the first case $x_s = 0$, while in the second $x_s = 1$.

We can treat the parameters x_s, y_s as predicted values of the population concentrations in the countries after a sufficiently long period of time: t>>(p_{xy} + p_{yx}),$^{-1}$ if the existing trends of migration are maintained. Fig. (**5**) shows the values x_s, y_s, z_s_s for population migration processes between Russia, Belarus, and the set of all other countries.

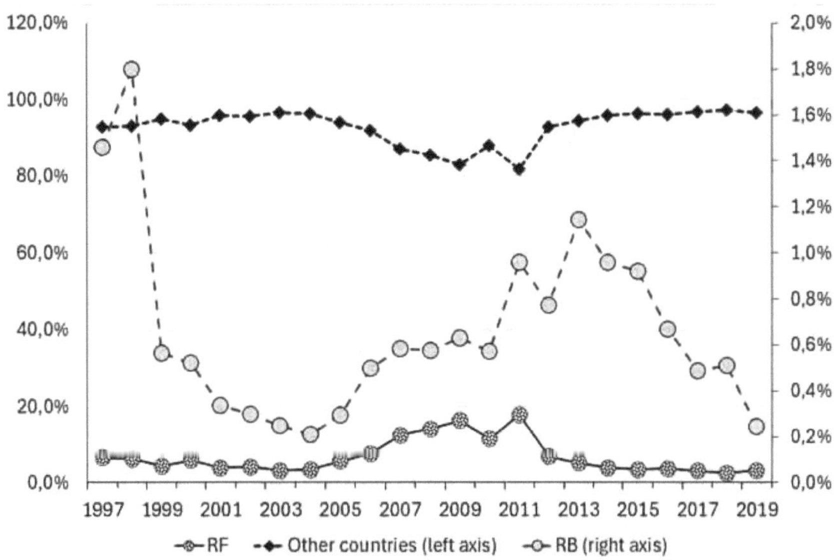

Fig. (5). The equilibrium concentrations (stationary points of the equations for concentrations) in migration processes between the Russian Federation, Belarus, and other countries; the results of the authors compiled on the data from https://rosstat.gov.ru/, https://www.belstat.gov.by/.

It is possible to note the clearly abnormal period 2005 – 2014 for the Russian Federation and 2006 – 2012 for the Republic of Belarus. The preservation of migration trends that existed at that time would have led, over a historically long period (hundreds of years), to a significant increase in the concentration of the world population in the Republic of Belarus and the Russian Federation, and with a simultaneous noticeable reduction in the share of the population living in other countries. It should be noted that with the current values of migration probabilities, the dynamics of $x(t)$, $y(t)$, $z(t)$, in accordance with (Equation 10a), has a relaxation character, with a small (on average 3,2) damping decrement and a long (about a thousand years) oscillation period. This can be verified by solving the corresponding equations of the model for the situation shown in Fig. (**6**) by standard methods (Feller, 1957; Gantmakher, 1988). However, it is necessary to mention that such a long time of establishing the equilibrium of migration flows (interesting, of course, only in a historical context) is due to the small value of the probabilities p_{ij} $(i, j = x, y, z)$. The latter is because in the definition of p_{ij}- (1) the denominators are the full population values N_x, N_y. Thus, it is assumed that absolutely all residents can migrate between countries. In fact, as can be seen from Fig. (**3**), more than 80% of migrants are people of working age. That is, it is more correct to use the number of the working-age population as N_x, N_y. In the Russian Federation on 01.01.2023, the share of the working-age population was approximately 57%, in the Republic of Belarus, about 53%. Thus, considering migration processes only with the working-age population approximately doubles the probabilities p_{ij} and, accordingly, reduces the time for establishing equilibrium of migration flows by the same amount.

Note that the value of x_s changes insignificantly, but now it should be applied only to the distribution of the working-age population between countries. However, the situation is even more complicated, since not all working-age population participates in migration processes, but only a certain and clearly not large part of it. Accurate determination of the number of people who can potentially participate in migration processes is relevant for modelling and forecasting migration processes. In this regard, it would be interesting in the future to conduct research on the profile of labour migrants, with their clustering by gender, age, level of education, profession, and marital status.

However, at present, the authors do not have a complete set of data for the Russian Federation and Belarus, which allows such a study. Thus, such an analysis will be the direction of further research.

Thus, the authors have considered the basic model of population migration between countries connected by socio-cultural, political, and economic relations. Moreover, all the listed factors influence the phenomena under consideration through the probabilities of population transitions from one country to another. Identifying the full set of factors influencing the probabilities of population migration between countries is a complex task and requires additional research.

For example, Fig. (**6**) shows the changes in the probabilities of migration from the Republic of Belarus to the Russian Federation and the reverse process based on data for the period from 1997 to 2022. It is evident that, despite the difference in the values of probabilities, the trends in their changes are quite similar. This indicates the presence of some factors common to both countries that influence migration processes. This will be discussed by the authors further in Chapter Three.

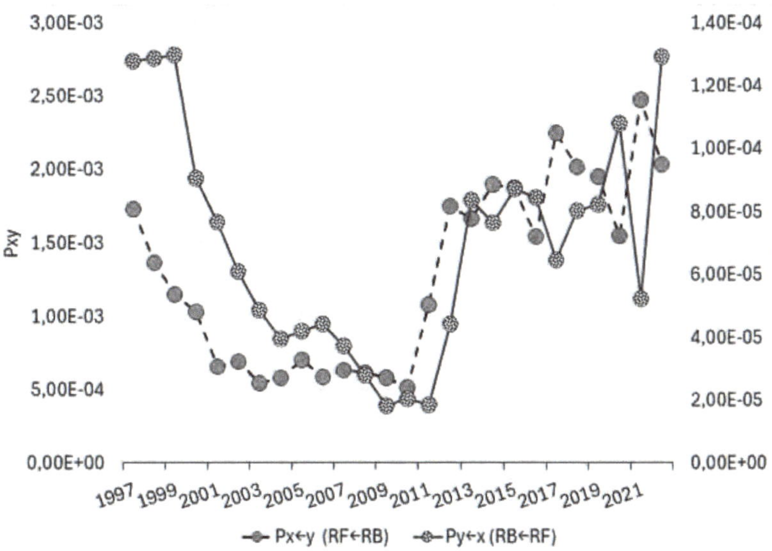

Fig. (6). The changes in the migration probabilities between the Russian Federation and Belarus, the results of the authors compiled on the data from https://rosstat.gov.ru/, https://www.belstat.gov.by/.

CONCLUSION

This chapter has explored the application of mathematical modeling to analyze labor migration processes between the Russian Federation and the Republic of Belarus within the framework of the Union State. The stochastic model based on Markov random processes has proven to be an effective tool for examining the complex dynamics of cross-border population movements and predicting long-term migration trends.

Our analysis reveals several important findings. First, the migration flows between Russia and Belarus demonstrate clear patterns over the 1997-2022 period, with Belarus primarily functioning as a labor exporter to Russia in recent years. Second, the model identifies an anomalous period (2005-2014 for Russia and 2006-2012 for Belarus) when migration trends, if maintained, would have led to significant increases in population concentration in both countries over the long term.

The model's calculation of equilibrium concentrations provides valuable insights into the potential future distribution of population between the two countries if current migration probabilities persist. However, the estimated timeframe for reaching this equilibrium (approximately 1,000 years) highlights the gradual nature of these demographic processes when viewed at the national level.

Importantly, our research confirms that migration flows are predominantly composed of working-age individuals (over 80%), suggesting that economic factors play a decisive role in migration decisions. This finding reinforces the need to focus on labor market conditions and economic disparities when analyzing migration patterns between the Union State members.

The similarity in the trends of migration probabilities between Russia and Belarus, despite differences in magnitude, indicates the presence of common factors influencing population movements in both directions. These shared determinants warrant further investigation to enhance our understanding of the socio-economic dynamics within the Union State.

While the current model provides a solid foundation for analyzing migration processes, its predictive power could be significantly enhanced through more detailed data collection and analysis. Specifically, future research should focus on developing comprehensive profiles of labor migrants, including characteristics such as gender, age, education level, profession, and marital status. Such demographic clustering would allow for more nuanced modeling and more accurate forecasting of migration flows.

In conclusion, the mathematical model presented in this chapter offers a valuable framework for understanding the complex interplay of factors driving labor migration between Russia and Belarus. As the Union State continues to evolve, this analytical approach can inform policy decisions aimed at optimizing labor market integration and addressing demographic challenges in both countries.

CHAPTER 18

The Socio-Technological Nature of the Organization of Labor in the Digital Environment of the Union State

Natalia A. Simchenko[1,*]

[1] *Department of Economic Theory and Economic Policy, St. Petersburg State University, St. Petersburg 199034, Russian Federation*

Abstract: This chapter examines the socio-technological nature of labor organization in the digital environment of the Union State of Russia and Belarus. As both countries transition toward innovative economic development models with an emphasis on digitalization, traditional labor organization approaches are being transformed. The study identifies how digital technologies are modifying labor content, processes, and relations, creating new employment platform models and ecosystem-based work organization structures. Particular attention is given to work rationing methods for IT specialists in digital environments, highlighting the convergence of analytical and summary approaches in modern practice. The research proposes functional points for IT project implementation on digital platforms and outlines factors affecting performance. The findings demonstrate that scientifically-based approaches to labor rationing on digital platforms can improve productivity, identify hindering factors, and create effective internal planning and control systems for project management in the Union State.

Keywords: Digital economy, Digital labor organization, IT specialists, Platform employment, Socio-technological transformation, Union State, Work rationing.

INTRODUCTION

Taking into account the influence of political, economic, and socio-technological factors, today the economic paradigm is changing in the Union State of the Russian Federation and the Republic of Belarus, and the model of economic development of fraternal countries is being transformed, focused on social and innovative development. In this regard, both countries have adopted a number of legislative acts related to the innovative and scientific and technical development

* **Corresponding author Natalia A. Simchenko:** Department of Economic Theory and Economic Policy, St. Petersburg State University, St. Petersburg 199034, Russian Federation; E-mail: natalysimchenko@yandex.ru

of national economies and individual industries until 2020, and extended until 2025 and 2030.

In accordance with the strategic planning documents[1], a list of initiatives for the socio-economic development of the Russian Federation until 2030 has been approved; this includes the following areas of development: social sphere, construction, ecology, digital transformation, technological breakthrough, and the state for citizens. Also, within the framework of the National Program "Digital Economy of the Russian Federation", as a tool for the strategic development of the country, nine federal projects are being implemented aimed at regulating the digital environment, training personnel for the digital economy and developing the human potential of the IT industry, the development of digital technologies and artificial intelligence, digital public administration, *etc.*[2] Among the listed areas, trends are being traced, focused on the introduction of digital technologies in all spheres of socio-economic development of the country, and, importantly, this is training for the digital economy. In the process of training personnel for the digital economy, forms and mechanisms of labor organization in the digital environment should be developed and proposed, since the digital economy modifies not only the content of labor but also the type of labor processes. Thus, the subject of work in the digital environment is information and digital data, which are presented exclusively in digital format; the means of work are digital devices, digital programs, and the result of work is information products (Savelyeva, 2018).

Within the framework of the Union State, the labor market of the Russian Federation and the Republic of Belarus has a similar structure and similar development vectors in the context of digitalization, namely:

- Creation of new jobs
- Investing in the workforce
- formation of a decent income
- Providing employment for the population
- Promotion of high labor standards as conditions for competitiveness
- Provision of other social and labor guarantees (Bengraf *et al.*, 2024)

---

1 On approval of the list of initiatives for the socio-economic development of the Russian Federation until 2030. Decree of the Government of the Russian Federation dated 06.10.2021 No. 2816-r (ed. from 03/14/2022) [Electronic resource].– URL: https://www.consultant.ru/document/cons_doc_LAW_397326/708a1dd4b9c098d56c63a4b0c948b8cdc3f39db0/ (accessed: 03/03/2024). (In Russ).

2 The digital economy of the Russian Federation. Ministry of Digital Development, Communications and Mass Media of the Russian Federation // Minutes of the meeting of the Presidium of the Council under the President of the Russian Federation for Strategic Development and National Projects dated 06/04/2019 No. 7. [Electronic resource]. – URL: https://digital.gov.ru/ru/activity/directions/858/?utm_referrer=https%3a%2f%2fwww.google.com%2f (In Russ.).

The team of authors M. M. Balog, S. E. Demidova, and V. V. Troyan noted that in foreign countries, there is a pronounced correlation between the use of digital technologies and labor productivity growth, but in Russia, such connections are absent due to imbalances in regional and sectoral development (Balog *et al.*, 2021).

In the Republic of Belarus, the problem of the relationship between the use of digital technologies and labor productivity growth is at the very beginning of its study. Nevertheless, there are known works showing that with the use of digital technologies, there is a redistribution of labor between humans and machines, partial replacement of human labor with machine labor, and the release of a significant share of the labor force, which ultimately increases labor productivity (Golovenchik, 2018; Maltsevich, 2023; *etc.*). It is also shown that labor productivity growth "... does not have a constant trend", but "... there are opportunities for its improvement within the framework of the concept of "Construction 4.0." (Maltsevich, 2023).

The author E.S. Sadovaya (Sadovaya, 2022) focuses on the fact that in the conditions of a new economic reality, "automation of business processes turns out to be a socio-technological prerequisite for employment platformization ... and labor relations are turning from social into computer algorithms" (Sadovaya, 2022). In other words, there is a transition from an industrial type of regulation of social and labor relations to a digital or platform type. A similar opinion was expressed by the authors E.V. Nekhoda and L. Pan, who emphasize that "the basic model of labor organization is the management of joint activities and empowerment of platform employment participants" (Nekhoda & Pan, 2021), that is, the organization of labor in a digital environment is carried out not on a vertical and horizontal division of labor, but on the basis of the integration of resources on a digital platform, with the help of which it is possible to attract more participants through online access, increase resources and form ecosystems by expanding the value chain.

It was considered necessary to supplement the changes and characteristics of the organization of work in the digital environment, compiled by scientists E.V. Nekhoda and L. Pan (2021). In their ecosystem-based work organization model (Nekhoda & Pan, 2021), changes in the content of work in the digital environment have led to transformations in the model, empowering all participants. Therefore, objects, means, labor results, and business processes acquire digital form and have a direct impact on the processes of distribution, exchange, and consumption in the digital economy. Also, in addition to technical and professional skills, employees in the digital environment are required to develop flexible skills aimed at personal development. In this regard, the process of digitalization transforms the labor market and social and labor relations and determines the importance of studying the socio-technological nature of the organization of digital labor in the context of the need to improve the efficiency of management of work rationing processes.

The components of labor organization, both in the industrial form of social and labor relations and in digital form, are work rationing procedures, on the basis of which it is possible to evaluate labor efficiency, analyze the use of working time, and determine whether the level of remuneration corresponds to the quantity and quality of work performed.

In the modern understanding of the process of labor rationing, it is necessary to identify three main principles of forming a methodological basis for work rationing in the digital environment:

- The principle of scientific validity of the established measures
- The principle of systematic norms (the presence of organizational and technical links in the labor process between labor, means, and objects of labor)
- The principle of dynamism (constant adjustment of established labor standards is necessary due to the influence of technical and technological factors).

Based on these principles, which form a single basis for the methodology for calculating labor standards, we have identified, generalized, and systematized the following groups of labor rationing methods, presented in Table **1**.

Table 1. Methods of labor rationing, in the author's interpretation.

A Group of Methods	Descriptive Characteristics of the Method
Analytical	Analytical and computational (formulas, standards, and calculated indicators are used; the Gauss method, graph-analytical method is used)
	Analytical and research (timekeeping, microelement division of labor, photography of working time, benchmarking)
Total	Expert (expert assessment)
	Statistical (analysis of statistical data for previous periods and forecasting based on them)
	The method of analogies (reasoning without dividing the labor process into elements)
Scientific	It is a method of observing labor processes.
	The method of studying the documents of the organization of labor rationing
Automated	A set of traditional rationing methods based on automating the collection of information about employee actions.

Taking into account the introduction of digital technologies in the practice of rationing, there is a tendency for groups of methods to converge. Thus, foreign companies apply the approach of labor rationing, which includes both groups of methods—analytical and summary (Anufrieva, 2021).

Currently, both in the Russian Federation and the Republic of Belarus, there is a main problem of organizing a labor rationing system – this is the lack of “centralized development and affordable/free distribution of regulatory materials on labor, taking into account industry specifics for many fields of activity” (Anufrieva, 2021). An example is the Soviet centralized rationing system, which was established in 1957 on the basis of the Scientific Research Institute of Labor, “the scale and areas of work of which allowed to normalize the work of almost 90% of workers in the country[3].”

To date, both in the Russian Federation and in the Republic of Belarus, there are specialized commercial consulting companies that can carry out labor rationing, but their services are paid for. At the same time, it should be noted that if we focus on the methodology of normative materials of the Soviet period, then such normative and methodological collections were developed mainly for manual labor. Soviet approaches and methods are not relevant for rationing work in a digital environment, taking into account the changing organizational and technical conditions of work and production.

At the same time, in modern conditions, methods and approaches of labor rationing in the digital environment of the Union State are being improved. This makes it possible to apply complex and cumbersome methods of labor rationing based on specially developed computer programs, digital technologies, and artificial intelligence, which allow “to form an intra-organizational base of labor standards and automate the work of standardizers to calculate new and clarify existing labor standards” (Anufrieva, 2021).

At the moment, the following stages of the process of labor rationing in the digital environment are known due to R.A. Dolzhenko and D.S. Malyshev:

1. Formation of a database of labor standards in the digital environment.
2. Digitization of the normalization results.
3. Automation of the collection of information about the actions of employees.
4. Online data analytics (Astratova, *et al.*, 2024).

---

3 Source: The Central Bureau of Labor Standards. The official website. [electronic resource]. – URL: https://cbnt.ru/(In Russ.).

That is why the process of labor rationing in the digital environment includes stages, the alternate implementation of which makes it possible to develop an effective mechanism for managing the labor rationing system, taking into account the impact of a socio-technological nature on the organization of digital labor.

Today, the IT industry is the basis for the formation and development of the digital economy of the Union State, since it is the result of the intellectual work of IT specialists and the implementation of IT projects that make it possible to determine suitable methods of work rationing. In order to form a system of methods for rationing the work of IT specialists, experts proposed to classify them into categories. For example, all IT specialists in a company can be divided into the following categories:

- System administrators, whose responsibilities include organizing a network within the company, installing and configuring software, and providing various services;
- Technical support specialists, whose responsibilities include the installation and configuration of computers, phones, network connections, servers, and printers, *etc.*
- Programmers, whose responsibilities include the development of websites and modules of accounting programs, the creation of their own software products, *etc.*

Based on the size of the company and its organizational structure, an IT service is being created, which will include the categories of IT specialists described above. Accordingly, the larger the company, the more significant the differences in the list of work in the implementation of IT projects, and the methods of labor rationing available for use will differ.

Economist S. Bushmin[4] proposed two approaches to rationing the work of IT specialists:

- Use direct rationing of labor costs;
- Use an indirect campaign based on the factors influencing the population rate.

These approaches to rationing the work of IT specialists and methods of their calculation are presented in Fig. (**1**).

---

4 Bushmin S.V. Methods of labor rationing for employees of business units // Portal for economists and labor engineers. – 2021. [Electronic resource]. – URL: https://www.nitt.by/aktual/vse-temy/metody-normirovaniya-truda-rabotnikov-it (accessed: 04/08/2024).

Direct rationing of labor costs:

- The method of timekeeping or photography of working time;
- A method based on suitable typical inter-industry norms;
- The method of expert assessment and conducting surveys of specialists, accumulated statistical data.

An indirect approach based on the factors influencing the number of employees:

- Regression method for calculating the number of IT specialists by factors;
- Correlation analysis of the influence of factors on the labor intensity of work;
- The method of functional points.

Fig. (1). Approaches to rationing the work of IT specialists and methods of their calculation, the author's interpretation

Depending on the complexity of the work performed when implementing projects on a digital platform, IT is advisable to normalize the work of IT specialists using a combination of the expert assessment method and the method of functional points, having previously determined their specific number and suggesting the subsequent correct application of time standards for each functional point.

Table **2** shows the approximate functional points of an IT project on a digital platform and the factors affecting the performance of each point. Note that the functional points presented in Table **2** have an enlarged form: when implementing an IT project on a digital platform, these points are divided into smaller, more specific tasks in order to carry out work rationing as an effective tool for managing work on the part of the project manager and identifying reserves for improving the productivity of IT specialists.

Table 2. Functional points of an IT project on a digital platform and factors influencing the performance of work, the author's development.

<table>
<tr><th>Functional point</th><th>Factors affecting the performance of work</th></tr>
<tr><td>Development of the technical specification of the project</td><td rowspan="5">– the scope of an IT project on a digital platform;
– the complexity of the implemented IT project on a digital platform;
– the degree of novelty of the implemented IT project on the digital platform;
–the degree of use of standard tools, approaches, modules, software, etc. in the implementation of an IT project;
– conditions and means of implementing an IT project on a digital platform.</td></tr>
<tr><td>Development of a preliminary design</td></tr>
<tr><td>Development of a technical project</td></tr>
<tr><td>Development of a technical project</td></tr>
<tr><td>Testing and commissioning of the project</td></tr>
</table>

As a result of applying such an approach to labor rationing in the Union State, duplication of work will be eliminated. Also, in the process of implementing an IT project, factors that hinder its effective implementation are identified and eliminated. In addition, the rationing of the work of IT specialists takes into account the optimal, rather than the maximum degree of labor intensity, and the organization of the labor process is aimed at the rational functioning of the work of IT specialists. Scientifically-based approaches used in the process of rationing work when implementing projects on a digital platform can improve performance and identify factors that hinder the productivity of IT specialists. At the same time, the labor rationing process will allow creating an internal planning and control system, which makes it an effective tool for managing the performance of work by the project manager and identifying reserves for improving the productivity of IT specialists on a digital platform.

CONCLUSION

The study of the socio-technological nature of labor organization in the digital environment of the Union State reveals significant transformations in how work is structured, evaluated, and managed. As both Russia and Belarus pursue innovative economic development pathways focused on digitalization, traditional approaches to labor organization are being fundamentally reshaped by emerging digital technologies and platform-based ecosystems.

Our research demonstrates that the digital economy modifies not only the content of labor but also labor processes themselves. In digital environments, information and digital data become the primary subject of work, with digital devices and programs serving as the primary means of work. This shift has profound implications for how labor is organized, regulated, and evaluated within the Union State.

The transition from industrial to digital forms of labor relations is characterized by several key developments. First, there is a movement from vertical and horizontal division of labor toward resource integration on digital platforms. These platforms facilitate broader participation through online access, increase available resources, and form ecosystems by expanding value chains. Second, the platformization of employment is transforming labor relations from primarily social interactions into computer-mediated algorithms, representing a fundamental shift in how work is coordinated and managed.

Our analysis of work rationing methods reveals the convergence of analytical and summary approaches in the digital context. The traditional principles of scientific validity, systematic norms, and dynamism remain important, but their application has evolved to accommodate digital work environments. The development of computer programs, digital technologies, and artificial intelligence now enables more complex labor rationing approaches that were previously impractical.

The four-stage process of labor rationing in digital environments—forming a database of standards, digitizing normalization results, automating information collection about employee actions, and implementing online data analytics—provides a framework for developing effective management mechanisms for labor rationing systems in the digital economy of the Union State.

For IT specialists specifically, we find that a combination of expert assessment methods and functional point analysis is most appropriate for work rationing on digital platforms. The functional points identified in our research (technical specification development, preliminary design, technical project development, testing, and commissioning) and their associated influencing factors (project scope, complexity, novelty, use of standard tools, and implementation conditions) offer a structured approach to rationing IT work.

The application of such scientifically grounded rationing approaches in the Union State yields several benefits: elimination of work duplication, identification and removal of implementation barriers, consideration of optimal rather than maximum labor intensity, and rational organization of labor processes. Importantly, this creates an internal planning and control system that serves as an effective tool for project management and productivity improvement.

Despite these advances, challenges remain. Unlike the centralized Soviet labor rationing system that normalized approximately 90% of workers' labor, current systems in both Russia and Belarus lack centralized development and free distribution of regulatory materials tailored to industry specifics. While commercial consulting companies offer labor rationing services, they come at a cost that may be prohibitive for some organizations. Additionally, Soviet-era normative materials, primarily developed for manual labor, have limited relevance in digital work environments with continuously evolving organizational and technical conditions.

As the Union State continues to develop its digital economy, labor organization approaches will need to further evolve to address these challenges. Future research should focus on developing more accessible and industry-specific regulatory materials, adapting rationing methodologies to rapidly changing digital environments, and exploring how artificial intelligence can enhance labor rationing processes. By addressing these areas, the Union State can create more effective and equitable labor organization systems suited to the digital era, ultimately enhancing productivity and competitiveness in the global economy.

CHAPTER 19

The Use of Digital Technologies in the State and Municipal Administration of the Russian Federation and the Republic of Belarus

Galina V. Astratova[1,*] and **Maxim V. Vlasov**[1]

[1] *Department of Regional Economics, Innovative Entrepreneurship and Economics (REIE&E), Institute of Economics and Management, School of Public Administration and Entrepreneurship (SPAE), Ural Federal University (UrFU), Yekaterinburg 620002, Sverdlovsk Region, Russian Federation*

Abstract: This study examines the implementation and usage of Digital Technologies (DT) in State and Municipal Administration (SMA) within the Russian Federation and the Republic of Belarus. The research investigates the current state, challenges, and potential benefits of digital transformation in the public sector compared to commercial enterprises. Based on expert surveys of civil servants in Yekaterinburg conducted in early 2024, the study identifies key applications of digital technologies in public administration, including process automation, automated decision-making systems, and manual task automation. The findings reveal significant gaps between the pace of DT adoption in public administration *versus* the commercial sector, primarily due to complex contracting processes and insufficient internal DT potential within government structures. Despite strategic policy documents in both Russia and Belarus aimed at creating innovative economies based on Big Data processing, the research highlights several unresolved issues in both the external application (public-facing electronic services) and internal application (management processes) of digital technologies. The study concludes by emphasizing the urgent need for solutions to enhance DT integration in public administration to improve efficiency, effectiveness, and productivity in government organizations.

Keywords: Digital technologies, Digital transformation, E-government, Public services, Republic of Belarus, Russian Federation, State and municipal administration.

* **Corresponding author Galina V. Astratova:** Department of Regional Economics, Innovative Entrepreneurship and Economics (REIE&E), Institute of Economics and Management, School of Public Administration and Entrepreneurship (SPAE), Ural Federal University (UrFU), Yekaterinburg 620002, Sverdlovsk Region, Russian Federation; E-mail: galina_28@mail.ru

INTRODUCTION

Digital technologies are understood in modern realities as "... a system of tools, methods and methods for creating, collecting, accumulating, storing, processing, transmitting and protecting information based on computer technology, used everywhere in various industries and spheres of economic activity" (Astratova & Bekshaev, 2024).

As a special information system, DT provides humanity with the following opportunities:

1. Increase the productivity/efficiency of management processes
2. Allow us to operate with a large amount of information (Big Data)
3. Increase the reliability of information
4. Give hope for the creation of an electronic model of universal system intelligent management (Astratova *et al.*, 2022; Bengraf *et al.*, 2024).

Using DT in the field of State and Municipal Administration (SMA) is extremely relevant in the context of the prospect of building an electronic state and the need for electronic communication between the state and society. In this regard, it is important that the digitalization of SMA is not only the development of public electronic services and web pages, but also the minimization of the time lag between obtaining results and the appearance of reporting data, reducing the risks of information security and data falsification, *etc*. (Astratova, 2023; Bengraf *et al.*, 2024; Dobrolyubova *et al.*, 2019; Kiselev, 2018; Lindgren and Veenstra, 2018; *etc.*).

Moreover, the use of DT in SMA also implies obtaining a number of additional features:

1. Involvement of all stakeholders at various stages of the development and implementation of public electronic services (Holgersson and Karlsson, 2014; Lindgren and Veenstra, 2018)
2. Understanding the needs, expectations, and values of users of electronic public services (Astratova, 2023b; Lindgren and Veenstra, 2018; Millard, 2015)
3. Transition of political communications to the Internet environment is a full-fledged digital marketing tool and a channel for interaction between the government and the population, political parties and society, which allows online "... analysis of opinions in social media about various party brands, personalities, analysis of the audience of blogs, *etc.*" (Chizhov, 2016, p. 335).

As the Yandex[1] query statistics show, the topic of digital/information technologies and their application in public administration is very relevant in Russia, since the number of requests is quite large (thousands and tens of thousands of requests, monthly) and it has an upward trend.

Moreover, the results of our expert survey[2] also show that the use of DT in the work of civil servants presents a lot of opportunities, and experts rate them very highly (Fig. **1**).

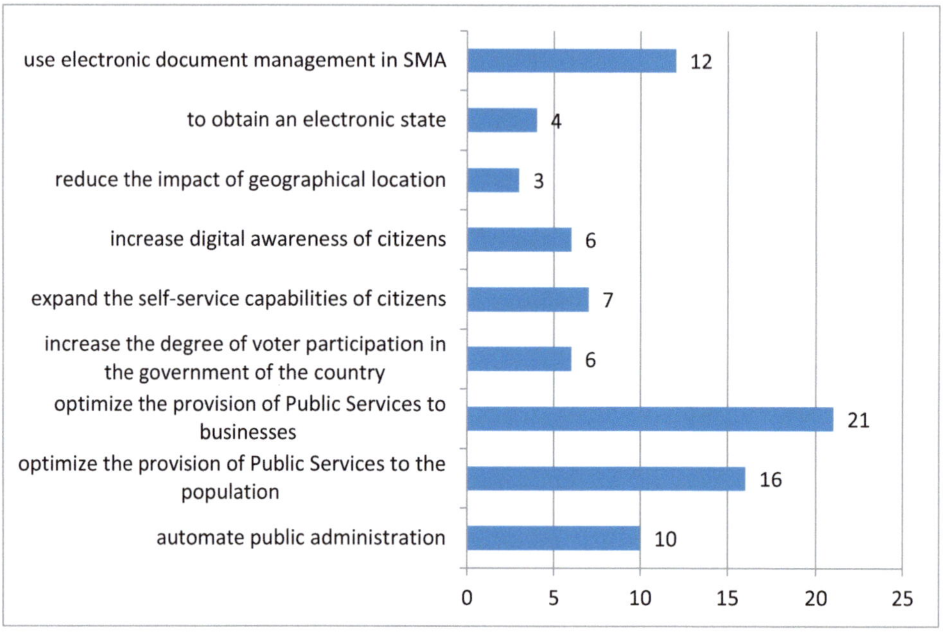

Fig. (1). Data from an expert survey of civil servants; respondents' answers to the question: "Do you think the use of digital technologies in state and municipal management allows ...", people (N=30; n=30; $K_k = 0.21$; $K_c = 0.76$). *Source: survey data in Google Docs and processing in Statistica; multiple responses from respondents were allowed.*

Fig. (**1**) shows that the use of DT in SMA, according to experts, allows optimizing the provision of public services to businesses (70.0% of respondents' responses)

---

1 Source: search on the Yandex resource (https://wordstat .yandex.ru /) a query concerning keywords

2 Employees of the SMA bodies of the city of Yekaterinburg were selected to conduct an expert survey. The expert survey of civil servants was conducted in January-May 2024. A questionnaire was developed based on the use of standard measurement and scaling procedures, consisting of three blocks: 1) Introduction; 2) Main content (8 questions); 3) Personal questions (5 questions). Through the use of an e-mail mailing list with a link to a questionnaire in Google docs, employees of the Yekaterinburg SMA authorities took part in the survey. The representativeness of the sample was determined by well-known statistical methods (Malhotra, N.K., 2002); the minimum required number of respondents should be at least 9 people. As of 06/01/2024, 30 questionnaires have been collected. All survey data were processed using Google docs, Microsoft Excel, and Statistica.

and the public (53.3%), as well as using electronic document management in SMA (40.0%) and automating public administration (33.33%).

It should also be noted that although the global spread of DT (primarily the Internet, mobile technologies, digital devices, *etc.*) is growing, they are still significantly ahead of the pace of benefits from digitalization (World DepRep, 2016).

Moreover, there are currently a number of effective examples of DT applications in the Russian Federation: Internet banking, marketplaces, e-commerce, electronic payments, electronic public services, *etc.* (Abdrakhmanova *et al.*, 2023 and 2020), but globally, governments[3] are generally slower to implement DT than the commercial sector. This is also confirmed by the data of our expert survey (Fig. **2**).

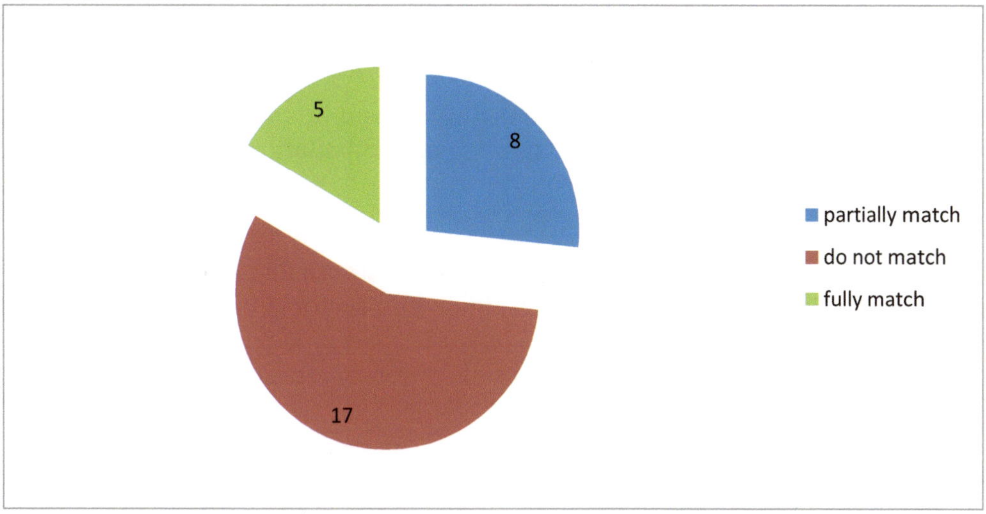

Fig. (2). Data from an expert survey of civil servants; respondents' answers to the question: "Do you think that at the moment the nature and pace of DT use in SMA correspond to the nature and pace of DT use in the commercial sector?", people (N=30; n=30; K_k = 0.20; K_c = 0.71). *Source: survey data in Google Docs and processing in Statistica; only a single selection of respondents was allowed.*

It follows from Fig. (**2**) that the absolute majority (25 out of 30 people, or 83.3% of the respondents) considers that the nature and pace of DT use in SMA does not fully or partially correspond to the nature and pace of DT use in the commercial sector.

3 The exception is the military–industrial sector, where digital innovations are implemented very quickly.

The main reasons for the lag in the pace of DT implementation in public administration, according to fundamental research by the Labor Center at the University of California, Berkeley, are the following factors:

1. Lack/lack of funding.
2. High public control over the activities of the authorities.
3. The complexity of the contracting processes (and often their high cost) for third-party technical work in the public sector.
4. Absence/lack of internal DT potential in the structures of SMA organs.
5. There are significant differences in size, resource potential, mission, political, and social context within the public sector.
6. Fragmentation and inconsistency of the activities of individual ministries and departments.
7. There is a risk of overloading employees of SMA bodies due to the fact that DT is superimposed on overloaded work processes (Hinkley, 2023, pp. 5-6).

In connection with the above, we interviewed experts and found that the key factors behind the lag in the pace of DT implementation in Russian public administration are the following two:

1. The complexity of the processes of concluding contracts (and often their high cost) for third-party technical work in the public sector (60.0% of respondents' responses).
2. Absence or lack of internal DT potential in government structures (53.3% of respondents).

The results obtained are illustrated in Fig. (**3**):

At the same time, both in Russia and Belarus, the introduction of DT in the field of public administration is an important strategic task. This is due to the fact that, as we noted in Chapter 1, both countries have policy documents aimed at creating innovative national economies based on the operational processing of Big Data and using the results obtained to improve the efficiency of activities in all sectors of the economy of the Union State and, above all, in the public administration sector. The latter is especially important in connection with the need to modernize public administration in order to increase efficiency, effectiveness, and productivity in government organizations and the introduction of such models as "Public Administration", "New Public Management" (or NPM), "Good Governance", "Electronic State", *etc.* Similar positions are noted in the works of Russian, Belarusian, and foreign authors (Astratova, 2023b; Barabashev,2016; Dolgikh,2017; Hood, 1995; Maratova, 2022; Pollitt & Bouckaert, 2000; *etc.*)

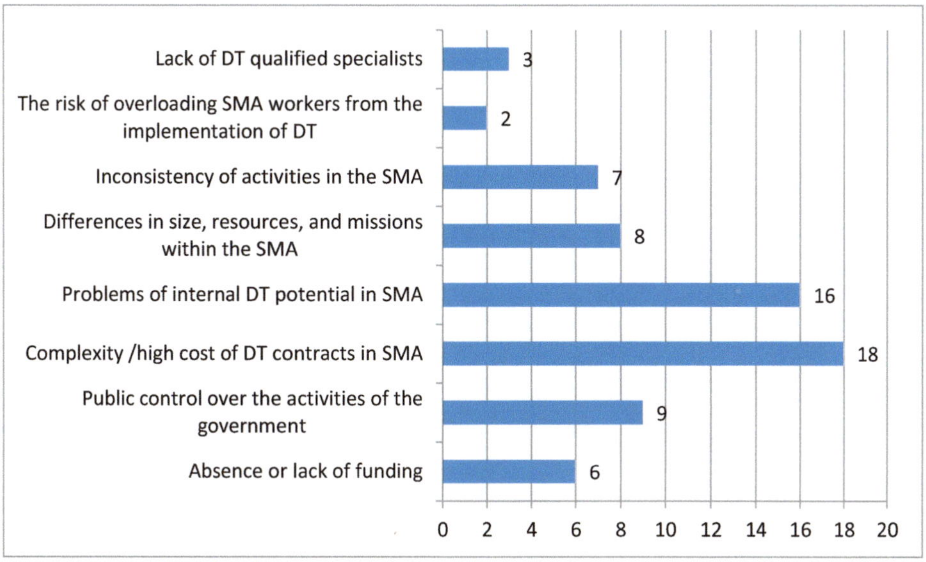

Fig. (3). Data from an expert survey of civil servants; respondents' answers to the question: "If you think that the introduction of DT in SMA lags behind the pace of DT implementation in the commercial sector, what are the main reasons for this situation?", people. (N=30; n=30; $K_k = 0.20$; $K_c = 0.74$). *Source: survey data in Google Docs and processing in Statistica; multiple responses from respondents were allowed.*

In the context of our research, it is important to consider how DT is used in public administration. An analysis of the literature sources available to us shows that at least five such areas can be distinguished:

1. Manual task automation.
2. Automation of processes.
3. Automated decision-making systems.
4. Integrated data systems.
5. Electronic monitoring (Chanmov, 2021, Dobrolyubova, 2018; Hinkley, 2023; *etc.*).

Accordingly, the data from our expert survey show that the main directions of using DT in the work of civil servants in the Russian Federation are the following three of the above:

1. Automation of processes (e-government, online payments, chatbots) – 80.0% of respondents' responses.
2. Automated decision–making systems (artificial intelligence, machine learning, predictive analytics) – 70.0% of respondents' responses.

3. Manual automation of tasks (using printers, scanners, robots, *etc.*) – 33.3% of respondents' responses.

The results obtained are illustrated in Fig. (**4**).

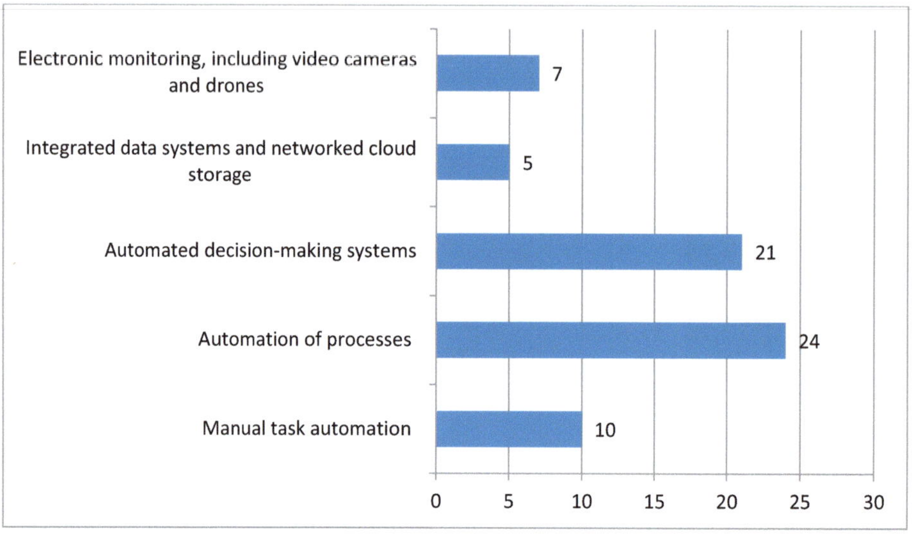

Fig. (4). Data from an expert survey of civil servants; respondents' answers to the question: "List the main directions of using DT in your work and/or the work of your colleagues", people (N=30; n=30; $K_k = 0.21$; $K_c = 0.75$). *Source: survey data in Google Docs and processing in Statistica; multiple responses from respondents were allowed.*

It is also important that research by the University of California, Berkeley Labor Center (Hinkley, 2023) shows that there are problems in the internal and external context of the use of DT by government employees.

So, as for the *external applicationof DT* (*i.e.*, public electronic services for citizens), the automation of public services has greatly facilitated public access to public services, and also freed civil servants from processing a huge number (Hinkley, 2023, p. 8). In this regard, we see a generally positive attitude of the Russian population towards the use of DT in public administration (Abdrakhmanova *et al.*, 2023 and 2020), as well as Russian and Belarusian students towards the use of DT in public administration (Figs. **3** and **4**, respectively[4]).

However, many more aspects of the external application of DT in SMA need to be discussed and clarified. For example, issues of customer service with limited access to electronic services, as well as problems of integrating DT with complex, specific, and peculiar knowledge that specialists (social workers, experts, consultants, parole officers, *etc.*) use on a daily basis to provide effective and personalized support to the population (Hinkley, 2023, p. 8).

As for the *internal application of DT* (*i.e.*, the use of digitalization for internal management processes in the SMA structure), advanced technologies (primarily new algorithms, artificial intelligence, robotics and process automation) have begun to significantly change the functionality of some government positions, supplementing or replacing elements of the decision-making process, especially in the fields of military, economic and public safety, as well as social security (Hinkley, 2023, p. 8-9).

Moreover, some experts express concern about the growing dependence of the government on DT in the process of making complex decisions and monitoring. This is also due to the fact that the public sector often outsources the performance of many DT functions, which leads to a significant dependence on "govtech"[5] companies and consultants. Accordingly, building up the SMA's in-house DT capacity could help solve some of the problems of cost overruns and unsatisfactory results associated with large DT projects (Hinkley, 2023, p. 8-9).

Thus, we can conclude that despite the relevance and demand for the use of DT in public administration, at the moment, there are many issues related to both external and internal use of DT in SMA bodies, which require prompt and urgent solutions both in the Russian Federation and in the Republic of Belarus.

CONCLUSION

The research demonstrates that despite the recognized relevance and growing demand for digital technologies in public administration, significant challenges remain in their effective implementation in both the Russian Federation and the Republic of Belarus. Expert surveys reveal that while DT offers substantial opportunities for optimizing public services, automating administrative processes, and improving documentation workflows, the pace of adoption significantly lags behind the commercial sector. This disparity is primarily attributed to the complexity and high costs associated with contracting third-party technical work in the public sector (60.0% of respondents) and the absence or limited internal DT potential within government structures (53.3% of respondents).

---

5 "govtech" – this is an abbreviation of the words "government technology", which means digital technologies used by the government.

The study identifies three predominant applications of digital technologies in Russian public administration: process automation through e-government initiatives, online payment systems, and chatbots (80.0% of respondents); automated decision-making systems utilizing artificial intelligence, machine learning, and predictive analytics (70.0%); and manual automation of tasks (33.3%). These implementations align with the strategic objectives outlined in policy documents of both nations aimed at creating innovative economies based on Big Data processing.

However, both the external application (citizen-facing electronic services) and internal application (administrative processes) of digital technologies in public administration require further development and refinement. While electronic services have improved citizen access to public services and reduced bureaucratic workload, issues remain regarding service accessibility for digitally disadvantaged populations and the integration of complex, specialized knowledge into digital platforms. Internally, concerns persist about growing governmental dependence on technology for complex decision-making and monitoring, particularly given the extensive outsourcing of DT functions to "govtech" companies.

To address these challenges, both countries must prioritize building in-house DT capacity within government structures, developing more efficient contracting processes for technical work, and ensuring that digital transformation initiatives align with the broader goals of public administration modernization. As Russia and Belarus continue to pursue innovative national economies based on digital technologies, resolving these issues will be critical to realizing the full potential of digital transformation in public governance and delivering more efficient, effective, and responsive services to citizens and businesses.

CHAPTER 20

Policy Synthesis: Advancing Socio-Economic Integration and Innovation in the Union State of Russia and Belarus

Chigozirim N. Onwusiribe[1,*], **Galina V. Astratova**[2], **Maxim V. Vlasov**[2] and **Longinus D.N. Nnadozie**[3]

[1] *School of Public Administration and Entrepreneurship (SPAE), Ural Federal University (UrFU), Yekaterinburg 620002, Sverdlovsk Region, Russian Federation*

[2] *Department of Regional Economics, Innovative Entrepreneurship and Economics (REIE&E), Institute of Economics and Management, School of Public Administration and Entrepreneurship (SPAE), Ural Federal University (UrFU), Yekaterinburg 620002, Sverdlovsk Region, Russian Federation*

[3] *Department of Agribusiness Management, Michael Okpara University of Agriculture, Umudike, Umuahia 7267, Abia State, Federal Republic of Nigeria*

Abstract: This synthesis integrates key findings from the 19 chapters analyzing the Complex Socio-Economic Systems (SES) of the Union State of Russia and Belarus (USRB). It emphasizes the critical role of digital transformation, Innovation infrastructure (InIn), human capital development, and adaptive governance in advancing integration. Key challenges include bureaucratic inefficiencies, R & D underperformance, labor market imbalances, and digital adoption gaps. Strategic recommendations prioritize harmonized policies, enhanced collaboration, and targeted investments to foster a resilient, knowledge-based economy. The USRB's experience offers globally relevant insights into regional integration amidst geopolitical uncertainty and technological disruption.

Keywords: Bilateral Cooperation, Complex Socio-Economic System, Eurasian Economic Union (EAEU), Socio-Economic Integration, Union State of Russia and Belarus (USRB).

[*] **Corresponding author Chigozirim N. Onwusiribe:** School of Public Administration and Entrepreneurship (SPAE), Ural Federal University (UrFU), Yekaterinburg 620002, Sverdlovsk Region, Russian Federation; E-mail: ndubuisichigo@gmail.com

INTRODUCTION

The dawn of the 21st century has witnessed an unprecedented acceleration in technological advancement and geopolitical realignment, fundamentally reshaping the landscape of regional integration and socio-economic development. Within this dynamic context, the Union State of the Russian Federation and the Republic of Belarus (USRB) stands as a pivotal experiment in post-Soviet reintegration. Born from deep historical, cultural, and economic ties formalized in the landmark *Treaty on the Establishment of the Union State (1999)*, the USRB represents more than a bilateral partnership; it embodies a strategic endeavor to create a cohesive socio-economic space capable of navigating global complexity and fostering shared prosperity. This Policy Synthesis Chapter consolidates critical insights from an extensive 19-chapter analysis, offering a comprehensive roadmap for transforming the USRB into a resilient, innovative, and globally competitive entity in the digital era.

The USRB's journey, spanning over three decades, has achieved significant milestones, notably a 2.6-fold increase in bilateral trade (2005-2021) and the implementation of ambitious joint programs like the 28 Union Integration Programs (2021-2023). These efforts underscore a commitment to deeper harmonization across defense, customs, agriculture, and technology. However, this integration occurs against a backdrop of intensifying global challenges: rapid digital disruption, fragile supply chains, geopolitical volatility (exemplified by sanctions regimes), and the imperative for sustainable development. While the foundational treaties and institutional frameworks provide a crucial scaffold, the Union State faces persistent and evolving bottlenecks that threaten its transformative potential.

This synthesis identifies these critical pressure points through rigorous analysis:

1. **The Innovation Paradox:** Despite substantial investments in R & D (averaging 1.1% of GDP in Russia, 0.8% in Belarus), outputs have markedly declined, with patent applications falling by 41% in Russia and 50% in Belarus (2015-2022). A disconnect persists between academic research and commercial application, hindering technological sovereignty and import substitution goals (Chapters 6, 7, 10).
2. **Governance Under Strain:** Bureaucratic inertia, complex contracting processes, insufficient digital competencies among officials, and corruption impede agile and effective public administration. These factors limit the responsiveness of State and Municipal Administration (SMA) to rapid socio-economic shifts and citizen needs (Chapters 8, 19, 12).
3. **Human Capital Mismatch:** While higher education enrollment surges,

particularly in digital fields (*e.g.*, tech enrollments rising from 25,000 to 68,000 in Russia and 12,000 to 30,000 in Belarus, 2020-2023), structural imbalances plague labor markets. An excess of general graduates coexists with acute shortages of skilled professionals in high-tech sectors. Migration trends further highlight this, with Belarus acting as a net labor exporter to Russia, driven by economic factors (Chapters 17, 13, 15, 16).

4. **Digital Divide:** Enthusiasm for digital education and AI tools (Chapters 13, 14, 15) contrasts sharply with implementation gaps. Critical infrastructure limitations, pedagogical integration barriers, and low effective utilization of digital platforms (*e.g.*, only 45% of Russian universities effectively use Learning Management Systems) hinder the digital transformation of public services and economic sectors (Chapters 19, 15).
5. **Integration Friction:** Asymmetries in economic size, institutional structures, and the dominant role of the public sector in Belarus create friction in deepening harmonization of legislation, standards (especially customs and technical), and financial markets, despite political commitment (Chapters 2, 3).

Simultaneously, external pressures, particularly comprehensive sanctions against Russia, act as a double-edged sword. They impose high economic costs and disruption, but also serve as a powerful catalyst, accelerating mutual import substitution efforts and reinforcing the strategic necessity of the Union State framework for economic security within the Eurasian Economic Union (EAEU) customs territory (Chapter 3). This complex interplay of internal challenges and external shocks defines the critical juncture at which the USRB finds itself.

The central question addressed in this synthesis is: How can the USRB leverage its unique integration framework, historical ties, and shared resources to overcome systemic bottlenecks, harness digital and innovation potential, and build a resilient, knowledge-based economy capable of thriving amidst 21st-century uncertainties? Answering this requires moving beyond conventional policy approaches. The analysis presented here treats the USRB not merely as a political union but as a Complex Socio-Economic System (SES), characterized by nonlinear dynamics, emergent properties, and intricate stakeholder interactions (Chapters 1, 11). Understanding these dynamics is paramount for designing effective interventions.

This chapter synthesizes evidence across diverse domains—from advanced simulation modeling of SES dynamics (Chapter 1) and the intricacies of economic cooperation (Chapter 3) to the transformative potential of AI in education (Chapter 14) and the socio-technological reorganization of labor (Chapters 17, 18). It presents a cohesive Strategic Vision for 2035: positioning the USRB as a globally competitive, digitally integrated knowledge economy anchored in sustainable growth and adaptive governance. Crucially, it translates this vision into actionable Key Recommendations and a detailed Integrated Roadmap (2025-2030), providing policymakers with concrete steps to:

- Revolutionize R & D effectiveness and technological sovereignty.
- Accelerate seamless digital transformation across governance and the economy.
- Align human capital development with future market demands.
- Deepen economic integration while respecting sovereignty.
- Strengthen collaborative governance and public administration.

The experiences of the USRB hold profound Global Relevance. Its efforts to build resilience through regional integration, navigate technological disruption, bridge the innovation-commercialization gap, and adapt governance models offer invaluable lessons for regional blocs worldwide (*e.g.*, ASEAN, AU, Mercosur) and nations grappling with similar challenges of digital transition, economic security, and sustainable development in an increasingly fragmented world order. This synthesis aims to contribute not only to the future prosperity of Russia and Belarus but also to the broader global discourse on managing complexity and fostering innovation in the pursuit of resilient socio-economic systems.

Recap of Key Themes

1. **Complex SES Dynamics:** Initial chapters (Chapter 1, Chapter 11) established SES as nonlinear systems requiring advanced modeling and adaptive policies. Challenges include parameter uncertainty, stakeholder diversity, and balancing efficiency with equity (Bertalanffy, 1962; Knyazeva, 2009).
2. **Integration Foundations:** Chapters 2-3 detailed the USRB's evolution, anchored in treaties (1999 Union State Treaty) and driven by trade growth (2.6x increase 2005-2021). Sectoral programs (*e.g.*, 28 Union Programs 2021-2023) and asymmetric funding (35:65 Belarus: Russia) underpin cooperation but face hurdles like institutional misalignment and public sector dominance in Belarus.
3. **Innovation & Digitalization:** Chapters 6, 7, 10, 16 identified underinvestment in R & D (1.1% GDP Russia, 0.8% Belarus) and declining patent outputs (-41% Russia, -50% Belarus, 2015-2022). Despite rising tech enrollments, gaps persist in university-industry collaboration, digital infrastructure (only 45% effective LMS use in Russian universities – Chapter 15), and commercialization.
4. **Labor Market and Human Capital:** Chapters 17, 16, and 18 highlighted migration trends (Belarus as a net exporter to Russia), skills mismatches (surplus graduates *vs.* tech skill shortages), and the rising importance of *creative human capital* and socio-technical labor organization in the digital

economy.

5. **Governance Challenges:** Chapters 8, 19, 12, 13 exposed bottlenecks: bureaucratic inefficiency, corruption, low digital competency among officials, complex contracting, and rigid regulatory frameworks hindering public administration and policy responsiveness.

Strategic Vision for the Future

The USRB must evolve into a globally competitive, digitally integrated knowledge economy by 2035. This requires:

1. **A Unified Digital Ecosystem:** Seamless data sharing, unified digital services for citizens/businesses, and AI-driven public administration.
2. **Innovation at the Core:** Transforming universities into R & D-Industry clusters, achieving technological sovereignty in critical sectors (microelectronics, biotech), and significantly increasing R & D effectiveness.
3. **Adaptive and Collaborative Governance:** Implementing New Public Management principles, fostering multi-stakeholder platforms, and ensuring policy agility.
4. **Future-Ready Human Capital:** Aligning education with digital economy needs, promoting lifelong learning, and optimizing labor mobility within the Union State.
5. **Sustainable and Resilient Growth:** Integrating SDGs into all policies, enhancing economic security through import substitution synergies, and building resilience against external shocks.

DISCUSSION

The synthesis reveals critical tensions:

- **Investment *vs.* Impact:** Despite funding, R & D outputs lag, signaling inefficiencies in resource allocation and knowledge transfer (Chapter 6, Chapter 7).
- **Integration Depth *vs.* Sovereignty:** Deeper harmonization (legal, market, education) must balance national autonomy (Chapter 2, Chapter 3, Chapter 12).
- **Digital Potential *vs.* Adoption:** Enthusiasm for digital education (Chapter 13, Chapter 15) and AI (Chapter 14) contrasts with implementation gaps in government and infrastructure (Chapter 10, Chapter 15).
- **Labor Supply *vs.* Demand:** Educational expansion hasn't resolved structural skill shortages in high-tech sectors (Chapter 17, Chapter 16).

Geopolitical pressures (sanctions) act as both a catalyst for accelerated cooperation (import substitution - Chapter 3) and a stressor on resources. The succcss of the 28 Union Programs is pivotal for demonstrating tangible integration benefits.

CONCLUSION

The USRB stands at an inflection point. Its deep historical ties and institutional framework provide a solid foundation. However, realizing its strategic vision demands overcoming persistent bottlenecks in governance, innovation, and human capital development. Embracing digital transformation holistically, fostering genuine collaboration between academia, industry, and government, and implementing agile, evidence-based policies are non-negotiable for future success. The USRB's journey offers valuable lessons for regional integration models globally, particularly in navigating complexity and leveraging partnerships for resilience.

Key Recommendations

1. **Accelerate Digital Transformation:**
   - Mandate interoperable digital platforms for public services (SMA) and establish a Unified Union State Data Space.
   - Launch intensive digital competency programs for civil servants (Chapter 8, Chapter 19).
   - Simplify procurement for digital solutions (Chapter 19).
2. **Revolutionize R & D and Innovation:**
   - Increase R & D funding to align with OECD averages (min. 2% GDP) with performance-based allocation (Chapter 7, Chapter 10).
   - Establish mandatory university-industry partnership frameworks and co-funded labs (Chapter 6, Chapter 16).
   - Create a centralized, accessible Union State IP registry and commercialization support fund (Chapter 4, Chapter 10).
3. **Modernize Education & Human Capital:**
   - Reform higher education curricula for digital/STEM skills and implement dual education programs (Chapter 12, Chapter 13, Chapter 16).
   - Scale up targeted upskilling/reskilling programs aligned with high-tech sector forecasts (Chapter 5, Chapter 16, Chapter 18).
   - Significantly simplify cross-border work permits and recognition mechanisms within the USRB (Chapter 17).
4. **Strengthen Governance & Integration:**
   - Implement a "regulatory guillotine" to streamline bureaucracy and adopt sunset clauses for regulations (Chapter 8, Chapter 12).

- Establish a robust, independent monitoring body for the 28 Union Programs using real-time data dashboards (Chapter 2, Chapter 3, Chapter 10).
- Deepen legislative harmonization, prioritizing customs, technical standards, and financial markets (Chapter 2, Chapter 3).

5. **Enhance Collaboration & Investment:**
   - Launch high-profile joint ventures in priority sectors (microelectronics, pharma, agritech) with tax incentives (Chapter 3, Chapter 4).
   - Create a Union State Venture Fund for start-ups and scale-ups.
   - Implement large-scale public awareness campaigns on integration benefits (Chapter 3).

The Integrated Roadmap (2025-2030) outlined in Table 20.1 provides a structured, phased approach to implementing the USRB's strategic vision. The Foundation Phase, which spans from 2025 to 2027, focuses on building critical capacity and launching key enablers. In the realm of Digital & Governance, this phase mandates digital competency training for officials, launches a Unified Data Space for citizen services, and simplifies digital procurement processes. In terms of R & D & Innovation, the roadmap increases R & D budgets by 25%, establishes five flagship University-Industry R & D hubs, and creates an Intellectual Property Registry and Seed Fund. Additionally, the Human Capital aspect reforms STEM curricula in 50% of universities, launches targeted upskilling programs, and implements a digital work permit platform.

Table 1. Integrated roadmap for policies (2025-2030).

Phase	Focus Area	Key Actions (2025-2027)	Key Actions (2028-2030)	Primary Actors	Metrics
Foundation (2025-2027)	**Digital & Governance**	1. Launch the USRB Digital Competency Initiative for officials. 2. Implement Unified Data Space Phase 1 (citizen services). 3. Simplify digital procurement rules.	1. Achieve 80% digital service adoption by SMEs/citizens. 2. Implement AI pilots in SMA (*e.g.*, permits, forecasting).	USRB Secretariat, MinDigital (RU/BY)	% Services online, User satisfaction; Procurement cycle time

(Table 1) cont.....

Phase	Focus Area	Key Actions (2025-2027)	Key Actions (2028-2030)	Primary Actors	Metrics
	R & D & Innovation	1. Increase R & D budget by 25%. 2. Establish 5 flagship University-Industry R & D hubs. 3. Launch IP Registry & Seed Fund.	1. Patent applications increase by 30%. 2. 50% of universities have active industry revenue streams. 3. Scale Seed Fund into Venture Fund.	Ministry of Science and Education (Russia and Belarus), Industry Assoc.	R & D % GDP; Patents filed; Industry co-funding; Start-ups funded
	Human Capital	1. Reform core STEM curricula in 50% of universities. 2. Launch 10 targeted upskilling programs (AI, biotech). 3. Implement a digital work permit platform.	1. 80% curricula reformed. 2. Track 70% graduate employment in target sectors. 3. Cross-border labor mobility increases 20%.	MinEd/Labor (RU/BY), Universities	Graduate employment rate, Skills gap index, and Cross-border work permits
Transformation (2028-2030)	**Deep Integration**	1. Full harmonization of customs/technical standards. 2. Operationalize Union State Venture Fund. 3. Implement SDG impact assessment for all major policies.	1. Establish a common financial market framework. 2. Achieve a top 30 GII ranking for RU/BY collectively. 3. Report annual SDG progress.	USRB Supreme Council, Central Banks, MinEcon	Intra-USRB trade growth; GII Ranking; SDG Index score
	Sustainable Ecosystem	1. Scale successful R & D hubs nationwide. 2. Embed circular economy principles in industry programs. 3. Full deployment of AI in predictive policy modeling (SES).	1. Become a net exporter in 2+ priority tech sectors. 2. Reduce resource intensity by 15%. 3. SES models are used for all major policy decisions.	All Ministries, Industry, Academia	Tech export value; Resource efficiency; Policy outcome *vs.* forecast

The Transformation Phase, covering the years 2028 to 2030, aims to scale successful initiatives and drive deep integration. This phase emphasizes Deep Integration by achieving full customs and technical standards harmonization, operationalizing a Union State Venture Fund, and integrating Sustainable Development Goal (SDG) assessments into policy. Furthermore, it seeks to create a Sustainable Ecosystem by expanding R & D hubs nationally, embedding circular economy principles, and deploying artificial intelligence for predictive SES policy modeling.

To ensure clear accountability and metrics, each action within the roadmap assigns primary actors, such as the USRB Secretariat, Ministries, and Industry Associations, while also defining measurable outcomes. These outcomes include metrics like the percentage of online service adoption, patent growth, graduate employment rates, and intra-trade growth. This structured approach guarantees focused execution and tangible progress tracking across the Union State's priority domains.

FINAL REFLECTIONS ON GLOBAL RELEVANCE

The USRB's integration journey offers profound insights for regional blocs worldwide. Its experience underscores that successful integration transcends economics, requiring robust socio-technical systems, adaptive governance, and shared human capital development (Florida, 2011). The focus on *technological sovereignty* and *import substitution* under sanctions (Chapter 3, Chapter 6) provides a relevant blueprint for nations navigating deglobalization or strategic autonomy imperatives. Furthermore, the challenges in digitalizing public services (Chapter 19, Chapter 15) and bridging the innovation "valley of death" (Chapter 6, Chapter 7) are near-universal. The USRB's experimental approach – using indicative planning (Chapter 10), testing ecosystem labor models (Chapter 18), and prioritizing creative human capital (Chapter 11) – contributes valuable empirical knowledge to global discourse on managing complex SES in the digital age. As noted by Nazarenko & Novikova (2023), digital transformation is a strategic public good; the USRB's efforts to build a unified digital space thus resonate with global efforts towards inclusive digital governance. Future research should compare the USRB model with other regional integrations (*e.g.*, ASEAN, AU) to identify transferable strategies for fostering resilience and innovation in an interconnected yet fragmented world.

CONCLUSION

Galina V. Astratova, Chigozirim Ndubuisi Onwusiribe, Maxim V. Vlasov

The Union State of the Russian Federation and the Republic of Belarus is in unique conditions: a previously unprecedented global socio-economic and military-political crisis, intensified by such phenomena as the protracted special military operation in Ukraine, suffering the consequences of the coronavirus pandemic, and facing intermittent local conflicts.

On the other hand, the successful coexistence of two fraternal states in the Eurasian space for a quarter of a century is not only the success of integration education in the post-Soviet period, but also the recognition that only the friendship of fraternal, Slavic peoples allows the "Russian world" to withstand the global military and political danger.

Despite the danger of World War III, it must be admitted that the world as a whole is moving towards the formation of a global digital economy based on R & D, higher education, and human capital development, and the Union State is striving to create a unified scientific and technological space. This is due to a number of objective factors, such as:

1. The global change in the role of the public sector and the importance of government regulation by sectors of national economies (primarily labor markets, HES, and R & D).
2. The universal nature of the introduction of digital/information technologies into the business models of organizations in the commercial and non-profit sectors.
3. Changing the formats of universities' activities and the nature of the work of teaching staff and researchers, as well as changing the nature and conditions of students' education.
4. Changes in the requirements for the qualifications and competencies of employees in the context of digitalization, which led to significant changes in the organization and nature of the work of personnel in the commercial and non-profit sectors.
5. The acquisition of the innovative infrastructure of the Union State of the Russian Federation and the Republic of Belarus as a key factor in import substitution and the development of the knowledge economy in the context of digitalization.

In this regard, complex, interdisciplinary studies of complex socio-economic systems—higher professional education, R & D, and the labor market of the USRB—and the problems of sectoral state regulation of these systems in the context of digitalization of the economy become particularly relevant. This is due to the work of the author's team, which resulted in this monograph, which examines three key issues: 1) Designing mechanisms for the optimal development of complex socio-economic systems (on the example of the union state of Russia and Belarus); 2) Challenges and perspectives of using digital technologies in new economic conditions; 3) Current issues of human capital development in the digital economy.

As a result of the research, the authors made the following main conclusions:

CONCLUSION:

The state policy of the development of the Union State of the Russian Federation and the Republic of Belarus is conditioned by global trends shaping the knowledge economy, digitalization, and innovative infrastructure. It is revealed that the strategic goal of the state policy in the field of higher education is to increase the availability of high-quality education that meets the requirements of the innovative development of the economy of the USRB, the modern needs of society, and every citizen of Russia and Belarus. The necessity of state participation in the formation of the knowledge economy has been proved, which necessitates further research to explore issues related to determining the most effective share of state participation in the management of the higher education system and the R & D sector. It is shown that the use of digital technologies in public administration, both in Russia and Belarus, has currently revealed many issues related to both the effectiveness of public administration in industries (primarily the HES sector) and the external and internal use of DT in SMA bodies. These issues need to be resolved as soon as possible and without delay.

Modern realities form multifunctional mechanisms for the development of the SSEC, as well as various approaches to the methodology for assessing the main indicators of the development of the CSES. The issues of assessing the processes of development of complex socio-economic systems in the digital economy of the Union State are considered. It is shown that the stated problem lies in the need to search for and further study the dependencies and relationships between a large number of values, parameters, and variables of the CSES. The solution to this problem is the subject of further and independent research in the context of a new scientific direction.

It is shown that in the context of state management of the innovation infrastructure of the Union State, the interaction between the CSES (higher education, R & D sector, and the labor market) plays a key role in ensuring and stimulating sustainable economic development of fraternal countries in the context of digitalization. It is established that for the successful implementation of this approach and the activation of the relationship between R & D, higher education and the labor market, the introduction of the "Triple Helix model" is required, where the spiraling interconnected and interdependent interaction between the elements of the innovation infrastructure – innovative agents of government, universities and enterprises – is carried out for the purpose of innovative production transformation and transfer of knowledge. It is concluded that higher education institutions are becoming a “crystallizing” core, a point of growth and development of innovative infrastructure. In the new economic conditions, the innovative infrastructure of the USRB is the basis for the further development of both countries and a key factor in import substitution.

The use of DT and AI in education, both in Russia and Belarus, has currently revealed many issues related to the technical and technological support of universities, as well as methodological, pedagogical, psychological, and educational problems. It is revealed that the behavior of the consumer of intellectual services (primarily HES and R & D) in the digital environment in modern conditions is a complex socio-economic, psychological, and digital phenomenon. The theory and practice of researching the main characteristics, motives, and factors of influence on the consumer are a problem area and are in the stage of active formation both in the Russian Federation and the Republic of Belarus, and beyond. The use of predictive, semantic, and sentiment analysis tools, as well as digital analytics methods in the process of evaluating the effectiveness of EdTech in universities, is also one of the urgent problems that requires a speedy solution.

It is revealed that the development of human capital—the key trigger of the innovative development of the SRB—should take place in the context of the integration of R & D and higher education in the digital economy. The socio-technological nature of the organization of labor in the digital environment of the Union State is revealed. The scientifically based approaches of work rationing in the implementation of projects on a digital platform are considered. The essence of creative human capital is considered, and the challenges of creative human capital in the digital economy are discussed. Finally, an assessment of key indicators of the development of complex socio-economic systems in the digital economy of the Russian Federation and the Republic of Belarus.

RECOMMENDATIONS:

To ensure the sustainability and further development of complex socio-economic systems in a turbulent external environment, scientifically based measures are needed that have a selective effect on key risk factors for the development of “critical points” of distress and take into account their long-term consequences.

In this regard, the authors consider it necessary to recommend further analyzing the developed strategies for the socio-economic development of the regions of

Russia and Belarus for the period up to 2035 from this point of view and making the necessary adjustments. Such measures and adjustments to strategies should be based on models and mechanisms similar to those outlined in this paper.

REFERENCES

Abd, R. A., Rowling, M., White, G., Mason-Jones, R. (2016). Public Sector Supply Chain Management: A Triple Helix Approach to Aligning Innovative Environmental Initiatives. *Foresight STI Gov., 10*(1), 43-52. [http://dx.doi.org/10.17323/1995-459x.2016.1.43.52]

Abdrakhmanova, G. I., Vasilkovsky, S. A., Vishnevsky, K. O. (2023). Digital Economy: 2023: A short statistical collection. *Higher School of Economics.* Moscow.

Abdrakhmanova, G. I., Vishnevsky, K. O., Gokhberg, L. M. (2020). Digital Economy: 2020: A brief statistical collection. *Higher School of Economics.* Moscow.

Abiona, O., Sodeinde, J. (2022). Utilisation of administrative theories and effective institutional administration in federal university of agriculture Abeokuta, Nigeria. *Int. J. Adv. Stud. Econ. Public Sector Manag., 10*(1)
[http://dx.doi.org/10.48028/iiprds/ijasepsm.v10.i1.09]

Abrami, P.C., Bernard, R.M., Bures, E.M., Borokhovski, E., Tamim, R.M. (2011). Interaction in distance education and online learning: Using evidence and theory to improve practice. *J. Comput. High. Educ., 23*(2-3), 82-103.
[http://dx.doi.org/10.1007/s12528-011-9043-x]

Agasisti, T., Shibanova, E. (2022). Actual Autonomy, Efficiency and Performance of Universities: Insights from the Russian Case. *Int. J. Public Adm., 45*(2), 121-134.
[http://dx.doi.org/10.1080/01900692.2021.1903496]

Agasisti, T., Egorov, A., Maximova, M. (2021). Do Merger Policies Increase Universities' Efficiency? Evidence from a Fuzzy Regression Discontinuity Design. *Appl. Econ., 53*(2), 185-204.
[http://dx.doi.org/10.1080/00036846.2020.1803488]

Agbazuere, A.C.B. (2020). Challenges of Public Policy Making and Execution in Nigeria. *Eur. Sci. J., 16*(7)
[http://dx.doi.org/10.19044/esj.2020.v16n7p130]

Aguaded, I. (2013). The MOOC revolution: A new form of education from the technological paradigm? *Comunicar, 21*(41), 07-08.
[http://dx.doi.org/10.3916/C41-2013-a1]

Ainslee, J. (2018). Digitization of Education in the 21st Century. Available from: https://elearningindustry.com/digitization-of-education-21st-century

Akmuradov, H. G. (2023). Mechanisms and tools of the world economy. *Symbol Sci., 5*(2), 78-79.

Alekseev, Yu.G., Dudko, N.A. (2018). University 3.0: Methodological approaches to the management of scientific and innovative development. *Digital Transformation,* (3), 14-19. In Russ., abstract in Eng.

Alekseeva, L. N. (2016). Creation of an electronic state as one of the stages of transition to the Good governance model. *Bull. Sci. Conf., 4-2*(8), 7-9.

Almasre, M. (2024). Development and Evaluation of a Custom GPT for the Assessment of Students' De-signs in a Typography Course. *Educ. Sci., 14*, 148.
[http://dx.doi.org/10.3390/educsci14020148]

AlQershi, N., Abas, Z. B., Mokhtar, S. S. M. (2021). How Intellectual Capital Dimensions Impacts Strategic Innovation In Manufacturing Smes. *Acad. Strateg. Manag. J., 20*, 1-8.

Andryushkevich, O. A., Denisova, I. T. (2014). Formation of entrepreneurial universities in the innovative economy. *Econ. Sci. Mod. Russ., 3*(66), 87-104.

Andryushkevich, O.A. (2012). Indicative planning in economies of different types // Capital of the country. Available from: https://kapital-rus.ru/articles/article/indikativnoe_planirovanie_v_ekonomikah_raznogo_tipa/

Ansoff, I. (1989). Strategic management *Ekonomika* (p. 519). Moscow. Scientific editor and introductory article by L.I. Evenko, pp. 11–32. In Russ.

Anufrieva, I. Y. (2021). Transformation of intra-organizational labor rationing in the context of digitalization. *Econ. Prof. Bus., 3*
[http://dx.doi.org/10.14258/epb202133]

Astratova, G.V. (2024). *Fundamentals of marketing: A short course of lectures. Textbook by G.V. Astratova..* Yekaterinburg: Ural University Publishing House. (In Russian)

Astratova, GV, Bekshaev, AA (2024). On the application of information technologies in public administration and the promotion of political parties in the Internet environment. *Bulletin of Eurasian Science, 16*(2) Available from: https://esj.today/PDF/20ECVN224.pdf

Astratova, G. V., Izmailov, A. M. (2024). Comparative analysis of the market of mass open online courses provided by institutions of higher education of the Union State of Russia and Belarus. *Fundam. Res., 6*, 14-27.
[http://dx.doi.org/10.17513/fr.43623]

Astratova, G.V., Sinitsyn, E.V., Laptev, V.M., Simchenko, N.A., Shamardina, I.A. (2024). Intercountry migration of the population in the Union State of Russia and Belarus: the development of a mathematical model in the context of the formation of the mechanism of interstate integration relations in the labor market in the context of digitalization. *Bull. St. Petersbg. Univ. Econ.* Accepted for publication. In Russ.

Astratova, G. V. (2024). Interaction of the system of higher professional education, R&D and the labor market in the conditions of digitalization of the economy of the Russian Federation and the Republic of Belarus: A collective scientific monograph. *Azhur Publishing House*Yekaterinburg. Available from: https://www.elibrary.ru/item.asp?id=76783678

Astratova, G. V. (2023). The Union State of Russia and Belarus: The effectiveness of development in new economic conditions. *Bull. Eurasian Sci., 15*(1) Available from: https://esj.today/PDF/61ECVN123.pd

Astratova, G. V. (2023). Sectoral policy of public administration in the system of higher education in the context of digitalization. *Bull. Eurasian Sci., 15*(5), 1-17. Available from: https://esj.today/PDF/58ECVN523.pdf

Astratova, G.V., Toshpulotov, A.A. (2023). Financial management in public administration of developing countries: Problems of effectiveness of foreign aid *Bulletin of the Samara State University of Economics. Economy,* (11), 22985-106. In Russ., abstract in Eng.

Astratova, GV, Izmailov, AM, Semenov, MM, Mitro, MS (2023). Problems of prices and choice of educational services for students in the context of digitalization of the economy (preliminary analysis). *Bulletin of Eurasian Science, 15*(3) In Russian; abstract available in English. Available from: https://esj.today/PDF/50ECVN323.pdf

Astratova, GV, Klimuk, VV (2022). On the issue of efficiency and effectiveness of scientific workers in the R&D sector. *Bulletin of Eurasian Science, 14*(1) In Russian; abstract available in English. Available from: https://esj.today/PDF/01ECVN122.pdf

Astratova, GV, Bedrina, EB, Klimuk, VV, Britvina, IB, Larionova, VA, Poshekhonova, GV, Rutkauskas, TK, Savchuk, GA, Sinitsyn, EV, Tolmachev, AV, Yashin, AA (2022). *Effects of the coronacrisis and new economic sanctions in the digital economy: Higher education and the labor market* Ural Publishing House.(Vol. 310). Yekaterinburg:

Astratova, G. V., Beleeva, I. D. (2021). Problems of cross-cultural communication in the context of modern linguistic technologies of higher education *World of Science. Pedagogy and psychology, 9*(6), 1-21. Available from: https://mir-nauki.com/PDF/03PDMN621.pdf

Astratova, G. V., Klimuk, V. V., Sandalova, N. V., Chashchin, M. R. (2021). Russia and China university's students values in the context of mass open online courses *Bulletin of Eurasian Science, 13*(2) Available from: https://esj.today/PDF/31ECVN221.pdf

Astratova, G. V., Bedrina, E. B., Larionova, V. A., Poshekhonova, G. V., Rutkauskas, T. K., Sinitsyn, E. V., Sinyakova, M. G., Tolmachev, A. V. (2021). Higher education and the labor market in the digital economy: The development of mathematical methods and tools for the study of complex economic systems. Scientific monograph *Publishing house "Pero"*. Available from: https://www.elibrary.ru/item.asp?id=47146122

Astratova, G. V., Astratova, S. V., Zhernov, A. A. (2019). Marketing of investment services for individuals and financial security of the banking sector in the digital economy. *Discussion, 95*(4), 6-20. [http://dx.doi.org/10.24411/2077-7639-2019-10032]

Astratova, G. V., Gnevasheva, V. A., Chashchin, M. R., Kocheryan, M. A. (2019). Values of students of Russian universities *BCI. Practical Marketing, 265*(3), 33-44.

Astratova, Galina V. (2018). A review of twenty years (1998-2018) research of the consumer behaviour study in different markets of goods and services, based on the author's interpretation of the system of values that influence market behaviour of the consumer *Eastern Academic Journal, 4*, 1-27. Available from: https://www.e-acadjournal.org/article-18-4-1.html

Astratova, G.V. (2018). Overview of the Consumer Behavior Study in the Markets of Food Products (1998-2018), Based on the Author's Interpretation of the Consumer's Requirements in the System of Values that Influence on the Consumer Market Behavior. *Proceedings of Business and Economic Studies, 11*(4), 1-28. b Available from: http://ojs.bbwpublisher.com/index.php/PBES/article/view/628 [http://dx.doi.org/10.26689/pbes.v1i4.628]

Babenkova, L.M. (2008). Theoretical aspects of labor market research as a system of socio-economic relations. *News of universities. The Volga region. Social sciences, 3*, 45-52. [In Russ.].

Balog, M. M., Demidova, S. E., Troyan, V. V. (2021). The impact of digitalization of the economy on the labor market *Stage: Economic theory, analysis, practice,* (5), 60-74. [http://dx.doi.org/10.24412/2071-6435-2021-5-60-74]

Barabashev, A.G. (2016). The crisis of public administration and its impact on the main administrative paradigms of the state and bureaucracy. *Issues of state and municipal management, 3*, 169-171. [In Russ.].

Barkhordari, S., Fattahi, M., Azimi, N. A. (2019). The Impact of Knowledge-Based Economy on Growth Performance: Evidence from MENA Countries *Journal of the Knowledge Economy, 10*(3), 1168-1182. Available from: https://doi.org/10.1007/s13132-018-0522-4

[http://dx.doi.org/10.1007/s13132-018-0522-4]

Becker, G.S. (1964). Human Capital *Columbia University Press.* Available from: https://www.nber.org/books-and-chapters/human-capital-theoretical-and-emp-rical-analysis-special-reference-education-first-edition

Belousova, D. R., Frolova, I. E. (2022). On the long-term scientific and technological development of Russia: Monograph. *Dynamic print* (p. 168). Moscow. (In Russ.)

Belenova, A. I., Arenkov, I. A. (2021). Transformation of consumer behavior in the context of a pandemic in the online education market *Creative Economics, 15*(7), 2921-2938.
[http://dx.doi.org/10.18334/ce.15.7.112316]

Bengraf, S. V., Astratova, G. V., Simchenko, N. A., Yanovskaya, A. A. (2024). Review of the state of the innovation infrastructure of the Union State of Russia and Belarus (research sector and higher education system) as a complex socio-economic system in relation to the labor market in the context of digitalization. *Deposit INION RAS* UrFU.(p. 227). Yekaterinburg-Moscow: (In Russ.)

Bertalanffy, L.von (1962). General System Theory– A Critical Review. *Gen. Syst., VII*, 1-20.

Bettman, J.R. (1979). *An information processing theory of consumer choice.*. Reading, Mass.: Addison-Wesley Pub. Co..

Bican, P. M., Brem, A. (2020). Managing innovation performance: Results from an industry-spanning explorative study on R&D key measures *Creativity and Innovation Management, 29*, 268-291.
[http://dx.doi.org/10.1111/caim.12370]

Biswas, S.S. (2023). Potential use of chat gpt in global warming. *Ann. Biomed. Eng., 51*(6), 1126-1127.
[http://dx.doi.org/10.1007/s10439-023-03171-8]

Bogdan, N. I. (2020). Innovative development of economics and law in the context of the digitalization model: A collective monograph. In: Klimuk, V. V., (Ed.), *Baranovichi State University (BarSU)* (p. 335). Baranovichi. (In Russ.)

Bolgova, V.V., Kalashnikova, E.B. (2015). Reform of public education management: some problems of goal formation *Modern problems of science and education,* (1), 12-19. In Russ.

Borenstein, A.L., Pozdnyakova, E.V. (2022). Problems of transformation of the Institute of public service in the domestic state. *Bull. Perm Univ. Leg. Sci., 57*, 427-453. In Russ., abstract in Eng.
[http://dx.doi.org/10.17072/1995-4190-2022-57-427-453]

Borodin, S.N. (2023). A model for assessing the sustainable development of the region based on the index method. *Ekon. Reg., 19*(1), 45-59. In Russ., abstract in Eng.
[http://dx.doi.org/10.17059/ekon.reg.2023-1-4]

Boroush, M., Guci, L. (2022). Research and Development: U.S. Trends and International Comparisons. Available from: https://ncses.nsf.gov/pubs/nsb20225 (Accessed: 11 Dec 2023).

Borowski, P.F. (2021). Innovation strategy on the example of companies using bamboo. *J. Innov. Entrep., 10*(3)
[http://dx.doi.org/10.1186/s13731-020-00144-2]

Bratanovsky, S.N., Demenchuk, D.V. (2018). Principles of public administration. *Humanization Educ.,* (6), 20-28. In Russ.

Brennan, J. (2004). The social role of the contemporary university: Contradictions, boundaries and change. *Ten Years on: Changing education in a changing world* Open Univ. Press.(pp. 23-54). Maidenhead, UK:

Brown, C., White, D. (2018). Research sector and economic development: A comparative perspective. *J. Econ. Dev. Res., 17*(2), 145-163.

Broucker, B. (2022). About the rise, the characteristics and future of New Public Management in higher education. *Int. Encycl. Educ.*
[http://dx.doi.org/10.1016/B978-0-12-818630-5.02116-3]

Broström, A. (2011). The Triple Helix: University–industry–government innovation in action – by Henry Etzkowitz. *Pap. Reg. Sci., 90*(2)
[http://dx.doi.org/10.1111/j.1435-5957.2011.00357.x]

Browning, C. (2006). Small, smart and salient? Rethinking identity in the small states literature. *Cambr. Rev. Int. Relat., 19*(4), 669-684.

Bula, A.K., Umnov, E.A., Umnov, A.E. (2017). Optimization of the Pareto set shape in multicriteria programming problems. *Proc. Moscow Inst. Phys. Technol., 4*(36), 120-131. In Russ.

Caprar, D.V., Walker, B.W., Ashforth, B.E. (2022). The dark side of strong identification in organizations: A conceptual review. *Acad. Manage. Ann., 16*(2)
[http://dx.doi.org/10.5465/annals.2020.0338]

Carayannis, E.G., Campbell, D.F. (2009). "Mode 3" and "Quadruple Helix": Toward a 21st century fractal innovation ecosystem. *Int. J. Technol. Manag., 46*(3–4), 201-234.

Carayannis, E.G., Barth, T.D., Campbell, D.F. (2012). The Quintuple Helix innovation model: Global warming as a challenge and driver for innovation. *J. Innov. Entrep., 1*(2)
[http://dx.doi.org/10.1186/2192-5372-1-2]

Casalino, N., Saso, T., Borin, B., Massella, E., Lancioni, F. (2020). Digital competences for civil servants and digital ecosystems for more effective working processes in public organizations. *Digital Business Transformation.* Springer.Cham:
[http://dx.doi.org/10.1007/978-3-030-47355-6_21]

Channov, S.I. (2021). The use of digital technologies in the field of public administration. *Proc. Saratov Univ. New Ser. Econ. Manag. Law, 21*(4), 419-428. In Russ., abstract in Eng.

Chen, L., Wu, Y. (2020). The gig economy and its implications for workforce development in the digital age. *J. Labor Stud., 22*(1), 45-62.

Chizhov, D.V. (2016). Formation of the image of Russian political parties on the Internet. *Monit. Public Opin. Econ. Soc. Chang.,* (1), 313-338. In Russ.

Chugunov, A.V. (2011). Indicator systems and monitoring of the development of the information society and the knowledge economy. Analytical materials of HSE. Available from: https://iorj.hse.ru/data/2011/04/14/1208610857/системы.PDF (Accessed: 24 May 2024). In Russ.

Chung, H.T., Fallick, B., Nekarda, C.J., Ratner, D.D. (2014). Assessing the change in labor market conditions. *Finance and Economics Discussion Series, Fed. Reserve Board.* Washington, DC. 34 pp.

Coursey, D., Norris, D.F. (2008). Models of e-government: Are they correct? An empirical assessment. *Public Adm. Rev., 68*(3), 523-536.

Crespi, F., Antonelli, C. (2011). Matthew effects and R&D subsidies: Knowledge cumulability in high-tech and low-tech industries. *Working Papers, Univ. Roma Tre, 140*, 1-24.

Crocker, L., Algina, J. (2010). Introduction to classical and modern test theory. Logos.Moscow: 668 pp. In Russ.

Custodio, M., Hadjikakou, M., Bryan, B.A. (2023). A review of socioeconomic indicators of sustainability and wellbeing building on the social foundations framework. *Ecol. Econ., 203*, 107608. [http://dx.doi.org/10.1016/j.ecolecon.2022.107608]

Cai, Y. (2014). Implementing the Triple Helix model in a non-Western context: An institutional logics perspective. *Triple Helix, 1*(1), 1-20. [http://dx.doi.org/10.1186/s40604-014-0001-2]

Danilchenko, A.V., Kharitonovich, S.A. (2019). Economics of knowledge in the context of post-industrial development of the Republic of Belarus. *News Sci. Technol.,* (1)*48*, 8-15. In Russ., abstract in Eng.

Dezhina, I., Kiseleva, V. (2007). "Triple helix" in the innovation system of Russia. *Econ. Issues,* (12), 123-135. In Russ. [http://dx.doi.org/10.32609/0042-8736-2007-12-123-135]

Diebolt, C., Hippe, R. (2019). The long-run impact of human capital on innovation and economic development in the regions of Europe. *Appl. Econ., 51*(5), 542-563. [http://dx.doi.org/10.1080/00036846.2018.1495820]

Dobrolyubova, E., Klochkova, E., Alexandrov, O. (2019). Digitalization and effective government: What is the cause and what is the effect? *Digital Transformation and Global Society* Springer.(Vol. 1038, pp. 55-67). Cham: [http://dx.doi.org/10.1007/978-3-030-37858-5_5]

Dobrolyubova, E.I. (2018). Public administration by results in the era of digital transformation: A review of foreign experience and prospects for Russia. *Issues State Munic. Manag.,* (4), 70-93. In Russ., abstract in Eng.

Dobrotă, (2019). Dobrotă, C.E., Marcu, N., Siminică, M., Nețoiu, L.M. Disparities, gaps and evolution trends of innovation, as a vector of economic development, in the countries of the European Union. *Rom. J. Econ. Forecast., 22*(4), 174-184.

Dobrova, E.D. (2021). The role of innovation infrastructure in ensuring the formation of the digital economy of Russia. *Issues of innovative economics, 11*(2), 485-506. [In Russ., abstract in Eng.]. [http://dx.doi.org/10.18334/vinec.11.2.112101]

Dolgikh, U.O. (2017). Good governance – an alternative way of public administration. *Nauka. Thought: An electronic periodical, 6*, 23-28. [In Russ.].

Dorina, E.B., Kadovba, E.A. (2019). The innovative potential of the region and the effectiveness of its use *Economic Bulletin of the University, 41*, 47-58. In Russ., abstract in Eng.

Doroshenko, Yu.A., Malykhina, I.O. (2014). The essence and mechanism of formation of the innovative infrastructure of a higher educational institution. *Bulletin of the Belgorod State Technological University named after V. G. Shukhov,* (1), 86-91. In Russ.

Drapkin, I.M., Mariev, O.S., Golenkova, A.D. (2019). Institutional factors of enhancing the attraction of foreign direct investment in the economies of developing countries. *Ekon. Reg., 15*(3), 952-966. In Russ.,

abstract in Eng.
[http://dx.doi.org/10.17059/2019-3-24]

Dvoretskaya, A.E. (2018). Innovative activity of Russian enterprises: An analysis of the current situation. *PRO-Economics.* Available from: https://proeconomics.ru/catalog/2018/7/dvoretskaya.pdf (Accessed: 03 Dec 2022).

Dudina, T.N., Tarasova, O.S. (2022). On approaches to the development of regional systems of indices and indicators of sustainable development. *Usp. Sovrem. Estestv. Nauk,* (1), 23-29. In Russ., abstract in Eng.

Dutta, S., Lanvin, B., Rivera León, L., Wunsch-Vincent, S. (2024). Global Innovation Index 2023: Innovation in the face of uncertainty. *Global Innovation Index.* 16th ed. 250 pp. Available from: https://www.wipo.int/edocs/pubdocs/en/wipo-pub-2000-2023-en-main-report-global-innovation-index-2023-16th-edition.pdf (Accessed: 06 Mar 2024).

Economics in Context Initiative, (2021). Comparative economic systems: Capitalism and socialism in the 21st century. *ECI Teaching Module.* Global Development Policy Center, Boston Univ. Available from: https://www.bu.edu/eci/files/2021/08/Comparative-Economic-Systems.pdf (Accessed: 26 Jul 2024).

Edwards, J. (2013). The role of universities in smart specialisation. *JRC IPTS – S3 Platform.* Berlin, 27 Nov 2013. Available from: https://slideplayer.com/slide/3406105/ (Accessed: 16 May 2024).

Eferina, T.V., Lizunova, V.O., Prosyanyuk, D.V., Shiyanova, D.A. (2017). Innovative infrastructure as a factor of interregional differentiation in the Russian Federation. *Issues State Munic. Manag.,* (1), 191-212. In Russ.

Efimova, M.R., Dolgikh, E.A., Pershina, T.A., Parshintseva, L.S. (2021). The methodology for multivariate statistical analysis of innovation potentials: The case of Russia. *Stud. Syst. Decis. Control*

Efremova, P.V. (2019). Indicators for evaluating the effectiveness of the development of innovative activities of universities. *Issues Innov. Econ., 9*(3), 989-1010.
[http://dx.doi.org/10.18334/vinec.9.3.41001]

Emelianov, A.A., Vlasova, E.A., Duma, R.V. (2002). Finance and Statistics.Moscow: Ed. by A.A. Emelianov. 368 pp. In Russ.

Ermakova, S.E., Bagrova, N.A. (2016). The impact of the transformation of consumer behavior on the company's activities in the era of informatization. *Russ. Entrep., 17*(20), 2655-2670. In Russ.
[http://dx.doi.org/10.18334/rp.17.20.36919]

Ermicheva, E.P. (2008). Strategic choice as a key stage of strategic management. *Ind. Econ. Manag. Technol.,* (3), 47-50. In Russ.

Escalante, J., Pack, A., Barrett, A. (2023). AI-generated feedback on writing: Insights into efficacy and ENL student preference. *Int. J. Educ. Technol. High. Educ., 20*, 57.

Eskindarov, M.A., Gruzina, Y.M., Kharchilava, H.P., Melnichuk, M.V. (2022). The role of human capital in the digital economy at the institutional and regional levels. *Ekon. Reg., 18*(4), 1105-1120. In Russ., abstract in Eng.
[http://dx.doi.org/10.17059/ekon.reg.2022-4-10]

Espeland, W. (2015). Narrating Numbers. In: Rottenburg, R., Merry, S.E., Park, S-J., Mugler, J., (Eds.), *The World of Indicators: The Making of Governmental Knowledge through Quantification.* (pp. 56-75). Cambridge: Cambridge University Press.

[http://dx.doi.org/10.1017/CBO9781316091265.003]

Etzkowitz, H. (2008). *University-Industry-Government: The Triple Helix Model of Innovation.*. New York: Routledge.

Etzkowitz, H., Leydesdorff, L. (1995). The Triple Helix – University-Industry-Government Relations: A Laboratory for Knowledge Based Economic Development. *Glycoconjugate Journal, 14*(1), 14-19.

Eucken, W. (1992). The Different Types of Economic System. *The Foundations of Economics.*. Berlin, Heidelberg: Springer.
[http://dx.doi.org/10.1007/978-3-642-77318-1_10]

Fayyaz, A., Chaudhry, B.N., Fiaz, M. (2021). Upholding knowledge sharing for organization innovation efficiency in Pakistan. *J. Open Innov. Technol. Mark. Complex., 7*(1), 4.
[http://dx.doi.org/10.3390/joitmc7010004]

Fedorova, (2023). Fedorova, E., Kalinina, O., Peng, X., Vilken, V. Human Capital in the Digital Economy: Search for a Perspective Field of Research. In: Dvořáková, Z., Kulachinskaya, A., (Eds.), *Digital Transformation: What is the Impact on Workers Today? // Lecture Notes in Networks and Systems, 827:1-10.*. Cham: Springer.
[http://dx.doi.org/10.1007/978-3-031-47694-5_1]

Felício, T., Samagaio, A., Rodrigues, R. (2021). Adoption of management control systems and performance in public sector organizations. *J. Bus. Res., 124*, 593-602.
[http://dx.doi.org/10.1016/j.jbusres.2020.10.069]

Feller, W. (1957). *An Introduction to Probability Theory and Its Applications / 1.* (2nd ed.). New York: John Wiley.

Ferlie, E., Musselin, C., Andresani, G. (2008). The steering of higher education systems: A public management perspective. *High. Educ., 56*(3), 325-348.
[http://dx.doi.org/10.1007/s10734-008-9125-5]

Fitzpatrick, K.K., Darcy, A., Vierhile, M. (2017). Fitzpatrick, K.K., Darcy, A., and Vierhile, M. Delivering cognitive behavior therapy to young adults with symptoms of depression and anxiety using a fully automated conversational agent (Woebot): A randomized controlled trial. *JMIR Ment. Health, 4*(2), e19.
[http://dx.doi.org/10.2196/mental.7785]

Flerov, O.V., Kutaitseva, O.N. (2023). Digital behavior as a psychological and pedagogical phenomenon (structural and content analysis). *Educ. Resour. Technol.,* (1), 51-61. In Russ.

Florida, R. (2011). *Creative class: People who change the future.* (p. 432). Moscow: Classic-XXI.

Florida, R. (2012). What critics get wrong about the creative class and economic development. *CityLab.*

Fonseca, T., de Faria, P., Lima, F. (2019). Human capital and innovation: The importance of the optimal organizational task structure. *Res. Policy, 48*(3), 616-627.
[http://dx.doi.org/10.1016/j.respol.2018.10.010]

Galcheva, A. (2022). The economist described the tactics of "survival" of Russian science under sanctions. *RBC.* In Russ.

Galvao, A., Mascarenhas, C., Marques, C., Ferreira, J., Ratten, V. (2019). Triple helix and its evolution: A systematic literature review. *J. Sci. Technol. Policy Manag., 10*(3), 812-833.

[http://dx.doi.org/10.1108/JSTPM-10-2018-0103]

Ganieva, A.K. (2022). Mechanism of creative human capital formation. *Digital content of social and ecosystem development of the economy* (pp. 133-134). Simferopol: Crimean Federal University. In Russ.

Gantmacher, F.R. (1988). *Theory of matrices.* (4., p. 548). Moscow: Nauka. In Russ.

Garcia, M., Patel, R. (2020). Fostering digital literacy in higher education: Challenges and opportunities. *J. High. Educ. Stud., 18*(2), 87-104.

Gavrikov, A.V. (2022). Specifics of protests in Belarus in the period from 2017 to 2020. *Studia Humanitatis,* (3), 34-43. In Russ., abstract in Eng.
[http://dx.doi.org/10.15393/j12.art.2022.3846]

Getzoff, M. (2023). Most technologically advanced countries in the world 2023. *Global Finance Magazine.*

Global educational economy (2022). *Global Educational OutlookHolonIQ*. Available from: https://www.holoniq.com/notes/2022-global-education-outlook

Global HES Rep. (2022). Global higher education market research report – forecasts to 2027. Market Data Forecast. Available from: https://www.marketdataforecast.com/market-reports/higher-education-market

Gold, E.R. (2021). The fall of the innovation empire and its possible rise through open science. *Res. Policy, 50*(5)
[http://dx.doi.org/10.1016/j.respol.2021.104226]

Golovko, E.R. (2020). Tools for analysis of complex economic systems. *Int. Res. J.,* (7-3), 146-149.

Golovenchik, G.G. (2018). Transformation of the labor market in the digital economy. *Digital Transform.,* (4), 27-43. In Russ.

Grishaeva, T.A., Beregovskaya, T.A., Kvachko, A.V. (2022). Consumer behavior in the digital environment: New forms of society segmentation. *Smart Nations: Global Trends in the Digital Economy*
[http://dx.doi.org/10.1007/978-3-030-94870-2_28]

Groves, T. (1973). Incentives in teams. *Econometrica, 41*, 617-631.
[http://dx.doi.org/10.2307/1914085]

Gunter, H.M., Grimaldi, E., Hall, D., Serpieri, R. (2016). *New public management and the reform of education..* New York: Routledge.
[http://dx.doi.org/10.12828/89612]

Güngör, A.S., Cadirci, T.O. (2022). Understanding digital consumer: A review, synthesis, and future research agenda. *Int. J. Consum. Stud., 46*(5), 1829-1858.
[http://dx.doi.org/10.1111/ijcs.12809]

Helbing, D. (2012). Modeling of socio-economic systems. *Social Self-Organization.* Berlin; Heidelberg: Springer.
[http://dx.doi.org/10.1007/978-3-642-24004-1_1]

Hinkley, S. (2023). Technology in the public sector and the future of government work. (p. 80). Berkeley: UC Berkeley Labor Center. Available from: https://laborcenter.berkeley.edu/technology-in-the-public-secto--and-the-future-of-government-work/

Holgersson, J., Karlsson, F. (2014). Public e-service development: Understanding citizens' conditions for participation. *Gov. Inf. Q., 31*(3), 396-410.

Hood, C. (1995). The “New Public Management” in the 1980s: Variations on a theme. *Account. Organ. Soc., 20*(2-3), 93-109.
[http://dx.doi.org/10.1016/0361-3682(93)E0001-W]

Hurdey, M. (2011). Generation C: Content, creation, connections and choice. *Int. J. Mark. Res., 53*(6), 749-764.
[http://dx.doi.org/10.2501/IJMR-53-6-749-770]

Ignatieva, E.D., Mariev, O.S., Serkova, A.E. (2019). A methodological approach to assessing the impact of infrastructural security on the socio-economic development of Russian regions. *Bull. Perm Univ. Econ., 14*(3), 434-447. In Russ., abstract in Eng.
[http://dx.doi.org/10.17072/1994-9960-2019-3-434-447]

Inakefe, I.G., Uduak, B., Ifenna, M.F. (2021). Political leadership and public accountability in post-colonial Nigeria. *Asian Res. J. Arts Soc. Sci., 14*(4), 30-42.
[http://dx.doi.org/10.9734/arjass/2021/v14i430242]

Ishkhanyan, M.V., Karpenko, N.V. (2016). *Econometrics. Part 1: Pair regression..* Moscow: MGUPS (MIIT). In Russ.

Ishmuratova, D.F. (2021). Human capital in the context of digitalization: Features of development. *Econ. Manag.,* (6), 203-207. In Russ., abstract in Eng.
[http://dx.doi.org/10.34773/EU.2021.6.40]

Ivanova, E.I., Vasilevskaya, I.V. (2019). Labor migration in the Union State of Belarus and Russia: Factors and problems of regulation at the present stage. *Sci. Pap. INEF RAS, 17*, 383-400. In Russ.
[http://dx.doi.org/10.29003/m826.sp_ief_ras2019/383-400]

Johnson, E., Smith, J. (2019). Innovation ecosystems and economic development: The role of research institutions. *Innov. Stud. J., 24*(4), 321-338.

Kaihua, C., Mingting, K. (2014). Staged efficiency and its determinants of regional innovation systems: A two-step analytical procedure. *Ann. Reg. Sci., 52*(2), 627-657.
[http://dx.doi.org/10.1007/s00168-014-0604-6]

Kim, S. (2019). Adapting higher education to the digital age: Strategies for success. *Int. J. Educ. Innov., 14*(3), 301-318.

Kirillov, K.O. (2023). Prospects for solving the problems of digitalization of Russian industry. *Bull. S.Y. Witte Mosc. Univ. Econ. Manag.,* (2), 74-79. In Russ., abstract in Eng.

Kiselev, A.S. (2018). Modern theoretical approaches to the concept of an electronic state. *Actual Probl. Russ. Law,* (6), 32-39. In Russ., abstract in Eng.
[http://dx.doi.org/10.17803/1994-1471.2018.91.6.032-039]

Klimenko, A.V., Klishch, N.N. (2013). Is it possible to save on bureaucracy? *Public Adm. Issues,* (3), 90-109. In Russ.

Klimuk, V.V. (2023). Comparative analysis of the development of the scientific and innovative infrastructure of Belarus and Russia in the model of the Union State. *Issues Innov. Econ., 13*(1), 583-596. In Russ., abstract in Eng.
[http://dx.doi.org/10.18334/vinec.13.1.117513]

Klimuk, V.V., Astratova, G.V. (2022). Analysis of the effectiveness of the use of scientific potential: Personnel renewal. *Reg. Econ. South Russ.,* *10*(4), 5-19. In Russ., abstract in Eng. [http://dx.doi.org/10.15688/re.volsu.2022.4.1]

Klimuk, V.V., Unsovich, A.N. (2021). Analysis of the development of the national innovation infrastructure of the Republic of Belarus. *Issues Innov. Econ.,* (3), 929-942. In Russ., abstract in Eng.

Knobel, A., Firanchuk, A. (2023). Dynamics of trade turnover between Russia and its main partners in 2022. *Monitoring of Russia's Economic Outlook.* Moscow: IEP. Available from: https://ssrn.com/abstract=4408221 [http://dx.doi.org/10.2139/ssrn.4408221]

Knyazeva, E.N. (2009). The world of elusive structures. *Philosophy of Science and Technology,* *1*, 103-116. [In Russ.].

Kolenik, T., Gams, M. (2021). Intelligent cognitive assistants for attitude and behavior change support in mental health: State-of-the-art technical review. *Electron.,* *10*(11) [http://dx.doi.org/10.3390/electronics10111250]

Koryttsev, M.A. (2009). Institutional structure and mechanisms of functioning of quasi-markets in the public sector. In: Belokrylova, O.S., (Ed.), *Southern Federal University* (p. 319). Rostov-on-Don. In Russian.

Koroleva, L.P., Yermoshina, T.V. (2014). Innovative infrastructure: composition and place in the innovative system of the economy. *Innovations,* (12), 59-61. In Russ.

Kosovsky, A.A., Malchevsky, E.S., Lyakh, S.I. (2017). Innovative infrastructure of the Republic of Belarus: The state, problems and ways to improve the efficiency of functioning. *News of Science and Technology,* (4), 26-34. Available from:

Kostyuchenko, I.Y. (2009). State administration of public education of the Russian Federation in the context of systemic reforms of the 1990s. *Bulletin of the Moscow University. Series 21: Governance,* *4*, 108-126. [State and Society].

Kotler, F. (1991). Fundamentals of marketing. *Progress Publishing House* (p. 651). Moscow. Translated from English; In Russian.

Kovalev, M.M., Avdonin, A.A. (2020). How to improve the efficiency of management of public organizations? *Journal of the Belarusian State University. Economy,* (2), 60-71. In Russ.

Kozopolyanskaya, A.V. (2018). The development of the humanitarian space of the Union state of Belarus and Russia since 1996. *Human Capital,* *120*(12), 9-20. In Russian; abstract in English. [http://dx.doi.org/10.25629/HC.2018.12.01]

Kuznetsova, I.A. (2015). Innovative infrastructure as a factor of increasing the efficiency of innovation activity. *Bulletin of the Irkutsk State Technical University,* *11*(106), 221-226. [In Russ.].

Larionova, (2019). Larionova, V., Sheka, A., & Vasilyev, S. Students behavioural patterns on the national open education platform. In: Orngreen, B R., Buhl, M., Meyer, B., (Eds.), *Proceedings of the 18th European Conference on e-Learning, ECEL 2019,* 313-319. [http://dx.doi.org/10.34190/EEL.19.126]

Laverov, N.P. (2004). Sustainable development: Resources of Russia. *Publishing Center of the D.I. Mendeleev Russian State Technical University* (p. 212). Moscow. Collective monograph; In Russian.

Lavrinenko, Ya.B. (2023). Innovative activity of universities of the Russian Federation and indicators of the

"Priority 2030" program. *Issues of Innovative Economics, 13*(3), 1675-1698. In Russian; abstract in English. [http://dx.doi.org/10.18334/vinec.13.3.119150]

Lazimov, I.K., O'G'Li, Nazarov, N.N., Ogli (2023). Modern strategic management issues. *Science and Innovation,* (Special Issue), 987-993.

Li, Q., Wang, H. (2018). Labor market dynamics in the digital era: Challenges and opportunities. *Journal of Labor Economics, 25*(4), 367-385.

Lindgren, I., van Veenstra, A.F. (2018). Digital government transformation: A case illustrating public e-service development as part of public sector transformation. *Proceedings of the 19th Annual International Conference on Digital Government Research (DG.O 2018).* [http://dx.doi.org/10.1145/3209281.3209302]

Lutsenko, E.V., Golovin, N.S. (2024). Revolution of the early XXI century in artificial intelligence: Deep mechanisms and perspectives. (p. 394). Krasnodar.*Kuban State Agrarian University* Monograph; In Russian.

Luzgina, A.N. (2017). International practice of building an electronic government system. *Journal of the Belarusian State University. Economy, 1*, 76-83. [In Russ.].

Lvov, D.S. (1990). Efficiency of management of technical development. (p. 255). Moscow.*Economics* In Russian.

Madgavkar, A., Schaninger, B., Smit, S., Woetzel, L., Samandari, H., Carlin, D., Seong, J., Chockalingam, K. (2022). Human capital represents two-thirds of wealth for the average individual – and work experience contributes almost half of that value. *McKinsey Global Institute,* 104. Available from: https://www.mckinsey.com/~/media/mckinsey/business%20functions/people%20and%20organizational%20performance/our%20insights/human%20capital%20at%20work%20the%20value%20of%20experience/mgi-human-capital-report-jun2022.pdf?shouldIndex=false

Malashenkov, V. (2023). Import substitution in Belarus and Russia: Growth points in 2023. January 24, 2023. Available from: https://eurasia.expert/importozameshchenie-v-belarusi-i-rossii-tochki-rosta-v-2023/ (Accessed: 05/13/2024). (In Russ.).

Malhotra, N.K. (2002). Marketing research. A practical guide. *Williams Publishing House.* Translated from English. 960 pp. (In Russ.).

Maltsevich, I.V. (2023). Modern trends in the development of digital products in the construction industry as a potential for increasing labor productivity. *Economics and Banks,* (1), 86-95. Available from: https://rep.polessu.by/bitstream/123456789/28882/1/Sovremennye_tendentsii.pdf (Accessed: 07/10/2024). (In Russ.).

Mamedov, A.A. (2011). State regulation in the field of higher education. *Bulletin of the Peoples' Friendship University of Russia (RUDN). Series: Legal Sciences,* (2), 29-39. (In Russ.).

Manokhin, V.M. (2012). Branch principle in public administration. *Bulletin of the Saratov State Law Academy,* (3), 80-83. (In Russ.).

Maratova, H.B. (2022). The evolution of the development of models of public administration: Public administration, new public management and good governance. *Public Service,* (6), (In Russ., abstract in Eng.).
[http://dx.doi.org/10.22394/2070-8378-2022-24-6-12-19]

Marčeta, M., Bojnec, S. (2021). Innovation and competitiveness in the European Union countries.

International Journal of Sustainable Economy, 13(1), 1-17.

Marushko, D.A., Ablameyko, M.S., Nguyen, Nhu Son (2017). On the issue of evaluating the effectiveness of e-government. *Journal of the Belarusian State University. Economy,* (1), 70-75. (In Russ.).

Marzuki, U., Widiati, D., Rusdin, , Darwin, , Indrawati, I. (2023). The impact of AI writing tools on the content and organization of students' writing: EFL teachers' perspective. *Cogent Education, 10*(2), 2236469. [http://dx.doi.org/10.1080/2331186X.2023.2236469]

Mazelis, L.S., Zemtseva, E.D., Krasova, E.V., Krasko, A.A. (2018). Assessment of the impact of human capital on social and economic development: Econometric modelling on the example of Russian regions. *Trends and Management,* (4), 97-110. (In Russ., abstract in Eng.). [http://dx.doi.org/10.7256/2454-0730.2018.4.28056]

McGee, R.W. (2023). Who were the 10 best and 10 worst US presidents? *2023 IEEE Global Engineering Education Conference (EDUCON).* [http://dx.doi.org/10.1109/EDUCON54358.2023.10125121]

Medvedeva, Yu.A. (2006). Directions for improving the system of sectoral management in the Republic of Belarus. *Bulletin of the educational institution Vitebsk State Technical University, 11*, 87-93. [In Russ.].

Merkulov, P.A., Malakhova, O.V. (2020). Modernization of public administration and public service in the context of digitalization. *Digital economy and electronic education: European experience,* Collection of scientific papers of the I International Scientific and Practical ConferenceStavropolMarch 10–14, 2020UshvitskyL.I.PenkovaI.V.Stavropol: SEQUOIA Limited Liability Company.260-264. (In Russ.).

Millard, J. (2018). Open governance systems: Doing more with more. *Gov. Inf. Q., 35*(4), S77-S87. [http://dx.doi.org/10.1016/j.giq.2015.08.003]

Mironov, A.V. (2002). Education as a sphere of state policy. *Socio-humanitarian knowledge, 6*, 32-48. [In Russ.].

Monteiro, P., Adler, P.S. (2022). Bureaucracy for the 21st century: Clarifying and expanding our view of bureaucratic organization. *Academy of Management Annals, 16*(2) [http://dx.doi.org/10.5465/annals.2019.0059]

Morimoto, T. (1963). Markov processes and the H-theorem. *J. Phys. Soc. Jpn., 18*(3), 328-331. [http://dx.doi.org/10.1143/JPSJ.18.328]

Mukhametov, R.S. (2020). Foreign policy of Belarus: A small state in search of asylum. *Koinon, 1*(1-2), 281-297. [In Russ.]. [http://dx.doi.org/10.15826/koinon.2020.01.1.2.016]

Mukametova, A.D. (2019). Methodology for the development of a strategy for regional development based on the effective use of human capital. *Economics and management of governance systems, 1*(31), 32-38. [In Russ.].

Musselin, C. (2018). New forms of competition in higher education1. *Socio-economic Rev., 16*(3), 657-683. [http://dx.doi.org/10.1093/ser/mwy033]

Mutanov, G., Zhuparova, A., Zhaisanova, D. (2020). Mutanov, G., Zhuparova, A., Zhaisanova, D. Measuring the knowledge-based performance efficiency in the oil-exported countries. *Montenegrin Journal of Economics, 16*(3), 109-122. [http://dx.doi.org/10.14254/1800-5845/2020.16-3.9]

Naidoo, R., Whitty, G. (2014). Students as consumers: Commodifying or democratising learning? *Int. J. Chin. Educ.*
[http://dx.doi.org/10.1163/22125868-123400]

Naylor, T. (1975). Machine simulation experiments with models of economic systems. (p. 392). Moscow: Mir. (In Russ.).

Nazarenko, T.S., Novikova, I.V. (2023). Digital transformation of public administration as a strategic public good. *Strategizing: Theory and practice,* (2), 140-158. (In Russ., abstract in Eng.).

Nekhoda, E.V., Pan, Li (2021). Transformation of the labor market and employment in the digital age. *Labor economics, 8*(9), 897-916.
[http://dx.doi.org/10.18334/et.8.9.113408]

Nelson, A.R., Strohl, N.M. (2014). Universities 2030: Learning from the past to anticipate the future. Available from: https://globalhighered.wordpress.com/2014/04/27/universities-2030-learning-from-the-past-to-anticipate-the-future/ (Accessed: 12/01/2017).

Nemeryuk, E.E., Romanovskaya, O.A., Kantemirova, G.A. (2020). Problems of functioning of the civil service as a social institution in the Russian Federation. *Izvestiya Saratov Univ. New Ser. Sociology. Political Science, 20*(4), 374-379. (In Russ., abstract in Eng.).
[http://dx.doi.org/10.18500/1818-9601-2020-20-4-374-379]

Nielsen, K. (2008). Indicative planning. *The New Palgrave Dictionary of Economics.* London: Palgrave Macmillan.

Noack, A., Jacobsen, H. (2021). Transfer scouts: From intermediation to co-constructors of new knowledge and technologies in Germany. *Res. Policy, 50*(4)
[http://dx.doi.org/10.1016/j.respol.2021.104209]

Noor, U., Younas, M., Aldayel, H.S., Menhas, R., Xu, Q. (2022). Learning behavior, digital platforms for learning and its impact on university students' motivations and knowledge development. *Front. Psychol.*
[http://dx.doi.org/10.3389/fpsyg.2022.933974]

Nove, A. (1987). Planned economy. *The New Palgrave: A Dictionary of Economics*

Novikova, I.N. (2022). Small countries in international relations: Some theoretical aspects. *Vestn. St. Petersb. Univ. Int. Relat., 15*(3), 219-242. (In Russ., abstract in Eng.).
[http://dx.doi.org/10.21638/spbu06.2022.301]

Obolonsky, A.V. (2014). The crisis of efficiency of the administrative-bureaucratic state and the search for a way out: The US experience (evolution of theory and practice of public administration in recent decades). *Issues Public Munic. Adm.,* (2), 145-170. (In Russ.).

Olmstead, L. (2024). 11 critical digital transformation challenges to overcome (2024). Available from: https://whatfix.com/blog/digital-transformation-challenges/ (Accessed: 06/06/2024).

Olojede, B., Ann, D. (2023). Tragedy of public administration in Nigeria: Implications for national development. *Int. J. Strateg. Res. Educ. Technol. Humanit., 11*(1), 99-110.
[http://dx.doi.org/10.48028/iiprds/ijsreth.v11.i1.09]

Orlov, D., Postnikov, E. (2022). The indicator of the relationship between the labor market and inflation. *Series of reports on economic research,* (96), 43. Available from: https://cbr.ru/StaticHtml/File/140042/wp_96.pdf (Accessed: 05/25/2024). (In Russ.).

Ozhiganova, E.M. (2015). Theory of generations by N. Howe and V. Strauss: Possibilities of practical application. *Bus. Educ. Knowl. Econ., 1*(1), 1-4. (In Russ.).

Pakhomova, I.Y. (2012). The "triple helix" model as a mechanism of innovative development of the region. *Economy. Comput. Sci.,* (7-1(126)), 1-6. (In Russ.).

Palchik, G.V., Volokh, N.V., Hasanov, A.P., Hermenchuk, V.V., Dubinko, N.A., Zabelov, S.M., Ignatyuk, A.Z., Kivayko, V.N., Krishtapovich, E.A., Lapina, S.V., Lisovskaya, T.V., Melnik, V.A., Mushta, A.A., Pecheneva, T.A., Starovoitova, T.F., Tomukcvich, O.T., Fablinova, O.N., Shibutani, M.S., Shchepov, V.A. (2020). Evolution of the public administration system: The Republic of Belarus. *Public Service, 20*(3/125), 86-118. (In Russ.).
[http://dx.doi.org/10.22394/2070-8378-2020-22-3-86-118]

Panikarova, S.V., Vlasov, M.V., Drashkovich, V. (2020). The system of higher education as a driver of innovative development of the country. *Univ. Manag.: Pract. Anal., 24*(1), 96-105. (In Russ., abstract in Eng.).
[http://dx.doi.org/10.15826/umpa.2020.01.007]

Pasmurtseva, N.N. (2020). Formation of the state strategic management system: Model and problems of implementation. *Moscow Economic Journal, 8*, 573-581. [In Russ., abstract in Eng.].

Pavlenko, I.G., Bukreev, I.A. (2020). Providing strategic planning of the development of entrepreneurial activity in the recreational sphere of the Republic of Crimea *Problems of modern economy,* (1), 73121-124. In Russ.

Pavlenko, I.G., Bezulyov, V.V. (2019). Cluster approach in the development of the tourism industry and its impact on the economic space of the region. *Bulletin of the Orel State University of Economics and Trade,* (1), 4795-100. In Russ.

Petrov, M.B., Gursky, V.L., Presnyakova, E.V., Serkov, L.A., Kozhov, K.B., Martynenko, A.V., Li, V.A., Verax, S.A., Rodevich, O.F., Solomko, M.V. (2022). Assessment of industrial and technological cooperation between Russia and Belarus: A macro-regional aspect. *Ural Branch of the Russian Academy of Sciences* (p. 216). Yekaterinburg. (In Russ.).

Piatrov, I., Kusá, A. (2019). Innovative approach to consumer segmentation in a digital age and their attitude to environmental issues. *Proc. Eur. Conf. Innov. Entrep.,* 788-792.
[http://dx.doi.org/10.34190/ECIE.19.170]

Pilgun, E.V., Leshenyuk, O.N. (2021). Public administration in the Republic of Belarus: Principles of sustainable development. *Law Manag. XXI Century, 17*(3), 27-40. (In Russ.).
[http://dx.doi.org/10.24833/2073-8420-2021-3-60-27-40]

Pirannejad, A., Ingrams, A. (2022). Open government maturity models: A global comparison. *Soc. Sci. Comput. Rev., 41*(3), 1-27.
[http://dx.doi.org/10.1177/08944393211063107]

Pleskevich, V.B. (2023). Analysis of the problems of implementation and application of digital technologies for managing the effectiveness of an organization's operational activities. *Bulletin of Eurasian Science, 15*(6) Available from: https://esj.today/PDF/39FAVN623.pdf (Accessed: 06/06/2024). (In Russ.).

Poletaev, D.V. (2021). External labor migration from Belarus: Prospects for Russia. *Eurasia. Expert,* (4), 32-37.
[http://dx.doi.org/10.18254/S271332140018169-2]

Policy brief: Education during COVID-19 and beyond. *United Nations Sustainable Development Group.* Available from: https://unsdg.un.org/sites/default/files/2020-08/sg_policy_brief_covi--19_and_education_august_2020.pdf (Accessed: 03/15/2021).

Pollitt, C., Bouckaert, G. (2000). Public management reform: A comparative analysis. *Oxford Univ. Press* (p. 409). Oxford.

Popikov, A.A. (2016). Creative human capital as a factor of development of the innovative economy of the country. *Power,* (3), Available from: https://cyberleninka.ru/article/n/kreativnyy-chelovecheskiy-kapital--ak-faktor-razvitiya-innovatsionnoy-ekonomiki-strany (In Russ.).

Popova, I.N., Sergeeva, T.L. (2022). Import substitution in modern Russia: Problems and prospects. *Beneficium,* (2)*43*, 73-84.ru
[http://dx.doi.org/10.34680/BENEFICIUM.2022.2(43).73-84]

Potreba, V.G. (2019). Features of the geopolitics of the Republic of Belarus as a small state. *BNTU Repository.* Available from: https://rep.bntu.by/bitstream/handle/data/44930/Osobennosti_geopolitiki_Respubliki_Belarus_kak_malogo_gosudarstva.pdf?sequence=1&isAllowed=y

Qadir, J. (2023). Engineering education in the era of ChatGPT: Promise and pitfalls of generative AI for education. *Proc. IEEE Glob. Eng. Educ. Conf. (EDUCON),* Kuwait.1-9.
[http://dx.doi.org/10.1109/EDUCON54358.2023.10125121]

Rajňoha, R., Lesnikova, P., Štefko, R., Schmidtova, J., Formanek, I. (2019). Transformations in strategic business planning in the context of sustainability and business goals setting. *Transform. Bus. Econ.,* (2)*18*, 44-66.

Ray, P.P. (2023). ChatGPT: A comprehensive review on background, applications, key challenges, biases, ethics, limitations and future scope. *Internet Things Cyber-Phys. Syst., 3*, 121-154.
[http://dx.doi.org/10.1016/j.iotcps.2023.04.003]

Razuvanova, K.S. (2016). The triple helix model: On the issue of studying and prospects for implementation in the Republic of Belarus. *Proc. Belarusian State Univ.,* Minsk.83-86. Available from: https://elib.bsu.by/bitstream/123456789/250466/1/83-86.pdf

Research EdMarket. *Research of the Russian online education market 2021 and trends 2022 from industry leaders., Netology,* 253. Available from: https://netology.ru/edtech_research_2022

Richards, M., Waugh, K., Slaymaker, M., Petre, M., Woodthorpe, J., Gooch, D. (2024). Bob or bot: Exploring ChatGPT's answers to university computer science assessment. *ACM Trans. Comput. Educ., 24*(1), 32.
[http://dx.doi.org/10.1145/3633287]

Rostislavsky, A.A. (2022). Analysis and assessment of the level of innovative development of the Russian Federation in the regional context. *Economics and Management: Trends and Prospects* (pp. 296-309). St. Petersburg: St. Petersburg State University of Architecture and Civil Engineering.

Roy, P., Datta, D. (2022). Theory and models of consumer buying behaviour: A descriptive study. *SSRN Electron. J., 11*(8), 206-217.
[http://dx.doi.org/10.2139/ssrn.4205489]

Federal State Statistics Service. (2022). Russian statistical yearbook. *Rosstat Moscow,* 691. Available from: https://rosstat.gov.ru/storage/mediabank/Ejegodnik_2022.pdf

Saad, M., Zavdi, G. (2011). Theory and practice of the triple helix model in developing countries: Problems and challenges. *Routledge* (1., p. 336). New York.
[http://dx.doi.org/10.4324/9780203838211]

Sadovaya, E.S. (2022). The mechanism of formation of inequality in the labor market in the digital age. *VNII Truda, Ministry of Labor of Russia.* Available from: https://vcot.info/blog/mehanizm-formirovani--neravenstva-na-rynke-truda-v-cifrovuu-epohu

Sadykhanova, G., Erezhepova, A., Nurmanova, B., Aitbembetova, A., Bimendiyeva, L. (2019). Efficiency of financing high-tech industries: The case of Kazakhstan. *J. Asian Finance Econ. Bus., 6*(4), 287-295.

Sav, G.T. (2016). Declining state funding and efficiency effects on public higher education: Government really does matter. *Int. Adv. Econ. Res., 22*(4), 397-408.
[http://dx.doi.org/10.1007/s11294-016-9602]

Sav, G.T. (2017). Efficiency evaluations of US public higher education and effects of state funding and Pell grants: Panel data estimates using two stage data envelopment analysis, 2004–2013 academic years. *J. Educ. Finance, 42*(4), 357-385.

Savelyeva, E.A. (2018). Digital labor organization: Directions, principles, approaches. *Labor Econ., 5*(4), 935-950.
[http://dx.doi.org/10.18334/et.5.4.39642]

Schubert, T. (2009). Empirical observations on new public management to increase efficiency in public research – boon or bane? *Res. Policy, 38*(8), 1225-1234.
[http://dx.doi.org/10.1016/j.respol.2009.06.007]

Secundo, G., De Beer, C., Passiante, G. (2016). Measuring university technology transfer efficiency: A maturity level approach. *Meas. Bus. Excell., 20*(3), 42-54.
[http://dx.doi.org/10.1108/MBE-03-2016-0018]

Siegel, D.S., Waldman, D.A., Atwater, L.E., Link, A.N. (2004). Toward a model of the effective transfer of scientific knowledge from academicians to practitioners: Qualitative evidence from the commercialization of university technologies. *J. Eng. Technol. Manag., 21*(1-2), 115-142.
[http://dx.doi.org/10.1016/j.jengtecman.2003.12.006]

Sergeev, V.M., Artyushkin, V.F. (2016). Indicators of the innovative potential of political and economic development. *Polis. Polit. Res., 25*(6), 114-126. Available from: https://www.isras.ru/index.php?page_id=2624&jid=5201&jn=polis

Shamardina, I.A. (2022). Formation of a single tourist market of the EEU based on the development of digitalization. *Prospects of Eurasian Economic Integration,* Minsk: Four Quarters.210-212.ru

Shibanova, E.Y. (2023). NPM policy in higher education: An overview of the impact of the “new public administration” on the effectiveness and productivity of universities. *Vopr. Obrazovaniya,* (2), 241-281.ru
[http://dx.doi.org/10.17323/1814-9545-2023-2-241-281]

Shirinkina, E.B. (2019). Digitalization of business processes in industries as a factor for increasing the return on human capital. *Res. Dev. Econ., 7*(1), 53-57.ru
[http://dx.doi.org/10.12737/article_5c598be6534ab0.00845034]

Shtrik, A.A. (2002). Macroeconomic indicators of the development of the information society and overcoming digital inequality between the countries of the world. (p. 240). Moscow: New Technologies.ru

Silakova, L.V., Grigoriev, E.A. (2021). Analysis of Russia's innovative development: Status, problems, prospects. *Econ. Environ. Manag.,* (2), 86-95.ru

Simchenko, N.A., Astratova, G.V., Klimuk, V.V. (2023). Creative human capital and assessment of its manifestation in organizational behavior in the context of digitalization of higher education. *Prospects Sci. Educ.,* (6), 647-672.
[http://dx.doi.org/10.32744/pse.2023.6.38]

Sinitsyn, E.V., Laptev, V.M., Komarova, K.S., Buzunov, A.N. (2022). Algorithms for the people intra-city flows analysis by the data on bank cards payments. *Sun Text Rev. Econ. Bus., 3*(2), 157.
[http://dx.doi.org/10.51737/2766-4775.2022.057]

Siparo, K.A. (2023). Problems and prospects of economic cooperation between Russia and the Republic of Belarus. *Regional problems of economic transformation, 2*(148), 7-13. [In Russ., abstract in Eng.].

Smirnov, V.E. (2019). The state as a subject of regulatory influence on economic development: Opportunities and limitations (sociological analysis). *Journal of the Belarusian State University. Sociology, 2*, 26-35. [In Russ.].

Smith, A., Jones, B. (2020). The Role of Research and Innovation in Economic Development: A Comparative Analysis of Russia and Belarus *Journal of Economic Development, 15*(2), 123-140.

Smol, M., Kulczycka, J. (2019). Towards innovations development in the European raw material sector by evolution of the knowledge triangle. *Resour. Policy, 62*, 453-462.
[http://dx.doi.org/10.1016/j.resourpol.2019.04.006]

Smorodinskaya, N.V. (2011). The triple helix as a new matrix of economic systems. *Innovations, 4*(150), 66-78. [In Russ.].

Soboleva, I. (2009). Paradoxes of measuring human capital. *Economic,* (9), 51-70. [In Russ.].
[http://dx.doi.org/10.32609/0042-8736-2009-9-51-70]

Solis, B. (2018). Defying demographics: Generation-C, today's hyperconnected consumer generation. Available from: https://briansolis.com/2018/01/defying-demographics-generation-c-todays-hyperconn-cted-consumer-generation/

Solis, B. (2015). X: The experience when business meets design. (p. 256). New Jersey: John Wiley & Sons.

Sridhar, P., Doyle, A., Agarwal, A., Bogart, C., Savelka, J., Sakr, M. (2023). Harnessing LLMs in curricular design: Using GPT-4 to support authoring of learning objectives. *Proc. Workshop on Empowering Education with LLMs,* Tokyo.1-12.
[http://dx.doi.org/10.48550/arXiv.2306.17459]

StatBul. (2024). Statistical bulletin "Population as of January 1, 2024 and the average annual population for 2023 in the Republic of Belarus by regions, districts, cities, urban-type settlements". *Statistical bulletin,* Minsk.30. Available from: https://www.belstat.gov.by/upload/iblock/486/uffrnge0ue8w5xizr44cc8qwaxwpk4a6.pdf

Stat SocEc. (2023). The socio-economic situation of the Republic of Belarus. *National Statistical Committee of the Republic of Belarus.* Available from: https://www.belstat.gov.by/ofitsialnaya-statistika/publications/izdania/public_bulletin/index_16223

Statistical yearbook of the Republic of Belarus. (p. 322). Minsk: National Statistical Committee of the Republic of Belarus. Available from:

https://www.belstat.gov.by/upload/iblock/0a7/lk1zigmat2zbcwvo3ljrfm1tow2f5zd2.pdf

Strauss, W., Howe, N. (1997). The fourth turning: An American prophecy. (p. 318). New York: Broadway Books.

Sukhanova, T.V. (2024). Indicators of the functioning of the national labor market in the context of the transformation of the global economic system. *Labor Econ., 11*(4), 431-440.ru [http://dx.doi.org/10.18334/et.11.4.120860]

Tarasova, N.P., Kruchina, E.B. (2006). Indiccs and indicators of sustainable development. *Sustainable development: Nature–society–man,* Moscow.127-144.ru

Tararyshkina, L.I. (2019). The role of the Union State of Belarus and Russia in the development of Eurasian integration. *Greater Eurasia: Challenges and opportunities,* Minsk: Belarusian State University.52-57. Available from: https://elib.bsu.by/handle/123456789/221595

Tatarkin, A.I., Pilipenko, E.V. (2007). Economics of knowledge: Problems of theory and methodology. (p. 284). Yekaterinburg: Institute of Economics, Ural Branch of the Russian Academy of Sciences.ru

Tolmachev, A.V., Sinitsyn, E.V., Brusyanin, D.A. (2019). Transport system modelling based on analogies between road networks and electrical circuits. *R-Economy, 5*(2), 92-98. [http://dx.doi.org/10.15826/recon.2019.5.2.010]

Thompson, M.J., Woerter, M. (2020). Competition and invention quality: Evidence from Swiss firms. *Technol. Forecast. Soc. Change, 156*, 120023. [http://dx.doi.org/10.1016/j.techfore.2020.120023]

Tretyakova, T.I. (2014). Index of intellectual development as an integrated indicator of intellectual potential assessment in a modern market economy. *Bulletin of the Samara State University, 8*(119), 228-234. [In Russ.].

Udaltsova, N.L., Krutskikh, D.A. (2021). Features of the formation and development of the innovation system of Russia in the context of the "Triple Helix". *Issues of innovative economics, 11*(1), 33-46. [http://dx.doi.org/10.18334/vinec.11.1.111894]

Van Vught, F.A. (1991). A public administration perspective on the study of higher education. *Higher Education in Europe, 16*(3), 57-77. [http://dx.doi.org/10.1080/0379772910160305]

Van Vught, F.A., de Boer, H. (2015). Governance models and policy instruments. *The Palgrave international handbook of higher education policy and governance* [http://dx.doi.org/10.1007/978-1-137-45617-5_3]

Vasilenko, L.A., Zotov, V.V. (2020). Digitalization of public administration in Russia: Risks, incidents, problems. *Digital Sociology, 3*(2), 4-16. In Russ., abstract in Eng.

Vasiliev, Yu.S., Volkova, V.N., Kozlov, V.N. (2020). Theory of systems as the basis of higher education under modern innovative technologies. *System analysis in design and management,* (1), 7-23. In Russ., abstract in Eng.

Vasilevskaya, I.V. (2019). Labor migration from Belarus to Russia in the context of interstate integration relations. *Bulletin of the Russian State University,* (1), 141-152. In Russ., abstract in Eng. [http://dx.doi.org/10.28995/2073-6401-2019-1-141-152]

Vlasov, M.V., Shardina, M.O. (2022). Factor analysis of innovative activity of the Russian Federation.

Bulletin of the Udmurt University. Economics and Law series, 32(4), 609-617. In Russ., abstract in Eng. [http://dx.doi.org/10.35634/2412-9593-2022-32-4-609-617]

Varlamova, T.A., Gokhberg, L.M., Ozerova, O.K. (2023). Education in numbers: 2023: A brief statistical collection. ISIEZ HSE.Moscow: 132 pp. In Russ.

Walczak, K., Cellary, W. (2023). Challenges for higher education in the era of widespread access to generative AI. *Economics and Business Review, 9*(2), 71-100. [http://dx.doi.org/10.18559/ebr.2023.2.743]

Wang, M., Platonova, E.D. (2019). The role of labor migration in the formation and development of global, Russian and regional labor markets. *Bulletin of Eurasian Science,* (1), 1-9. In Russ.

Wentzel, E.S. (2002). *Probability theory: Textbook for universities.* Vysshaya shkola.(8., p. 575). Moscow: In Russ.

Wentzel, E.S., Ovcharov, L.A. (1991). *Theory of random processes and its engineering applications.* Nauka.(p. 384). Moscow: Chief Editor of Phys.-Math. Lit. In Russ.

Williamson, B., Hague, C. (2009). Digital participation, digital literacy, and school subjects: A review of the policies, literature and evidence. Futurelab. Available from: https://www.nfer.ac.uk/publications/digital-participation-digital-literacy-and-school-subjects-a-review-of-the-policies-literature-and-evidence/ Accessed: 07/06/2024.

Women and men of Russia. Glotko, O.L., Ivanova, A.M., Moruga, A.S., Nikitina, S.Y., Strakhova, E.V., Fatyanova, L.N., Chumarina, V.Zh., Elefterova, M.P. (2022). Rosstat.(p. 208). Moscow: Available from: https://rosstat.gov.ru/storage/mediabank/Wom-Man%202022.pdf Statistical collection. Accessed: 06/19/2024.

World development report 2022: Finance for an equitable recovery. World Bank. Available from: https://www.worldbank.org/en/publication/wdr2022 Accessed: 09/05/2023.

World development report 2016: Digital dividends. World Bank. Available from: https://unctad.org/system/files/non-official-document/dtl_ict4d2016_01_WDR_pptWorldBank_en.pdf Accessed: 07/14/2022.

Yakovleva, E.A. (2014). Analysis of key indicators of the Russian labor market. *Naukovedenie,* (6), 16. Available from: http://naukovedenie.ru/PDF/177EVN614.pdf In Russ., abstract in Eng. [http://dx.doi.org/10.15862/177EVN614]

Yanovskaya, A.A., Simchenko, N.A. (2024). Socio-economic aspects of the transformation of forms of labor organization. *Labor economics, 11*(2), 135-154. In Russ., abstract in Eng. [http://dx.doi.org/10.18334/et.11.2.120478]

Yarushkina, E.A., Kobeleva, A.A. (2018). Human capital: The essence and role in improving the efficiency of the organization. *Scientific Bulletin of the YUIM,* (1), 30-34. In Russ.

Yunchits, E.M. (2016). Improving the efficiency of scientific and innovative development of the regions of the Republic of Belarus on the basis of the "triple helix" model. *Proceedings of the Belarusian State University "Trends in economic development in the XXI century",* Minsk.268-274. Available from: http://edoc.bseu.by:8080/bitstream/edoc/70262/1/Yunchits_E._M._s._268_274.pdf Accessed: 03/04/2024. In Russ.

Yusupov, V.A. (2013). The concept and features of services provided by public administration bodies (administrative and legal aspect). *Bulletin of the Eurasian Academy of Administrative Sciences, 3*(24), 8-16.

[In Russ., abstract in Eng.].

Yuzhuo, C. (2013). Enhancing context sensitivity of the Triple Helix model: An institutional logics perspective. *Triple Helix Journal. A Journal of University-Industry-Government Innovation and Entrepreneurship,* *1*(1), 1-22.

Yüksel, A., Gök, M.Ş., Özer, G., Ciğerim, E. (2022). A new theoretical approach to intellectual capital: Meta-synthesis definitions of innovative literacy. *J. Intellect. Cap., 23*(6), 1435-1460. [http://dx.doi.org/10.1108/JIC-12-2020-0379]

Zaytsev, Y.K. (2021). Russia's approach to official development assistance and its contribution to the SDGs. In: Chaturvedi, S., (Ed.), *The Palgrave handbook of development cooperation for achieving the 2030 agenda.* Palgrave Macmillan.Cham: Accessed: 12/10/2023. [http://dx.doi.org/10.1007/978-3-030-57938-8_22]

Zbyshko, B.G., Stepus, A.F. (2022). Search for new approaches to rationing intellectual labor. *Economics: Yesterday, today, tomorrow, 12*(2A), 240-258. In Russ., abstract in Eng. [http://dx.doi.org/10.34670/AR.2022.67.79.002]

Zemrani, A. (2019). Budgeting in the United States: From Theory to Practice Using Higher Education. In: de Vries, M.S., Nemec, J., Špaček, D., (Eds.), *Performance-Based Budgeting in the Public Sector..* Cham: Governance and Public Management. – Palgrave Macmillan. [http://dx.doi.org/10.1007/978-3-030-02077-4_2]

Zhang, C. (2021). Triple helix theory as the conceptual platform for innovative talent cultivation in digital economy. *State and Municipal Management. Scholar Notes,* (4), 246-252. Accessed: 03/23/2024. [http://dx.doi.org/10.22394/2079-1690-2021-1-4-246-252]

Zhavoronkova, A.A. (2023). Theories of generations in Russia: Myth or reality? *Education. Science. Scientific staff,* (4), 189-192. In Russ., abstract in Eng. [http://dx.doi.org/10.24412/2073-3305-2023-4-189-192]

Zhalezko, (2022). The use of technical analysis and indicators in algorithmic trading / B.A. Zhelezko, A.O. Stadnik, O.A. Sinyavskaya. *Economics today, 15*, 119-130. [In Russ.].

Zhelezko, B.A., Daineko, A.E., Danilchenko, A.V., Ustinovich, I.V., Glubokiy, S.V., Grintsevich, L.V., Yakushenko, K.V., Zubritskaya, I.A., Makarevich, N.V., Prots, T.A., Kharitonovich, S.A. (2020). *International competitiveness of the export potential of the Belarusian industry.* Law and Economics.(p. 286). Minsk: In Russ.

Zimina, I.V. (2016). Educational networks in the "triple helix" model. *Creative Economics, 10*(11), 1195-1206. In Russ. [http://dx.doi.org/10.18334/ce.10.11.36990]

Znamensky, D.Y. (2012). State policy of the Russian Federation in the field of education, science and innovation: Problems of an integrated approach to formation and implementation. *Bulletin of the State University of Management, 4*, 1-5. [In Russ.].

SUBJECT INDEX

A

B

C

Galina V. Astratova, Maxim V. Vlasov, Chigozirim Ndubuisi Onwusiribe & Longinus D.N. Nnadozie (Eds.)

E

I

K

L

S

T

U

V

W

Y

www.ingramcontent.com/pod-product-compliance
Lightning Source LLC
LaVergne TN
LVHW070947210926
848482LV00002B/123